CM0117573?

THE BAREFOOT COACH

THE BAREFOOT COACH

LIFE-CHANGING INSIGHTS FROM COACHING THE WORLD'S BEST CRICKETERS

PADDY UPTON

SPORT

First published by Westland Sport, an imprint of Westland Publications Private Limited in 2019

1st Floor – A Block, East Wing, Plot No. 40, SP Info City, Dr. MGR Salai, Perungudi, Kandanchavadi, Chennai – 600096

Westland, the Westland logo, Westland Sport and the Westland Sport logo are trademarks of Westland Publications Private Limited, or its affiliates.

Copyright © Paddy Upton, 2019

The views and opinions expressed in this work are this work are the author's own and the fact are as reported by him, and the publisher is in no way liable for the same.

Paddy Upton asserts his moral rights to be identified as the author of this work.

All rights reserved

No part of this book may be reproduced, or stored in a retrieval system, or transmitted in any form or by any means, electronic, mechanical, photocopying, recording, or otherwise, without express written permission of the publisher.

ISBN: 9789387894983

10 9 8 7 6 5 4 3 2 1

Typeset by SÜRYA, New Delhi
Printed at Thomson Press (India) Ltd

CONTENTS

INTRODUCTION   1

PART 1: IN THE BEGINNING

1. SEARCHING FOR THE AUTHENTIC GARY KIRSTEN   15
2. COACHING. NO, NOT COACHING. *COACHING*.   26
3. THE CHANGING LANDSCAPE OF LEADERSHIP   35

PART 2: THE INDIA JOURNEY

4. ARRIVING IN INDIA   53
5. PLAYING TO STRENGTHS   62
6. INDIA AT WAR   76
7. SHED THE BLAZER AND TIE   85
8. THINKING DIFFERENTLY   98
9. CHARACTER AND VALUES   109
10. EGO: THE BATTLE WITHIN   124
11. EGO AND MY GREATEST PROFESSIONAL ERROR   136
12. GETTING THERE: BIRTHING THE WORLD CUP STRATEGY 141
13. GETTING THERE: THE SIX INCHES BETWEEN THE EARS 149
14. THE MYTH OF MENTAL TOUGHNESS   165
15. INTUITIVE LEADERSHIP   175
16. FAILURE: PART ONE   182

17. FAILURE: PART TWO — 191
18. RIDING THE WAVES OF FEAR — 198
19. THE ZONE OF DEATH, THE NORTH POLE AND THE WORLD CUP — 208
20. THE WORLD CUP: COMETH THE HOUR, COMETH THE TEAM — 228

PART 3: LIFE IS BUT A JOURNEY

21. HARNESSING COLLECTIVE INTELLIGENCE — 249
22. PERSONAL MASTERY — 270
23. SELF-AWARENESS: A JOURNEY OF UNINTENDED CONSEQUENCES — 281
24. THE PROTEAS IN SWITZERLAND — 288
25. ALPHA LEADERS — 299
26. THE PAINFUL LOSSES — 317
27. NO 'ZEN SHIT' — 322
28. OUT OF THE BOX — 332
    POSTSCRIPT: MADIBA'S SLEEVE — 351
    ACKNOWLEDGEMENTS — 356
    REFERENCES — 358
    INDEX — 365

www.thebarefootcoach.net

INTRODUCTION

In the mid-1990s, I was living the dream life. I was travelling the world with the South African cricket team as cricket's first ever full-time fitness trainer, and working with the late South African captain Hansie Cronjé and the late and highly respected coach Bob Woolmer.

It was my first real job, which I had been offered while studying for a PhD in Sport Science at the University of Cape Town, in my home city. Accepting it at age twenty-five meant having to retire from my cricket and rugby-playing career and to take my studies onto the road with me as I joined my new travel partners: Hansie, Allan Donald, Gary Kirsten, Jacques Kallis, Brian McMillan, Dave Richardson, Mark Boucher, Lance Klusener and Jonty Rhodes, to name a few.

Over the next few years I became friends with most of the players, many of whom I already knew from having played with or against them. Travelling and working together brought us even closer. I was very well paid to watch international cricket at the world's best stadiums and from the best seats in the house. I met and sometimes had a drink with greats like Sachin Tendulkar, Rahul Dravid, Shane Warne, Steve Waugh and Brian Lara. I met the Queen of England in person and twice met President Nelson Mandela. We got free tickets to whichever music concert was on in the city we were in. We stayed at the best hotels and, several nights a week, ate at the best restaurants in Mumbai, Sydney, London, Barbados, Auckland, Colombo, Cape Town, Karachi, Dubai and others. Most times, the restaurant manager would come over, meet the famous cricketers I was dining with, and announce that the meal was on him, as his way of honouring us.

We would often frequent the city's popular night spots after a day's play. In those days, we played less cricket. The players didn't all conduct themselves as professionally as they do today. Most significantly, there were no cell phone cameras and, of course, social media was non-existent.

This meant there were more opportunities for night-time fun than are available to sportspeople today. The group I was with always attracted the lion's share of female attention in the pub or nightclub. Oakley, the sports equipment company, gave me free sunglasses—more pairs than I could wear. The guys from Nike would invite me to load up a trolley of free clothes and shoes a few times a year, and the South African telecom company MTN gave me free cell phones and airtime. What's more, although employed full-time between 1994 and 1998, I enjoyed about four months of paid leave every year. I was, indeed, living the dream.

It was during the Australian tour of 1997 that I became vaguely aware that something was missing. At the time, I didn't understand, nor could I explain, what that 'something missing' was.

Looking back, it was the beginning of an emptiness somewhere in the pit of my stomach. As I touched this void within myself, I recall thinking that I could sense it in some of the players too. More tangibly, I couldn't get rid of the feeling that the individual cricketers—and the team as a whole—were performing below their potential. I could not say how or why, but the sense that things could be a whole lot better was strong.

We were the fittest team in the world—the only team with a full-time fitness trainer, after all. Under the visionary Bob Woolmer, we were a very innovative team. With seven players who were university graduates, we were also a highly educated team, and we had great talent. Everything we could do to be the best in the world at the time was being done; there were neither obvious flaws nor problems in the system.

In fact, other than occasional personality clashes and power games, relations within the team were particularly healthy and professional. Despite all this, I felt we were not where we could be—that there was something missing.

I knew I wanted to resign, but did not know why. I also had no sense of where, or what, I would move to next. I recall the day I told Hansie of my decision. The two of us were driving from George to play a One Day International (ODI) in Port Elizabeth. The team flew, but Hansie and I drove because we wanted to bungee jump from the 216 metre-high Bloukrans Bridge. On the same day that we took the plunge and jumped off that bridge in early 1998, I took the plunge and resigned from my 'dream job'.

I left, not sure what I would do next, and with no clue about where to look to find the 'something missing', within me or within the team.

BECOMING A NOBODY

Over the next three years, as I worked towards submitting my PhD thesis on the prevention of schoolboy rugby injuries, trained a professional rugby team and backpacked across Southeast Asia for six months on a budget of eight US dollars a day, the search for the answer to the 'something missing' remained active at the back of my mind.

Sometime in 1999, I recall sitting in a dingy Vietnamese Internet café, mulling over a recent and profound insight. I had been on the road for about four months by then, sleeping in cheap youth hostel dormitories and travelling and eating as cheaply as possible. Since nobody knew cricket or cricketers in Vietnam, Laos, Cambodia or Thailand, no one was impressed with my credentials. And no one ever asked me what I did. It was not relevant. Fellow travellers were interested in the kind of person I was. No one cared about the number of degrees I had—they never even asked if I had finished school. I would often sit cramped up next to someone on a third-class train trip or on the roof of an overcrowded bus. We would talk for an entire day without either of us ever asking the other's name. It did not matter what our names were.

Sitting in that Vietnamese café, I typed these words: 'Resigning from the South African cricket team and becoming a complete nobody in the subculture of the international backpackers' world has given wind to the sails of my soul.' I felt more alive and fulfilled in a world that made no distinction between high school dropouts and postgraduates; between so-called successful business people and barmen; between the rich and the poor. This subculture was equally unconcerned about nationality, creed, colour and religion.

It was then that the thought occurred to me: The international cricket world had been a playground for my ego. It had been about looking good, appearing to be in control, always seeming happy, forever smiling and being the popular guy—and I had played that game well. I had been frolicking in the shallow and superficial depths of a so-called dream life. I had plastered on a permanent 'smiley face' mask, and many had envied me.

Yet, somehow, it wasn't the dream I had expected. I can't say exactly what I had hoped to gain from being apparently 'successful' and almost famous by association, but I guess I had hoped it would at least feel as good as it looked. Only, it didn't.

Simply put, my life lacked depth and substance.

After typing that email, I started to realise that nothing of what I was unconsciously seeking—joy, peace, freedom, contentment, love and more—derived from the name, fame, money, privileges or even the vices that I had thought might deliver them. Four months after being stripped of the identity that the cricket world and I had constructed for myself, and giving up all that I had held so dear, I finally started to feel truly alive. It was as though I had inadvertently stumbled upon what I had been seeking for so long—the 'something missing' that had driven me to resign from a dream job. Something clicked into place, and my own inner journey towards personal mastery gained impetus. It was time to scratch a little deeper below the surface of life—and still have loads of fun.

THE SCHOOL OF HARD KNOCKS

Back in South Africa, I learned to wear shoes again and revelled in the simple pleasure of shaving with hot water while looking in a mirror. In six months of backpacking, I had worn shoes only twice, and very few places that I had stayed in were upmarket enough to have both warm water and a mirror in the washroom.

The next part of my post-cricketing journey took me through two failed businesses and three years on the streets of Cape Town's Central Business District (CBD), working intimately with the youth who lurk in the dark shadows of the city's underbelly. I went from the global cricketing high life to the shocking reality of my city's destitute and criminal low life.

I found myself enmeshed in the darkest recesses of the territorial gang system with its drug-peddling, retribution stabbings, rape and tourist crime, and also came face-to-face with the city's methods of 'removing the problem'. My work took me into police cells, the youth courts, boys' towns and the Western Cape prison system, with its notorious numbers gangs. It was very hard to digest the reality of extreme child abuse and dysfunctional parenting, such that an eight-year-old child would rather sleep in the open, in the cold and stormy Cape Town winters, hoping to not get beaten up, stabbed or raped too often, and constantly under the threat of contracting AIDS or tuberculosis, than be at home with his parents.

It all started with a girl playing soccer and drawing with kids while she was working in the movie industry, filming advertisements in Green Market Square at the centre of Cape Town. Her name was Linzi. Her chance encounters with the kids progressed to weekly soccer matches on an abandoned piece of land behind the Artscape Theatre (then the Nico Malan Theatre) on the Cape Town foreshore.

The numbers swelled each week, as more and more kids joined the Tuesday evening soccer games. I received an invitation from Donne Commins, a volunteer and a lawyer who would go on to become one of the most respected athlete representatives in professional cricket, to join them. To be honest, I started going to the games every week mainly to get in some fitness and to look good—pretending to be doing something for the less fortunate. As I got to know some of the kids, however, I started to spend more and more time chatting with them at the street corners where they hung out, as I shuttled between business meetings.

The sports conference business I had been involved with was limping along and in the process of collapsing, leaving me with plenty of free time, which I was now spending on the streets. Soon it became something I did full-time, day and night. I did not become a street worker through a religious experience, and I am certainly not a bleeding heart who wants to save the world. I was single at the time and not sure if I even liked kids all that much. But the streets never sleep and I felt an urge to get more deeply involved.

I became interested and then fascinated by the parallel life that went on in my city, something largely invisible to the tourists and business people who frequented it regularly. Somehow, I knew I could make a difference. One day, we invited all the leaders of the dozen or so territorial gangs to Linzi's movie production office. These gang leaders were effectively the self-appointed parents of the kids. We wanted to learn from them how we could really help, beyond the ad hoc stuff we had been doing. It turned out that the leaders of these groups had never been in one room together, let alone an office. Most of them had only visited offices in town in the course of a 'midnight shopping spree' wearing balaclavas.

By the end of that day, they had taught us a great deal about how the streets and the city actually worked. They went into detail about what kind of social help worked and what didn't, how to operate so that we could stay safe, and so much more. They really let us into their lives that day. They also agreed to work with us to help the children. Our organisation was given a name: Street University (it would later change to Street Universe).

Linzi's office was transformed from a movie production office to a homeless children's office; an office where the 'staff' were leaders of the street gangs and some of the toughest street criminals in Cape Town. It would be the beginning of long-standing battles with landlords, as we were (understandably) expelled from each location that we moved to.

One of these landlords, David Barnes of Central Boating, deserves a special mention. He leased us the office next to his business, and it wasn't long before the kids drove him nuts, turning what hair he had left grey, and many times even compromising his own business. But he had a soft spot underneath the business exterior and his support held out the longest among all our landlords. Sorry, David. And thank you.

In 1999, Street Universe was registered as a non-profit organisation, with a mandate to rehabilitate the hardened street children of the Cape Town city centre. Linzi and I became the two founders, directors and financiers. The gang leaders arrived at the office on most days, almost always washed and cleaned. In a city that does not have washrooms for the homeless, this was something of a miracle, but they were a resourceful bunch.

Along with this unlikely group of gang leaders, the now ex-movie industry girl and the ex-fitness trainer set out to make an impact, armed with will and commitment, only a vague idea of what they were getting themselves into, and without any real qualification to do so.

Seasoned and qualified street workers told us that we should never get the different territorial gangs, of between five and fifteen youth, to mix. Apparently, they only mixed when they were attacking each other with fists, knives or broken bottle necks. Fortunately, we were only told this six months into running what had become twice-weekly soccer games, for which over a hundred youth from several different areas in the city would assemble, willingly handing in their weapons and drugs before playing. Soccer dominated the proceedings, mostly without incident, until darkness eventually brought the game to a close. It was perhaps just as well that we hadn't yet been given the advice from those so-called experts about not mixing the groups—we might have paid heed to it. Unknowingly, this experience would prepare me for a conflict situation I had to deal with, a whole decade later, when an informal soccer match between Indian cricketers got heated.

During the games, Linzi, a few volunteers and some of the street girls would light fires beneath Cape Town's Eastern Boulevard Bridge, preparing food for the hundred-plus hungry footballers. We would camp there deep into the night, cooking, eating and listening to hilarious and disturbing stories of life on the street. Often, I would head home at around midnight, leaving Linzi alone with Cape Town's most hardened criminals. No harm ever came to her or to any one of the numerous volunteers who would later join us.

In the early days, we spent most of our time on the streets, building relationships with homeless children and those negatively affected by them. We were constantly reacting to problems at ground level: in the courts, police cells, hospitals and prisons. In time, our efforts gradually progressed to being less reactive and more proactive, as over 400 children and youth from Cape Town and neighbouring suburbs started to participate in weekly soccer, cricket, rowing, sailing, drumming, cross-country running, music, art, weekend camping trips and various other forms of temporary employment. Admittedly, they were seldom able to hold down a job for long. I gravitated to working with youth from the age of about sixteen and older. Linzi worked more with the younger kids. Volunteers from around the world also joined the organisation during this time.

We would take gang leaders or street youth with us to all meetings with businesses, police, government departments, potential funders and other non-profit organisations. Strangely, the street dwellers had almost always been excluded from these meetings where people were talking about them. Later, this approach of including the opinions of the people I was leading would become one of the hallmarks of my approach while working with international athletes.

After a year of self-funding, comprehensive financial support came in from various businesses and the Laureus World Sports Foundation. The latter was thanks to the wonderful, caring support of former South African rugby captain, the 1995 World Cup Rugby winning manager and laureat, Morné du Plessis. Through this initiative, the kids were even afforded the opportunity to spend a few days with Morné himself, along with former American 400-metre hurdler Edwin Moses, ex-British decathlete Daley Thompson and erstwhile Argentinean rugby fly-half, Hugo Porta.

Friends often remarked on the polarity between this life and my previous cricketing high life. In truth, I saw more similarities than differences. The international cricketers I had spent time with were the best in their field. They had to work incredibly hard to stay at the top in a fiercely competitive and cutthroat world. On and off the field, they were always under close public scrutiny. Only a few, with the necessary skills and talents, would survive and thrive.

The street kids were no different. Most of those who came to the city in search of a better life and the so-called riches on offer didn't survive the harsh conditions beyond a few days. They were chased off from one gang's territory to the next, or to another district, or back home—often after being injured or violated. Those who managed to stay had to constantly fight for their survival, and only the toughest actually thrived. They were always under scrutiny, including that of the police, security guards, fearful tourists, city improvement initiatives and government policies.

I found myself again dealing with the best, only this time it was in the very different game of survival. As a sport scientist back in the 1990s, I had offered cricketers the best of my fitness training knowledge and experience, with the aim of helping them do even better in the game of cricket. My support for the hardened street kids and youth of Cape Town took the form of whatever I could muster—contacts in the sports and business world, my people skills in conflict resolution and my care and concern, all with the aim of helping them live a better life.

I went through a veritable lifetime of experiences in those three years: love for murderers, fear for my life, exasperation, elation, desperation, optimism from the extent of caring, support and humanitarianism on display, anger and despair at the indifference of the world, respect for the police and disappointment with them. As in the cricket world, I again had to face up to my ego as publicity mounted for the work the organisation was doing and the acknowledgement I started to receive for apparently being so selfless. This time round, I recognised my ego and its wanting to look good, something I had been oblivious to during my earlier cricket days.

I was not planning to share what follows here. It may even affect sensitive readers. But I do so to honour my commitment to this book, to be truthful and not just speak of the things that looked good or led to success.

In the course of my work with the gangs, I had become close to one person who was quite candid about the fact that he didn't know how many had died by his hand. His first killing was as a eleven-year-old, when he murdered the priest who had molested him.

On another occasion, I watched another street dweller repeatedly stab his girlfriend as she clutched their newborn baby to her body, attempting to use the child as a shield against the thrusting knife. This person was known throughout the Western Cape underworld by a name that, translated into English, meant 'Horrendous'. He stabbed all around the tiny body, just missing it each time as the knife thrust into his girlfriend's chest and thighs. It happened late at night in a place called Observatory, just outside the city—in an area I should not have been in, that night. Noticing me slip into a dark corner in an attempt to call the police, he cornered me and then turned the knife on me. I was terrified, knowing the man's capabilities.

As he pushed me into the corner, telling me how he was going to cut me up, something incredulous happened. It felt like I saw straight into his heart, and what I 'saw' was an image of a terribly hurt young boy. I was compelled to extend my arms to embrace him; to hold him tightly, to comfort him. I have never been able to recall the words that came out of my mouth in that moment. All I know is that he dropped the knife, wrapped his arms around me and embraced me in one of the single most powerful emotional experiences I've ever had.

What happened in those moments is even now beyond my understanding. Still deep in the embrace, Horrendous asked me for a favour: Would I listen to his confession? He had a secret that he had carried for over twenty years, and he was ready to tell it.

The next day, I took him to a psychologist friend of mine. Over the next hour, he told us how his mother's drunken boyfriend had brutally sodomised him, night after night. He would wake up early to wash the blood off himself and the makeshift platform that was his bed, filled with fear and embarrassment. Not able to take it any longer, he eventually told his mother, whose response was to beat him for making such an accusation. He was six years old at the time.

Since leaving home some twenty odd years prior, he had regularly taken his rage out by raping, stabbing, pouring petrol on and lighting more people than he could count. As he related his story, it almost seemed like the demons were being physically purged from his body. His muscles, veins and eyes bulged almost unnaturally as he spoke. He used an entire box of tissues to mop up the sweat, tears, mucus and even blood that poured from his eyes, nose and pores as he purged. In the end, he was calm and spent. His parting words expressed a desire to go home and kill his mother and her boyfriend. He was grateful that finally someone knew the truth—a truth, he said, he would happily tell in court at his murder trial.

I did not see him for a long time after that day, and I never discussed any part of it with anybody, including my psychologist friend. His secret was locked away in that office. Over a decade later, when writing this part of the book, I asked my friend about her professional experience of the confession that day. Try as she might, she had no more than a distant and vague recollection of me visiting her offices with a street dweller. Experiencing his confession had been so traumatic that, as it sometimes happens with victims of extreme trauma, her brain had erased the memory.

We had both broken our professional vows that day of the confession, by not telling the authorities of a pending murder. It was a choice I made, one I am neither proud of, nor comfortable sharing. And perhaps I would have never confessed it here, if I hadn't seen Horrendous two years later. He proudly showed me his clean hands— he had given up smoking Mandrax (a popular drug in South Africa at the time) since the day of that confession. He told me that he did go home to kill his mother and her boyfriend.

He explained how he had walked into their shack, armed and ready to kill. A smile came across his face as he explained how, when he saw them after all those years, he was overcome with forgiveness and did not proceed as planned. He was still living on the streets, but had changed his name back to the one given to him at birth. He did not want to be called nor behave like the old Horrendous. Also, he said he now visited home from time to time. Standing in the middle of Breë Street in Cape Town, we hugged, and I was overcome with emotion—a strange mix of joy, wonder and gratitude.

On another occasion, a letter arrived at my home from the Brandvlei Correctional Centre (maximum-security prison) in Worcester, Western Cape. The letter contained beautifully written words and art from a life prisoner, declaring his undying love for me as the father he never had. It reduced me to another teary combination of pain and gratitude. Three years of working with these so-called criminal street children, these angels with dirty faces who had become hardened by life, had softened me.

Street Universe eventually merged forces with another non-profit organisation, Foundation for a Brighter Future, which operated from Claremont in Cape Town's southern suburbs. The patron of the organisation was an international cricketer by the name of Gary Kirsten. As it turned out, his path and mine would cross again a short while later, under quite different circumstances.

Part 1

IN THE BEGINNING

1

SEARCHING FOR THE AUTHENTIC GARY KIRSTEN

Gary Kirsten dreads the anticipated telephone call. It has been six years since he made his international debut as a Test cricketer. And now, in the summer of 1999, he feels more at home vacationing with his family in the South African Eastern Cape than on cricket's finest stage. An in-form English team has recently arrived in South Africa. And, in the first two Tests, Gary has been out of form.

He knows he is not the most skilled cricket player ever to represent his country. Even in his own family, there have been more skilled batsmen. But his hours of grafting and crafting have helped him gain recognition as an industrious left-handed opening batsman who regularly frustrates the living daylights out of the world's finest bowlers.

Not lately, though.

It has been more than a year since he scored 210 in Manchester, and apart from a century each in January and February of 1999, he has been delivering performances below his own high standards. In Johannesburg, he scored 13 runs off 47 balls, but was spared a second outing as the Proteas bludgeoned the visitors by more than an innings. In Port Elizabeth, he scored 15 off 29 and then 2 off 23.

With the Boxing Day Test in Durban looming, Gary understandably fears that telephone call. Not the one informing him that he has been dropped, but one that tells him he has been called up for national duty again! The thirty-two-year-old is actually questioning his own merit as a representative of his country.

The phone rings and Durban it is. Gary opens the batting, and his persistent fears and doubts are justified as Andy Caddick rips through the home side's top three batsmen of Kirsten, Gibbs and Kallis for a mere 24 runs. Gary contributes 11.

'Gazza, that's it. You're done.'

At the team hotel, he tells his wife that this is his last Test. His confidence is shattered. Temporarily sheltered from the opinions and judgements of fans, selectors and the cricketing world, Gary and Debbie spend a quiet evening in each other's company. They surrender their anguish in pray, handing Gary's destiny over to God. *Que sera, sera.*

In the second innings, Gary bats for more than fourteen hours, recording his highest score of 275. It is still the second-longest Test innings in history, and is only surpassed by the 1958 innings of Pakistan's Hanif Mohammad that lasted more than sixteen hours. Gary plays shots that he has never played before, and the leather leaves the willow in a way it hasn't done for months. Supported by a neat 69 from Jacques Kallis and 108 from Mark Boucher, they save the Test for South Africa, and Gary revitalises his career.

Whatever happened in those quiet hours preceding Gary's record innings, it didn't include video analysis or net sessions. It didn't include expert advice or instruction. Frankly, it didn't include any cricket whatsoever.

Gary has often said it is not your skill but your character that is being tested in these make-or-break moments in life and that tips the scales when it comes to the crunch in big Tests. Since his best innings didn't come about after technical fitting-and-turning to his game, the traits that inspired his innings had to have been present in him even when he lost his wicket in the first innings for just 11 runs. That something had to be rediscovered.

In many ways, it was a flowering of potential Gary already possessed and the development of a better understanding of himself as an individual and as a player, since character is not limited to one or the other; it's all-encompassing. In Gary's case, that actualisation included a spiritual aspect. It was through prayer that he was able to surrender the outcome of his next innings, and of his career. He let go of the unconscious mental chatter of the 'thinking brain', with its need to succeed and its worry about failing. As this temporary veil of thought was lifted, it revealed the more permanent qualities that were always there and underpinned so much of his prior success: his innate cricketing intelligence, trust in his own skill, belief in himself, and the ensuing state of flow (the zone).

Gary had to learn to master the self—a cornerstone of the coaching philosophy he and I would later employ with the Indian cricket team, with South Africa, and the many other teams we coached, together and separately, in the years to come.

Gary would eventually go on to score 12 more of his eventual 21 Test centuries in the three-and-a-half years that followed. During that same period, I went outside of sport into business, philosophy, academia and spirituality, as I found myself drawing from, and combining these, for their application in sport.

During this time, a friend told me about a master's degree in executive (business) coaching at Middlesex University, which I decided to pursue. There I was exposed to some of the most innovative companies, business leaders and academics in the world, and from them I gained a much deeper and broader understanding of how to get the best out of people. The best leadership philosophies employed by the best companies worldwide enable them to attract the best talent, keep them the longest, and simultaneously to get the best out of the rest.

In recent years, leadership approaches in the business world have shifted emphasis towards true people management, or more accurately to 'coaching', away from the old-school command-and-control and instruction-based style. Today, leaders seek to help people become the best they can be. They facilitate growth by serving their employees' or athletes' needs ahead of their own needs. It's no longer about leaders believing that they know more about the game or the industry than anyone else and therefore telling others what to do and what processes to follow.

[Handwritten annotation: CALM/COMPOSED IN A DIFFICULT SITUATION]

To make that shift and to master the art of leading people, you need to acquire a totally different skill-set. You need to have a fairly high level of competence and also equanimity in most aspects of your life. And if you can pull it off, it is undoubtedly better than the old way. This approach makes even more sense now than at the time I did my research more than a decade-and-a-half ago, because young people who enter the business or the sports world are really not interested in being told what to do. What they are looking for is someone who can help them learn, grow and develop so that they can realise their potential to the fullest.

My master's thesis was on the coaching methods employed by South African provincial and national cricket coaches between 1991 and 2004 and it viewed these methods in the light of new insights through which successful companies managed their people. My hypothesis was that the old methods were ineffective because the coaches were instruction-based and thus created an over-structured and excessively result-focused environment.

I interviewed twenty-one senior provincial cricketers (averaging 257 caps per player), eight of whom were also national players (averaging 100 international caps per player) and sought to understand their personal experiences of being coached. At that stage, and in the fourteen years or so since South Africa's re-entry into international sport, the Proteas (cricket) had had five coaches, the Springboks (rugby) nine and Bafana Bafana (soccer) fourteen. I wanted to establish why, under most of these coaches, the teams never delivered to what many perceived to be their full potential. I investigated this from a player's perspective, to understand whether the coach managed the players in the best conceivable way in order to get the best out of them. I also drew comparisons with the business world.

Armed with this research, I approached Cricket South Africa in 2004. I was able to prove that cricket coaching at the top level locally was ten years behind the best practices in the business world, and was still rooted in old behavioural models. I argued that there was a fundamentally better way to lead people, and I was convinced that South Africa would be far ahead of the rest of the cricket world if they could apply that thinking locally.

To my mind, advances in people management, more so than science, was the next great differentiator in sport. In a way, I said this at my own expense, having been one of the early sport scientists in international cricket, under Bob Woolmer, Hansie Cronje and Professor Tim Noakes.

Those earlier innovations all fell within the external, visible and measurable world of sport science and technology. The world saw them, copied them and then innovated even further. Science contributed immensely to cricket, and most other sports, for about two decades, starting somewhere in the early 1990s. Because we understand things much better nowadays, we have been able to fine-tune those sports and take them to new levels. Video analysis, fitness analysis, big data, biomechanics, diet, rehabilitation, medical care and nutritional supplements—all these things and more have helped tremendously. But while they remain vital, they are no longer differentiators between teams and athletes.

We live in an era of information and technology and so, it's very easy to copy science. Today, there is very little scientific data that is not widely available to anyone with an Internet connection, a budget for consultants or the ability to mine data. With information so widely available, we need to ask where the next significant advances in sport will come from. A diligent search will reveal that those advances have been around for a long time—in the business world.

This brings us back to human beings and how we can create an environment in which they can come into their own.

Between 1999 and 2004, my views on sport changed. I graduated from a purely scientific approach to a more holistic view of the human being. At that stage, many in the South African cricket setup were not overly interested in what I was proposing. The business world was hungry, though. So I ended up working as an executive (business) coach. But sport was still closest to my heart, and I started doing private sessions with (South African cricketers) Jacques Kallis and Ashwell Prince at first.

During the 2003-04 cricket season, Gary and I found our paths converging again and so powerfully that it would determine much of our future in the years that followed. It was in Gary's last season—three years after he had thought in Durban that his Test career was at its end—that I coached him around his mental game, related to both batting and to life. In that season, he went on to score five of his twenty-one Test centuries, which included two against England, in a series where he scored 462 runs at an average of 66. This swansong season became his best ever as an international cricketer; he became the first South African to earn 100 Test caps, and he became a living, breathing example of what he and I would come to regard as one of the most important aspects of being a coach: guiding players on their journey towards personal mastery.

In 2005 and after his retirement, Gary and I, along with Dale Williams, the same friend who had first introduced me to executive coaching, started a business that was based on helping create 'performance through awareness'.

Our work focused on helping people to become their own best coach, guiding them to become masters of their profession and of their own lives. Like Gary had done.

Whilst he was still playing and in a letter he wrote to me in 2004 after one of our sessions, Gary made the observation that as a professional sportsman, 'ego makes showing emotion, vulnerability and weakness taboo, while what becomes important is pride, a sense of belonging, adopting the values of society, and living up to the public's perceptions and expectations'. With a newly-found awareness of these somewhat common trappings of fame, Gary went on to ask, 'If not this, then what is it that I am looking for?' His answer:

> I'm searching for the authentic Gary Kirsten—someone who is accepting of his shortcomings and is confident in the knowledge of who he is. One who is not locked into the perceptions of society, but one who is willing to have a positive influence and add value to society in my own unique way. I want to make a difference to people's lives and give them similar opportunities to those I have had. My perception of success is not about how much money I can earn in the next ten years, but rather, what impact I make on people I come into contact with.

Gary had spent thousands of hours mastering his stroke play, which has brought him great success and recognition. To this pursuit of professional mastery, he added personal mastery. In life as in cricket, it's who you are inside, your character and your values, rather than what you do, what results you achieve or possessions you gain, that will determine your true contentment, your enduring success and how you will ultimately be remembered.

Sachin Tendulkar is a cricketer who has long pursued personal mastery alongside mastering his profession. He says, 'When I meet someone, they will remember the impact I have on them as a person long after they have forgotten my statistics.' (See Chapter 9, *Ego: The Battle Within*). The wide-ranging public respect for Tendulkar extends beyond his statistics, as does his own contentment.

Personal mastery is many things to many people. It is a journey towards living successfully as a human being, first and foremost. It is a commitment to learning about yourself, your mind and your emotions, in all situations. It is a strengthening of character and deepening of personal values, like the roots of a tree. It is an increased awareness of self, others and the world around us; living from the inside out, not the outside in.

Peter Senge, one of the original creators of the idea of personal mastery, defines it as 'the discipline of personal growth and learning' that allows people with a high level of personal mastery to live in a continual learning mode.[1] They never 'arrive'. It is also a pursuit that seems to command relatively little interest in the world of 'celebritydom'.

This concept may already be sounding too touchy-feely for the John Rambos and Chuck Norrises out there. But before dismissing the concept, know that it translated to Gary's most successful international season; it underpinned Hashim Amla's remarkable performances, and grounds Tendulkar's extraordinary fame. And there are several others like them.

Conversely, the lack of personal mastery has undermined many celebrities' personal and/or professional lives. Have you heard about the guy who was a brilliant batsman but whose peers thought he was overly selfish and divisive, who got fired before he was actually done, and after retirement had no real mates? Or the guy who had talent and opportunity, but never managed to deliver on it? We will never know of all the failures that may appear to have been caused by technical weaknesses but which were actually due to a flaw in character or temperament, causing the player to repeatedly succumb to inner obstacles, fears, insecurities and self-imposed limitations.

We all know how 'greats' like Hansie Cronjé, Mike Tyson, Ben Johnson, Salman Butt, Marion Jones, Diego Maradona, Lance Armstrong and even Tiger Woods may be remembered, at least partially. Perhaps, personal mastery would have helped.

As with any journey, there is always a map. The same applies to personal mastery. Personal mastery is a shift in attitude that drives a shift in behaviour. It deepens the roots of one's life, making the tree grow taller and healthier, and holds it firm in the face of inevitable adversity, challenges and stormy weather.

Personal mastery is a shift in attitude …

… from placing over-importance on results to placing importance on the processes that set up the best chance of success; from defining one's contentment by results, to deriving contentment from the effort made in the pursuit of those results.

Personal mastery is a shift from the importance of looking good outwardly, to the importance of inner substance and strength of character. It is not about trying to be a good person, but about allowing the good person in you to emerge. From worrying about what others think about you, to knowing that what others think about you is none of your business. There are people who speak ill of Nelson Mandela, Mahatma Gandhi and Mother Teresa, never mind Jesus, Buddha or Prophet Muhammad. So what makes you so special that everyone should like you?

Personal mastery is a shift from thinking you have the answers to knowing you have much to learn. From balancing talking and telling with listening and asking. From pretending to be strong and in control and covering up ignorance, faults and vulnerabilities, to acknowledging these normal human fallibilities while still remaining self-confident.

When things go wrong, it is a shift from pointing fingers and blaming others to taking responsibility. It is first asking, 'What was my part in this?' before looking elsewhere. It's a shift from being reactive to being proactive; from withdrawing or getting pissed off by criticism to accepting that it's one of the things that could help you grow.

It is a shift from an attitude of expecting things to come to you, to earning your dues through your own efforts, and then feeling gratitude for what does come. It is a shift from focusing on yourself to gaining awareness of what is going on for others and the world around you. Not everyone is naturally compassionate, but everyone can be aware.

Personal mastery is a shift from expecting to be told what to do, to taking responsibility for doing what needs to be done. A shift towards becoming your own best coach as you learn more deeply about your game, your mind and your life, in a way that works best for you. It is about developing social, emotional and spiritual intelligence in addition to building physical muscle and sporting intelligence.

As coaches, Gary and I would encourage players to make decisions for themselves. Bowlers set their own fields, and batters took responsibility for their game plans, decisions and executions. In the Indian and the South African teams Gary and I led, there were no rules to govern behaviour, no curfews, no eating dos and don'ts, and no fines. Players were asked to take responsibility for making good decisions for themselves, at least most of the time. They decided amongst themselves which errant behaviours required addressing, and how these would be addressed, and thus the team became largely self-governing.

Personal mastery is about pursuing success rather than trying to avoid failure. It is an acceptance that failure paves the path towards learning and success. It's important for leaders to be okay with their athletes' mistakes. Many a coach will display visible signs of disappointment when an athlete makes a mistake, yet prior to that will have told that same athlete to go and fully express themselves. Their words and actions do not line up—and, every time, it's their reactions that speak more loudly than the words. Show me a coach who reacts negatively to mistakes, and I will show you a team whose performance is inhibited by a fear of failure.

Personal mastery is about knowing and playing to your strengths rather than dwelling on your weaknesses, knowing that developing strengths builds success far more effectively than fixing weaknesses does. If you're a good listener, it's about becoming even better, or if you're naturally compassionate, it's about fully living that gift.

It requires an awareness of how you conduct yourself in relation to basic human principles such as integrity, honesty, humility, respect and doing what is best for all. It means having an awareness of and deliberately living personal values as one goes about one's business. It's about knowing how one day you want to be remembered as a person—and living that way today.

When a top athlete does well, it's about receiving the praise fully and expressing gratitude in equal proportion, knowing that no athlete achieves success without the unseen heroes who support him or her. Praise plus gratitude equals humility. One needs only to listen to Rahul Dravid, V.V.S. Laxman or Hashim Amla receiving a man-of-the-match award to witness humility.

Personal mastery is a path that leads through all of life, bringing improved performances on the field and a more contented and rewarding life off it. It's a journey out of the shadows of the ego and into the light of awareness; it's a daily commitment, not a destination.

The bonus is that while personal mastery leads to a happier and more rewarding existence, it also leads to better performance. Gary adds: 'I spent years fighting a mental battle with my perceived lack of skill. Towards the end of my career, I dropped this, as well as trying to live up to others' expectations. I went on to score five Test centuries and have my best year ever. As a coach, I now know that managing myself and others well, being aware of who I am and why I do things, is of far more importance than technical knowledge of the game.'

When Sunil Gavaskar contacted Gary at the end of 2007 about the Indian head coach position, Gary had never coached a cricket team in his life. And the two main roles I was given, which we'll discuss in some detail in Part II of the book, did not yet exist in international cricket.

We knew a few things, though. From playing against them, and from observing them, we knew the Indian team was somewhat divided by class, region, seniority and skill level. So, the team had to be unified. And we knew the team wasn't happy under their last full-time head coach, Greg Chappell. So, there was room for improvement on the happiness scale. We also knew that no other cricket-playing nation puts as much pressure on their players to perform, as does India. At that time, India had a 39 per cent win ratio in Test cricket and 51 per cent in ODIs. So, the team had to win more often.

Sitting in an aeroplane flying over to coach the Indian national cricket team, we agreed and wrote down four main goals for Team India:

1. Become the number one Test side in the world.
2. Win the 2011 ICC World Cup.
3. Create a happy team environment.
4. Help players become better people (player self-mastery).

Neither Gary nor I had any experience in ticking the first three boxes. But we knew that if we did our utmost to support the players on their individual journeys to become the best person each of them could be, the other three goals might well look after themselves. It turned out to be a really good bet.

2

COACHING. NO, NOT COACHING. COACHING.

Ask ten players, officials or administrators what they think the role of a head coach is, and you'll get close to ten different answers. Ask those same individuals what they think the definition of a successful team is, and you'll likely have a ten-man choir singing 'We are the champions' back at you. Now, ask them how they intend to achieve that winning status, and again you'll be listening to ten different sets of answers.

When a group of MBA students from Stellenbosch University Business School posed the first question to cricket professionals as part of a leadership group assignment in 2016, there were differing views on what the role of the head coach was. There will be some overlap here, since I coached all the teams involved in the study, but here are some of the answers:

The role of the coach is to keep players happy. Happy players train well, play well, and they'll fight and play for their coaches.
—Chris Morris, all-rounder for the Proteas and the Delhi Daredevils

Provide all the necessary resources for a player to improve and get the most out of himself.
—Mike Hussey ('Mr Cricket'), retired Australian Test batsman and captain of Sydney Thunder at the time of the study

> *The head coach is the head of the family. He guides players, upholds the culture and environment. He facilitates contact with the different departments (players, staff, administration, etc.)*
> —Sameen Rana, Chief Operating Officer and team manager of Lahore Qalandars in the Pakistan Super League

> *The role of the head coach differs from someone coaching a provincial side to someone coaching a T20 or international team. (But the overarching responsibilities of the head coach include) maintaining momentum (performance), keeping the side's morale up, and making sure players understand their game plans. Thus, the head coach provides role clarity, momentum and vision.*
> —Nick Cummins, former General Manager of Sydney Thunder and Chief Executive Officer of Cricket Tasmania[1]

The study questions above, along with the sample answers, produced just one constant: teams want to win. Considering that on any given match day only about 50 per cent of teams will be victorious, there's a lot of potential pressure on coaches to manage the legion of expectations of how they must help players and organisations achieve the one goal everyone shares: winning.

As coaches, parents, managers and teachers, there are different ways available to us to help people learn, grow and succeed. And those different ways work with different people in different situations and at different times. Although we discuss learning styles and the changing landscape of leadership in more detail in the next chapter, here is a brief introduction to the five most prevalent methods used to help others.

I. INSTRUCTION

Instruction is the most commonly employed method of helping people. I'm the expert, so let me help you by telling you what to do. I have the power, and what is expected of you is to obey my instructions. It was historically the most common method of managing and coaching, and continues to be so today. It is also one of the least effective.

The advantages of this method are that it is quick, easy and familiar to many leaders and coaches. It is useful in a very limited sphere, like with people who are really young, with inexperienced people, and with teams that are new. It's also recommended in situations where there might be imminent danger. But, even here, it is overused.

The disadvantages of this method are many, including that it is disempowering, athletes report it as being frustrating, and it compromises learning. Research suggests that people who are told what to do forget up to 90 per cent of what they've been told within three months. Being told what to do creates robotic followers of instructions who are unable to think for themselves. When one hears a frustrated coach, boss or parent saying, 'How many times do I have to tell you?', you know they've been using an instruction-based approach. A number of South African rugby coaches have been accused of being over-prescriptive, and of coaching (instructing) game intelligence out of players.

This style of management gives the coach a feeling of being in power. But they're actually neither in control, nor in power; they are deluding themselves. This is particularly so in the case of older or more experienced players or workers. It is a very ineffective method, and people report feeling demotivated, frustrated and tired of acting subserviently in the face of an instruction-oriented leader.

II. ADVISING

Advising, or suggestion, is where I give you my opinion of what is best for you. As with instruction, it assumes that I am the expert, that I know and you don't. However, with advising, I don't tell you what to do—I make a suggestion and you decide for yourself. Making a suggestion that someone is compelled to follow is an instruction (or a threat) dressed up to look like a suggestion.

III. MENTORING

Mentoring is a very specific, focused way of helping, and it requires an experienced senior in a specific domain passing on knowledge to a junior within that domain.

As an example, since Gary Kirsten was an opening batsman in Test cricket and ODIs for South Africa, he could mentor another opening batsman. But he can't mentor a fast bowler because Gary has no experience of being a fast bowler. Allan Donald or Brett Lee could do that job.

The way a mentor would do their job is to say, 'When I was in that situation, this is what I did'. They then leave the young mentees to make sense of that for themselves. If a mentor were to say, 'This is what you must do', that would be instructing. If a mentor were to say, 'This is what I suggest you do', that's advising. But when a mentor truly mentors, they would say, 'This is what I did', and then leave the young mentees to decide for themselves.

IV. ABDICATING

With abdicating, I leave it to you as the player to figure things out for yourself. With the modern-day requirement of coaches to shift from a coach-centered approach towards an athlete-centered approach (which has been discussed in detail in Chapter 3), coaches can fall into the trap of saying, 'I'm not going to tell you what to do. I'm going to leave it all up to you.' But by leaving someone to his or her own devices, I'm abdicating, and most times, it's not a very helpful method.

V. COACHING

Coaching is a very misunderstood concept among coaches. For centuries, sport has used the term 'coach', but given that the majority of coaches still spend the majority of their time telling athletes what to do, it would be more accurate to call them 'instructors'.

The concept of a 'coach' or 'executive coach' in business emerged a few decades ago, and it has become a fast growing profession since. Better understood in business than in sport, coaching means to help you find the best answer for yourself. Modern-day coaches understand that they are there as coaches for only a short period of the individual's journey, to help the individual learn, grow and ultimately become their own best coach, to become the expert on their own life. The coach is not there to *tell*—they are there to *help*.

What does good coaching require? It is about asking good questions to gain clarity on where you want to go or how you want to improve, checking the intention behind that desired outcome, then working with you to brainstorm all possible options. When assisting you in picking the option that seems most appropriate, it is about listening to answers and helping fine-tune your thinking. Once a plan is agreed upon for the athlete's improvement, it is about giving accurate, supportive and non-judgmental feedback and support. As coach, I do more asking than telling, and I help the sportsperson think, so that they may come up with what is best for them.

Trust is critical in this coaching space. Trust only develops when the player or the person being coached genuinely understands and knows that, as coach, I'm here to serve them and their agenda. It is not about me (the coach), and about what I want—it is all about the sportsperson and the team, and what serves their best interests.

So, essentially, in coaching I'm helping you become an expert in your own game and life. As a coach, I'm an expert in helping you, or your team, to find your best answers.

Coaching is time-consuming and requires considerable skill. But it's a learnt skill, so one can learn to do it. It is important, though, when someone is introducing coaching into a previously instruction-based environment, that it should be done gradually and slowly.

In 2016, Professor Mike Ewing from Deakin University's Faculty of Business and Law led a leadership study, for which his team interviewed twenty-five players in two Indian Premier League teams and one Australian Big Bash League team whom I had coached.[2] Ewing found that 'inexperienced players may need to go through a process of "unlearning" the asymmetric hierarchical model that they likely experienced from previous coaches. They then need to learn the new symmetric model centred on self-awareness and professional maturity. Players refer to this process as a gradual evolution from directive coaching to being self-driven.'

While adopting this style and philosophy of coaching is not easy, the advantages far outweigh the disadvantages. It empowers the individual and maximises learning. With instructing, you have up to a 90 per cent forget rate after three months, but with coaching, you have about 85 per cent retention of information. It helps people to think for themselves, and therefore, they are able to make better decisions—not only when they are being coached, but also later in life. Coaching creates smart individuals and smart teams who think for themselves, far more so than players and teams who receive instruction.

Fundamentally linked to coaching, as defined in this chapter, is the concept of servant leadership, which was foundational to the approach Gary and I employed jointly and individually, wherever we've been involved in coaching.

SERVANT LEADERSHIP

The notion of leaders placing others' needs ahead of theirs is certainly not a new one. As early as 1970, AT&T executive Robert Greenleaf coined the term 'Servant Leadership' in the context of management and organisational behaviour:

> It begins with the natural feeling that one wants to serve, to serve first. Then conscious choice brings one to aspire to lead... The difference manifests itself in the care taken by the servant-first leader to make sure that other people's highest priority needs are being served. The best test, and difficult to administer, is this: Do those served grow as persons? Do they, while being served, become healthier, wiser, freer, more autonomous, more likely themselves to become servants? And, what is the effect on the least privileged in society? Will they benefit or at least not be further deprived?[3]

Servant leadership is not about making coffee and running around and cleaning up other people's mess behind them. It's also not a touchy-feely, feel-good philosophy. Greenleaf speaks about unlocking potential and abilities in others, delegating responsibility, collaborating and engaging others in participative decision-making, and about helping them become the best they can be.

As a frame of reference for what we'll discuss next, in Ewing's study of twenty-five professional T20 cricketers, he cited two core dimensions of servant leadership ('humble service' and 'effective action'), before breaking those down into five attributes.

ATTRIBUTES OF A SERVANT LEADER

1. HUMBLE SERVICE

1.1 Humility	The ability to put one's accomplishments and talents in perspective; admitting one's fallibility and mistakes; understanding of one's strong and weak points

1.2 Standing back (modesty)	Gives priority to the interest of others first and gives them the necessary support and credits; retreating into the background when a task has successfully been accomplished
2. ACTION	
2.1 Empowerment	Encouraging autonomous decision-making, sharing information, and the coaching and mentoring of individuals for increased innovative performance
2.2 Accountability	People feel responsible for their results
2.3 Stewardship	The common interest and the good of the whole are taken in account, while establishing a comprehensive framework for providing meaning to work and ensuring consistent action

Source: Sousa and van Dierendonck 2017[4]

Keep the two core dimensions and the associated coaching values and behaviours in mind as we now consider some of the most significant findings from an Eastern Washington University (EWU) study of servant leadership and high school athletes. The study, following earlier research done on 251 collegiate athletes, examined the impact of perceived servant leadership behaviours on 195 high school basketball athletes, aged fifteen to nineteen. They looked at how coaches, who were perceived by their athletes to possess servant leadership characteristics, were associated with their athlete's use of mental skills, motivations, satisfaction and performance (compared to teams and athletes of 'non-servant coaches').

Here are some of the most significant findings:

- (A)thletes who were coached by servant leaders felt they were getting better training and instruction than athletes of non-servant leader coaches. This is an interesting phenomenon, especially considering the strong probability that many of the 'non-servant leader' coaches in this study undoubtedly were good trainers and instructors of high school basketball.

- (A)nalysis indicated that six of the twelve ... mental skills variables (tested) differed significantly between the servant leader groups, with goal-setting, self-confidence, and commitment differing to the greatest degree ... These results seem incongruent with the sentiment that the servant leader model might produce athletes who are 'soft'. Many coaches believe that an autocratic coaching style is a necessity in order to instill mental toughness and promote the growth of mental skill in their athletes. The results of this study seem to suggest that the 'keys' to promoting mental toughness do not lie in this autocratic, authoritarian, or oppressive style. It appears to lie, paradoxically, with the coach's ability to produce an environment, which emphasises trust and inclusion, humility, and service. This paradoxical approach to developing toughness may well serve as a foundational skill for coaches of the future as older fear-based models of coaching go by the wayside.
- The servant leader coaches in the present investigation were also the most successful (at winning), suggesting that 'winning-at-all cost' coach behaviours are not necessary, nor desirable, for winning outcomes.

The EWU researchers concluded that 'high-school athletes who perceive their coach to be a "servant leader" also display higher intrinsic motivation, are more satisfied with their sport experience, are mentally tougher, and seem to perform better as a team and individually when compared with athletes coached by non-servant leaders.'[5]

For many coaches, it's challenging to move from making decisions for players to engaging them in making decisions for themselves and in doing so, to let go of some degree of power and control. It is difficult to move from having winning as a primary coaching focus to focusing on growing self-determining and autonomous athletes or employees, especially if results don't follow very soon and your boss or the parents of the kids you're coaching don't understand or agree with this new approach.

There are a number of team owners and coaches, and even athletes, who don't agree with how I coach, and I've been fired because my employers didn't see the value in what I was doing. Yet, the clearer I've become about my approach and why I'm doing what

I do, as well as the value it can bring to others, the less I'm swayed by those who don't hold the same coaching and leadership values.

I foresee a number of coaches, bosses and managers over the next decade or so having to navigate the same resistance to change, to a newer and more empowering leadership approach; a change that is going to take place, regardless of the resistance to it. For, in my experience, coaching as an expression of servant leadership has the best chance of all the coaching methods of creating happy, engaged players and employees. And happy people are more productive than unhappy people.

3

THE CHANGING LANDSCAPE OF LEADERSHIP

The Franciscan friar Richard Rohr wrote: 'Mystery is not something you cannot understand. It is something that you can endlessly understand. There is no point where you can say, "I've got it." Always and forever, mystery gets you.'[1]

I believe the same holds true for coaching, or any form of leading or growing others for that matter. To acknowledge the mystery that presents itself when working with people is to open oneself to an endless journey of discovery and reinvention, forever. In this acknowledgment resides the humility to say that I do not know everything, but what I do know, I would love to share with you—*for you*. It is to step away from a worldview governed by black and white, absolute rights and wrongs; even from seeking answers in the grey. It is to open oneself to a multicoloured palette of possibilities. The mystery of coaching is as much about unknowing as it is about knowing. It is about discarding some knowns we hold for the sake of feeling personally secure in having a chunk of 'the truth', to making ourselves vulnerable and, therefore, receptive to new ideas, to new manifestations of the mystery. Each new discovery may improve performance by, say, 10 per cent. And then another 10 per cent, and another 10 per cent. Until we've improved 200 per cent from our base level. But we can never be 100 per cent knowledgeable. There can never be a 100 per cent of knowing. Coaching is like chasing a light beam. You can never be ahead of the ray of knowledge, but you can ride its coat-tail for infinity, all the while progressing endlessly.

To illustrate this analogy, I will quote from David Bodanis' book $E=mc^2$: *A Biography of the World's Most Famous Equation*.

> When a light beam starts going forward, one can think of a little bit of electricity being produced, and then as the electricity moves forward it powers up a little bit of magnetism, and as the magnetism moves on, it powers up yet another surge of electricity, and so on like a braided whip snapping forward. The electricity and magnetism keep on leapfrogging over each other in tiny, fast jumps—a 'mutual embrace'. (Albert Einstein) began to explore the leapfrogging of light waves (...) If light was a wave like any other, Einstein mused, then if you ran after it, could you catch up? (...) Light is not like that, however. Light waves keep themselves going only by virtue of one part moving forward and so powering up a next part. (The electricity part of the light wave shimmers forward, and then 'squeezes' out a magnetic part; then that magnetic part, as it powers up, creates a further 'surge' of electricity so the rushing cycle starts repeating.) Whenever you think you're racing forward fast enough to have pulled up next to a light beam, look harder and you'll see that whatever part you thought you were close to is powering up a further part of the light beam that is still hurtling away from you.[2]

There is no point at which you can say, 'I've got it'. Always and forever, mystery gets you ...

Our role as coaches is not to bring our players to where we are, but to bring them to a place and point where they can surge 'ahead of us' by virtue of our own magnetism powering up new bursts of energy in them; a magnetism generated by being present where the mystery reveals new knowledge and understanding all the time. That is when boundless growth can happen in teams and individuals—when the coach is a catalyst for growth and not the pinnacle of it; when a coach doesn't only impart knowledge and understanding to an athlete, but also empowers him or her to develop that knowledge even further. Exactly because of this infinite surge of new knowledge, a coach can never be 100 per cent knowledgeable. Yet, in one's acknowledgment of unknowing lies what Socrates regarded wisdom to be: The unceasing pursuit of truth (note: not *the* truth) *and* the simultaneous admission of one's own limitations.

This brings me to my own journey in search of truth and my attempts to grapple with the mystery of coaching. As mentioned before, I spent time at Middlesex University gaining an understanding of the smartest academic theories on how to best manage people, and how truly successful companies did this in practice.

Three or four decades ago, the CEO of a company or the coach of a sports team reached that position because he or she was the content expert. They knew more than anybody else about their particular field. Their thinking and actions revolved around their knowledge and understanding of what to do—*and* telling others what and how to do it. Many people were happy enough to follow someone who knew more than them, but this has fundamentally changed over the last twenty years, primarily due to the dawn of the information era and associated technologies. The content expert is no longer the sole fountain of knowledge—information has become freely available to anyone with a device connected to the Internet, which in turn has influenced how people perceive their leaders' application of knowledge and wielding of authority.

Research conducted by three different companies—Forbes, Gallup and Saratoga—covering over a million people at over 200 different corporations, in sixty different countries, found that 74 per cent to 84 per cent of employees would rather leave their jobs than stay in their current employment. When asked why, the main reason was their boss. People leave bosses, not companies.[3]

This does not suggest that bosses are necessarily wrong and employees are always right. But it's true that a company is most likely to suffer through reduced outputs from disgruntled employees. The same can be said for athletes in an unhappy team. Research in business has shown that happy people are 30 per cent more productive than unhappy people.[4] As in business, so in sport.

We are living in a world that is changing faster than ever before. Although performance, coaching and leadership are all subject to these same global forces of change, not all industries, bosses or coaches have moved with the times. The disconcerting statistic of disgruntled employees attests to this. Today, old-school sports coaches still do the thinking, planning and decision-making and then instruct players what to do. They decide what each player and the team should be doing at practice, what the game plans will be and how players should behave. Many coaches still assume responsibility for in-competition decision-making as they direct proceedings from the sidelines. In cricket, we see the coach's instructions being run onto the field via the twelfth man carrying replacement batting gloves or drinks. Some professional South African sport coaches even devised clever systems of coloured lights on stadium rooftops to instruct players what to do next. Water boys run the coach's instructions onto the field in rugby and some other team sports, and in sports like football and water polo, coaches simply shout from the sidelines—as do some over-excited parents, who embarrass themselves by forgetting their children are just children, mostly playing to have fun. The role of the athlete in these teams is to obey and follow instructions, under threat of reprimand for poor execution or disobedience.

Performance in business and sport underwent a significant upgrade around the early 1980s when computers became more widely available. Processes, strategies and behaviour were analysed, directed and monitored using scientific measurement of efficiency, data-driven analytics, and detailed process- and time-management systems. Combining video with computers saw a leap in performance through technical skill analysis, biomechanics, injury prevention and other specialisations within the field of sport science. These advances in technology also gave birth to specialist coaches, or 'technical coaches'. To some athletes, this meant there were now more people to deliver more specialised instructions.

Professional cricket first saw the use of computers and video analysis in 1995, some fifteen years after it was actually available and being used in other industries and sports. The late Bob Woolmer was responsible for this breakthrough, under the guidance of Professor Tim Noakes from the University of Cape Town. Prior to this, all professional cricket teams had only one coach who performed the role of batting coach, bowling coach, fielding coach, fitness trainer and data analyst. Today, professional cricket teams might have up to five coaches and will have upwards of ten support staff members. Through a David Leadbetter golf-coaching programme, Bob became the first coach to introduce a computer and video analysis programme in cricket. Admittedly, in those early days, very few South African players took the computer programme seriously, mainly due to the concept being so new and because the golf software had not yet been adapted for cricket. The cricketers who played golf did however take it seriously. I filmed Gary Kirsten's golf putting stroke in the change room after he had got out during a Test match (I still have the video). When uploaded, he was able to see clearly that he was cutting across the ball. Other players also reported returning from those first few tours with improved golf swings. Since then much has changed, with most professional, club and even school teams making good use of technology.

Moving a few years ahead, the Internet kick-started the information age. It drove content expertise down the chain of command from 'bosses' to so-called 'subordinates'. I met a fifteen-year-old bowler who lives on the cricket-starved island of Mauritius, who learned through YouTube to bowl beautiful in- and outswing. Sydney Thunder finger spinner Arjun Nair learned how to bowl like Sunil Narine in the same way, through YouTube. The knowledge era requires knowledge leadership, which has fundamentally different requirements for how leaders lead and others 'follow'. Authority is granted to the person with the best answers, or access to the best answers, whilst the designated leader is required to be a facilitator rather than an instruction-giver. By relinquishing power and authority, the leader gains influence, which has become the 'new' power.

As mentioned earlier, I drew on these leadership insights for my master's thesis on the coaching methods employed by South African cricket coaches between 1991 and 2004. The players I interviewed spoke of their preferred coaching approaches or methods, which I then compared with the coaches' actual methods, and with business best practices. The section that follows deals with the statistically significant differences between players' wishes and coaches' methods. Interestingly, although few, if any, of the players would have read books on business leadership, the approaches they preferred corresponded strongly with international best practices in companies that were at the cutting edge of their industries.

INSTRUCTION VERSUS COLLABORATION (ATHLETE-CENTERED COACHING)

Instruction-based coaching is characterised by an authoritarian, dogmatic and dictatorial approach where the coach's word is law. The collaborative style is essentially where coach and player work together to achieve what is ultimately best for the player and the team, with the coach employing influence more than power, and the player assuming a degree of responsibility for their decisions and actions.

At the time of my study, the common language used in sport to describe this alternative to the instruction-based coaching style was 'collaboration'. As the concept became more popular, it was gradually distilled into what today is becoming known as 'athlete- or player-centered coaching'. This evolution in the language of coaching was more than semantics. It represented an essential acknowledgement on the part of coaches that we are in the business of serving athletes and not ourselves. The early idea of a 'collaborative style' was effectively a halfway house between the old-school, coach-centered, instruction-based style and today's player-centered approach, since the objective of 'collaboration' was never to collaborate, but to facilitate the growth of the player as an athlete and person. Hence, the more accurate 'player-centered' philosophy took root in the modern coach's lexicon.

A coach who employs a coach-centered approach will feel the need to be in control. It's an approach where coaches assume the role of being the expert and set the agenda, which is most commonly about winning. And this is understandable, as most coaches are judged, hired and fired based on results, even though this remains a woefully incomplete and narrow measure of coaching success. It's like measuring a businessperson's success solely by how much money they make. Some businesses do make good money, yet might employ environmentally unhealthy practices, produce harmful products and/or suffer high staff turnover and high absenteeism. One financially successful business I consulted with had such an unhappy workforce, courtesy of a tyrannical leader, that over 50 per cent of the middle managers were on strong anti-stress and antidepressant medication.

A player-centered approach places the athlete in focus, with the coach's primary role centred on developing the player as an athlete and as a person, based on the player's needs and goals in terms of performance, as well as their personal life. Instead of doing all the thinking and telling, in this approach the coach asks the players what they require, and then listens to their answers. The coach first seeks to understand what and how the athlete is thinking, before adding his own thoughts. Instead of winning being the only measure of success, this approach fosters the athlete's improvement in skill or learning, their personal growth, autonomy or the ability to make smarter decisions, both on the field and in life. A well-executed player-centered coaching approach sets an athlete up for a lifetime of success, well beyond sport.

With this as the background, my study revealed that the average coach had a preference for instruction-based coaching, which they employed 53 per cent of the time, whereas the average player preferred it only 43 per cent of the time. Differently put, coaches collaborated 47 per cent of the time whereas players preferred it 57 per cent of the time. All the players in the study, both provincial and national, were upset with those coaches who had a rigid or dictatorial style. In those environments, the players reported being frustrated, unhappy and unmotivated. Over time, a kind of apathy had set in among some of the players because they were openly criticised or punished when they didn't do things the coach's way. If players spoke up about this, their discipline was questioned.

Sir John Whitmore, the author of *Coaching for Performance*, wrote that the appeal of the instructional style from a coach's viewpoint is that it makes for quick decision-making. It makes the coaches feel as if they are in control. But Whitmore points out that the converse, which has been called the 'power paradox', is actually applicable here—the more power coaches appropriate to themselves, the less power they have in reality.[5]

When power becomes a driving force in coaching, the intellectual flame that lights up the path to knowledge and progress is smothered. What is already known becomes the law. What has become the law has been proven before and is therefore not open for questioning. Power, or ego, upholds the status quo, and in a static environment, a coach's magnetism declines over time until it can no longer energise athletes to propel themselves to new levels of performance.

In discussing Socrates and leadership in *The Open Society and its Enemies,* Karl Popper wrote:

> The secret of intellectual excellence is the spirit of criticism; it is intellectual independence. (...) The authoritarian will in general select those who obey, who believe, who respond to his influence. But in doing so, he is bound to select mediocrities. For he excludes those who revolt, who doubt, who dare to resist his influence. Never can an authority admit that the intellectually courageous, i.e. those who dare to defy his authority, may be the most valuable type. Of course, the authorities will always remain convinced of their ability to detect intentions. But what they mean by this is only a quick grasp of their intentions, and they will remain forever incapable of seeing the difference.[6]

EXTERNAL FOCUS VERSUS INTERNAL FOCUS

The second area of significant difference between players' preference and coaches' methods is related to the focus of coaching. An internal focus addresses more abstract things such as thoughts, feelings, attitude and team spirit; facets of the game that are neither visible nor directly measurable, thus falling within the 'art of cricket'. An external focus is more on visible, tangible and measurable aspects, such as technical skill, fitness, tactics, strategy and management structures. These are the easier to teach (or prescribe) skills, and fall within the 'science of cricket'. Both these focus areas are vitally important at the elite level, but most coaches (and coaching courses) tend to have a greater external focus. The different aspects of these two areas are summed up in the matrix below (which I have adapted for cricket from Ken Wilber's map of human potential):

MATRIX OF INTERNAL AND EXTERNAL FOCUS

	INTERNAL	EXTERNAL
	Intangible/subjective/ immeasurable *Art of coaching* *Transformational leadership*	*Tangible/objective/ measurable* *Science of coaching* *Transactional leadership*
INDIVIDUAL	Thoughts, Feelings, Attitude, Character, Values, Intentions, Motivations, etc. *Art*	Technical skill, Talent, Physical fitness, Physical health, Personality traits, Behavioural habits, Measurable results *Science*
TEAM	Team values, Team culture, Team spirit, Team cohesion, Cultural integration **Moral standards**	Laws of the game, Competition rules, Match strategy, Match tactics, Management structures, Codes of conduct/discipline *Science*

In this case, too, the preferences of the coaches and the players were reversed. The coaches indicated an average of 58 per cent preference for the external approach, while players had a 58 per cent preference for the internal focus. The implications were that coaches had a more scientific and mechanical approach to coaching—therefore, with a greater focus on how the players trained, played and behaved.

While these aspects were also considered important, the players preferred an approach that Gary and I were to adopt later: encouraging individual players to reflect on, analyse and try to understand their own game, techniques, body, mind and feelings, in an environment in which all the players determined the team values, the team culture and the team spirit. This approach was formulated as follows in my thesis: 'In order to have "thinking players" who can make in-the-moment/on-the-field decisions, and adjust their game plans, players would need to have been actively involved in the reflection, analysis and planning, and not have it simply imposed on them by the coach.'

This is illustrated in the first graphic below, which I've adapted for sport from David Kolb's experiential learning cycle.[7] It shows how players learn. The first step comes from *playing* the game. Later, we use video and stats to *review* the match—reflecting on and analysing what worked, what didn't work; what happened, what didn't happen—and drawing lessons about how and where to improve. The review might also include what players might have been feeling or thinking, specifically at key moments, and how these affected decisions and/or execution. At school or club level, where there might not be video cameras or statistical analysis, the review is generally done based on what the coach saw and heard, and by referring to the scorecard. We then move our focus to *planning* for the next game, armed with lessons from past performances, plus an understanding of our opponents, expected conditions of play and

Creating thinking players

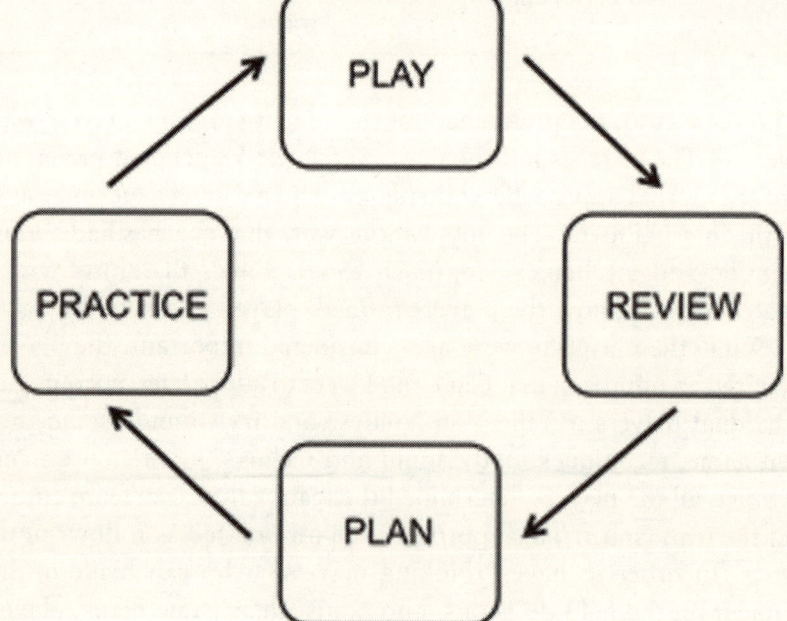

PLAY → REVIEW → PLAN → PRACTICE → PLAY

whatever else might be relevant for strategising. The next step is to take these plans onto the training field and *practice* according to them, followed by execution in the next game.

The more times we repeat this cycle, the more experience we gain and the more we learn. By involving players in all four stages, we create thinking players.

However, in sport, many coaches are responsible for creating *non-thinking* players. This happens by breaking the learning cycle in half through employing an instruction-based coaching approach.

Creating *non-thinking* players

In the top left, playing and practising (training) are the 'doing' functions of the learning cycle. Reviewing and planning happen off the field, and these are the 'thinking' functions. In most sports, coaches generally do the majority of the reviewing and planning (That's all I can do as coach, because I don't get to practice or play). At the post-match debrief, often armed with reams of information from the video analyst, the coach delivers a blow-by-blow account of how he or she saw the game unfolding and what they as the coach learned. This is traditionally where coaches get to show their expertise, and get to be seen to be doing their job. What happens? Fifteen minutes into this impressive presentation, if they can get away with it, players will start texting underneath the table, or at least start thinking of something other than what's actually happening in the room. What the coach has succeeded in doing is to create players who might appear to be looking at the presentation and nodding in agreement, but who are actually disengaged and/or bored. A similar thing might happen in the pre-match meeting where a coach presents a detailed match strategy, including an impressive analysis of the opposition players.

Once these players are put under pressure again, by default they go back to their old ways since they were not part of the processes that generated the thinking that went into their plans. Thus, we often see players make the same mistakes over and over again. Coaches, administrators and spectators will then exclaim, 'What were you thinking?' But that's exactly the issue: the players weren't thinking at all. That's what they had been repeatedly coached to do—to not think.

In my study, players weren't only showing a preference for a more collaborative coaching style, but also for an internal focus. And this is where trust and relationships carry much more weight than a coach's technical know-how and facilitation skills. I'm jumping ahead of myself with the following example, but it illustrates the importance of using these two preferences in tandem.

I would often ask batsmen, for instance, how many times they got themselves out through their own error, compared to how many times they got out because of a good delivery by the bowler. The standard answer was that batsmen got themselves out between 80 per cent and 95 per cent of the time. (Sorry bowlers, batsmen don't think you're as good as you think you are!). The follow-up question was: 'What is the actual root cause of your getting yourself out?' In almost every instance, the batsman would say it was an error in thinking—the pressure got to me; I was nervous; I had decided beforehand which shot I was going to play; I acted outside of my game plan; I was too aggressive; my shot wasn't well thought through; I was scared of failure or injury, and the like. These are all errors in thinking. Not one player said that the main cause of their dismissal was a technical problem. Interestingly, I've done the same exercise with elite rugby, soccer and hockey teams, and both the percentage of self-induced errors as well as the causes of these are literally the same!

As an example, when a batsman has a fear of the bouncer—the short fast-pitched delivery aimed at his head—the anticipation of this delivery sees them getting into a defensive position with their weight slightly more on the back foot than is ideal. What we see both live and on the video review is that he doesn't get into a strong front foot position to the fuller pitched delivery. With his weight hanging back, his hands go at the ball, and he maybe nicks it and gets caught behind, or misses it and gets out lbw or bowled. When reviewing the dismissal, the coach correctly points out the visible technical errors. The most common approach is then to go into the nets, where the coach throws full-pitched deliveries and asks the batsman to get into the correct front foot position. From the very first throw-down, they get it 100 per cent right. After thirty-or-so throws, both batsman and coach walk out of the nets, with the coach happy that he has addressed and remedied the error. No word is spoken about the fear that caused the batsman to hang back. This happens all too often in cricket these days—perceived technical errors are corrected in the nets. This is despite the fact that batsmen acknowledge that 80 per cent to 95 per cent of their errors are mental errors, which then play out as visible technical errors.

The coach cannot see the mental error that precedes the visible technical error associated with the ensuing dismissal. I would ask to re-confirm: 'Who in this team has ever got out because of mental errors such as fear of failure, fear of the short ball, premeditation, nerves, doubt, lack of confidence, and/or overconfidence?' Each time, everyone's hand would go up. I would follow this up with the question, 'When reviewing these dismissals with your coach, who uses these words to explain the reason for getting out?' Not one hand would go up.

It becomes obvious then, that players never actually address the vast majority of their errors. Almost every athlete and coach you ask will say that '80 per cent of success lies in the mental game'. I'm not sure how we got to this 'rule of thumb' number. I'd challenge it, suggesting that individual success derives 50 per cent from the technical (the science) and 50 per cent from the mental/emotional game (the art). The skewing lies in the fact that coaches spend probably 80-90 per cent of their time focusing on technique and skill, and almost no time really addressing the mental game. The main reason for this is the hierarchical approach of traditional coaching. If a batsman were to tell his coach that he folded under pressure or succumbed to doubt or a lack of confidence, he may not get picked again. If he were to say that he is scared of the short ball, it's unlikely he would get to open the batting again. (I refer to the masculine here, as males are generally more predisposed than females to hiding their vulnerabilities or insecurities.)

Coaches want players who are supposedly mentally tough. I'm of the view that out of the 150 top international cricketers, there are perhaps five players who are 'mentally tough'. There are uncertainties, vulnerabilities and cracks inside every single human being, including almost every single professional athlete. But given the way most coaches work with their athletes, they are discouraged from talking about these cracks.

Arguing the importance of an *internal* coaching focus in sport, Timothy Gallwey, author of *The Inner Game of Tennis*, suggests that the opponent within one's head is more formidable than any external opponent.[8] He claims that if a coach can help a player remove or reduce the internal obstacles to his or her performance, an unexpected natural ability will flow forth without the need for much technical input from the coach.

Also, after studying more than fifty of the world's top performers in more than twenty different sports codes, ex-Olympian and author David Hemery found that *attitude* or *state of mind* (an internal factor) was key to performance of any kind, way above technique or fitness (external factors), neither of which guarantees excellence, or is even indispensable.[9]

Personally, I have yet to meet a batsman who is not in some way scared of a bouncer—and I'm sure the same goes for coaches who were once players. As a cricketer, I was certainly scared. And that's fine. It's high time we started talking about and addressing the ripest area for athletic development, the normal, human frailties that lead to 80-95 per cent of errors—the errors in thinking.

As Leonard Cohen wrote in *Anthem*: 'Forget your perfect offering / There is a crack in everything / That's how the light gets in.'

PERFORMANCE FOCUS VERSUS PERSONAL FOCUS

The third and last framework that emerged in the course of my study is possibly the most fundamental of all. It relates to the distinction between treating a person based on the performance they deliver, and treating them as a person first, separate from performance or results.

A performance focus and a personal focus represent two different approaches to leadership. Here I found the biggest discrepancy between coaches' preferences and players' needs. While the players indicated a preference for a more personal approach, ideally wanting 52 per cent of the coaches' focus to be on who the player is as a unique individual (and 48 per cent on their performance), the coaches had a 33 per cent preference for this personal focus, and a 67 per cent preference for their focus to be on performance, on things like results, skills and fitness.

Sachin Tendulkar provides a beautiful illustration of a player's preference for the personal focus. Shortly after being appointed as the Indian head coach, but before officially reporting for duty, Gary Kirsten accompanied the Indian team to Australia for a Test series. He went along in an observational capacity, having one-on-ones with each player in order to understand what they wanted from him as coach. Sachin answered: 'I want you to be my friend.'

You won't find Sachin's coaching preference prescribed anywhere in a traditional coaching manual.

All twenty-one of the professional cricketers I interviewed felt that man-management was a more important coaching requirement than knowledge of the game; that knowledge of the game (technical and strategic expertise) and knowledge of coaching (enhancing skill and getting the best out of players) were two fundamentally different skill sets, and the former did not necessarily lead to the latter. What players wanted was similar to what the best leaders in business were doing to bring the best out in their employers, yet both were measurably different from what professional cricket coaches in South Africa were doing.

In the years following my academic and corporate exploration of leadership, I spent a lot of time coaching professional athletes, from over ten professional sports, around their mental game. One of the biggest learning experiences on my journey towards becoming a team coach—something I didn't intentionally pursue at the start—was that in my estimate, about 80 per cent of the obstacles to performance that players raised in these conversations related to either the team environment and/or their personal lives.

Some of the common concerns raised were: 'I'm asked to play a role that's not ideal for my game/skills'; 'I don't like the way I'm treated'; 'Many players don't agree with the way things are being done; we over-train, we feel there is a much better way', etc. This insight into players' minds would prove to be invaluable when Gary and I arrived in India to work with one of the biggest brands in cricket. The changing landscape of leadership I studied could not but inform the type of environment we tried to create when working with people. Yet, moving from an academic conviction to implementing the underlying principles in a real world sporting environment was a journey rather than an event, as we would soon learn.

Part 2

THE INDIA JOURNEY

4

ARRIVING IN INDIA

When Sunil Gavaskar contacted Gary Kirsten at the end of 2007 about the position of the Indian head coach, Gary didn't respond to the message at first. He thought it was a prank, since he had never coached a cricket team in his life, not even his sons' Under-9 school team.

Sunil persisted, and eventually Gary went to India for an interview. I got to hear about it while I was doing maintenance work at home in Cape Town, when my wife brought me the telephone. It was Gary. He said that if he was offered the job, he wanted me to come with him. In the weeks that followed and before he departed for the interview, he and I discussed the opportunity at some length. Gary didn't prepare a formal presentation to the board. Instead, he told them, 'You asked me to apply for the job. So, ask me any questions and I'll answer them.'

In the end, Gary was appointed, and after some convincing, he managed to have my appointment approved. It was difficult to explain to the Indian authorities exactly what I would do, but I was effectively going to be the mental conditioning coach, and because I had previous fitness experience, I was going to be the physical conditioning coach too, as well as the 'strategic leadership coach'. The last role, which did not exist in cricket at the time, would focus on the strategic leadership of people and team culture, as opposed to imparting strategic cricketing expertise.

Gary had never coached a cricket team prior to this assignment. I had never worked as a mental conditioning coach for a team, and my other role of strategic leadership coach still required definition. Neither of us registered on the international coaching radar. A while after being appointed, we were told that one of the Indian Cricket Board (BCCI) members and interviewers had left Gary's job interview saying, 'I thought Kepler Wessels was very good in there.' On the day of the interview, whilst sitting in a waiting room at the BCCI's Mumbai (Wankhede Stadium) offices, Gary bumped into the then India Test captain, Anil Kumble. He, too, didn't know what Gary was doing there.

We went in as green as any coaches could possibly be, to lead the biggest brand in cricket and one of the biggest brands in world sport. In India, cricket has for long been the popular sport of choice, built on the God-like adoration players enjoy in the eyes of the worshipping masses. Since Kapil Dev's side won the 1983 World Cup, the marketing value of Indian cricket has also grown exponentially.

Nike, the world's biggest sports brand, is a case in illustration. One might expect that it would be as involved in cricket as it is in many other sports. But in February 2015, *Forbes* reported: 'And yet, despite its involvement in seemingly every corner of the sports world, the top brand's iconic swoosh adorns the jersey of just a single team (at the 2015 Cricket World Cup): India. Nike joined up with India back in 2005 on what was reported to be a five-year deal worth just under $45 million, or roughly $9 million per year. That original agreement was later extended to include the 2011 World Cup, a savvy move considering that India went on to win the tournament on home soil that year. Shortly afterwards, Nike fought off a competing Adidas bid and re-upped with India for five additional years at more than $12 million per year.'[1]

In 2017, the Chinese smartphone manufacturer Oppo won the bid to become India's next team sponsor, committing $162 million over a period of five years ($32.4 million per annum). This is easily cricket's biggest team sponsorship to date.

At the time of writing, India's Virat Kohli had moved ahead of the FC Barcelona and Argentina football star Lionel Messi on the *Forbes* list of the most valuable brands among athletes. Swiss tennis legend Roger Federer was numero uno at $37.2 million, Kohli seventh at $14.5 million, and Messi ninth with $13.5 million.[2]

And here we were, Gary and I, a hillbilly from Cape Town (Gary) and a barefoot surfer from Houtbay (me). We had our work cut out for us!

Sitting in an aeroplane flying to India, we thought up some really ambitious goals for the team. We wanted to win the ICC (50-over) World Cup, something India hadn't done in twenty-seven years. We wanted to help them to the number one World Test Ranking, a position they hadn't yet got to. We knew we had to create a happy team environment. And the fourth thing we set out to do was to help players become better people through our interventions.

We didn't share this last goal with anyone, firstly because we had not been employed to help players to become better people; we were supposed to make them win, and, secondly, due to our own doubts over the possible arrogance of the goal. Who were we to think we could help other people become better human beings? We knew, however, that by being more rounded, grounded individuals who were secure in themselves, the players could go a long way towards achieving those other goals.

So, if these were the four goals we were setting out to achieve, the fundamental question we asked ourselves was: What could we introduce to the environment that could help the players and the team improve their performances? How could we be of real service to Team India?

A few months earlier, after spending time with the team in an observational capacity during their Australian tour, Gary had managed to have conversations with each of the players, and the majority had indicated that what they wanted was direction—a clear strategy going forward. The previous coach, Greg Chappell, had left them in an unhappy space and for some months they had been working with a caretaker coach.

Stories about the team's discontent with the previous coaching 'regime' would reach us upon our arrival in India. It became clear to us that the unhappiness hadn't sprung from Chappell's ideas around cricket—his cricketing brain was second to none. But he had used a very dictatorial, strongly instruction-based approach to get his message across. The Indian players didn't like somebody ordering them to do things. From my understanding, Chappell had very good information, but employed a fairly ineffective way to get players to buy into his considerable cricketing expertise. Also, players accused him of using the Indian coaching platform to further his public profile.

We took stock of the players in the team: Anil Kumble, Sourav Ganguly, Sachin Tendulkar, Rahul Dravid, V.V.S. Laxman, M.S. Dhoni, Yuvraj Singh, Harbhajan Singh, Zaheer Khan, all great cricketers. Whatever facilities we required were available. Greg Chappell had brought in some of the best thinking in terms of individual game plans and strategy. Yet, all that had delivered was a 39 per cent win ratio in Test cricket and a 51 per cent win ratio in ODIs, culminating in the team being eliminated from the 2007 ICC Cricket World Cup in round one. We weren't going to come up with any new or better players, better thinking or improved systems. We had to do something completely different with exactly what Chappell had to work with. And we had no experience whatsoever.

Still, Gary had learned that we primarily needed to give the team direction; that we needed to do that in a collaborative style; and we couldn't do what we were going to do in a self-promotional way.

Gary is an extremely diligent individual and, in the months leading up to our departure to India, he'd had many conversations and planning sessions with leadership experts, personal mentors and business coaches—most often at the Vineyard Hotel in Cape Town. Before our departure for India, we had created a vivid strategy that we were going to present to the players during our first three-day camp with them.

We couldn't have been better prepared—mentally, physically and theoretically. Gary was to present the strategy to the players, and as I would end up doing over the next three years, I would closely observe their levels of engagement, while also observing Gary's verbal and body language. The aim was to deliver the message in a way that had the best chance of landing with the greatest number of players, and to make sure that it served their needs, not only ours. I would give him feedback on his use of language, his body language, and whatever we thought could improve the effectiveness of his message. One of the key principles in our strategy was to give the players nothing to resist or push back against. Our message had to be fluid enough to create a dialogue if a player didn't see something the same way we did. Another hostile environment was exactly what the Indian team didn't need.

These ideas were the building blocks with which we arrived in India. And they survived a mere ninety minutes. Coaching is a mystery, you see!

As Gary presented our vision and strategy to the players, they nodded, smiled, and said they were happy with what we had laid out in front of them. But there was something insincere and unconvincing in their approval. As Gary and I sat down for a cup of tea after the first session, we looked at each other and almost simultaneously said, 'Oh shit! That didn't land.'

All that effort, all those deliberations, all the hard work Gary had done for months in advance, and our message to the players didn't land. We couldn't tell why, but intuitively we knew we had to change course immediately. From that day on, feeling and intuition became a very strong part of our leadership style in India.

In the fifteen minutes between sessions, we reworked the schedule and did a complete 180-degree turnaround in our proposed strategy. When Gary spoke to the players again, he told them that they were a relatively successful international team, so there had to be certain things that were working well for them. We proceeded to divide the players and support staff into groups of about seven, and asked them to discuss and write down all the things in their environment they felt were working well or even fairly well: strategy, training, team meetings, logistics, supporting structures, whatever. The different groups then fed those things back into a conversation we had as a team, which I captured on a flip chart.

During lunch, Gary and I organised this player feedback into a basic template of on-field performance, off-field systems and team values/culture. He then presented the reworked strategy to the team as the 'starting strategy' for this new Indian unit working with a new head coach. The players' response to the 'new strategy' was fundamentally different from the first attempt. They were engaged, the smiles seemed more sincere, and although I didn't yet understand the Indian head wave, it felt more like a 'yes'. It became crystal clear that all the things the players heard and saw in the presentation that afternoon were the things that were already working for them. We had just confirmed and reinforced what they already knew, even if it wasn't yet articulated in a way that made strategic sense. It was their own words and sentiments, so there was nothing to resist.

That was a key learning experience on the very first morning: If you want to present to these players what they want, don't think you can go in and present to them what you *think* they want. That's what Gary and I had done in coming up with the original strategy. If you want to know what people think, ask them. When we did that, we took the first steps in handing ownership of the team back to the players. There was early and sincere buy-in. Not once did we ask what wasn't working and what needed fixing. We improved the environment by highlighting and then seeking to enhance the existing strengths within the team.

We defined the coaching and support staff functions as: to protect the team environment from potentially destructive outside forces (administrators, ex-players' criticism, some media, etc.) and internal forces (cliques, fractures, unhealthy competition, power games, etc. that can plague the team from the inside), and to nurture players by praising, protecting, inspiring, motivating, encouraging and serving them, individually and as a group, in their quest to become the best cricketers and team in the world. It was all about serving the players' needs and best interests, and not our own. We captured this in one PowerPoint slide and, over the next three years, would regularly begin our support staff meetings with this reminder.

The first practice session was where the rubber really hit the road. This, too, was an undeniable moment of growth for both of us as coaches. Helping the players improve was an academic goal until we arrived at the first practice where bowlers were actually bowling and batsmen were actually hitting balls.

I stood some distance away from the players. For the first time since arriving in India, I was really nervous. The reality had hit home for this barefoot surfer, now dressed in new sponsored Nike running shoes and Indian cricket apparel. I felt exposed and remember thinking: How on earth am I going to help these guys? This was the first of many occasions when I felt like a bit of a fraud and asked myself whether I really had all that it took to be in my role. Some of the best coaches I've met have subsequently shared, somewhat sheepishly, that at times, they also feel the same way. It's a relief to know I'm not alone.

Back at that first practice, I looked over to where Gary was standing behind the bowlers, and went to stand next to him, hoping to be comforted by his calmness. But I could sense the uncertainty in him too. I said, 'Gazza, how are we going to help these guys?' I can't recall exactly what we said to each other. It was more nervous chatter than anything else; an attempt to ease our own anxieties.

But by the time we had watched the first three groups of batsmen practising in the nets, my confidence had started to grow. We began to see where we could really make a difference. For top international players, many of them prepared poorly. With the exception of Rahul Dravid, Sachin Tendulkar and one or two others, most of them seemed to just go through the motions. All they did was the stock standard net sessions. They would bat, sometimes even fool around, get out five times, and then leave the nets. Given the level at which they performed, there was a definite lack of quality in their training. Rahul and Sachin would practise stuff that would have relevance in the Test they'd be playing in three days' time, but there seemed to be little thinking or match-specific training going on with some of the others. And we knew we could help them with that. We were anxious, yes, but if nothing else, we knew we could create an environment where professional preparation could support the kind of ambitious goals the team had set out for themselves.

Eventually, India went from a side that prepared poorly to one that turned preparation into a defining quality. A year into our tenure with the side, I overheard a conversation between Gary and Rahul Dravid. Gary asked him: 'What has changed that the players are now such good preparers?' Rahul answered: 'It's because *you* work so hard.'

Gary worked up such a sweat throwing to players in the Indian heat, that even his socks and shoes were dripping wet after some training sessions, as if he had gone swimming with his shoes on. But if the player asked him whether he wanted to rest, his response was always the same: 'No, I'm here for you. I'll keep throwing until you feel prepared.' We didn't tell people what to do. We never had a single conversation with the players about how they needed to improve their preparation. Rather than telling, Gary demonstrated what he wanted from the players. The advantage of this kind of servant leadership is that players step over the boundary rope knowing that they have prepared as well as possible, with the coach leaving no stone unturned in supporting the players' preparation. Players took the responsibility and worked in close cooperation, consultation and negotiation with the coach on what they believed needed rounding off. This is by no means a model that allows a coach to sit on his hands. You dirty your hands precisely so that the players can grow, learn and think for themselves.

The growing and learning were not, of course, limited to the players. We, too, had much to learn, especially given our lack of coaching acumen.

Through research and experience, Gary and I would come to understand that the Indian players were definitely not used to giving negative or critical feedback. Whenever Gary and I came up with a new or innovative idea with which we thought we might be onto something but weren't sure, we'd present it to the players, believing that they would be able to knock it into something worthwhile. In the beginning, almost all the players agreed with almost everything we said, which made it difficult to know what they did really agree with, or what, out of respect for authority, they were only *saying* they agreed with. In those early days, they never openly disagreed or were critical of our ideas.

Typically, we'd all get together before practice or a match, and Gary would give his inputs to the team, mostly on points of strategy and high level reminders. In my dual roles, I felt I had a lot to offer. I would therefore always make a brief contribution around some aspect of the mental game. I never really knew whether it was working, but since the players were looking at me and appeared to be listening, I assumed that my inputs were valuable.

Unbeknown to me, I had been getting something wrong, as I would soon find out.

About three months into our tenure and after about twenty such contributions from me, we walked away from yet another team meeting. M.S. Dhoni, who was captain of the one-day side, came to me, put his arm around my shoulders and said, 'Paddy, don't feel that you always have to say something.'

It was subtly put, but it hit me straight in the ego!

After that, I remember struggling to know when to speak and when to keep quiet. What did the players want to hear and what didn't they? I'm still wondering about that. It remains a good lesson, to check in with myself and my intentions behind speaking; am I doing it for the sake of speaking, to tick a box, in an attempt to be seen to be doing my job, or to be seen to be clever, or am I saying it because I genuinely believe it is for the players' benefit, and not only mine? Thank you, MS!

As I spent more time in his company, I would come to deeply appreciate Dhoni's way of thinking and leading.

In trying to get the players to give us feedback on what needed to happen for the team to achieve their goals, we once asked them how important it was to be on time, considering that we were a large group of people moving together and had to attend various functions at specific times during the day.

Everyone agreed that being on time was important. So, how should we deal with being late? We threw that question back to the players, knowing that the standard practice was some punitive measure administered by the coach or management.

After some discussion amongst the Test team, captain Anil Kumble concluded that if a person was late, the meeting or bus would continue without them, and they would be fined 10,000 rupees. When we put the same question to the one-day side a short while later, MS listened to the team's views and then decided that if someone was late, every single person should be fined 10,000 rupees. I was fascinated by the impact their differing approaches had on me personally.

I'm someone who skates on the edge of time. All it takes is for a lift to stop on every floor, or something unexpected to happen, and I could be late. V.V.S. Laxman and I were similar in that respect.

Now, with the Test team, I was never overly concerned about being late. If I was late, I'd pay up. But I was never late with the one-day side, since my being late would also impact other people's pockets. I had huge admiration for both Anil and MS, but somehow Dhoni kept me on the very tips of my toes—always!

5

PLAYING TO STRENGTHS

Gary's and my first assignment with the Indian team was a Test series in March 2008 against our home country, South Africa. As the Indian batsmen got ready to face the formidable fast bowling attack of Dale Steyn, Morné Morkel and Makhaya Ntini, opening batsman Virender Sehwag prepared to bear the brunt of it. He played a naturally attacking game, but Sehwag had one major flaw at the time.

He was a compulsive hooker of the short-pitched ball, meaning if the bowler bowled a short-pitched delivery that bounced to head height, he would compulsively attack the ball. This was a high risk shot, and if well-directed by the bowler, could only get hit in the air and the batsman could be caught. The three South African bowlers would target him with this tactic, with deep square leg and deep fine leg fielders positioned for the catch.

Gary suggested that rather than going into the nets to get better at the hook shot, why not eliminate the shot by ducking under the bouncer? Sehwag's response was, 'They would keep bouncing me then, but if I hit them enough, maybe they will stop.' After some discussion, though, he agreed to try ducking. He set about diligently practising all through the next week, with Gary using a tennis racquet to serve hard rubberised balls at his head, at speeds of over 150 kilometres an hour, and from about 18 metres away (less than the 20.12 metre cricket pitch length). It helped that Gary is a very handy tennis player.

To his credit, Sehwag eradicated this weak area from his game in that short time. He focussed on his strengths by attacking the fuller pitched deliveries, and with two fielders placed for the bouncer, it meant one less fielder in the areas he chose to target.

In the first Test in Chennai, in March 2008, the South African pace attack set about bouncing Sehwag when he came to the crease late on day 2 of the game (South Africa had batted first). He ended the day on 52 not out. The next day, the barrage of bouncers continued, and continued. By the end of the day, Sehwag had ducked under all of them, and left the field on 309 not out, having amassed 257 runs in the day. He was finally dismissed for 319, which would not be a one-off success. The first Test was drawn, South Africa won the second, and much to Gary's relief, and mine, India won the third to draw the series. It was clear to both of us that professionalism (wanting India to win) trumped patriotism.

Sehwag never played at another head-high fast-pitched delivery that year, ducking under each one. At the end of the year, he was crowned Wisden Leading Cricketer in the World, and in the following year the International Cricket Council (ICC) Test Player of the Year.

It's becoming increasingly known that the most successful people in the world do the things they are really good at, most of the time. They spend thousands of hours learning and upskilling in the areas where they have natural talent, developing these into core strengths. They then spend the bulk of their time playing to these strengths, which delivers excellence.

The majority of people, however, still believe that focusing on fixing weaknesses or 'areas of growth' will help them become more rounded and thus successful. This is simply not true. Playing to strengths delivers excellence; merely fixing weaknesses does not.

When it comes to focusing on strengths versus weaknesses, which have you been prescribed most often by your parents, teachers, coach or boss? When you came home with your report card, which marks did your parents (or do you as a parent) focus on: the high or low ones? When you bat or bowl in the nets, or you have finished playing a game, does your coach focus more on the things you did well, or on the things you got wrong and need to improve on? How much time do you spend focusing on your own mistakes and the areas where you need to improve, versus the things you are good at, that you enjoy and do really well?

Gallup, one of the world's top performance-management and research companies, interviewed 1.7 million people from 101 companies across 63 countries and found that the majority of the world's population thinks that the secret to improvement lies in fixing weaknesses, rather than building on strengths.[1] They learned that only 20 per cent of people in these businesses played to their strengths every day, which mirrored their finding that most organisations operate at 20 per cent capacity. And on the question of what parents focus on when looking at an exam report, Gallup found that 77 per cent of parents noticed and focused on the low scores. It's likely that a similar high percentage of parents are lured into conducting a coaching workshop in the car on the way home from their child's sporting event, focusing on the things they did wrong.

These key points are worth repeating and remembering:

- Playing to strengths delivers excellence.
- Patching up your weaknesses will never lead to excellence.
- Because the majority of the world still believes that fixing mistakes is the way to succeed, a wonderful opportunity exists to move ahead of the pack.

HOW DOES ONE PLAY TO STRENGTHS?

There is an important difference between talent, a strength and a learned skill. Talent is something you were born with; it holds the potential for you to do well. But talent alone is not enough to achieve lasting success. When talent is repeatedly worked on to the point that it constantly produces near-perfect performance, it becomes a strength. When you spend time working to improve a weakness or something that is not a natural talent and you become fairly good at it, it's known as a learned skill. Examples of developing a learned skill may include Sehwag playing a bouncer, a marathon runner working on her sprint speed, or a creative person trying to do her own accounting.

Talent + Smart Work = Strength
Non-talent + Smart Work = Learned Skill

Developing a talent into a strength will take you part of the way to achieving excellence and consistent results. The next part requires you to play to your strengths for the largest portion of your practice and match time, or your time at the office. It's like buying a really good fishing rod that is strong enough to land a trophy fish. Having the rod is not enough to catch the fish; you need to use that rod often enough to give yourself the best chance of success.

In contrast to playing to a strength, regularly playing to a learned skill (a weakness that you have fixed) can lead to good results, but not excellence.

Strength + Regular Application = Excellence
Learned Skill + Regular Application = Good

How do you differentiate between a strength and a learned skill? One way is to observe how you feel after a day at practice or work. Playing to strengths is generally easy and enjoyable. You can do it the whole day and at the end still be full of energy. It may even feel like you haven't actually been working.

In contrast, spending a day working at a learned skill is more difficult, less enjoyable, and energy-sapping. You may feel a sense of accomplishment, but you will probably be exhausted and will feel like you have worked hard. Office administration feels like hard work to me; I am not drawn to do it and it tires me out, even though I can do it pretty well. I know this is not my area of strength. Giving my bookkeeping and tax to someone else to do, someone who thrives on this kind of work, has been a huge relief.

Neurophysiologist Katherine Benzinger showed that when using natural or preferred learning strengths, people learned easily and rapidly, with increased concentration, fewer errors, and a heightened sense of personal satisfaction and well-being.

On the other hand, Professor Richard Haier, Professor of Psychology at the University of California, used brain imaging studies to demonstrate that the brain needs to work as much as a hundred times harder when the individual is not using his or her natural work preferences. Normally the brain uses approximately 20 per cent of the oxygen taken in through the lungs. As more and more oxygen is demanded by the brain to perform unnatural or non-preferred ways of learning, less and less is available to the body, resulting in a variety of symptoms such as difficulty in mastering a skill, a higher than normal error rate, difficulty with concentration, stress, fatigue and listlessness. I wonder how many school children who are diagnosed with Attention Deficit Disorder (ADD) are that way due to being asked to do things in an environment that simply does not suit their learning preferences and natural talents—and how many of them are prescribed drugs as the solution. A time may well come, and hopefully soon, when we look back on this madness and shake our heads at our ignorance.

DEVELOPING A TALENT INTO A STRENGTH

Developing a talent into a strength takes a lot of input. I deliberately use the word input and not work, because focusing on strengths often does not feel like work. It does, however, require a considerable investment of time, a hunger to learn, and focused practice. When I present this part of the discussion on strengths, I am frequently asked about Malcolm Gladwell's often-quoted 10,000-hour principle (in his book *Outliers*), which holds that it takes 10,000 hours of deliberate practice to become world-class in any field.[2] Whilst Gladwell is fascinating to read, and I've learned loads from his unconventional views on conventional subjects, I'm not entirely convinced by his 10,000-hour principle.

If I were to spend 10,000 hours learning the piano, with my unfortunate lack of musical talent, I might become very good, but will still not become a great concert pianist. If I spent that same time surfing good waves, apart from being the happiest man alive, I will have an excellent chance of winning surf contests, thanks to my natural bodily-kinaesthetic talent (body movement control).

Let's say someone works an average of eight hours per day for five days a week, and takes four weeks' leave per year. This equates to 1,920 hours of work per year, which means that according to Gladwell's theory, it would take this person just over five years and two months to become world class. Okay, few people really work eight hours a day. So let's say with natural avoidance tactics, social media distractions, smoke breaks and talking around the coffee machine or water cooler, this same person does four hours of work per day, which is more realistic. According to Gladwell, they should still achieve world-class status in just over ten years. We all know this does not happen.

The original authors of the study that Gladwell popularised with his 10,000-hour rule suggested his interpretations weren't very accurate.[3] What Gladwell's principle does not account for is talent, quality of input and different professions. To achieve the excellence akin to the people Gladwell studied, one needs to:

a) Invest considerable time in an area of natural-born talent.
b) Have a hunger to learn and constantly improve.

The principle of applying thousands of hours to achieve excellence is also more applicable in predictable and stable professions such as music and sport. The scrap heap of talented athletes who never make it, who never deliver on their potential, is piled high. Among the main reasons for this is that they are already so good at a younger age and things come so easily that many simply do not invest the amount of time or the quality of training required to develop their talents into strengths. Thanks to their natural talent, possibly further enhanced by an early growth spurt and the early-age success it brings, they often don't learn the commitment, determination, grit or resilience that comes from having to fight from behind, all of which underpin sustained success in most sports, and life.

Late developers and those with adequate talent who have to really apply themselves just to stay with the game tend to enjoy more success later in sport and in life. At the time of writing my first master's thesis (on rugby injuries), of all the rugby players selected to play for the South African national team, the Springboks, only one in ten had made the national under-19 team; the other nine developed post the age of nineteen. Another study showed that only 24 per cent of inter-provincial under-13 rugby players went on to later be selected at the provincial under-18 level, which represents a 76 per cent dropout rate.[4] This is another example showing that early-age sport success is not a good indicator of success in high school years and beyond.

Also, too many athletes spend too much time working on their weaknesses, misdirected by well-meaning coaches or parents who are constantly focusing on where they are not doing well. Spending too much time working on, and thinking about, areas of weakness decreases energy, motivation and self-confidence. I don't blame an athlete for not wanting to spend thousands of hours training under these circumstances. In fact, few athletes or musicians will be able to grind their way through 10,000 hours if they are not naturally talented, and if they are not in an environment where they are able to naturally thrive. Too much repetitive training at younger ages (up to the age of fifteen or sixteen) leads to boredom, decreased learning, and earlier than necessary dropout rates from the sport, whilst too many hours of training leads to injury and early burnout. The only people who likely put in more than 10,000 hours in an area of non-talent or in an unfavourable environment are people who *have to* work. Their engagement and productivity are likely to be low despite the investment of time.

DEVELOPING STRENGTHS INTO EXCELLENCE

Once a talent has been developed into a strength, one should find a profession and an environment where that strength can be routinely applied. The gift of being able to regularly play to strengths, with only a small amount of time being spent on other skills, translates to the best chance of achieving excellence through consistent near perfect performance. It is important for leaders to understand this and to recognise that the majority of people in the world, including in sport and business, still believe in fixing weaknesses and dictating to people what and how to do their work. The opportunity to forge ahead of the pack lies in the ability (and courage) to shift from the old management or coaching philosophy towards a more empowering and strengths-focused environment.

The Gallup survey revealed that people who play to strengths are six times more likely to be engaged in their job (versus simply going through the motions) and are over three times more likely to have an excellent quality of life compared to those who spend their time fixing weaknesses. Businesses that allow people to focus on strengths engage about 73 per cent of employees compared to 9 per cent being engaged in businesses that do not.

In summary, developing talents into strengths requires:

- Majority of training time to be focused on areas of natural talent.

- A constant hunger to learn and improve. The opposite of this is arrogance and a 'know-it-all'/'I have arrived at the top' attitude.
- Preparing with purpose and direction, not just whittling away the hours by going through the motions.
- And hopefully a coach, parent or boss who employs a player-centric coaching approach, allowing people to play to their own natural learning preferences, brain styles and strengths within an environment of growth and learning rather than of fear, control and obedience.

Sachin Tendulkar was born with a great cricketing talent. He was lucky in his schooldays to be able to spend many hours developing this talent. And as he navigated his way through his professional career, he never let up on seeking to further develop, learn and advance on his batting strengths.

It is fairly well known that when Sachin was still in his early teens, his coach would drive him around Mumbai from one cricket match to the next, so that he could bat in three and sometimes four matches per day. At the end of it all, his coach would put a coin on top of a stump and local kids would bowl to him, spurred on by the reward of the coin if they hit the stump. In this way, Sachin probably hit more cricket balls in advancing his talents than possibly any other child in India at that time. On the other side of the world, I personally watched the tiny figure of Jacques Kallis spending hours in the cricket nets as a young boy, his father endlessly throwing to him, day in and day out. Both Tendulkar and Kallis became examples of what dedicated, focused and deliberate practice can do in an area of strength. Both achieved consistent, near-perfect skill.

In my tenure with the Indian team, which was in Sachin's eighteenth to twenty-first year of international cricket, the professor of batting almost always hit more balls in any given practice week than any of his teammates. This was despite the fact that he had earned the right to take things easy. But he didn't. In fact, only in one practice session in three years did I see him hitting aimlessly at balls, playing loose shots and visibly distracted. Most players have a few off days like this, but I had not seen Sachin have one, and I must admit it was unexpected. Something was bothering him, and it must have been fairly significant because it took well over two hours to get the frustration out of his system.

I went to his room later that day to see if he wanted to talk about whatever was bothering him. After unsuccessfully fishing around for what it might be, I mentioned that he had practised differently that day. He agreed instantly. He said he had completed his one-day batting preparation earlier in practice. Thereafter, his plan had been to practise bending down into his stance, playing a shot and then standing up again, for two-and-a-half hours. He explained that as we were near the end of the ODI part of the tour, he wanted to get his body, specifically his lower back, ready for longer periods of batting in the Test series which was due to start in ten days' time. So he was in fact following a clear plan. He wasn't 'batting' as much as he was 'exercising' his lower back.

THE PROBLEM WITH FIXING WEAKNESSES

Business managers are common perpetrators of the weakness focus. Gallup's research with 80,000 managers from hundreds of organisations around the world showed they had two flawed assumptions about people:

1. Each person can learn to be competent in almost anything.
2. Each person's greatest room for growth is in his or her areas of greatest weakness.

They suggest that one way to check whether your own organisation holds these assumptions is to look for these characteristics:

- Your organisation spends more money on training people once they are hired than on selecting them properly in the first place.
- Your organisation controls performance by placing a heavy emphasis on work rules, policies, procedures and 'behavioural competencies'.
- Your organisation spends most of its training time and money on trying to plug the gaps in employees' skills or competencies. It calls these gaps 'areas of opportunity'. Your individual

development plan, if you have one, is built around your 'areas of opportunity', your weaknesses.
- Your organisation promotes people based on the skills or experiences they have acquired. After all, if everyone can learn to be competent in almost anything, those who have learned the most must be the most valuable. Thus, by design, your organisation gives the most prestige, the most respect, and the highest salaries to the most experienced, well-rounded people.[5]

The focus on weakness persists not only in business and sport, but also in the fields of research and academia. Martin Seligman, former president of the American Psychological Association and front runner in the field of positive psychology, found that the number of studies done on depression disproportionately outweigh those on the subject of joy, happiness or fulfilment by more than ninety-five to one.[6] Traditional psychology epitomises the focus on diagnosing and fixing problems. Removing the problem, getting someone to be 'not sick' or able to cope with life, is deemed a success. Not sick is quite different from being vibrant and healthy. Fortunately, the new and exciting field of positive psychology, largely pioneered by Seligman, is bridging the gap between coping and thriving in life.

Marcus Buckingham and Donald Clifton, in their book *Now, Discover Your Strengths*, lament that unfortunately most of us have little sense of our talents and strengths, much less the ability to build our lives around them. Instead, guided by our parents, teachers, managers, and by psychology's fascination with pathology, we spend our lives trying to repair these flaws, become passably good in our areas of weakness, while all along our strengths lie dormant.

Since these areas continue to remain our weaknesses, we always run the risk of making mistakes and being exposed. This can create fear either fear of our weaknesses, fear of making a mistake, or fear of being exposed. For many people, this fear undermines their confidence to the extent that it overshadows their confidence in their strengths.

WHEN FIXING A WEAKNESS IS NECESSARY

If you have a weakness or non-talent, which generally will also be something you don't like doing, try your best to delegate this skill to someone who is good at it.

If you genuinely cannot delegate the weakness and it is career-threatening, then do the necessary damage control and upskill this area to just above a pass mark. Get your F up to an E so that it doesn't cause you to fail. In cricket, a really good bowler who can't catch or throw should practice enough to be able to catch the easier catches or to throw the ball to the wicket, even if it is with one bounce. If a batsman scores well off the front foot but gets out to the bouncer, practice ducking under the bouncer—like Sehwag did. This practice should still use up less time and mental energy than working on the strengths that got them into the team in the first place. Similarly, if a really intelligent manager is a very poor speaker, have him or her improve basic speaking skills and no more.

A word of caution here, on misinterpreting 'playing to strengths' as an excuse for not working on something that is important and that falls within the gambit of your strength. Hard-hitting batsman Richard Levi (South Africa) burst onto the international cricket scene with a record 45-ball 100 in a T20 game against New Zealand in February 2012, which saw him go from unsold in the IPL auction a few weeks earlier, to getting a multimillion rand (ZAR) contract by the next morning. Levi had a discernible weakness against left-arm spin bowling as well as when playing the ball on the off-side (which constitutes 50 per cent of the playing field). Because he was new on the international scene, the New Zealanders did not know this at the time of his remarkable innings. Levi himself showed a reluctance to work on his areas of vulnerability, at least with the level of dedication required at the international level. He went on to play only 13 T20 internationals, recording double figures only once in his last 9 innings. After only 6 IPL matches at an average of 13, he went back to being unsold in the auction. To succeed as a batsman in international cricket, it is necessary to have enough strengths to score off most types of bowling, and enough learned skills to survive the rest without getting bogged down or dismissed.

THE WAY FORWARD

Bob Dylan sang, *Come gather 'round people/ Wherever you roam/ And admit that the waters/ Around you have grown/ And accept it that soon/ You'll be drenched to the bone/ If your time to you is worth saving/ Then you better start swimmin' or you'll sink like a stone/ For the times they are a-changin'.*

The best teams and organisations of the future will not only understand and embrace the fact that people are different, they will actively capitalise on these differences. *For the times they are a-changin'.* They will help unearth each person's natural talents and then create as many opportunities as possible to play to and develop these talents into genuine strengths. Such organisations will not first decide on roles and then try to fit people into them, but will understand people's strengths and create roles to match. Truly great organisations will redesign how they select, and then measure and develop their people, building their strategy and success around each person's strengths. *For the times they are a-changin'.*

Buckingham and Clifton predict that such companies will dramatically outperform their competitors. And that the two assumptions that will guide the world's best managers in these great companies are:

1. Each person's talents are enduring and unique.
2. Each person's greatest room for growth is in the areas of his or her greatest strength.

But although the times they are a-changin', not everyone is quick to start swimmin'. Some years after my time with the Indian national side, I was again involved with two different professional T20 cricket teams, where the same opponent was discussed in an important pre-game strategy meeting. That opponent was M.S. Dhoni, then still captain of India, and one of the most skilled hitters of the cricket ball towards the end of a batting innings, which is a time when the game is often won or lost.

In the first instance, I was an observer. The coach and video analyst were leading the team meeting, presenting their well thought-through strategy for the next day. Statistics correctly showed that Dhoni had the least success scoring off the wide full-pitched delivery, called a wide-yorker. The coach told the two main 'death' (the last 4 overs of the game) bowlers to bowl this delivery to Dhoni, and the ensuing discussion revolved around what field placing the two bowlers preferred.

Walking out from that meeting, I asked one of these bowlers how he felt about bowling wide-yorkers to Dhoni, when the pressure and stakes would be at their highest. He replied somewhat sheepishly, 'I'm not really confident about my wide-yorkers at the moment, but I'll try.' Dhoni (and his Indian team) prevailed the next day.

In the second instance, just six weeks later, I was leading the meeting as head coach of the Rajasthan Royals. We were discussing the same player, and the same wide-yorker statistic emerged. Australian James Faulkner would potentially be bowling 1 or maybe 2 overs to Dhoni near the end of the game.

I asked what deliveries he preferred to bowl, and he replied that he wasn't comfortable with his execution of the wide-yorker at that particular moment. He said he'd rather set a field to bluff Dhoni, to lead him to think he was bowling a wide-yorker, but then bowl a deceptively slower ball hitting him on the hip. *That* was Faulkner's best ball, his strength at the time. He chose to stick with what he was good at in a pressure situation, and was happy to let the best man win.

A hand went up in the room. One of the IPL's less experienced players, Pravin Tambe, had done some research of his own. He pointed out that Dhoni was slower to score early on in his innings, and asked if he could bowl to him during that period. Tambe was a slow bowler, and had plans to reduce Dhoni's run scoring even further, as well as a plan to then get him out. Even the most experienced in the room hadn't thought of that particular plan, but all of them supported it.

[margin note: IMPORTANT COACHING POINT]

The result? The spinner kept Dhoni's runs down in the early part of his innings, which forced the error he had predicted, and resulted in him dismissing Dhoni as planned. Planning for opponents' weaknesses and planning for your strengths are two different approaches. Our team won that encounter, and it may just have been as a direct result of having players involved in the planning phase *and* knowing and sticking to their strengths.

Unfortunately, our strengths are often not easy to identify. When asked, most people draw a blank; they do not know what they are really good at. One of the reasons is that our strengths are the things we do easily, without effort or much conscious thought. When someone asks how we do something we do well, the answer is often, 'I don't know, I just do.' We also don't know our strengths because our parents, teachers and coaches generally spend very little time highlighting and discussing them. Because they tend to spend the majority of their time focusing on our weaknesses, we know these well.

There are a number of ways to begin to understand your strengths, a combination of which could include:

- Approach a few people who know you well, asking what they think you do really well.
- Reflect on the things that you enjoy, which have brought you success with the most ease and joy, and the things that, given a choice, you would love to spend most of your professional time on.
- Take the relevant Strengthsfinder tests, either online (www.gallupstrengthscenter.com) or by buying one of the books.

According to Buckingham, developing your strengths is being true to yourself; it is honouring your birthright or God, if you believe your talents are God-given. Spending too much time developing your weaknesses is almost irresponsible. If you want to avoid failure and enjoy average levels of success at best, then fix your weaknesses. If you want to achieve success, build your strengths.

6

INDIA AT WAR

In 2008, when Gary and I started our Indian journey, there were no such things in cricket as the Spidercam, LED bails, day-night Tests or pink balls. The same can be said about some of the shots that are played in the game today. If you wanted to see A.B. de Villiers create the sort of magic that earned him the nickname Mr 360, you needed a remote control and a Sony PlayStation. In a very short span of time, the game has moved from simulation to real-life enchantment. And it will undoubtedly evolve to a stage where simulation and real-life converge as virtual reality becomes commonplace in our lives.

In ten years' time, many of the concepts and innovations discussed here will sound ancient to a generation coming of age during the next evolutionary stage of cricket, which we can only try to imagine. But the route to whatever that future will look like will start with questions and learning.

In T.H. White's *The Once and Future King,* the wizard Merlyn offers some sage advice:

> You may grow old and trembling in your anatomies, you may lie awake at night listening to the disorder of your veins, you may miss your only love, you may see the world about you devastated by evil lunatics, or know your honour trampled in the sewers of baser minds. There is only one thing for it then—to learn. Learn why the world wags and what wags it. That is the only thing which the mind can never exhaust, never alienate, never be tortured by, never fear or distrust, and never dream of regretting.[1]

INDIA AT WAR | 77

In my role as strategic leadership coach of the Indian national side, I had to learn 'why the world wags and what wags it'. The point of departure was to ask four questions around innovation that needed deeper exploration before we could come up with satisfactory answers:

- In five years' time, are the best coaches and players going to be doing the same things they are doing today? Probably not.
- So, what are coaches and players going to be doing in five years' time? The choice would be to either follow, waiting to see what others come up with, or lead by unearthing and bringing in those new innovations.
- Closer home, are we doing everything possible to set this Indian team up for success? Are there new or other things we could be doing?
- A fourth question, which delivered more value and 'innovation' than the preceding one: Is everything we are doing setting us up for success? In other words, are our current practices relevant and helpful in the pursuit of our goals of becoming the number one team in the world in Test cricket and at the World Cup in 2011?

I had to understand the trends that were unfolding in performance, technology, fitness, diet, leadership and people management before extrapolating these themes to cricket. I had already taken the leadership trends from the sharpest minds in academia and business and extrapolated these to what was going to happen in the future of cricket. That was the easy part, since other industries had already got there.

Extrapolation without contextualisation is a senseless exercise, however. India and Indians were as foreign to Gary and me as we probably were to them, and yet, that was our context. So, before we could try to answer any of the aforementioned questions, we needed to develop at least some understanding of this unknown world we were trying to influence for the better.

If, for instance, the Indian team were an individual, what would its psyche look like? We had to try and understand the Indian DNA, much as I would in later years try to understand the 'chokers' element that seemingly underpinned the South African psyche in ICC tournaments. What was that unseen, intangible psyche of the unit that manifested itself through the actions and behaviours on the field?

I read, researched and spoke to a lot of people. I read books by Indian authors who wrote specifically for foreigners doing business in India. I read foreigners writing about doing business in India. I tried to understand the differences between Eastern philosophy and thinking and Western philosophy and thinking, since Gary and I were coming in with a Western mindset. I followed business mythologist Devdutt Pattanaik's work on ancient mythology, seeking to understand the fundamental differences between India's cyclic, fuzzy logic, relative, multiple-life thinking and the linear, binary logic, absolute, one-life worldviews of the Western world.

I remember I was reading a business book during a four-day warm-up match when Robin Singh, our fielding coach at the time, spoke to me. He had played cricket for India, but had grown up in the West Indies before moving to India at the age of nineteen. He was forty-four at the time, and had lived in India for twenty-five years, but he spoke no language other than English. He said to me, 'Paddy, you can read as much as you want, research as much as you want, and you can spend ten years learning. Just know that you'll never fully understand India or Indians.' This wasn't Robin being difficult; this was an 'outsider' of twenty-five years giving advice to an outsider coach who was trying to conquer unknown territory in just a few months. After working in India for over a decade now, I still find Robin's advice invaluable. No matter how much I come to understand India and Indians, I know there is much left to know. I keep asking questions, keep listening to answers, and keep getting baffled by India's mysteries.

One of the books I read during this period alluded to some of India's war efforts, and as I read, I noticed some striking resemblances with Indian cricket efforts. As I turned my search towards the history of India at war, I was amazed to find that it was actually helping me understand how that same Indian psyche played itself out on the cricket field. I eventually presented my findings to the team in the form of a narrated homemade video, with *Elysium* from the movie *Gladiator* as background music. After a brief exercise to get the players fully present and into a mindful state, this is what was presented:

Home versus away: Unlike most major civilisations, India has rarely pursued a war outside of the greater Asian subcontinent. Unfamiliar with doing battle outside the borders of its mother country, as is required in international cricket, India during the years 1983 to 2003 won a meagre 20 per cent of games played outside its borders, compared to a win ratio of 52 per cent at home. In Test cricket, the ultimate battle played out on the cricket fields, India had won only 10 per cent of matches away, compared to 57 per cent within its borders.

Attacking first: Modern India has never been an aggressor at war. It has never been first to strike. It has never taken the battle to the opposition. In the 1971 war with Pakistan, the Pakistan Air Force struck a number of airfields in northern India before India officially declared war. In comparison, and historically, Indian cricket teams were not known to attack first or to dominate from the start of a cricket series. Between 1983 and 2003, India went 1-0 up in only 20 per cent of the series the team played, compared to going 0-1 down in 80 per cent.

Fighting back: India's war efforts have always been founded on resilience. Once attacked, India excels at fighting back—fuelled by passion and pride in defending country and honour. A good example of this is the 1971 war, which was over a mere two weeks after Pakistan attacked. The Indian Army had overrun erstwhile East Pakistan (Bangladesh) and taken 93,000 prisoners of war. It was one of the swiftest military campaigns in recent history. Similarly, Indian cricketers have performed best when their backs were to the wall. This is best illustrated by the 2001 fightback against Australia. Often hailed as the greatest Test series ever, Australia won the first Test, and in the second, scored 445 and forced India to follow-on after dismissing them for 171. With their backs firmly to the wall, India went on to score 657 with V.V.S. Laxman and Rahul Dravid scoring 281 and 180 respectively in a partnership of 376. Australia were bowled out for 212 and lost the match, with India going on to win the next, clinching the series 2-1.

Handing back the advantage: India at war has been uniquely forgiving, either handing back territories or not pushing home the advantage. Without going into unnecessary detail, this was illustrated in 1965 when Prime Minister Lal Bahadur Shastri generously returned the strategically located Hajipir Pass in Jammu and Kashmir to Pakistan. Again, in 1971, Indira Gandhi handed almost all military gains back to Pakistan. Similarly, the warriors of Indian cricket had been known to hand the advantage back to the opposition, becoming complacent once ahead. During our time in India, complacency was often identified in team meetings as the team's biggest 'red flag'.

Divide and conquer: India as a nation has long been divided along regional and cultural lines; north against south, state against state, Hindu against Muslim, and caste against caste. Exploiting this to their advantage, foreign rulers held on to their power by maintaining these inherent divisions amongst the nation's people, conquering them by division. Dating back some time, Indian cricket too was known to be a team divided by region, culture and even seniority. In response, opposition teams have openly acknowledged working to fragment the team, seeking to divide and conquer—a tactic that reportedly worked on many an occasion. It was a tactic Gary and I were completely aware of when we joined Team India. From playing against them, and from observing them, we knew the Indian team was easy to divide into factions based on class, seniority, skill level.

Individualism: Further illustrating division or individualism in battle, India's finest warriors, the Sikhs, Jats, Rajputs and Gurkhas once fought in isolation rather than together, and more often against each other than against a common enemy—a fragmentation that saw their regions being subjugated to the rule of outsiders. In comparison, the Indian cricket team has historically been characterised as one where individuals are often placed ahead of the team. Like their soldiers at war, they have been known to do battle in isolation rather than as part of a unified team.

Talk versus action: Indians have often been accused of confusing talk with action. An example of this was the revolutionary movement to overthrow the English during their occupation of India. Many Indians agreed with the young rebels' violent tactics, but few acted on this and followed suit.

In the video, I went on to suggest that 'sport is a modern-day version of warfare, where fuelled by the pride of doing battle, one nation pits their finest competitors against the other. Using every means of combat and strategy available, each nation's warriors seek the spoils of victory and try to avoid the disappointment of loss'. I spoke of how history has a habit of repeating itself, until someone has the insight to say 'enough' and then has the courage to act to change it.

I then presented a direct challenge to the Indian team:

- If history were to be repeated, India would continue with an average win ratio abroad when compared to the ratio at home. To rewrite it, we would need to prepare well enough to win under all conditions and in all countries.
- If history were to be repeated, India would continue to take the fight to some of the opposition, and only some of the time. Rewriting history would require that we take the fight to all the opposition, attacking first and taking the lead from the outset of battle, all the time.
- If history were to be repeated, we would play best when coming from behind. To rewrite history, when ahead, we would have to commit ourselves to drive home the domination until the last battle is fought.
- History would continue to be repeated if we became complacent and handed back the initiative, compared to making winning a habit and relegating complacency to the history books. History would be repeated if individuals only acted in their own best interests and played more for themselves than for the team.
- The team may once have been divided along lines of seniority, regionalism, background and culture, so history would be rewritten if the players were to place the team first and team unity became one of our core strengths, with everyone enjoying one another's company and success, and differences being embraced.
- History would be repeated if we spoke about being the best in the world, but did not have or show the courage to act.

The video ended with a call to action: 'To rewrite history would require us to act, practise and prepare our skill, our bodies and our minds as professionals, taking full responsibility as individuals and as a team, to do what it takes. As India moves to conquer the world on the cricketing battlefields, we will remain humble in our processes, humble in victory, and become known as a team that dies trying, even in defeat.'

Most players visibly resonated with the comparison between India's war versus cricketing efforts. A fascinating conversation ensued, during which details were added to our existing strategy towards world cricket domination. At the time, Yuvraj Singh referred to the side as 'the new Indian cricket team', a phrase that went on to be regularly used as we went about rewriting history.

T.E.A.M. INDIA

Based on this new perspective and previous workshops with the ODI team, a team strategy was formulated that would remain unchanged until we reached the World Cup in March 2011. Based entirely on the inputs and the actual words that players used, the strategy was based around the acronym TEAM, which meant:

- Team comes first: Specifically, players would talk positively about teammates in the media, they would back each other fully on and off the field, perform as a unit, enjoy and celebrate each other's success, and settle any concerns internally.
- Excellent Entertainers: 'Excellent' meant setting world standards of best practice, specifically with a commitment to impressive and specific training (which we often referred to as 'putting money in the bank'). 'Entertainers' meant displaying great skill with bat and ball, including superb fielding and running between wickets, being energetic, and being fit.
- Attitude of winners meant being match winners from every situation, being fighters with the will to win every game, becoming known as the toughest team to play against, giving 110 per cent, being fearless, ruthless and passionate, having belief in ourselves and taking pride in playing for India.
- Mature individuals meant having clear thinking, being smart cricketers, good and clear communicators, each committed to our roles, and determining that we would all be good role models.

At both pre- and post-match meetings, Gary or I would regularly give specific examples of various aspects of T.E.A.M. in action, reinforcing the message for the players. I was all too aware that a strategy like this is useless if it only exists as a poster on the wall in the team dressing room. To deliver on its inherent value, the message needed to be constantly reviewed, refined and embedded in the minds and actions of players.

CHOOSE YOUR BATTLES WISELY

Something rather quirky happened soon after I had presented 'India at War' to the players. It was October 2010, and I was trying to coerce Dhoni to lead the team into a battle with Ricky Ponting's Australian team; a battle which most Indian players were oblivious to.

It happened on the opening morning of the two-Test series for the Border-Gavaskar Trophy, and before the first ball was bowled. I was leading the Indian team's warm-up and stretch at the PCA stadium in Mohali, initially doing some running on the outfield, which was still a bit damp from the morning dew. We moved to stretch on the pitch, which had been covered overnight and was quite dry. As we sat down to begin, Ponting led his men for a warm-up lap around the boundary. Halfway around the loop, I noticed him redirect his team. They cut across the field and Ponting led them to run directly through and in between our stretching session. It was deliberately confrontational and it certainly got my blood pumping.

As we completed our stretches, the Aussies sat down at the other side of the field to begin theirs. I went up to Dhoni and told him that we should return the favour and run our team through their warm-up.

Dhoni replied, 'I agree. But let's not bother. Most of the players wouldn't even have noticed that it was a challenge.'

He reminded me that the concept of personal space is different in India, both culturally and due to the sheer numbers. People are used to and comfortable being in close quarters with others and to having others in their space. Later, I asked a few players about the incident, and most of them said that Ponting's gesture didn't really bother them; one of them said he hadn't even noticed it.

I still had lots to learn.

What did happen, though, is that India took the battle onto the field, and delivered a remarkable victory five days later.

Australia piled on 428 runs, thanks to a Shane Watson century. India replied with 405, and then bowled Australia out for 192, leaving a victory target of 216. On a fast deteriorating wicket, India slumped to 124 for 8, still 92 runs short. But (an injured) V.V.S. Laxman was at the crease, and anyone who follows Test cricket knows that there are few better at absorbing the pressure of a fourth innings fight than Lax.

The post-lunch session on day 5 was one of the most dramatic in Test history. Australia would give Laxman a single off the first ball of the over, and pepper the number 10 batsman, Ishant Sharma, with bouncers and verbal abuse for the next five. And so it went on, over after over; Lax would take the single he was offered, and Ishant would get the odd single and boundary himself. This went on for nearly two hours, before Ishant was given out lbw for 31 off 92 deliveries, to a ball which television replays showed had clearly missed the stumps. This was one time India almost paid for refusing to use review technology when all other countries did.

A few moments later, the favour was, however, returned by umpire Billy Bowden, who gave our last batsman, Pragjan Ojha, not out after being clearly struck in front. With 7 runs to win, Ojha set off for a risky single to Steve Smith, who threw at the stumps for a direct hit. The throw missed, was not backed up, and continued for 4 overthrows.

With two needed, Ojha nudged a Mitchell Johnson delivery down leg as we ran through for victory (216 for 9). Laxman was still at the crease on 73, once again proving himself a nemesis for Australia, turning certain defeat into glorious victory as he had already done in Kolkata in 2001, Adelaide in 2003 and Perth in 2008.

India went on to win both 'battles', clinching the Border-Gavaskar series 2-0. The 'India at War' narrative had clearly impacted our thinking in many ways. But the war was far from over. Although we could learn from history, our focus would be on the future and fighting for the ambitious goals the team had set for itself: winning the ICC World Cup, becoming the number one Test team in the world, and being a happy team.

Both Gary and I realised that in our efforts to understand why the world wags and what wags it, a commitment to innovation would be essential. But that innovation turned out to be something completely different from what we had thought it was. When Gary and I left three years later, we found that our biggest innovations weren't the new stuff we had brought in, but the old things we had stopped doing because they were no longer relevant.

7

SHED THE BLAZER AND TIE

When South African teams go to India for a Test series, the players wear their blazers and ties on the first morning of a match. This has always been the case. But it's incredibly uncomfortable, especially when you play in Chennai, where the temperatures easily cross 40 degrees Celsius and the humidity is lethal.

You end up sweaty, and if the players and support staff forget to take their blazers, smart shoes and pants back to the hotel after the first day's play, which was almost always the case, they would spend five days cluttering an already cluttered change room. Typically, the Proteas left their hotel rooms in their formal gear, boarded a bus in a cordoned off security area, got driven to directly outside their change room, alighted, and got undressed immediately—they were never seen in public wearing those blazers on the first day of a Test. And yet, the convention is still upheld. I'm really not sure about the merits of this practice in international cricket in the twenty-first century.

While the blazer in Chennai is ludicrous, the blazer in itself is not silly. In his book *Rowing Blazers*, Jack Carlson writes that the rowing coats worn by Cambridge University's Lady Margaret Boat Club were blazing red, from which the term 'blazers' apparently originated. Different designs for different clubs would eventually make it easier for spectators to differentiate between competing boats.

But wait, there's more.

'The first blazers were meant to be worn in boats by rowers at Oxford and Cambridge. They were very loose-fitting, sort of the equivalent of a modern-day windbreaker, and *were meant to keep rowers warm during chilly training sessions* and races on early mornings.'[1] (Italics mine)

The emphasis in italics is my own, but the daftness is there for all to see. Why would anyone wear an English blazer in the middle of summer in sweaty Indian conditions? It just goes to show how absurd people can be, doing things only 'because that's how things have always been done'.

During our time in India, Gary and I would question anything and everything we did, and the blazer and tie would become our theme: In the world of cricket, what were the metaphorical blazers and ties in the Indian team?

Why did we practise? Why did we have team meetings before the game? What were we hoping to accomplish with them? Was net practice the best way to prepare? Why were we having bowlers' meetings? What were we doing that amounted to little more than ticking the box?

This questioning of everything—of every possible blazer and tie noosed around the team's neck—led to a lot of significant changes, none more than the implementation of optional practice and fitness sessions.

PRACTICE IS OPTIONAL

The best sports people in the world understand their game better than anybody else. *They* are the real experts of their game. *They* are their own best coach, but they use other coaches and people to add to their library of knowledge of themselves. Even as I write this, Sachin Tendulkar and Rahul Dravid come to mind.

These days, in a professional cricketer's career of say, ten years, he or she will probably be coached by upwards of fifteen coaches across state/provincial and national teams, as well as the various global T20 league teams they might represent. Hence the need for players to understand their own game better than any one of these other transient coaches who will come and go during their careers. Change the word coach for manager, and this is probably quite similar for many people entering the job market today.

One way to help more players have a better understanding of their game is through optional practice. Most professional cricket teams have by now adopted optional practice, but since Gary and I were the ones to introduce it as a regular approach with India, I'm not sure how many adopters fully appreciate the thinking that underpins this approach. For there is much more to optional practice than the 'come if you feel like it, don't if you feel you need to rest' attitude.

One way to approach these practices or training sessions is to have players view their game through the eyes of the opposition. All our opponents at the professional level have extensive libraries of video footage and streams of analytics on every aspect of our players' game. I ask our players what the opposition will be studying about them, what strengths and weaknesses they might be highlighting, and what strategies they might devise to limit their strengths and exploit their weaknesses.

Most times, the player responds with a blank stare and an 'I'm not entirely sure.' We then ask them to go figure it out, suggesting they sit with our own analyst and turn the mirror to face themselves. (I would have already asked our analyst to prepare for this.) What is the opposition studying about *you*, and what are *you* going to do to stay one step ahead of them?

Veteran Australian bowler Clint McCay had a fairly average (by his high standards) 2015 Big Bash series for Sydney Thunder. In 2016, I asked him what the opposition were most likely saying about how to play him, specifically at the end of an innings. His assessment revealed they'd be saying, 'Hang back and wait for his slower ball, which he bowls about 4 out of every 6 balls.' Based on this, I asked what his counter strategy could be, to which he replied, 'Wow, I've never looked at it like that. I'm not going to give them what they're expecting.' He went on to be one of the tournament's top performers, as opposition batsmen continued to hang back to wait for the slower deliveries that never arrived.

We asked the players to understand their game in greater detail. If a game was to begin in an hour's time, were they 100 per cent ready on that wicket and against that opponent, and were they clear and ready to execute their best game plan?

If the answer was 'yes' and they had studied the whole book for the exam, then it was their decision whether they felt like going to practise, or whether a rest and a massage would actually be better for them.

If the answer was 'No, I'm not as 100 per cent ready as I could be', then they were to ask themselves what it was that they could do in one or two practices to be 1 or 2 per cent readier than they were. And that's the thinking you came to practice with.

In the traditional way of coaching, prior to training, the coach would have already decided who was going to practice what skills, having written on the whiteboard who would bat in which nets, in what order and for how long, and which bowlers would bowl to them. They would also decide on the fielding drill each player would follow, and for how long. Other sports had their equivalent of the coach doing the same level of planning for what players would do at training.

Who, in that model, is deciding how these professional players need to prepare for a game? To me, it's fundamentally flawed that a coach must decide how a professional athlete must prepare. (I'd go so far as to extend this to club and school level, imploring that coaches should engage players to some degree about what they want to work on in training, and how they feel they could best do that. Engage them, get some buy-in and, in so doing, foster some game-intelligence and own-game awareness.)

When we started doing optional practices with the Indian team (which eventually was the case for probably 75 per cent of our sessions), we'd ask why a player was there and what he wanted from the session. In the beginning, the general response was, 'I don't know, coach. What's the plan?' They were used to someone else planning what they needed to do. After three or four such conversations, however, they started to anticipate the questions and started thinking about the answers before coming in. The best players in the world arrive at practice already knowing what they want to work on. But the majority wait for someone to tell them what to do. A player might say to me, 'I want to work on my cover drive and sweep and I want to take a couple of slip catches.' I will then ask a player how he wants to work on each of these elements.

'I don't know, coach. What do you reckon?'

No, how do *you* want to do it? Do you want a bowler, throw downs, bowling machine, new ball, old ball, spinner, seamer, left arm, right arm? Players eventually get used to arriving at practice knowing *what* part of their game they want to work on and *how* they want to do it. Sure, there needs to be some structured team activity in training for most team sports, but even that should be done with athlete input.

When players tell me what they want to work on, and how, I regularly ask, 'What's your thinking behind this?' I want to know what they want, but I also want to understand and support how they are thinking about upskilling and preparing for the next game. This approach is about creating thinking players, so it's important to discuss the thinking that led to their decision.

When Gary and I first introduced optional practices in India, all the players arrived thinking it was our way of testing commitment. When Zaheer Khan and Harbhajan Singh, two senior players who really needed to rest, missed a practice, some of the others asked whether Gary had spoken to them about not attending. The answer was 'no'.

Realising that optional practice was not a test, more players started not coming, and that's when we started the questioning process:

Why are you here, and what do you want to get out of this?

Slowly, they got used to it. The system, if implemented well, transforms players who are waiting to be told what to do and for the coach to analyse their game, into players who are thinking about their own game, analysing it, assessing it and starting to become experts in their own game, which is the ideal place to be. You want thinking players, and the coach's job is to test and question their thinking, maybe add to it, to help players become their own best coaches. I sometimes see myself as a player's 'thinking partner'.

The advantage is that over time (never overnight), you create really intelligent players who have an awareness of their own game. When you have an entire team of intelligent, thinking players on the field, you almost always have an advantage over any opposition.

The downside is that there are some people who take advantage of it. There are players who do cut corners, and when that happened, we would ask them what their thinking for not coming to practice was. To a man, this conversation led to a player realising they had not applied their best or most thorough thinking to their preparation, which they'd then do. There were times when I didn't see the logic in a player's explanation, but as long as they had thought it through, even if I didn't agree with it, I'd accept it.

Once their training was completed, in twenty minutes or two hours, players could return to the hotel in their own time and without having to inform any coaches. We trusted them to understand what they needed to do, to get that done, and to go and get the rest that is often in short supply in the busy international cricket schedule.

At the T20 World Cup in England in 2009, this backfired. There were some players in the team who missed out on quite a few of the optional morning trainings. We came to know that they had been coming back to the hotel late at night, or more accurately, early in the morning, after enjoying the offerings of London's nightlife. The Indian team didn't fare very well at the tournament. Honest conversations were had, and the players acknowledged that they hadn't come to training because they'd had late nights and they wanted to sleep rather than train.

We asked them how they wanted to navigate and manage this on future tours. We mentioned the option of going back to the old system where practice was compulsory for all, or we could keep the same system, with these specific guys needing to come to the party with more accountability and responsibility. The guilty players owned up to the fact that they had taken advantage and were not serving the team in the best way they could. They then committed to placing the team first, specifically to placing their preparation and professional obligations ahead of socialising. This was an ideal result, as we really wanted to keep an environment where choice was the norm, where players were treated like adults and responded accordingly.

A word about younger kids and optional training. When I relate the idea of optional practice to parents and coaches of school athletes, they often remark that their kids don't yet know enough about their own game to make decisions about how to practice or train. They argue that younger kids in particular need to be instructed by someone who has the requisite knowledge and experience. To my mind, as long as this thinking (and execution) prevails, kids will never get to think for themselves—which is not very good preparation for sport, or life for that matter. You can prepare kids for a lifetime of success by coaching them from a young age to (gradually) making their own decisions (whilst expecting and accepting the inevitable mistakes associated with learning new skills).

THE STORYTELLING PROBLEM AND GAMBHIR'S SHOES

Another important aspect of the Indian team's practices, even the compulsory ones, was that what players did at the practice was optional. If someone wished not to bat or not to bowl and they had a good reason for it, they could just be with the team and add value to the younger players' practice when possible. If, on the other hand, they wanted to bat in the net, for however long they felt they needed to, we'd support them in whatever way possible.

In his book *Blink*, Malcolm Gladwell writes about the 'storytelling problem'. Essentially, he suggests that people are too quick to come up with explanations for things for which they cannot have explanations. For example, when playing a forehand topspin in tennis, Gladwell wrote that people say, at impact, you must roll your wrist over the ball to impart spin on it. However, when analysing this shot with digitised imaging (which allows you to analyse wrist spin to an eighth of a degree), it became apparent that top players, like André Agassi in this analysis, didn't roll their wrist at all—the spin came from the angle of the racket. Only once the ball had left the racket did players roll their wrist over the shot. But many coaches continue to tell their young charges otherwise, and end up causing a whole lot of elbow problems.[2]

The second part of the storytelling problem is that when we come up with explanations for things we can't have explanations for, we generally use our favoured theory. Why? Gladwell says, 'Our world requires that decisions be sourced and footnoted, and if we say *how* we feel, we must also be prepared to elaborate on *why* we feel that way.'

But, sometimes, we just don't know why. Does that really matter if we're getting the desired results? To illustrate this point, I'll cite two examples—one from Gladwell, and another from a net session with Gautam Gambhir that shows the importance of coaching in an optional practice environment. First, Gladwell.

Gladwell wrote about Vic Braden, one of the world's best tennis coaches at the time, who had the ability to accurately predict when a player was about to double-fault (consecutive faulty serves on the same point). Braden died in 2014 at the age of 85, but even in his old age, the former pro player, coach and broadcaster was regarded as someone who knew 'as much about the nuances and subtleties of the game as any man alive'.

Braden didn't need to have any prior knowledge of a tennis player to 'know' when he or she was about to double-fault. Gladwell wrote, 'It didn't seem to matter who was playing, man or woman, whether he was watching the match live or on television, or how well he knew the person serving. "I was calling double-faults on girls from Russia I'd never seen before in my life," Braden says. Nor was Braden simply lucky. Lucky is when you call a coin toss correctly. But double-faulting is rare. In an entire match, a professional tennis player might hit hundreds of serves and double-fault no more than three or four times.'

This ability scared Braden himself. He decided to test his intuition at a significant pro tournament held at Indian Wells, near his home in southern California. Keeping track, Braden ended up correctly predicting sixteen out of every seventeen double-faults. He said, 'It literally scared me. I was getting twenty out of twenty right, and we're talking about guys who almost never double-fault.'

Here was a man who had played professional tennis and who, over more than fifty years, coached, counselled and got to know some of the sport's greatest ever players. Understandably, he had developed a sharp eye for the game of tennis. As Gladwell wrote, 'It really isn't any different from the ability of an art expert to look at (a piece of art) and instantly know that it's a fake. Something in the way the tennis players hold themselves, or the way they toss the ball, or the fluidity of their motion triggers something in his unconscious. He instinctively picks up the "giss" of a double-fault.'

While Braden might have known *why* he developed the ability to know, he remained frustrated by his inability to figure out *how* he knew. Sometimes, we just don't know. As in the case of Gautam Gambhir's struggle to hit a drive through the extra cover region.

Gautam almost always hit the ball square of the wicket on the off-side. Although he wanted to hit it straighter, something would happen that led to the face of the bat opening up on impact, which would cause the ball to travel through point or backward point.

Consequently, in one-day games, the opposition would employ a gully, a backward point, a point and someone just in front of point against Gautam. For those not familiar with cricket, they would place four fielders in the narrow part of the field where Gautam's cover drives would generally go and leave a big, open gap between extra-cover and mid-off, the area through which they knew he couldn't hit the ball. They would block his shots, because he'd hit them all into the congested area. This wasn't dissimilar to how Gary Kirsten played early in his career. He also hit most shots to this same area square of the wicket on the off-side, using the pace of the ball, because he didn't yet have the power or technique to hit it back down the ground.

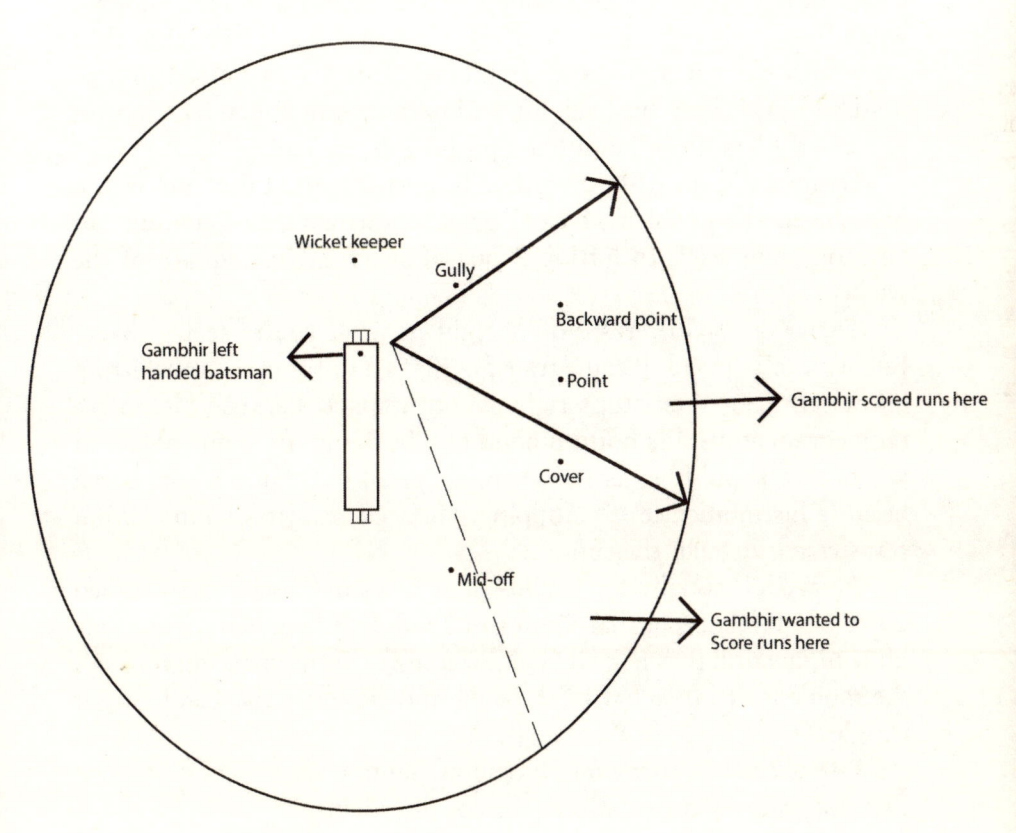

During a net session, I was throwing to Gautam and he was trying to hit the ball straighter, towards extra cover. He hit the odd one there, but he would mostly carry on with the open face of the bat and the ball going square.

Gary and Sachin were standing behind me, talking about it. Then Eric Simons joined them. While I was throwing to Gautam, I listened to their conversation that turned into one of the most fascinating master classes in batting technique that I have listened to.

It started with Sachin, who said that on contact, Gautam's back hip was coming through a little early and forcing his bottom hand to push ahead, which in turn led to the bottom-handed drive. This recollection of mine is the explanation-for-dummies version of what Sachin said, which was way more intelligently phrased than I'm able to accurately recall. I was listening to Sachin and watching Gautam when I remember thinking, *that's it*—Sachin's nailed it! Sachin then came into the net and showed Gautam a drill that helped him to hold his shape, keep his back hip and back foot in line, which in turn prevented his bottom hand from pushing at the ball.

Gautam did the drill, it worked beautifully, and I thought Sachin had solved the problem. I went back to throwing to Gautam, but he soon went back to hitting 2 out of every 3 balls square of the wicket.

Then Gary said, 'Yes, you're right in what you're seeing, Sach. But it's actually his weight-transfer that's faulty. He's transferring his weight, but then stops right before impact. Because his body's momentum stops, his bottom hand and back hip are going ahead of where they should be, as you correctly point out, but it's happening because his momentum is stopping. He needs to get his momentum transferred through the shot.'

Amazed, I thought, flip Gazza—that's my boy! You actually drilled down one level deeper than Professor Tendulkar had. Gary then came up with this drill that helped Gautam transfer his momentum through the moment of impact with the ball, and true as nuts, Gautam got it right.

I went back to throwing, but soon Gautam went back to hitting two out of every three balls square of the wicket.

Then Eric (*the bowling coach!*) said Gary and Sachin were both right, but …

'Yes, Gary, he is stopping; and yes, Sachin, because he's stopping, you're seeing his back hip and bottom hand coming through. But through all this, he is making contact with the ball *in front* of his eyes. He needs to be hitting the ball beneath his eyes.' And I thought, wow! Can you believe that? Eric, the bowling coach, is actually right!

So, he, too, had this drill where he made Gautam hit the ball under his eyes. He had to make sure he hit the ball into the ground within about two metres of where he made contact. In order to do that, Eric said, Gautam had to hit the ball beneath his eyes. After Eric did that drill with Gautam, all those things fell into place. He had simplified the problem beautifully.

When I went back to throwing, Gautam went back to doing the old stuff. I retell this story knowing full well that it takes time for a new skill or technique adjustment to come into play. When Gautam finally walked out the net, he was still a little confused, thinking of these three things. He came to me after the session and asked that I throw him some more balls; he wanted to continue working on the issue.

When he got it wrong, he'd ask me, 'What did I do? What am I doing wrong?' I stood there thinking, he has just had the best batting master class ever from Eric Simons, Gary Kirsten and Sachin Tendulkar. And now, he's asking *me* what he did wrong! That in itself was just wrong. So, I decided I'd use a coaching approach. I said, 'I'm definitely noticing something. I'm not quite sure what, but I'm noticing a difference.'

He would then hit the ball perfectly, and I would say I definitely saw something different. When he asked me what, I'd say, 'I'm not sure, Gauty. What did you do differently?'

I kept throwing it back at him. In reality I saw nothing, because technically I'm not as astute as Sachin and Gary to see whatever minor thing he was doing differently. But there must have been something different, so I just kept saying that to him. He kept asking, and I kept saying, I'm not sure, but there is 'something you're doing differently, and we need to figure out what that thing is'.

He started hitting more and more balls in the right area. Gary and Sachin came and stood behind us again and watched. Sachin said, Gautam's got his hips and hands in the right place now. Gary said, he's got his momentum going through the ball.

When Gautam came out of the nets, he gave me a fist pump and said, thank you very much. After he unpadded, I went to him, asking what that different thing I had noticed was. He said, 'I've got it figured out now. I take my stance and I look down. Then I look up at you, and then I need to look back down at my shoes. And then look up again. As long as I look down at my shoes for a second time, I hit the ball in the right area.'

In the next two years, Gautam went through many bats, pads and pairs of gloves, because the players get given all these things for free. But he kept those same pair of shoes; he kept getting them stitched up. And as long as he looked at those shoes, he was able to hit the ball straighter, more often.

Now, imagine putting that in a coaching manual. If you want to hit the ball straight, just look down at your shoes for a second time. But that's what Gauty figured out for himself.

There is a lesson about coaching in this story. And it isn't just about Gautam Gambhir. There was Lasith Malinga from Sri Lanka, who, for a long time, was the world's premier fast bowler in limited overs cricket. Everyone says you should release the ball with a nice high arm action, but Malinga released the ball at shoulder height. Now, what was more important? That he got his technique right and his arm up, or that he landed the ball in the right area almost every single time? Coaching has often been too much about getting the technique right, whereas it should be about the result, regardless of technique. The same was true for Hashim Amla, whose batting technique was heavily criticised by experts before he became one of the world's great cricketers. He didn't change his technique. One of the best ever players under pressure in Test matches, V.V.S. Laxman, and current Proteas captain, Faf du Plessis, both grip their bat with the top hand at the top of the handle and bottom hand at the bottom, with a big gap between their hands. The coaching manuals recommend keeping your hands together. Graeme Smith, who averaged over 50 in Test matches, hit full-pitched balls through the leg side when they were pitched outside off, despite the manual saying these should be hit through the off-side. The list goes on.

If you're always going to try to provide the answers, you might succumb to the pitfalls of the storytelling dilemma and fall for your own theories, whether they're right or not.

I once asked Dale Steyn how many pieces of advice around his bowling he had received from someone who knew what they were talking about—and not from a drunk punter in a pub. He said, comfortably over a 100, but probably more than 200. I asked him how many of those made a material impact or were valuable for him. He said one, possibly two. I've asked a number of professional cricketers the same question. And what comes back is that when you give someone advice about what to do, particularly someone at a higher level, consider that about 98 per cent to 99 per cent of the time, your advice is going to be useless. Not necessarily wrong, but useless; that's just how players deal with advice. In fact, the best advice I can give on giving advice is, think twice about giving it and then don't give it. Rather, elicit the answer from the person you're tempted to give it to. That's coaching.

If you want to help someone with their technique, I would suggest showing them a video (I can't imagine there's a training session happening anywhere in the world without a smartphone present). Get them to look at their video, and get the player to figure out what he or she could do differently. There might be advice you could give the player, but the player needs to own their own game plan and want to change something, and they need to understand why they are making changes. This giving of unsolicited advice is coaching from another era, where the coach is the fault analyser and fault fixer. It's overused and mostly ineffective.

Instead, give the player the end result, like hitting the ball through extra cover, and keep throwing the ball to them while they're figuring out their own explanation. They, too, will succumb to the storytelling problem, since their explanation for what they've done and how they did it is quite likely to be inaccurate or plain wrong. But that doesn't matter—it's their explanation and they need to own it. As long as their explanation connects with the correct neuromuscular pathway in the body, nothing else matters.

8

THINKING DIFFERENTLY

BE FIT ENOUGH TO REMAIN GOOD ENOUGH

As de facto fitness coach, I wanted players to be the best managers of their own bodies and their own energy. The advent of fitness trainers brought a prescriptive style to sports, and it also created an inability for players to tune in and really listen to their own bodies. Like we do when taking a car to a mechanic, so we do with our body. Too many athletes give too much responsibility for their bodies to a fitness trainer (and the physiotherapist).

I remember an individual session with captain Hansie Cronjé when I was still the fitness coach for the Proteas in the 1990s. I asked him to 'do a few push-ups' to loosen up, and he told me to tell him how many and he'd do them. I asked him again, and Hansie became quite adamant that I come up with a number; he was not going to decide that for himself, regardless of how his body felt. Hansie was a fitness fanatic, but even he didn't want to own the process of managing his body for a simple warm-up exercise. He wanted to be told what to do.

In India, as with the thinking behind optional practice, we wanted the players to gain an in-depth understanding of how to manage their own bodies and fitness. We would provide whatever support they needed in this pursuit.

I had not done fitness training on a full-time basis since 1999, and the two previous fitness trainers with the Indian team had been

Adrian le Roux and Greg King. Jointly, they had been with the team for seven years.

Although it was clear that the Indian team was not the fittest in the world, I'm very grateful to both of those guys. They very generously gave me all their fitness programmes and training reports from the past seven years. In looking through it all, it became clear that I wasn't going to come up with any smarter, better or cleverer programmes because the existing ones had been created by two of cricket's best fitness trainers in the world at the time.

Despite such excellence, the team was still quite unfit. I ran a battery of fitness tests with the players and, by international standards, nearly half of them failed a number of the tests. The same had been happening under le Roux and King.

Gary and I discussed whether we should bother to test the players, if it was only a 'tick the box' exercise. Nobody held the players accountable for poor test results. Were we really going to drop Tendulkar or Dhoni because they had failed the running fitness test?

Rather than dropping the players, we dropped fitness testing altogether. Then we tried something really risky. The prescribed training programmes were not getting the results required, and the bulk of the players were resisting them. A big part of Greg Chappell's approach had been to impose things on players, which created resistance. We weren't interested in doing more of the same.

We redefined fitness into only two criteria:

- You need to be uninjured to play the game.
- When you are playing, you need to be fit enough to deliver on your skill, in order to be continually selected to play.

We basically said players had to be on the field, and they had to deliver results. Whatever they needed in order to do that, they could let us know and we would provide it for them. If they didn't know, we'd help them figure it out.

If a player was injured, he was obviously not going to play. If he was not delivering results, he was going to get dropped. Since they wanted to play for India, they had to do whatever they needed to be doing to play in the first XI for their country. This was our fitness criteria.

At the time that we presented the stats to the team, ten players who had been in contention had been ruled out of selection due to injury in the preceding five months, between June and October 2008—an unnecessarily high injury rate.

I had been witness to one of those injuries as it happened. I had watched fast bowler Ishant Sharma tense up after delivering a ball in a Test match, and then immediately reach for and massage his buttock muscle. He walked back to his mark, rubbing it and clearly in some discomfort, likely with a minor muscle strain. To my dismay, he turned to bowl another delivery. I felt like screaming from the pavillion, 'Don't do it!' (Not that I would have been heard in a stadium with over 20,000 spectators.) He ran in, bowled again, and predictably tore the muscle a lot more severely. This was the lack of body awareness I wanted to help players overcome.

Effectively, we made all fitness training optional. You decide what you want, and another trainer or I will help you get there. Or, as a group, share what each of you are doing and figure it out among yourselves. See what works and what does not. Do whatever you need to do in order to play cricket for India, and I'm here to help in any way you want. Most of the players had worked under Adrian le Roux and/or Greg King and could draw from the expertise and training programmes they had provided.

This went on for nearly a year, and in that year not a single player approached me to oversee their training in the gym. Not one! There are no fitness records for that year, but what is on record is that during that entire time, when fitness training was completely optional, the team incurred the least number of injuries during our three-year tenure.

Again, the thinking behind this was to get the players to understand their own bodies. If you need to train to get fit, to stay strong, to score runs, then do it. If you need to rest in order to stay fit, in order to take wickets, then do it. But tune in and listen to your own body. If you eat badly, you are going to get overweight and will run into trouble. The consequence will be on your shoulders, because you are the one who will get injured or dropped.

In the current knowledge era, there is no shortage of good information and guidelines, and not knowing what to do is no longer a valid excuse. Most people know what they need to do to get fit and stay healthy, or they know where to find this information, but they lack the discipline, or a good enough reason for following through. These Indian cricketers all had a good enough reason *why* they should stay fit.

It was a complete redefinition of fitness training, and it was obvious that it made some people uncomfortable that there were no fitness and training prescriptions for the Indian team. But there was a distinct lack of injuries, the team was winning a lot of cricket matches, and the players were happy.

Yet, it made some of the administrators uneasy. Prior to one of our tours abroad, when the team met at the airport, I noticed an unfamiliar guy in the same travel clothing as the rest of us. I asked Gary, captain M.S. Dhoni and a few others who he was, and no one knew. We did have a different manager on every tour, but I had already met the one for this particular trip. When I checked with him, he told me that this guy was the new fitness trainer. That's how Gary and I learnt, then and there, without any consultation, of his appointment.

I fully understood the board's position, and that of anyone else who thought Gary and I were crazy. But we had figured that if the best fitness and training information and protocol in the world had produced an unfit team, I was never going to come up with anything better. We just looked at the same situation with very different eyes, and we established what was actually important. Runs on the park or shuttle-run test results for Sachin Tendulkar? We all know what is actually important, so we made the important stuff important. As it turned out, we would arrive at the World Cup in 2011 with possibly the least, or second-least fit team at the tournament, a situation that would prove inconsequential in our quest for the summit.

This approach to fitness training did, however, take on a comical twist in our second year with the Indian team. We were based in Dambulla in Sri Lanka for a triangular series when Harbhajan Singh said to me, 'I don't have the self-discipline to train by myself,' which was wonderfully honest, as only Harbhajan can be. He said, 'I need you to push me. I need you to come knock on my door at ten in the morning and take me for a run.' He was excited and super enthusiastic about it—Harbhajan really is a zero-to-a-hundred, all-or-nothing kind of guy. So, I knocked and we went for a run on the dirt road, through the bushes and around the dam at Dambulla.

As we set off, a security vehicle with heavily armed military men started up a short distance behind us. When we turned to run through the bushes, they said we should stay on the road, which we didn't. There was a quick conversation amongst them before one hopped off the vehicle and fell in behind us, on foot. The temperature was already in the high thirties, and we were in running shorts and vests, but the poor military dude was in full overalls, boots, helmet and bulletproof vest, carrying a walkie-talkie in one hand and a heavy semi-automatic rifle in the other. I admit, we added a kilometre or two to our run to see how our shadow would handle it, but we soon realised that he wasn't tiring, so we returned to the hotel. I learned later that he was the local military long-distance running champion, and a champion boxer. Our run was a leisurely stroll for him!

Since Bhajji is a 100 per cent guy, right after completing our first run, he said we'd do it again the following morning. I recommended that we only go every second day, and he agreed. In the middle of our third run, his excitement about running and getting fitter had him mimicking the finely-tuned athletes he saw on TV, which led directly to a strained calf muscle. He was doing way too much, too quickly—guided more by his enthusiasm than by his body. I knew I had failed Harbhajan by joining in the fun rather than forcing him to slow down. Sorry, Bhajji. But I just loved his honesty and enthusiasm. Thankfully, he was soon back to playing, and this time he left the running to runners.

There was always a reason why Gary and I did things differently. Considering the fundamental shift in the performance and leadership terrain, we needed to constantly update older and more traditional approaches, and bring in new innovations. We needed to loosen the metaphorical tie and shed the blazer if we were going to outsmart and outpace the rest of the cricketing world.

Our philosophy was to create an environment that empowered players to think and decide for themselves. For the players to be able to make good decisions, they needed to become *and be treated as* the leading experts on their own lives, physical, mental and spiritual. No one knows you better than you do, and sometimes you just need a bit of help in allowing that understanding to emerge from within you. *That* is coaching, and it is beautifully illustrated by the way Gary nudged Rahul Dravid towards a revival in his Test career through 2009.

Less than a year after we had arrived in India, Gary was confronted with the prospect of dropping Rahul from the Test team. In this thorny situation, he put himself in the player's shoes by tapping into his own personal experience as a player when, on the verge of being dropped, he had produced that extraordinary innings of 275 runs, which we discussed at the beginning of the book.

By December 2008, it had been almost nine months since a struggling Rahul last scored a century (111 against South Africa) and there was enormous media pressure on Gary to omit him from the squad for the home series against England. He had performed poorly in a recently concluded series against Australia, and the selectors seemed keen to see what young Virat Kohli could achieve in the Test team.

Rahul did play in the first Test in Chennai, and although we beat England by 6 wickets, his contributions of 3 and 4 runs in the 2 innings didn't help his cause.

But omitting a player of Rahul's stature would have been considered sacrilege and the selectors ducked the decision to drop him by keeping him in the squad of fifteen players for the second Test in Mohali. Gary and I discussed this dilemma, noting that if Gary left Rahul out, he could have people stoning his house and burning effigies, as had happened when Greg Chappell dropped Sourav Ganguly. Omitting him could have unpleasant consequences. I really wasn't sure how I could contribute to resolving the issue, so Gary took the conversation to captain M.S. Dhoni.

Gary and MS had the option of either picking Rahul for the playing eleven or leaving him out of the series-decider. While Rahul's experience counted in his favour, his recent run drought was a problem. MS wasn't convinced one way or the other, which led to them agreeing on an unconventional approach to this selection quandary.

Gary went to Rahul's room about twenty minutes before the team meeting. To any player, a knock on the door so close to a meeting means only one thing: He is being informed of being dropped in person, before it is announced in the group. Rahul, a true gentleman, understood the difficult situation in which Gary found himself and stated that he would support his coach, regardless of what he decided.

Gary took Rahul by surprise by saying that he was the one who had to cross the ropes, no one else could do it for him. He was the one under pressure from the fans' expectations, the media's critique and the selectors' axe, and so it was he who had to make the decision.

'I'm faced with a dilemma,' Gary said. 'And I've now come to ask you whether you want to play or not. You are the best person to make that decision, because you are the only person who truly knows whether you're ready.'

By shifting the decision-making to the player, Gary stumped Rahul. He had assumed the visit was to inform him that he was being dropped. But there was no doubt in his mind that he wanted to play; he said he was ready and that he truly believed he could still make a contribution. He also said that in the future, if he felt otherwise, he would tell Gary. The very next day, he batted for just under eight hours to amass a critic-silencing 136 runs in the first innings of the Mohali Test, setting up a draw. India went on to win the series 1-0, with the foundation laid by Rahul's timely return to form, just like Gary's return to form in 1999, which denied England victory in Durban. Once again, it was England that suffered.

Rahul went on to score five fifties and two centuries in 2009, with eight more tons to follow before he retired from Test cricket in 2012.

LOOKING AT THE SAME THINGS DIFFERENTLY

One of the four main goals we had set at the outset of Gary's and my tenure was for India to become the number one ranked Test team in the world, a position it had not attained since the ranking had been officially introduced in 2003.

Gary believed that our batting line-up of Gambhir, Sehwag, Dravid, Tendulkar, Laxman and Dhoni was as good as any batting line-up in the world, so on the batting front we had what it took to be number one. But when we compared our bowling attack to those of other teams, we were probably the fourth best in the world in terms of skill, behind Australia, South Africa and England. Spinner Harbhajan Singh and medium-fast bowler Zaheer Khan were top class bowlers, while the rest cycled in and out of the team. They included spinners Pragyan Ojha and Amit Mishra, seamers Ishant Sharma, Jaydev Unadkat, Umesh Jadav, and the skilled but highly unpredictable Sreesanth, none of whom were established international bowlers at the time.

Either way, this Indian attack was not going to instill much fear in opposition batsmen.

As Gary studied the bowlers, trying to figure out how we could compete with far superior bowling attacks around the world, an idea came to him. He figured how our attack would not only compete, but be even better than the rest, and he did this by looking at bowlers from a very different perspective. He devised a plan that would make a significant contribution to India actually becoming the world's number one ranked Test team. Interestingly, although many wrote about and commented on how India eventually did get to the ranking, nobody seemed to recognise this part of our strategy.

Winning Test matches requires you, if batting last, to score more runs than the opposition, and if bowling last, to bowl them all out for fewer runs than the posted target. Runs and wickets. That's it. Gary scratched his head. We needed runs and wickets. Over the year, we needed more of both. And our bowling was limited.

So, what was his plan? Score even more runs.

At the time he devised this strategy, the total number of runs that batsmen 8 to 11 scored per Test match, across the top five teams in the world, was 45. We would work on the batting skills of bowlers, known as tailenders, who generally do not spend much time working on their batting. They are not expected to score too many runs, and opposition bowlers generally expect to improve their wicket tally when bowling to these 'rats and mice' at the end of an innings.

Over the next many weeks and months, Gary would spend tireless hours working with these tailenders, coaching them on how to survive bouncers aimed at their heads, which were meant to scare them and force them into making errors. He worked on their techniques and run-scoring options so that they could add bonus runs to the tally and give our weaker bowling attack (themselves) more runs to defend.

There was a second thing this strategy would achieve. Those who play double innings cricket would know that when the tailenders come in to bat, the bowlers often get greedy as they look to raise their wicket tally. They often bowl differently to these tailenders, either very short or full-pitched deliveries, and seldom bowl the good length balls they bowl to top-order batsmen. While this is going on, the top-order batsmen in the fielding team are starting to prepare their minds to bat, which they expect to do as soon as the last wicket is taken and after the standard ten-minute break between innings. The longer the tailenders stay at the crease, the more the bowlers will get frustrated, the more the fielders start losing their sense of humour, and the top-order batsmen, unknowingly, start to become mentally fatigued from continually planning to bat, on top of the building frustration. If the tailenders can keep a team out in the field for anything over an hour, or even two, it not only adds valuable runs, but it also mentally erodes their opponents.

When India finally achieved the goal of being the number one ranked Test team in the world, we still had a bowling attack that was possibly only the fourth best in the game. But these same bowlers were our tailend batsmen, and over the course of that year, while the total runs scored by batsmen 8 to 11 in all other teams in the world was on average 43 per game, the total per game for India's tailenders was 83.

Add these additional runs to the physical and mental fatigue and frustrations the extra time in the field caused opponents, and the value of looking at the same things differently becomes apparent.

ONE, TWO, CHA CHA CHA

Some years later, when I was head coach of the Rajasthan Royals team in the IPL, we would apply this same approach in a different way.

As will be elaborated upon in Chapter 17, the Royals were a team of underdogs that had not done well for some years. The T20 cricket statistics at the time, and even today, suggest that the team that hits the most 4s and 6s—the crowd-pleasing big shots over the boundary—wins. And the main way to prevent this from happening is to take wickets; to get the big hitters in the opposition out of the game.

The Royals' batting line-up in 2015 simply did not have the kind of big hitters that almost every opposition team boasted—we were not competitive in this all-important boundary-scoring department, and our bowling unit was no more than average. With Australian Steve Smith as captain for much of the season, we looked to gain advantage through the details: by accumulating the small wins; firstly, by scoring more singles and doubles than the opposition, and then by shutting down these runs in the opponents' batting innings.

From the seventh to the twentieth over in T20 cricket, teams are allowed a maximum of five fielders on the boundary to defend the all-important 4s and 6s, which leaves a minimum of four fielders (wicket-keeper and bowler excluded) who are obliged to be in the 'inner ring', which is the area within about thirty metres of the batsmen and where the fielders' job is primarily to stop the singles. Our batsmen might not have been powerful hitters, but they were mostly young and fast, so we pushed to score as many singles and doubles as possible.

Most opponents had the standard four close-in fielders defending these 'less important' runs. In contrast and for much of the season, we would keep five and sometimes six fielders in these close-in single-saving positions, for as many overs as possible, and often deep into the game. This meant we had less fielders defending the boundary, but in order to reach the boundary, opposition batsmen would have to take a greater risk by hitting the ball in the air and over the extra fielder(s) positioned in the inner ring.

It's very attractive for most teams and businesses to chase victory by making the big plays, hitting the 6s, signing the big deals and working to record the 'public' wins that look good. This 'grand strategy' mentality is often prevalent in large corporations that were successful in the past due to the scale and scope of their operations, but who are now being disrupted by new technologies, more agile competitors and/or changing customer demands that require of them to shed the blazer and tie if they are to remain relevant and competitive.

No batsman in cricket ever scores a century without accumulating the small, less important, less impressive and less applauded ones and twos. What are the small wins, the micro habits, the details that you can attend to on a daily basis, which in course of time will translate to your team or business scoring those metaphorical 1 or 2 runs more than your opponents? What personal wins are available to you in this same way; the small yet regular changes that you can make to your preparation, your training, your skill acquisition, relationships, finances, to your health, or whatever else is important to you? Every one of us can be healthier, gain fitness, lose weight, have more energy, or whatever we want, by making small and seemingly inconsequential changes in daily habits; scoring the proverbial ones and twos that over time deliver significant results. These small wins might not make the highlights package at the end of the day's play, but if they are regularly acknowledged and celebrated, as we did at the Royals in 2015, they might well become a new habit.

After fourteen league games, our team of underdogs qualified for the play-offs. Our opponents scored an average of 18 runs per game more than us in 4s and 6s, but when tallied up, we had scored on average 21 more runs per game than all our opponents, in singles and doubles.

9

CHARACTER AND VALUES

About six months into our tenure with the Indian team, Test captain Anil Kumble announced his retirement from the international game. As a leg spinner, he had played 132 Tests and 271 ODIs for his country, claiming 619 wickets in Tests (including eight ten-wicket hauls) and 337 in one-dayers.

Anil the man was known to be level-headed, mature and intelligent, and he was greatly respected by those within and outside the game. From the short time I worked with him, I knew that he was always open to learning and exploring ways to improve his game and captaincy. But the most impactful memory I have of him was the result of something unexpected, and it had little to do with cricket.

It happened at one of the many felicitation ceremonies that the team attended towards the end of 2008 to honour Anil. It felt like some of the ceremonies were conjured up more for the host's benefit than Anil's, so we weren't always alert and listening as one longer-than-necessary speech rolled into the next.

At one such ceremony, the MC called onto the stage a lady to speak on behalf of a charity for the physically challenged, which Anil apparently supported. The previous speakers had used up a lot of airtime, so ears were only vaguely tuned in. It is a fairly common practice for famous athletes to link their names to charities, offering support that ranges from genuine giving driven by care and concern, to getting something for themselves, like good marketing exposure and PR.

Ms Vasanth Raghuvir came up onto the stage and shared a story that completely changed the atmosphere. She spoke of how Anil had agreed to preside as chief guest at the Shakti Foundation's annual fundraiser in Chennai. The function was arranged to coincide with a short window Anil had between two appearances for India. The day after the Test match finished, he was scheduled to fly from Mumbai to Chennai on a 7 a.m. flight to attend an evening fundraiser along with approximately 1,000 guests.

This was a particularly early start for any player the day after a Test match. As fate would have it, an Air France plane crashed on the Chennai runway in the early hours of that morning, forcing all flights into Chennai to be cancelled. Anil phoned Vasanth at 6 a.m. to inform her of the delay, and tell her that according to reports of the damage to the runway, it seemed no flights would be landing in Chennai that day. He was not calling her to cancel, however, but to inform her that he had booked a flight from Mumbai to Bangalore, and from there, would drive to Chennai, a six-hour journey. And he did. He booked a flight, drove for six hours, engaged with guests till the end of the ceremony, and delivered 'an emotional and touching speech'.

Sometime after that function, I phoned Vasanth in India to confirm the finer details of this story. She choked up and cried tears of gratitude as she told me how Anil's 'innate goodness and caring, at the height of his career, had such a powerful impact on (her son) Velan's life'. Velan was terminally ill, and died in May 1998.

Vasanth's story of Anil's personal commitment to a charity, his friendship with a terminally ill boy, and his determination to keep his word possibly had more of an impact on those who sat with me than any part of his illustrious career on the field being celebrated that night. Such was the emotion in her story that it moved many to tears, and I recall being self-conscious about holding mine back even as I realised that players and dignitaries around me were doing the same.

In my follow-up communication with Vasanth, she told me something else. She said Anil had met a total stranger at the airport in Mumbai, who also desperately needed to get to Chennai, and had offered to take him along.

When I asked her how Anil came to know her son, she told me this story. 'The introduction to Anil Kumble followed from an accidental meeting with Rahul Dravid at Sunny's restaurant in Bangalore. I explained to Dravid my son's predicament and his love for cricket. Dravid immediately volunteered to meet Velan along with Anil Kumble and Venkatesh Prasad at the Chinnaswamy Stadium in Bangalore, where they were having their net practice. True to his word, he requested Anil and Venkatesh to stay back after practice. All three of them met Velan. That was the first time Anil and Velan met, in May 1997, and the bond that developed between them grew stronger until my son's demise in May 1998.'

For me, this story defined Anil's character more than his record-breaking statistics on the field did.

WHAT IS SUCCESS?

A time will come for most of us when we retire from work or move on to a new chapter in our lives. If you're young, maybe you will leave your current or next workplace in five years' time. For some, retirement may be around the corner. The values that we live by, those invisible things that drive our behaviour, on and off the field, at work and at home, will ultimately define how people experience us, and how we will be remembered. Anil's value system drove his decision to stick to his commitment in Chennai, to do what he had said he would do, and not take the very attractive (and acceptable) excuse that was offered by the Chennai airport being closed.

Values are like the rudder of a yacht, invisible to the naked eye but critical in determining the direction of travel. They define what our priorities are, and what's important and valuable in our lives. They are the principles, standards and qualities that serve as our guiding lights, ideally towards living our best life. Whether you believe in them or not, they exist; you already have them, and they directly influence your decisions and behaviour, and thus your impact and effectiveness in life.

The fourth goal Gary and I had set ourselves for the Indian team—to help the players become better people—connected directly with the values that the team and the individual players endorsed. Being in a high-performance environment, it was important for us to first know how we defined and valued 'success'.

Shortly after arriving in India, I facilitated a session with the players where we tried to answer the following questions:

- What is success?
- What undermines success?
- What is the value of values?

To the first question, I proposed the following: Is success

- Becoming undisputed champion of the world, amassing US$300 million in career earnings; *MIKE TYSON*
- Winning five Olympic medals; *MARION JONES*
- Being a 100-metre world record holder; *BEN JOHNSON*
- Being voted 'America's most innovative company' for six consecutive years. *ENRON*

All agreed these were good measures of success. Until we unpacked them further. Do you remember Mike Tyson, the undisputed heavyweight boxing champion of the world who earned US$300 million over his career? He was also jailed for sexual assault, drinking and driving; was a self-confessed drug addict who became bankrupt by 2003. In 2005, he said, 'My whole life has been a waste. I've been a failure.'[1]

Do you remember Marion Jones, winner of three Olympic gold medals and two bronzes, who took steroids, lied about it to two grand juries, was banned for life, and handed back her medals?

And then there was Ben Johnson, a world record holder in the 100-metre dash, who was caught doping and left the sport disgraced.

And do you remember Enron, named America's most innovative company for six consecutive years before being unmasked as the world's most spectacular corporate fraud?

What then is success? What undermines success? And what are our values? I posed these questions to the players.

Different players had different thoughts about success. Gautam Gambhir suggested that making regular contributions that led to the team's success was better than being personally successful; Harbhajan Singh spoke about being a 'good guy', someone who was respected both on and off the field, as well as about the importance of forgiveness; Rahul Dravid spoke of consistently staying in the processes that were important for him, and detaching from whatever results might follow, highlighting things like hard work, resilience, commitment and training, enjoying the challenge and remaining relaxed. Staying true to these processes was one aspect of success for him. V.V.S. Laxman felt that success for him was saving the team when it was in a 'miserable situation', and helping teammates when they were down. Sachin Tendulkar placed more importance on being remembered for the kind of person he was, than for the runs he scored.

Everyone acknowledged the importance of wanting to score runs, take wickets and win games, but also acknowledged that these were very incomplete measures of success. Some players found it easier to view their success through the eyes of others, and what these others thought about them, while other players preferred to depend on their own evaluation of it. What was important was that, as often as possible, they were true to themselves and their values.

We spoke of the fact that the players' public identity as Indian cricketers was separate from, and should not to be mixed up with, who they were as human beings. They were ordinary people with a special talent. Every player in the room had worked tirelessly to convert their talent into the success they were enjoying as international cricketers, and we discussed how similarly diligent work was required to become the kind of people they would one day want to be remembered as. We spoke not about trying to become good, but about the fact that most players are innately good. Being celebrities was not about being liked, but rather about being likeable persons.

The workshop was concluded with a quote from Einstein: 'Try not to become a man of success, but rather try to become a man of value.'

I am not proposing that people become saints or that they should live perfect lives, and I cannot claim anywhere near either for myself. But the fact is that as humans, we all have flaws and imperfections. Few, if any, are able to live up to the teachings in the Bible, the Koran, the Bhagavad Gita, the Kabbalah or any other wisdom guides to living a wholesome life. But having these and other useful guiding texts do help us to know when we are on course and when we might be straying.

One such guideline is our personal values; the rudders of our personal yacht. They influence or underpin many of our choices and behaviours, the consequences of which impact the way we live.

Athletes are faced with choices all the time, many of which have varying degrees of consequences. The choices off the field include whether to sign an autograph or turn the person away, to answer an overexcited fan's question, however silly it may be, or ignore it, to respond or ignore comments on social media, to react to abusive spectators or walk away. On the field, a fielder or bowler may choose to insult or verbally abuse a batsman, or not, to stay within the spirit of the game or go outside of it.

Greg Chappell ordering his younger brother, Trevor, to bowl underarm to Brian McKechnie in 1981 will always be more infamously remembered than the fact that Australia won the game against New Zealand. It was the final ball of the match, the Kiwis needed a 6 to draw level, and it was legal at the time to deliver the ball underarm and along the ground. Contrast this with the gesture of golfer Bobby Jones, who on the final play-off for the US Open tournament, caused a minor movement of his ball when addressing it. So small was the displacement that the marshals did not see it move, nor did the TV cameras or anyone in the gallery. Only Bobby knew, and so the marshals left it up to him whether to call a stroke on himself or not, which he did. He lost the match that day by one stroke, but he did not lose his integrity. Today, the Bob Jones Award is the highest honour given by the United States Golf Association in recognition of distinguished sportsmanship in golf. Some might recall the story of G.R. Viswanath, the Indian Test captain who famously called England's Bob Taylor back after being given out caught behind in the 1980 Golden Jubilee Test played in Mumbai. Realising Taylor had not touched the ball with his bat, Viswanath withdrew his appeal and Taylor resumed his innings. After India ended up losing the match, Viswanath said, 'If it were to happen again, I would do the same thing.'

The more successful a team is, the more susceptible it becomes to questionable or unethical conduct, often driven by the need to win at all costs. The game of cricket has become increasingly plagued, from the international to the schoolboy level, by the practice of sledging, which is the act of verbally abusing opponents in an attempt to distract them. The Australian cricket team has led this practice in the game for decades. But the most respected athletes in the world do not engage in sledging. That's one of the reasons they're so respected.

They use their skill and sporting nous to gain an advantage over opponents. It's hard to imagine Rahul Dravid, Hashim Amla or Mike Hussey verbally abusing an opponent. Those who choose to sledge are generally the least respected amongst their peers. Ask yourself: 'What kind of person sledges?' And then decide whether you want to be known as that person.

Ball-tampering is another popular yet illegal practice in cricket, which sees players altering the condition of the ball in order to get it to reverse-swing* and thus gain an unfair advantage in a game. Perfected in the 1990s by Pakistan's Waqar Younis and Wasim Akram, the ability to (illegally) alter the condition of the ball without being spotted by the TV cameras has been a sought after skill. Many have been caught and fined, but none more spectacularly than when the Australian youngster Cameron Bancroft was caught using sandpaper on a ball in a Test match against South Africa at the Newlands cricket ground, in March 2018. An investigation revealed that he had been coerced into doing this by senior player David Warner, and that captain Steve Smith knew about the plan but did nothing to prevent it. Smith and Warner received twelve-month bans and Bancroft a nine-month ban. Warner was additionally banned for life from holding any position of leadership in Australian cricket, and Smith banned from any leadership position for twenty-four months.

Decisions carry consequences: to drive drunk or not, to use a condom or not, to be faithful to your partner or not, to fight or to walk away from a hostile situation, to take those performance-enhancing or party-enhancing drugs or not, to use sandpaper on a cricket ball or not, and sometimes even to speak up or not.

---

*Conventional swing happens either due to seam position or one side of the ball being smoother (shinier) than the other. Air travels faster over the smooth than the more worn side, causing the ball to deviate towards the worn side. Reverse swing is likened to the dimple effect of a golf ball, where the worn side of the ball develops a turbulent layer of air that provides even less resistance than the smooth or shiny side, and thus the ball swings towards the shiny side (a dimpled golf ball travels about twice the distance of a smooth ball). Because it takes time for the turbulent air to form around the worn side of the ball, the ball swings later in its flight path than with conventional swing, making it much more difficult to see and thus play. A drier pitch and outfield will wear a ball far quicker than lush grass, and thus reverse swing happens earlier in these dry conditions. Although illegal, a ball can also be artificially 'worn' with the use of a thumbnail, dirt, shoe spikes, pants zipper or sandpaper.

Compared to sport, the business and political terrain offer a far greater bouquet of options to choose from, for gaining an advantage or financial reward via unethical or illegal means. But in most cases, the illicit gain is short-term. People who get away with it might try again. Yet, each time, the win is temporary, as success or financial gains always are. The implications and cost of getting caught are almost always far more permanent, and damaging. Think of the long-term legacy that their indiscretions have left behind for the likes of Hansie Cronjé, Lance Armstrong, Diego Maradona, Zinedine Zidane, and other fallen heroes. Whichever country you live in, look for a politician or politicians who might fit this bill—I have little doubt you'll find them. There's a plethora of examples in the business world, of people caught chasing a quick win and suffering a lifetime of consequences, often condemning their organisation to the same fate. Think Enron, Bernie Madoff, Lehman Brothers, Worldcom, Tyco, Steinhoff—the list is long.

In the ball sandpapering case mentioned above, banned Australian cricket captain Steve Smith inherited a culture, created and perpetuated by his predecessors, where verbal bullying of opposition players, and even their own, was deemed as acceptable, even when the rest of the cricket world felt differently. The turning point came when the desperation to gain a momentary advantage saw Cameron Bancroft manipulating the ball. Being caught brought to a head the long-standing win-at-all-costs attitude that had gradually seen the lines blurring between ethical and unethical conduct. Whilst this is not the only team in the world to have engaged in ball tampering, the team's leadership eventually paid the price.[2]

Literature on team development has long highlighted a common and generic shortcoming of successful teams, that 'they can become overly self-admiring, arrogant and overly-competitive, and because dissent and criticism are stifled in this environment, the team can have difficulty correcting its own errors'. The Australian team was very successful, so I guess nobody felt it necessary to change anything.

As a young leader given the reins of a team in which a bullying, sledging and ball-tampering culture was entrenched, it could be argued that Steve Smith also lacked the courage, guidance and/or support to bring about a shift in culture. This is certainly not the first time in sport that a captain, or coach for that matter, has been appointed into that position for their first time, only to receive very little leadership support.

Professional athletes who arrive at the next level of success are provided a plethora of support to settle and then advance at that level, courtesy a bevy of coaches and managers, as well as medical, fitness and dietary experts, and possibly even media and social media training. All with the assumption that the athlete is not the finished product and could benefit from guidance in their required areas of expertise. Why then do coaches and captains who are placed in key leadership positions so seldom receive the corresponding leadership coaching, guidance and support?

Given that success can make people even more susceptible to unethical conduct, I'd suggest that especially when rewards are showered on individuals, teams or organisations, they humble themselves and undergo a rigorous review and alignment of ethics, values and integrity. Every one of the players mentioned above, and others who have been caught in the act, probably thought they didn't need to do this exercise.

After receiving the news of his ban, the now ex-Australian cricket captain Steve Smith publicly stated, 'If any good can come from this, if there can be a lesson to others, then I hope I can be a force for change.'

DIFFERENT STROKES FOR DIFFERENT FOLKS

No one set of personal values is better than the rest. The reality is that people develop their value systems as a result of the parenting and upbringing they had, and according to their life situation.* Someone who has lost everything in a war or environmental disaster will value shelter, food and water the most. A teenager may value freedom and independence more than a bank manager who may value trust, integrity and status, or a headmaster who may value tradition, discipline and truth. An entrepreneur may value independence, innovation and material wealth more than a charity worker, who may value community, compassion and making a contribution to

---

*A value 'system' in this context refers to a set or group of complementary values. For example, honour, tradition and discipline are complementary. Spontaneity and innovation do not complement these, thus would not fall within that system.

society. Bill Gates started out as an entrepreneur focused on building his empire and material wealth before undergoing a fundamental shift in value systems, to become the philanthropist and humanitarian he is today.

Sportsmen also differ in their value systems. Some are impulsive, spontaneous and express themselves regardless of others; some value tradition, self-discipline, respect and belonging whilst others may value achievement, success, excellence, ambition and profitability. Towards the end of their career, some may move to value personal growth, self-awareness, quality of life and peace of mind.

I recall an intriguing moment during a practice session with the Indian Test team, when nineteen-year-old fast bowler Ishant Sharma was struggling with his bowling in the nets. His frustration levels were clearly increasing, and at one point, as the ball came rolling back down the pitch towards him, he kicked out at it, sending it flying into the adjacent empty net. This was not unusual, for a competitive person to show his frustration, but what was out of the ordinary was that Sachin Tendulkar, who was standing nearby, walked into the net to fetch the ball. He took it back to Ishant, not throwing it, but walking to him. As he handed it over, I heard him tell Ishant in a calm and measured tone, but with gravitas, that it was because of this ball that he had the privileges he was currently enjoying in life. He said that without this ball, Ishant had nothing. He then told him to treat that ball, and every other cricket ball, with respect. Sachin Tendulkar had, and still has, the utmost respect for the game of cricket—he would not stand by and watch a youngster compromise this value.

Like players, fans and spectators identify with different values. Some might enjoy watching a fight between ill-disciplined and impulsive players and happily get themselves into a physical fight with opposition football fans after a game. Some may promote the pride and honour of wearing the team jersey, badge or cap, of respecting history and tradition, as well as the game and the opposition (think cucumber-sandwich-eating Lord's faithful wearing their MCC ties). Some may embrace the values of the professional era where money supersedes loyalty and tradition, and yet others may be more interested in how players conduct themselves as role models in serving the community and those less fortunate than themselves. The reality is that most people are centered in any one of these value systems, even if they subscribe to some of the values from another system. Our values are linked to how we view the world, with no one way being more right than the others.

Knowing what is important gives you a map to navigate decisions and actions, each of which comes with its own consequences. If you like chocolate cake and you like being healthy, you will need to decide what proportion of each you would like. Both are nice, but you can't have lots of both.

At the time they made the decision to spot-fix in cricket matches, the likes of Hansie Cronjé, Salman Butt, Mohammed Asif, Mohammad Amir, Mohammed Azharuddin, Ajay Jadeja and S. Sreesanth would have valued money more than their integrity, honour or doing the right thing. There are many athletes who value winning over doing the right thing, as illustrated by a World Anti-Doping Association (WADA) study that showed that 30 per cent of athletes at the 2011 World Championships and 45 per cent at the Pan-Arab Games had used banned substances during their careers.[3] During the Lance Armstrong era, it is thought that up to 95 per cent of professional cyclists chose doping and winning above following the rules and the spirit of the sport.

Knowing and intentionally living your values is important and even critical in some instances. Some values are more self-oriented, such as independence, competitiveness, power, ambition, status and winning while others are more oriented towards serving others or the greater good, such as honour, tradition, faithfulness, loyalty, caring and empathy. As a player, Anil Kumble valued his rest and his private time, yet his values of commitment and caring superseded his need to use the closed runway as an excuse.

Of the many value-creation exercises that are available, I have gravitated towards and often employ one that presents a playful way of making your values explicit, and another that is more of a checklist. I would recommend that you try the exercise that works best for your learning preference.

Imagine that at your eightieth birthday party, you get to invite five really special guests who would make the occasion the best ever. Who would you invite? These people do not need to be alive, or even real. You can have Jesus Christ, Nelson Mandela, Mahatma Gandhi, Steve Jobs, Elvis Presley or Mickey Mouse, if you wish. This is how the exercise goes:

1. Write their names down.
2. Next to each name, write down words to describe what makes them so special to you.
3. When you're done, make a list of all the different words you have used to describe these individuals, without repeating a word.
4. Next to each word, score how important that quality or characteristic is for you, in your life. (1=not important, 10= extremely important).
5. Make a note of the top five rated words, with the highest rated on top. These are likely to closely represent your personal values. Next to each of these five words, write:

    a) What happens in your life/relationships/ sport when you are like this?
    b) What happens when you compromise on this?
    c) In what ways is this value important to you?

6. Reflection. Write down your main takeaway from this exercise.

I remember a time when a very well known international cricketer undertook this exercise. In an earlier coaching conversation with me, he had brought up the issue of being unfaithful to his girlfriend at the time. He was a young man, unlikely to get married in the next three to five years, and was not even sure if he wanted to marry his current girlfriend.

His dilemma was not uncommon: What was he to do when the opportunity to be with another girl presented itself while travelling abroad, especially as it was unlikely that anyone would find out that he had been unfaithful. To be honest, I had been unfaithful to my previous girlfriend whilst on tour, so I was not in a position to advise him. When we did the exercise, his top two values were *freedom* ('to have the experiences I want') and *loyalty*. After deep consideration, he gave loyalty 9/10 and freedom 8/10.

He realised in that moment that despite the temptation, he would feel better about himself by remaining loyal, even if he didn't eventually marry his current girlfriend. Whether he ended up following his conviction or not, at least he now had a moral compass for making his decisions and knowing what was driving the conflicting messages.

The second exercise to help one determine one's values is the 'Values checklist'.

Below is a list of possible values:

- Impulsive, have fun in the moment
- Doing whatever I want, without guilt
- Conquer, dominate, outfox
- Important to avoid shame
- Non-conformist, will not follow rules
- Be the hero
- Belonging (to a team or group)
- Approval by others
- Security
- Order
- Stability
- Tradition
- Structure
- Loyalty
- Self-discipline
- Self-sacrifice
- Truth
- Achievement
- Success
- Excellence
- Opportunity
- Competitiveness
- Profit
- Ambition
- Intelligence
- Winning
- Innovation
- Status

- Power
- Personal growth
- Self-awareness
- Peace of mind
- Connection
- Community
- Respect
- Tolerance
- Compassion
- Equality
- Emotional well-being
- Cooperation
- Quality of life
- Learning
- Understanding
- Flexibility
- Big picture perspective
- Best man for the job

1. Read through the list of values and rate each on a scale of 1 to 5, where 1=not at all important, and 5=very important to you.
2. Look at all those you ranked 5 (very important), and make a separate list of these, with the most important ones at the top. Identify your top five values, and next to each of these five words, write:

    a) What happens in your life/relationships/ sport when you are like this?
    b) What happens when you compromise on this?
    c) In what ways is this value important to you?

3. Reflection. Write down your main takeaway from this exercise.

In the previous chapter, we discussed the World Cup T20 tournament in London where some players chose the 'fun' of London's nightlife ahead of 'commitment' to morning training and preparation as professional athletes. One of the essential differences between these values, if we can call them that, was that the 'fun' was for the players' personal benefit and compromised the team, whereas saying 'no' to a very late night and 'yes' to optional training (or a good night's sleep and quality rest) would have benefited the team. Every decision we make, every action we take, and even everything we say, has an impact on others, and at the core of each decision sits the intention to serve ourselves, to serve others, or to serve both. With values as the rudder that direct the metaphorical yacht of our lives, the question is, how do *you* want to sail the inevitably calm to the stormy seas of life.

10

EGO: THE BATTLE WITHIN

Sachin Tendulkar is an example of someone who has in equal parts talent, confidence and humility, and plenty of all three. It is a fairly rare combination in sport.

Talent is innate, a gift at birth. It is not earned, and having it is not an accomplishment. Confidence and humility are different, although I don't fully agree with the dictionary definition, that humility 'is a modest or low view of one's importance'. Humility without confidence tends towards insecurity, and confidence without humility tends towards arrogance. Humility and confidence should ideally exist in equal parts, and in abundance.

It's uncommon, however, that humility is in balance with talent and the confidence it sprouts. Our ego—an opposing force to humility—is constantly competing for the attention that talent attracts. Ego wants to receive praise, take the credit, and is reluctant to give much of either. Yet talent, confidence and humility characterise Sachin Tendulkar's unrivalled international cricket career of twenty-four years.

As I listened to him address his teammates at our hotel during the 2011 Cricket World Cup campaign, I reflected on how much poorer cricket would have been if, many years ago, a friend hadn't pulled the sixteen-year-old Sachin aside in an effort to bring the whiz kid's feet back to earth.

We often had breaks of four to five days at the World Cup (more about that later). These breaks were longer than the standard break of two or three days between ODIs and they were significant because they allowed more time for players to think about the next game, but also more time for pressure to build up. Players will often play the game over and over in their heads before match day. Too much of this intensifies the experience of pressure and anxiety, and is likely to leave them mentally exhausted before the first ball has even been bowled.

In his book, *A New Earth*, spiritual teacher Eckhart Tolle speaks of 'the anxiety gap', which is the space in time between our physical body in the present and our mind as it attempts to deal with a conceptual situation some time in the future.[1]

At the World Cup, the challenge of these long waiting periods between games was exacerbated by the fact that players could not leave the hotel. They would have been mobbed had they attempted to do so, and also, the local security regulations prevented the World Cup teams from leaving their hotels for anything but practice and matches. All the teams would have been equally affected by the potential for both anxiety and boredom. Gary and I were constantly on the lookout for ways to manage this, and one idea we came up with was to arrange informal group learning sessions within the inner sanctum of the squad.

For the first one, we asked Sachin if he would take the hot seat and allow players to ask him whatever questions they wished. In his twenty-first year of international cricket, we knew he would have insights that could help most of the squad members, and they were asked to come prepared with questions for him. No media, no outsiders, and no recording devices were allowed.

Midway through the session, one of the players asked Sachin what the most memorable event of his career was. His answer took many by surprise.

He said it happened when he was sixteen years old and soon after he had become the world's youngest ever player to make his country's senior national team. However, it was not this milestone that he deemed most memorable, but rather an incident that happened afterwards. When he returned from the tour to rejoin his local Mumbai teammates, one of his close friends, another sixteen-year-old, pulled him aside and asked if he could speak freely. Then he went on to say that he was speaking on behalf of many of their teammates.

'We all recognise that you are a better cricketer than we are, but since you've played for India, you're acting like you are a more important person than us. We don't like that.'

Sitting in that Bangalore hotel room, Sachin shared his story with sincerity and humility. He also recalled advice that his father had given him as a young boy: 'He said, who I am as a person in my true nature is permanent. My results on the field are temporary—they will go up and they will go down. It is more important that I am consistent as a person. This I can control, my results I cannot. People will criticise me for poor results or praise me for good ones, and they will soon forget these when the next result comes, but they will always remember the impact I have on them as a person. This impression will last forever.'

These few words from his father and a teenage friend helped shape and ground Sachin Tendulkar the person to the extent that he considered it one of the most significant moments of his twenty-one-year-long career, a career that was strewn with more highlights and milestones than any other cricketer's in history. It's hard to imagine an arrogant, self-serving Sachin, and the impact this might have had on the game and on literally hundreds of millions of Sachin fans. With the level of fanaticism that exists in India for the game of cricket and its heroes, one of Sachin's greatest achievements is his ability to remain humble amidst the God-like worship that has followed him for well over two decades.

This quality was manifest to me one morning, once again, when we were preparing to leave our hotel for the start of an ODI against New Zealand. As Sachin and I entered the hotel elevator, a very nervous mom asked if she could take a picture of him with her two young children. We risked being late for the bus, but Sachin obliged, letting the elevator go without him. The nervous mom was shaking so much she couldn't get the camera to work, while the precious seconds ticked by. As the next elevator arrived, I moved to usher him in, to which he responded, 'Pads, won't you help her with the camera, help her to get a nice picture.'

Far lesser players and less successful public figures have been caught up in, and then fallen from, the lofty heights of self-importance that is superficially propped up by the ego's attachment to name, fame and fortune. This chalice of the ego—one that a sixteen-year-old Sachin Tendulkar thankfully swore off—is the source of many of life's greatest catastrophes.

The ego is as self-serving as it is cunning, charming and deceptive. It stalks in the shadows of our personality, waiting for the opportunity to flourish in the fertile environment provided by ignorance, unconsciousness or lack of awareness. Every one of us has an ego, and it drives us to fight for four things:

- to look good
- to not look bad
- to be right
- to not be wrong

Every time we behave, dress and speak in a way that is driven by wanting to look good in the eyes of others, it's our ego manifesting itself. Almost every argument we have with someone close to us comes from our need to be right, and if we can't be right, then our ego fights to not be wrong. Nobody likes to look bad or be wrong. When it does happen, the ego is pricked, and its natural reaction is to defend itself or attack others, with its favourite weapons being blame, justification and explanation. When driven by the ego, it's our own needs and agendas that receive the highest priority. We are not serving others, and often not even considering their needs. As coaches and players, it is essential to be aware of that.

Between 2008 and 2011, managing the ego was one of the most important factors in nurturing the growth and performance of the Indian team, players and coaches. And it needed to start with Gary and I managing our own egos, both leading by example and placing the team's and players' needs ahead of our own needs for looking good, being right and gaining recognition.

In August 2008, India toured Sri Lanka for a five-match ODI series. It was an excellent opportunity for the players to show that they had turned the corner from what had been identified as the key areas for taking Indian cricket to the next level on the international stage. In preparation for the series opener, the team and each individual player committed to attack from the outset, showing aggressive intent. The conditions for the first game suited the Indian team much better than they did the Sri Lankans, and we also identified how to avert the long-standing red flag of complacency.

Sri Lanka won the first ODI with 8 wickets in hand and 91 balls remaining. Almost to a man, the Indian players succumbed to all of the oft discussed complacency-related red flags, things that were within our control.

The loss was bitterly disappointing for everyone (although we would go on to win the series 3-2). We as coaches had spent months helping the side prepare mentally and physically for the battles they had assured us they wanted to fight. Then Sri Lanka happened. Gary and I had a rule that we never spoke to the team after a game. When you win a match, emotions run high, but there could still be someone who was out for a duck, someone who had dropped a catch, or someone who had bowled a bad spell. The team is happy, but a few individuals may be unhappy. When the team loses, there will still be someone who scored 80 or took 3 wickets, so they are happy to some extent, but the team as a whole is not. Either way, a heightened emotional state is not conducive to learning. So, we would always talk to the players the following day, once the emotions had settled and we could have a measured conversation about the game.

But coaches also have egos. We also want to look good, which happens when the team wins and others judge us positively. When a team loses, the coaches look bad, feel bad, and others judge us negatively. This prompts our ego's need to save face by blaming umpires, the conditions or other factors, reprimanding players or the team for not doing their job, or justifying or explaining away the situation. All of this activity is directed at serving our need as coaches, and not that of the players.

After the Sri Lanka game, Gary came to me in the dressing room and said that this was possibly one of those rare times (for us) when it might be necessary to address the team. I agreed. It did seem appropriate that he should have stern words with his players—they deserved it!

But the first thing was to determine exactly what Gary wanted to convey to them. I acted as his sounding board to help him come up with a clear message. Then we discussed how he was going to get it across—direct and forthright, the way we might in South Africa, or gentle and a little bit suggestive, which seemed to be more in keeping with how the Indian players communicated. It was important to tailor the message in a way that ensured the best chance of it landing with the majority of the players.

When Gary was clear on the message and the best way to deliver it, I asked him just one more question: 'Gazza, is this something you honestly believe the team needs to hear? Is it for their benefit, or is this something you're wanting to get off your chest?'

After a moment of self reflection, Gary said it was probably more a case of him wanting to get it off his chest. My response was, 'Okay cool, then let the two of us step outside the change room, and whatever you want to say, say it to me. Don't worry about what you're saying or how you're going to say it, just get it off your chest.' I grabbed a couple of beers, off we went, and Gary did just that.

He ended up not talking to the players. He realised that had he done so, it would have been a case of him serving himself and his needs, and not necessarily of value to the players. They were already disappointed and knew that they had let themselves and the team down—they did not need to be told this. A key learning here is the need for self-awareness, especially before delivering a harsh message to a team. Consider what you're saying, how you're saying it, whether it's the right time to be saying it, and most importantly, who the message is serving—you as coach, or the team? Like the alien mineral that deprives Superman of his powers, ego's kryptonite is the light of awareness.

A REPRIMAND FOR REPRIMANDING

Had Gary issued his 'reprimand' in the change room that night, it would have served to erode the players' confidence, retard the learning that was available from that failure, and possibly undermined his relationship with the players.

It would also have added to the players' fear of failure, which itself is one of the biggest mental obstacles to success. Show me a team with a coach who shouts at players for making mistakes, and I'll show you a team with a fear of failure. For some, it may not so much create fear of failure as fear of the repercussion of failure. Most players don't like being responsible for upsetting their coach or their parents.

Each time one of these people demonstrates their disappointment or unhappiness, the fear within that player grows. If done often enough to a child, there is a good chance of creating in someone a lifelong and self-limiting mental narrative of 'I'm not good enough'.

Interestingly, having players who are focused on trying to not make a mistake is actually one of the formulas for making mistakes—and it's certainly not the formula for delivering success.

If reprimanding a player is so ineffective and sometimes even destructive, why then do so many coaches (and parents, teachers, managers) do it?

A lot of the time, a reprimand comes from the ego and its unconscious need for power or control over others. It comes from coaches who have put hours of time and energy into preparing and planning for the team's success, and who have then told players how they need to play. An (often unconscious) expectation from the coach is that the players will do what they are told, so that the team can win and the coach then gets to look good and be judged positively. The reprimand usually follows when the players don't meet the coach's expectations, when they don't do what the coach told them to do, or when they don't do it with the commitment or energy the coach expects. Especially when a player makes a mistake that causes the team to lose or produce a poor showing, it reflects badly on the coach, and so his ego looks for someone to blame for it.

In short, the reprimand is a tool primarily used to serve the coach's own ego, blaming someone else for them not looking good. It is a largely ineffective and overused tool that hails from an earlier era. The process described above applies equally to pushy parents with unrealistically high expectations of their kids, controlling bosses and authoritative teachers.

'Not making a mistake' is a very reasonable expectation for a production line where anything from a widget to a motorcar is being manufactured. The same still applies for some functions in fields like manufacturing, engineering, accounting and computer programming, where one cannot afford to make mistakes. However, in creative and innovative pursuits in today's VUCA (Volatile, Uncertain, Complex, Ambiguous) world, which includes sports like cricket, hockey, rugby, soccer and others, mistakes *will* happen, and athletes *will* fail. Failing is integral to learning and succeeding. What's important is to pursue success far more actively than looking to avoid failing. Especially in these environments, the reprimand is ineffective, disempowering, disengaging and, dare I say, annoying.

Two ways to address failure or an error are 1) go back and unpack the error in the past, and 2) look towards the solution in the future. When the coach focuses on the mistake in the past, the athletes ego is pricked because it reignites the memory of them looking bad or being wrong. The reprimand exacerbates this and turns the volume up on their ego's need to blame, justify or explain the situation away, either by defending itself or attacking others. This ego reaction (in the thinking brain) closes the mind to learning, undermines the player's confidence, increases fear of failure and also erodes the relationship between the player and the person doing the reprimanding.

In neurophysiological terms, when someone is criticised, the negative emotion causes the body to produce higher levels of the stress hormone cortisol, which is designed to shut down thinking and trigger a conflict and defense (fight or flight) mechanism. We should all know by now that the error should almost never be pointed out in front of others, and certainly not in front of the whole team.

The ideal way to address failure is to view it in terms of a solution in the future. The first step is to acknowledge the mistake with the non-judgmental and unemotional understanding that mistakes happen, that they are a very necessary and normal part of the learning process. One player who stands out in this regard, and whom I have a very high regard for, is Proteas cricketer J.P. Duminy. He is secure enough within his insecurities, and able to put his ego aside enough to own his errors in a team meeting: 'I felt pressure to get up with the run rate, and thought if I hit a 6 it would relieve the pressure. In hindsight, I realise this was more a panic reaction than a smart option. Sorry guys, getting myself out in this way put pressure on the remaining batsmen.' My response to this would be to praise the level of honesty and assumption of responsibility, and hope that it encourages others to do the same.

Once the error is acknowledged, it's time to look ahead. The key question to ask is, 'Next time you are in that situation, what would you do differently?' In Duminy's case, it would be, 'Next time, I'll absorb the pressure longer, looking to play strong cricket shots along the ground, and give myself more of a chance. There is always more time than one thinks.'

This focus on both the solution and the future accesses the creative part of the brain, which engages whole-brain thinking. Creatively designing solutions for the future increases the chances of learning, builds confidence and improves the relationship between the athlete and the person helping them to learn.

The positive experience of designing solutions boosts the body's production of oxytocin, a feel-good hormone that increases our ability to communicate, collaborate and trust others. Additionally, oxytocin activates networks in our prefrontal cortex that lead to increased creativity and more expansive thought and action. Good moods produce better solutions.

Compared to cortisol, which is released in response to criticism, the feel-good hormone, oxytocin, metabolises much faster. The effects of a positive interaction are therefore less dramatic and enduring than those of a negative one. This is the neurophysiological foundation for the recommendation of four compliments to balance every one piece of criticism or negative feedback. It's also why negative feedback is so much more impactful and remembered longer than compliments and positive feedback.

For such solutions-focused conversations to really work, players need to trust that the coach is genuinely trying to help them, and that they will not be judged, punished or reprimanded for making *and* owning the mistake. In a position of leadership, like coaching, managing and even parenting, our job is to serve the players' needs, and not to serve ourselves by getting things off our chest.

Players, especially younger ones, should never be the dumping ground for our own frustrations and emotions. If we wish for them to perform and grow as players and people, the battle with the ego within needs to be fought just as hard as, if not harder than, the battles we fight on the outside. For player-centered coaches, contemporary leaders and people-managers, this level of self-awareness will help navigate some of the toughest situations coaching can throw at you. Like dealing with difficult players.

FROM MR ROWAN ALGIE TO 'THE SOCCER BULLY'

In 1984, when I was in Grade 10 at Wynberg Boys' High, we were not allowed to play cricket in the corridor. Duh. I was a leader in the school, excelled at sport, and was 'one of the guys'. Despite it not being allowed, I found myself batting at the intersection where two corridors met, playing the pull shot down the length of one and the cut shot back down the other, with enthusiastic boys trying to catch me out. As one of the teachers came out of his classroom, the ball hit the light fitting just above his head, sending it crashing to the floor and shattering right at his feet. I knew I was in deep trouble. Back then, we still received corporal punishment. The new headmaster, Mr Rowan Algie, had been at the school for just three or four weeks, but as a provincial squash player, he already had a reputation as someone who could wield a cane. On my way to his office, I tried to predict whether this was a four- or six-cut offence. It had to be one of those; it couldn't be less. When I entered Mr Algie's office, he looked at me and said: 'Mr Upton, how unfortunate for us to have our first meeting under these circumstances.' So he clearly knew who I was. Then he asked, 'Would it make any difference to your understanding of your offence if I gave you four or six cuts (across the buttocks with the cane)?' The obvious answer was 'no'—whether he caned me four or six times would make no difference in my understanding of my wrongdoing. Mr Algie decided not to cane me, and let me leave his office with a message that made a huge impression on me: 'Try not to put the two of us in this position again, would you?'

For the remainder of my two years in high school, each time the temptation arose to do something I knew I shouldn't, Mr Algie's words rang in my ears. I was not as frequently naughty, and when I was, at least it was with far more awareness than before that incident. Thoughtless and senseless mistakes were largely eliminated. But, as we will see in the next chapter, the ego is cunning and saw to it that my mistakes were not entirely behind me.

In my final year, when I became a prefect and had to deal with difficult peers, I would often employ that same line, and it worked. When you give someone the punishment they expect, it serves as a reset button; we're all square now. Rather than giving wrongdoers the punishment they expect, remove your ego (and its need for power and control over others) from the situation and give them respect. I continue to be amazed at how often the benefit of this respect-based approach is returned, with interest.

We had a similar experience with the Indian team. One of the senior players in the side was a very strong personality and if not managed well, he could be a threat to the team environment, sometimes disrupting his teammates and the culture. One day, we were playing soccer during a training session. In order to avoid injuries, players were told not to contest a 50-50 ball on the ground or in the air. Most players would back off from a physical contest, except this same senior player who was more interested in getting the ball for himself. During one such game, a youngster contested the senior, and showed him up by taking the ball off him more than once. It happened once too often, leading to the senior player retaliating by kicking out quite violently at the younger player's legs.

The game paused awkwardly as everyone wondered what would happen next. Gary did nothing. Mike Young, an American-Australian fielding consultant who was with us at the time, marched over to him and told him he had to take the player aside and let him know that his behaviour was unacceptable. But Gary just told him to let it go. The game got back underway, and soon after that Mike approached Gary again, unable to understand why he was not addressing the matter. He even asked me whether Gary was scared of conflict. He again told Gary that he understood the culture we were trying to establish, and that such conduct undermined it completely. Again, Gary told him that they should leave it.

To be honest, we didn't really know what to do. But we knew what not to do. In the same way that any adult knows when they have made a mistake, we trusted that the senior player would realise that he had been wrong.

Later that afternoon, the same senior was helping one of the other young players with his bowling action. Gary walked up to him and told him that by helping like this, he was adding real value to the younger players and to the team. Gary wanted to let him know that he had taken note of what he was doing for that player, and that he really appreciated it. We knew the players with whom we worked. I'm not saying that one should only react to the positive things and ignore the negative things—not at all. But we knew who we were dealing with and the potential we could help unearth by treating players as adults.

After the training session, while boarding the bus for the hotel, that same senior apologised to captain M.S. Dhoni and to the junior player he had kicked. He then came and sat down next to Gary. He admitted that he had erred earlier that afternoon and that his actions were not in keeping with the culture the team had established for itself. He went on to acknowledge the pattern in his behaviour, and committed to spend some time with me to better understand and eliminate it, which he did. His ownership of his error, and genuine and heartfelt apology helped make the whole team stronger. Growth had taken place.

WHEN IS EGO A GOOD THING?

In practical terms, ego can be a huge asset. Specifically, it is an asset for an athlete on the training ground or in the gym, because it drives them to want to be stronger, better, fitter, to want to practise longer, look good, beat an opponent, and enjoy the spoils of victory. Ego drives people to prepare better, study more, work longer hours, to do whatever is required to avoid failure and to get recognition, acknowledgement, reward and success.

But the moment an athlete crosses the ropes and the game begins, their ego works more against than for them. It goes from being an asset to being a liability.

Knowing when to be energised by the ego and when not to be is just as important as being aware of the ego's existence. As an example, in his debut Test for South Africa against Australia in Adelaide, in November 2012, Faf du Plessis faced a seemingly impossible task of saving the game for the Proteas. He needed to bat for nearly eight hours and see out 125 overs. With an attacking field in place and his score on 98, he proceeded to defend 24 consecutive deliveries without attempting to score. An attacking field meant there were many gaps in which to score 2 runs for himself and reach his century on debut. The team's need to play out time prevailed over the ego's need to achieve this rare personal milestone. Thankfully, he succeeded on the twenty-fifth delivery.

11

EGO AND MY GREATEST PROFESSIONAL ERROR

THE SEX DOSSIER

My most painful professional experience was also my greatest lesson in coaching and leadership. It happened in 2009. The Indian cricket team had started performing better and better. They enjoyed the environment and would speak openly about it. People who were watching India could see that there was increased enthusiasm, energy and professionalism compared to what they had become used to in recent seasons. The players were no longer just individuals, they were a team.

Noting the difference, the media wanted to know what Gary Kirsten was like as a coach. The players all spoke very highly of him, and along with improved results, this led to more media on 'Guru Gary'. Between the players and delighted journalists, he was increasingly put in the limelight, a position he doesn't like all that much.

The few times Gary agreed to do interviews were generally when we had lost, so he could face the music and take the flak for the players. At interviews, he would always speak about the players, how *they* were doing, and about *their* efforts. Gary never made it about Gary. People who followed us knew our entire approach was about the players and putting *them* centrestage. But the more Gary made it about the players, the more the media made it out to be about the 'selfless' and 'humble' demigod of a man affectionately known as Gazza.

This went on for about a year before my professional ego went, 'Hang on—what about me?' People close to me were saying, 'Paddy, you're not getting any recognition for what is happening in the team. But when Gary speaks, I can hear he's using the language you've been using for ten years. When the players are speaking, they're using your language.'

At first, when friends and family said to me that I was not getting any recognition, I would answer that I knew there were only a handful of people in the inner circle of my professional life that needed to know what I was doing. Wherever I was going to go after the Indian experience, it was these key individuals who were going to influence my career (this turned out to be true). It really didn't matter what the person sitting on the couch at home thought or didn't think, whether they knew me or didn't know me. Also, as a qualified executive (business) coach, my job was to work with a leader or a high performer, and to help *them* lead better, or perform better, and gain recognition. If they wished to acknowledge me, that was fine. But my job was not to be seen to be doing a good job. It was to do a good job. Period.

But the ego needs to look good, and my ego would actually have liked some recognition for what I was doing. It was around this time that Rahul Dravid spoke to me about it. He and I had a lot of conversations, and we spoke about life and philosophy, not just about cricket. Cricket was always secondary in our chats. Rahul is a deep thinker, and he was always seeking to learn new things. We'd spend a lot of time in front of my computer as I shared some of my ideas and presentations. On that specific day he said, 'Paddy, I just want to acknowledge the work that you're doing with this Indian team. I can see your influence and ideas in a lot of what Gary presents to the team.'

The feelings I was battling with were exacerbated by my understanding that, in the Indian community, there was a definite sense of respect for a senior figure. Players respected what Gary said far more than they would respect it if I said exactly the same thing. From my personal conversations with players and a close observation of what made them tick, I would often make suggestions to Gary about what message he should convey to a specific player. With 101 Test matches to his name, a message was always going to have more impact coming from him than from me. In this way, much of my communication to the players would go through Gary. But as a result of this dynamic between Gary and me, from the players' perspective, they got a limited view of my actual input into the team.

In October 2009, the ICC Champions Trophy in South Africa would provide me with the opportunity to set the record straight. There was something extra in this tournament for Gary and me, since we would get to come home and our work would be on show, more tangibly than would have been the case if the tournament were being hosted elsewhere. Also, it was an ICC tournament, so more preparation went into it than for a normal bilateral series.

We prepared striking leather-bound folders with the players' names embossed in gold on the front. In those folders were notepads that we'd use in the workshops leading up to the tournament. Also included were some materials that I had generated for the players—some pretty cool stuff on diet, the mental game, preparation and so on. One topic that people didn't really talk about, but which I felt needed to be addressed, was the impact of sex on performance. I looked at it from various angles: from the psychological angle, the emotional angle, a spiritual angle, from different religious perspectives, from a social-conscience perspective. I looked at it from a Chinese medical perspective and a purely biological perspective, at what happens with the biology of testosterone.

While writing all of those pieces, I knew the players weren't going to sit and read four-page documents. I needed to write in a way that would hold their interest. Just so I could get the players' attention, the introduction to the sex document was, '*Does sex increase performance?*' And to get them reading a bit more, I wrote, '*Yes, it does. So go ahead and indulge.*' The next line read, '*Okay, so that's the popular answer, the one that everyone wants to hear. I know that if I want to have this article quoted widely, I should just leave it at that.*' I went on to elaborate over three more pages. As with all the other documents, there was quite a bit of tongue-in-cheek stuff in the copy. They were written in a light-hearted tone and were mostly topics for discussion and not guidelines or rules governing the team's behaviour while at the Champions Trophy.

As it happened, I knew a journalist who was a fan of my thinking and philosophies. I also knew that information gets leaked to the Indian media all the time, and that those leather-bound folders containing my written documents might well be leaked somewhere along the line. The folders were printed at the BCCI office, they were embossed in some other place, and everything was put together in someone's office before being distributed to the players. The players could also have left them lying in a team room or even leaked one to a media contact.

Knowing this, I took the entire folder to this journalist because I wanted him to see the articles I had written, the philosophies I ascribed to, and the work that I had put in behind the scenes for the team. I hoped that he would write an article about the great work Paddy Upton was doing in the engine room of the revived Team India. Having that done in South Africa would make the article's publication even sweeter.

Nothing like that happened. When I woke up the following morning, news had broken in India that Gary Kirsten promotes players having sex before a game. In India, it is almost taboo to speak about sex publicly. Some of those tongue-in-cheek statements I made were taken completely out of context, and it was made to seem that Gary was proposing that players go out and have sex while they were away from India, away from their families, and if they couldn't get sex, they should masturbate while imagining having sex with as many people as they could—that this was part of their preparation for the Champions Trophy tournament. It became a massive media scandal, both vilifying and making a laughing stock of Gary.

I was devastated. I had acted purely out of ego in order to get recognition for my work and myself. My self-centred actions had led to the media crucifying Gary. I had hurt a very good friend who trusted me. In one selfish move, I had pulled the rug from under the person whom I had spent eighteen months supporting and building up. The fact that Gary and his family had a very high standing in the Christian community aggravated the situation. I knew Debbie's family well, and her father Michael Cassidy is a well known evangelist, preacher and author. The scandal caused considerable damage to Gary's image, and to Debbie and her father. Back in India, the reputation of the coach who was all about the players was seriously tarnished.

What drove an arrow through my heart—a physical pain—was when the team got together for practice that morning. Sachin Tendulkar didn't speak often, not in team meetings, nor at practice. But when he did talk, people listened because he always had a point to make. On that day, he gathered us together, and although I can't recall exactly what he said, every word was like a dagger through my heart: 'Someone here has leaked that document. It's hurt our coach. It's completely unacceptable, it's not right, and we need to pull together and rally together as a team. Now.'

I was *that* guy. I had acted out of self-interest, out of ego, in order to get recognition for myself. What I had succeeded in doing was to hurt one of the persons in this world whom I least wanted to hurt.

I went to Gary afterwards and told him I had done it, and why I did it. 'I wanted some recognition back in South Africa for the work I have been doing. It has backfired, but what makes it ten times worse is that it hasn't backfired on me; it has backfired on you and your family.' Things had got so far out of hand by now that Gary was on the point of offering his resignation should the BCCI need a scapegoat.

I recall meeting Debbie Kirsten outside the team hotel in Sandton and, with tears rolling down my cheeks, stumbling out a very emotional apology. Even as I write this, I can feel the emotion welling up inside. It was only because of the special relationship I'd had with Gary, over a number of years, that I was able to be totally honest and to have him accept my apology. My mistake, born of my ego, had consequences beyond anything I could have ever imagined. Debbie and my wife were very close at the time, and a lot of rebuilding had to go into our relationships because of what I had done.

At the time, Gary said the players didn't need to know that I was the guy who leaked the document. 'Because we have work to do. The team doesn't need this,' he said. But we let it be known in the media that I had written the article.

Looking back now, I don't think I could have had a more painful lesson in what happens when a coach acts out of ego and self-interest. When I messed up, I had to own up and be honest about why I did what I did. Few of us will ever transcend our ego or have it fully die. But we can at least try to shine the light of self-awareness on the shadows where our ego lurks.

12

GETTING THERE: BIRTHING THE WORLD CUP STRATEGY

In June 2010, during the triangular Asia Cup series, our stay just outside Dambulla had all the potential to be a memorable and significant one. Well, at least for me, and for reasons that had little to do with the job at hand.

This gorgeous mountainous region of north Sri Lanka is extremely isolated. We stayed in the Kandalama Hotel, one of the most majestic places I have ever lodged in. It is built right up against the Ritigala mountains, overlooking the rock fortress of Sigiriya in the distance. The hotel's façade is entirely overgrown by bottle-green vegetation, reclaiming the multi-storeyed structure back for the wilderness, as if man's attempts to assert himself in this ancient land had long since been defeated by Mother Nature. Except inside. There, luxury meets tranquility.

In the hotel restaurant, where we spent a lot of our time, three of the four walls are made of glass from floor to ceiling. One window is five metres away from the mountain's rock face. Another overlooks the Sri Lankan countryside of dense forest, embracing the Kandalama Lake where Gary and I would fish, and where wild elephants escaped temperatures reaching into the upper thirty degrees Celsius.

Barring the final of the Asia Cup (for which we only had two days to prepare), we had three days' rest between all the regular matches. On those days, given the isolation, our options for recreational activity were limited. Mainly, one could drink coffee, lounge around the rim flow pool, go for long runs or fish in the nearby lake. All perfectly pleasurable, but not entirely what I had in mind when I strapped a surfboard to the Indian team bus, heading inland.

I have often joked, tongue not so firmly in cheek, that I coach cricket to support my surfing and fishing habits. Dambulla might be in the middle of nowhere, and catching (and releasing) lazy freshwater fish would soon lose its novelty factor, but a surfer's paradise awaited me not too far from there. Arugam Bay, one of the ten most consistent right-hand point-breaks in the world during that time of the year, was a nine-hour bumpy taxi drive away from Dambulla. And so, I disappeared for a day-and-a-half, taking our video analyst Dhananjay with me to experience surf culture.

I must admit, however, that the significance of Dambulla 2010 had very little to do with my surfing expedition, and that it had almost everything to do with the Cricket World Cup that would take place in India in ten months' time. (Nevertheless, one does not surf Arugam Bay when it's that good and keep quiet about it. And it definitely added to the Dambulla trip, remaining one of my fondest memories from that time).

On the morning before the Asia Cup final—after having ticked Arugam Bay off my bucket list—Gary Kirsten, Eric Simons and I were sitting in the hotel restaurant right against the window that overlooked the lake. An inspiring view, to say the least. I can't recall who asked the question, but it was this: If India were to play in the World Cup final tomorrow, were we ready?

The answer was 'no'. We didn't feel we were ready, and the conversation we had that day between breakfast and lunch, at that same table, was about what needed to be done to alter that. The Kandalama Hotel in Dambulla was where we created the roadmap we would follow in pursuit of the team's dream of conquering the biggest wave of their professional lives.

The World Cup was to be hosted in India, and we knew the Indian conditions better than anyone else did. When it came to hotels and venues, we would be in our comfort zone, while all the other teams would be outside theirs. But being at home during a World Cup meant the added pressure of meeting local expectations. It's always easier being the underdogs. So, we had two major considerations: playing smarter cricket, which was Gary and Eric's domain, and dealing with the pressure of playing at home. That's where I came in.

With Eric's inputs, Gary offered a strategic perspective on what was needed to be done to improve our 50-over game. For one, we weren't very fit. Although fitness training was still optional, Ramji Srinivasan had joined us as fitness trainer in 2009 (remember the guy mentioned in Chapter 8, *Thinking Differently*). He was a lovely guy and I think he may have been the only fitness trainer in the world who smoked, couldn't run, and had a potbelly. But the players enjoyed being with him, and his contribution to creating a happy team environment was tangible. In keeping with our coaching philosophy, he never forced anything on the players but supported them diligently with plenty of interesting options, great information and loads of encouragement.

The mental game was a key piece of our World Cup strategy, since we needed to prepare for a home final in Mumbai, on Sachin Tendulkar's home ground, in his final World Cup game for the Indian one-day side. If we made it to the final, it would be the maximum pressure any team would have played under in a World Cup. In all likelihood, for every team, the mental game would feature as the most crucial ingredient in pursuit of cricket's ultimate crown.

During our inspired coffee house conversation in Dambulla, we concluded that as things stood, at least on the mental side of the game, the odds were stacked against India. We discussed what needed to be done, based on an assessment of the current potential obstacles to success. The following is a summary of that conversation, taken directly from a document sent to the Indian cricket authorities, outlining the obstacles that had to be overcome while preparing the team for the World Cup finals.

> *Home pressure:* Historically, the additional pressure of playing a World Cup at home seems to have taken its toll on participating teams, illustrated by the fact that in all nine World Cup tournaments up to this stage, the home team has never won.
>
> A home tournament and final in Mumbai will bring with it the highest possible pressure on Team India. Adding to this pressure is the fact that India will likely be tournament favourites, and that

Indian fans and media, possibly above all countries, place the highest amount of pressure and expectation of results on its players.

The most significant factor in this increased pressure is that it affects the Indian team negatively. When discussing it, players report that they struggle with the pressure of results under normal circumstances, particularly when playing knockout games in India. The effect of this perceived pressure is best illustrated by India recording only three wins out of a total of twenty-one tri- or quadrangular ODI finals played over the past decade.

Pressure and the current team: The current team has performed better in the previous two years than in the past decade, with a near 70 per cent win ratio, and with significant wins in the 2007 World T20 tournament, as well as the 2008 Commonwealth Bank Series against Australia and Sri Lanka. Unlike the 2011 World Cup, though, both those tournaments were played away from home, and, therefore, India did not carry the expectation and pressure of being the favourites.

Despite these recent successes, the tendency to succumb under high pressure remains. This was evinced by the early exit at the World T20 in 2009, where India were defending the title they had won in 2007, and again when pursuing an imminent number one ODI ranking by handing back a clear 2-1 advantage to a severely weakened Australian team in 2010.

Without the necessary attention, this long-standing trend of under-delivery under pressure cannot be expected to simply disappear by 2011.

Except for a fortunate minority, most sportsmen and teams are negatively affected by pressure associated with big moments. In order to address this phenomenon, we need to understand the contributing factors that exist within this specific group of individuals.

First, the players are affected by what others say about them: Except for one or two unique individuals, the majority of players in our ODI side are overly concerned about what other people think or say about them. They report being significantly affected by other people's expectations and particularly criticism of them, reporting experiencing more of this type of pressure when playing in India than when abroad. The increasing popularity of social media and players' fixation with it gives previously anonymous fans direct access to players. All of a sudden, critics are able to travel home on the team bus with us, as players read and react to comments and criticism delivered to their smartphones.

Some players have an over-focus on results: Except for a few, and this goes beyond the Indian team, players have a tendency to place an unhealthy value and sense of well-being on their personal results or achievements—becoming visibly puffed up by good performances and depressed by poor ones. A desperation or need to score runs or take wickets leads to unforced errors. It also gives rise to the so-called confidence player who does well when he is feeling good, and tends to under-deliver when he is not feeling good, or under pressure.

The need to look good: More often than not, players exhibit an over-emphasis on the need to look good or not look bad, both on and off the field. Typically associated with ego-dominance, this trait is fairly common amongst younger males and reflects a normal insecurity at that age. Even if it appears outwardly confident, the ego is ultimately vulnerable and insecure, leading to the vulnerability in high pressure situations on the field.

Sourcing motivation from outside the individual: For most players, an unhealthily high amount of motivation for performance lies in factors external to themselves and in the world outside, over which they have no control. The outside world and the game situation determine players' motivation. Thus it requires ideal external conditions and levels of pressure to set players up for ideal performance.

Common external factors affecting the players' confidence or motivation include: playing at home or away, with significant others watching them or not, against opponents they are confident matching up to versus not, under playing conditions that suit their game versus those that don't, and the different levels of perceived match pressure. Some players are low pressure experts, in that they tend to perform best when pressure is low; others are medium pressure experts, and only a very few like M.S. Dhoni, and possibly Gambhir, are genuine high pressure players. None of the players are equally good under all three levels of pressure, an indication that they are all affected by external situations or conditions.

Apart from losing eighteen out of twenty-one (high pressure) finals in the past decade, the team also shows a tendency to win narrowly and even lose in low pressure games. The latter is due to the tendency we have previously identified, of players relaxing when ahead, and thus allowing the opposition back into the game. (Recall Chapter 6, *India at War*)

Consistently high performers have the source of their motivation within themselves, thus they are less influenced by external situations, expectations or pressure, whether high or low. If India are to win the World Cup at home, our strategic and mental preparation has to address all the potential pitfalls identified above.

Most of the mental obstacles mentioned are true to varying degrees for many cricketers in all other participating teams. In order to strengthen India's chances, we simply need to have better mental resolve and emotional management than our opponents, particularly in the key game-changing moments.

This was a reality check regarding the challenges facing our mental preparation for the World Cup, none of which was shared with the players or captain Dhoni. In line with our philosophy of playing to strengths, we also took clear stock of those, with the intention of focusing on and further improving all that was working well, specifically the things that had seen this team take their ODI win record from 51 per cent to nearly 70 per cent in the two years since we had joined them. The players liked this approach of focusing on what was working, as Gary and I had learned on the very first morning we met the team.

While listing all that was working, we referred to the matrix of internal and external focus as a basic framework or guideline to ensure that we would cover all aspects of the team's campaign.

We considered both the measurable and immeasurable aspects related to the game, the art and science of it. At the individual level, this meant analysing the players' attitudes, character and mental game assets, and on a team level, the team environment and culture.

The measurable aspects included reviewing individual strengths related to batting, bowling and fielding skills, as well as fitness levels (which were never really a strength, and were unlikely to be in the lead up to the World Cup). We just needed everyone to get a pass mark here, which Ramji was seeing to. We also listed our strengths with regard to team systems (off-field management and logistics), team processes (meetings, practices, etc.) and team strategies (on-field).

Some of the key strengths which would go on to play a significant role in the World Cup campaign included noteworthy improvements in preparation and practice, improved strategic thinking and execution of ODI strategy, increased attention to detail in most aspects of our game, a heightened work ethic, a genuinely happy and supportive team environment, and undoubtedly, M.S. Dhoni's example: both his captaincy and the fact that he repeatedly performed under high pressure. His personal performances with the bat had won a number of games that otherwise may have been lost. And true to form, MS and Gautam Gambhir would do the same in the World Cup final.

I recall how my energy changed when going from assessing our perceived weaknesses or areas where we were not yet ready, to brainstorming on what was working well—our strengths. The first left me quite depressed with what seemed like a huge mountain we still had to scale, while the latter left me feeling upbeat and optimistic, certain that 'we can do this'.

TALK THE WALK

After that morning's conversation in the Kandalama Hotel dining room, Gary, Eric and I doubled down to the task of planning for India's first world championship win since 1983. By midnight that same day, the Indian team had taken the first step by beating Sri Lanka in the Asia Cup final. Defending a first innings total of 268 for 6 in their allotted 50 overs, India bowled Sri Lanka out for 187 in the 45th over. As it turned out, the next time these two teams met in a final would be on the game's greatest stage.

From that day onwards, our language changed. At every meeting we had in the next ten months—whatever the next game or tournament was—we would say, '*When we play in the final in Mumbai ...*' or '*When we play on the 2nd of April ...*', the day the final was scheduled for. Only once we had started a conversation by prefacing it with 'When we play...' would we talk about the immediate match or tournament we were involved in. However, we never said, 'When we *win* the World Cup', since that would have loaded avoidable pressure on the players.

Our language was subtler. We wanted to get the players' minds around getting to the final. So, if and when we got to the final, we would have been there mentally numerous times before. We needed to be as prepared as possible, physically, emotionally and mentally, for that moment.

As mental coach, if all went as planned, I would get the once-in-a-lifetime opportunity to deliver the final team talk on the night before the World Cup final. I was so looking forward to my Al Pacino/*Any Given Sunday* moment. I'd be lying if I said that, ten months out from the occasion, I hadn't already started thinking about a speech that would get the players so motivated they'd be ready to run through a brick wall for the team.

13

GETTING THERE: THE SIX INCHES BETWEEN THE EARS

Following the review of the challenges facing us in the lead up to the World Cup, it was time to plot how we would make it to the finals day in Mumbai on 2 April 2011, fully prepared for whatever might be thrown at us. Not only prepared, but better prepared to win the game than any opponent—who in their own ways would also be doing all they could to arrive as the best prepared team at the tournament. The race was on.

FINDING THE ZONE

The zone, or state of flow, is that mental state from which optimal performance naturally emanates. Little else delivers victory better or more regularly than an athlete in the zone. Much is written about it, athletes and coaches regularly speak about it, but neither the underlying mechanisms nor the way to achieve it are well understood.

What we do know is that athletes in the zone report having laser-like focus, an intense yet effortless present-moment awareness, with an accompanying effortless execution of skill at the highest level of their ability. The athlete is totally absorbed in a state of undistracted concentration on the task at hand. There is no thinking. Time is distorted, in that it passes so quickly, yet things seem to happen in slow motion. Instinct and intuition are heightened as players merge with their environment, somehow seeming to know what will happen next. It leads to individuals being the best version of themselves, delivering their best performances, with ease and flow, and it leaves them on a high afterwards. A.B. de Villiers, Virat Kohli, Roger Federer, Kelly Slater (the surfer) or any of the great athletes of our time performing in a state of flow, especially in a big game, are a truly majestic sight.

Some of the aspects that are understood about the underlying mechanisms of 'the zone', which then offer clues towards pursuing this state, include:

- The focus is entirely *external* (on what's happening 'out there'). The athlete is focused on the task at hand, such as a batsman focusing on the ball or a bowler on their target down at the other end of the pitch. There is correspondingly little or no internal focus (on what's happening inside the head or with any aspect of technique, such as balance, footwork or back lift).
- The zone happens when someone is *optimally challenged* by the task. If the task is too easy, athletes will be under-aroused and are likely to get bored or easily distracted, and if the task is too difficult or the pressure too high, stress and anxiety are likely to lead to choking or panicking.
- On a side note, my experience, as well as the natural distribution curve or Bell curve, suggests that the majority of athletes will be at their best or at just either side of medium levels of pressure. Only a few athletes are optimally challenged when the pressure is really high, which then brings out the best in those lucky few, who become known for their 'big match temperament'.
- There are high levels of *intrinsic motivation*. Athletes need to be doing something they enjoy, are drawn to do and are good at; they need to be playing to their strengths. It's unlikely they will find a flow state when forced to follow a coach's instructions.
- Motivation, trust, cooperation, supportiveness and team work are words also associated with flow states, and thus, finding the zone is more likely where there is a *healthy team culture*.

The reality is that very few athletes are able to access this state at will. The zone mostly just 'happens', generally when most of these and other favourable factors happen to align on a particular day. The Indian team could not rely on this phenomenon for results, so we would have to work on a number of other ways for players to manage their minds.

THE FOCUSED MIND

The mental condition that is possibly closest to the zone is a (correctly) focused mind, specifically one that is focused on the right things at the right time. The idea of an athlete 'not being focused' or the coach telling an athlete to 'focus' is flawed, because athletes are almost always focused; it's just that they are not always correctly focused. We wanted the Indian players to improve their understanding *and* management of their focus, specifically in terms of:

- Past, present and future focus, using a past focus primarily to gain lessons (not to feel bad or lose confidence), a future focus to make plans (and not worry, feel pressure or fear failure), and a present moment focus, to be fully present to events as they unfolded in real time (from when the bowler starts their run-up, until the ball becomes dead).
- Broad to narrow focus, understanding when to broaden (or relax) their focus (between deliveries, which we called switch-down time), where it's appropriate to take in lots of information from all around, such as the game situation, scoreboard, field placing and so on. And understanding when to narrow (or sharpen) focus onto the task at hand (as the ball is about to enter play, called switch-up time), when batsmen focus narrowly and only on the ball, and bowlers on their target, and;
- Internal versus external focus, understanding when to focus on what's going on inside (on things like thoughts, feelings, footwork, balance or any facet of their technique), and when to focus outside of themselves (on the ball, the opposition, field placing, etc.). Cricketers in poor form generally get stuck there because they (and their coaches) are too focussed on

correcting technical errors (which is an internal focus), at their end of the pitch, rather than focusing on what is happening down the other end, whether it's a batsman needing to focus on the bowler and the ball, or a bowler on his target. Just as a public speaker needs to focus on their audience out there, and not on what they are thinking or doing on stage.

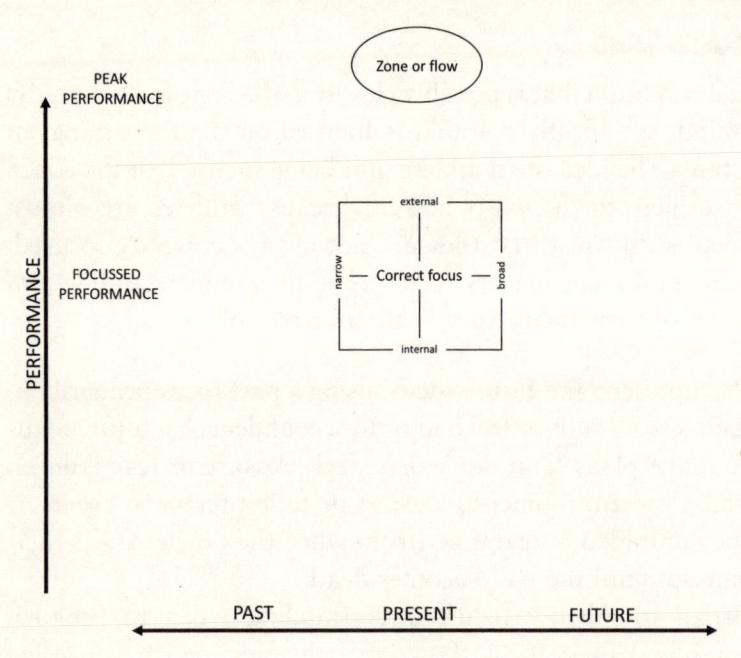

```
                    ┌─────────────┐
              PEAK  │Zone or flow │
       PERFORMANCE  └─────────────┘
                         
                           external
                        ┌──────────┐
       FOCUSSED      narrow  Correct focus  broad
    PERFORMANCE        └──────────┘
                           internal

PERFORMANCE

           PAST        PRESENT        FUTURE
```

As mentioned, players are almost always focused; it's just that in key moments, they're not necessarily focused on the right things, or in the right way. Short of being in the zone, having the right focus at the right time is a major key to winning the big moments. Unlike with the zone, which athletes have little control over, players do have control over being correctly focused.

A note here: There is a difference between focus and concentration. Focus refers to breadth and concentration to depth. Concentration refers to how deeply and detailed the mind is observing whatever the attention is on—regardless of whether on one thing (narrow focus), or a large number of things (broad focus). An athlete can focus on the coach and what they are saying, but this does not mean they are concentrating on what they are saying. If concentrating, they would be taking in what the coach is saying, the subtle body language and non-verbal communication, whilst processing what it all means for the athletes themselves.

THE DISTRACTED MIND—A MAP OF MENTAL ERRORS

When play is underway in sport, the mind is 'distracted' if it is not in the zone or correctly focused on the task at hand. In reality, the majority of us humans spend upwards of 90 per cent of our waking hours in a distracted state—not in the zone or state of flow, and also not fully present to what is happening in the moment. In mental game workshops I've run with over 500 professional cricket, rugby, hockey and soccer players, they report that between 80 and 95 per cent of all their errors are a direct result of errors in thinking (a distracted mind), which then play out as visible technical or tactical errors.

When a player is in the zone, or fully present and appropriately focused on the task at hand, errors seldom occur. Sure, a batsman might get out, or a bowler get dominated, but that is not an error. Rather, it's the opponent being better in that moment. This happens as a normal part of any game, and does not require any more attention than acceptance of what happened. Errors mostly occur when a player's mind is in a (temporarily) distracted state.

From over a decade of my work as a mental coach to some of the world's best athletes from a number of different sports, across cultures and countries, it emerged that almost every error players make can be placed on a fairly simple 'map of mental errors'. It also emerged that these errors were often predictable according to a player's natural personality style. Helping the Indian players find their unique errors was the first step towards managing their distracted minds. Awareness is the key.

On the following page is a map of mental errors that shows the four main areas (quadrants) of distraction, each populated with real world examples of athletes' most commonly reported mental errors.

At the key moment of performance, the distracted mind will either be focused on the past, stuck in a memory of something that has already happened, or focused on the future, grappling with or anticipating something that has not yet happened. And whether past or future, the distracted mind will either be thinking positively about

	PAST FOCUS	**FUTURE FOCUS**
Positive (success)	Over-confidence Arrogance Complacency Boredom	Premeditation Impatience/ over-eager Trying to be the hero Arrogance Go out of game plan Overly aggressive Poor shot selection
Negative (failure)	Doubt Lack of confidence Lack of self-belief Hesitant Insecurity Over-analysis Frustration Negative self-talk Blame Intimidated	Fear of failure Failure of reprimand Fear of injury Pressure Panic Choking Apprehension Tentative Indecision

Map of mental errors

things that went well in the past or about success in the future, or negatively, about things that went wrong in the past or might go wrong in the future.

Sentimental or past-oriented people will tend to make errors associated with their mind being stuck in the past, as they struggle to let go of things that have already happened. Future-oriented people will tend to have their mind running ahead, trying to manage the future. As a batsman, all my errors were future-oriented.

Pessimists will tend to get distracted by things that went wrong in the past or that might go wrong in the future. Sentimental pessimists will get overly caught up in memories of times when they failed, when an opponent got the better of them or when they got injured. This category of thoughts mostly leads to them losing confidence and becoming doubtful or hesitant. Such folks also tend to over-analyse problems.

Future-oriented pessimists will find themselves getting anxious about the prospects of losing, getting injured, being dropped or being embarrassed. These fear-based concerns are likely to make them apprehensive, tentative or risk-averse. Fear itself is one of the biggest mental obstacles to success in sport, and is almost always associated with the mind worrying about something going wrong in the future.

Optimists will tend to dwell on things that went well in the past or that they envisage going well in the future. Sentimental optimists will find themselves replaying scenes of the successes and victories of glory days gone by. Initially this builds confidence, but if replayed often enough, it tends towards over-confidence, arrogance or even boredom from a 'been-there-done-that' attitude. Future-oriented optimists will tend to dwell on fabricating success in the future, imagining themselves dominating their opponent and being the hero. In their rush to get to that success before it's actually time, they premeditate, get impatient or force things that they want but that the situation doesn't allow or warrant.

I was somewhere in the middle of this pessimist-optimist continuum as a cricketer, so my errors were either fear of the short ball against fast bowling, causing errors from being overly-tentative (future, negative), or premeditating and thus being overly-attacking against the medium pace bowlers and spinners in an attempt to chase victory and be the hero (future, positive). I have yet to work with an athlete who makes more than the two primary mental errors identified in the matrix on the following page.

One top-ranked international batsman I worked with during the Dambulla series got out in three very different ways in three consecutive innings: bowled when defending, run out, and caught in the deep. All these were a result of the same error—premeditation—trying to force a result he wanted, but that the situation did not warrant. (Note: This would have been impossible for any coach to know. Only the player [and his trusted mental coach] could have known that all three dismissals were caused by the same mental error.)

In the lead-up to the World Cup, I would run team workshops and do individual sessions with players to help identify their default errors (distractions), to recognise these early (around the time the bowler is about to begin his run-up), and have a pre-programmed

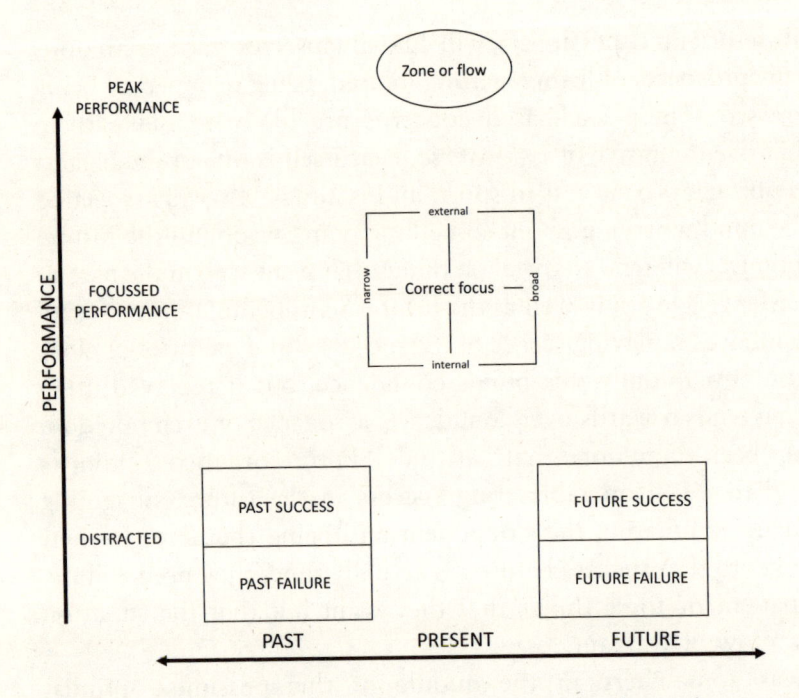

```
                    ┌─────────────┐
                    │ Zone or flow│
                    └─────────────┘
   PEAK
   PERFORMANCE
   ↑
   │                      external
   │                    ┌─────┬─────┐
   │ FOCUSSED        narrow─ Correct focus ─broad
   │ PERFORMANCE        └─────┴─────┘
   │                      internal
PERFORMANCE
   │
   │              ┌──────────┐    ┌──────────┐
   │              │PAST      │    │FUTURE    │
   │ DISTRACTED   │SUCCESS   │    │SUCCESS   │
   │              ├──────────┤    ├──────────┤
   │              │PAST      │    │FUTURE    │
   │              │FAILURE   │    │FAILURE   │
   │              └──────────┘    └──────────┘
   └──────────────────PAST──PRESENT──FUTURE──→
```

response that would force their attention back to the present and correctly to the task at hand. To be thus 'deliberately focused' is one small step away from being in the zone. As a player and when feeling tentative (fearful) facing up to fast bowlers, I'd imagine myself getting into 'strong positions', and say the word 'courage' to myself. Against slower bowlers, when I found myself wanting to over-attack, I'd focus on being 'patient' and 'playing each ball on its merit'.

WHAT'S IMPORTANT *NOW*?

One way to prompt the process of going from being distracted to deliberately focused is to ask the question, 'What's important *now*?' (which has the rather relevant acronym WIN). In most ball sports, what's important is to focus on the ball, now, in this moment. With some of the pro surfers I've coached, it's been three questions: What score do I need, where will I get a wave that will offer that score, and how will I ride it? Ex-Springbok rugby captain Jean de Villiers would implore his charges to 'Know your job. Do your job.'

Most athletes also develop a trigger that helps them focus correctly as play is about to begin. Sri Lankan bowler Lasith Malinga would kiss the ball, South African Morne Morkel would walk in a tight circle, most batsmen tap their bat or touch some part of their body, Gary Kirsten would say 'trust', Jacques Kallis would remind himself to 'watch the ball' and Virender Sehwag would hum his favourite song.

As a comical side note, I remember a specific incident when watching Virender Sehwag opening the batting in a ODI for India. We got off to a great start, and then all of a sudden, Virender was visibly out of sorts for 3 or 4 balls before losing his wicket. It appeared as if something was wrong or something had got to him. A little while after he had reached the pavilion, I went to him and said, 'Viru, something changed. What happened there?' Viru is an honest and very funny guy. He answered, and I quote verbatim, 'Shit! I always sing one of my favourite songs, but I spent 2 overs at the non-striker's end, and when the bowler turned to start his run-up to bowl at me, I had forgotten the words to my song.' (Okay, not quite verbatim; there were a few more expletives!) He was fighting so hard to remember the words of his song that it completely derailed him from refocusing himself in the present. That was his mental dilemma. And it is still a fond memory. Incidentally, singing in key moments of performance is more common amongst professional athletes than you'd believe. It is a powerful way of quieting the thinking mind and to access the instinctive mind. Try to sing and think at the same time; it's almost impossible.

BREATHE

Another way to direct attention back into the present moment is to intentionally focus on the breath, ideally breathing slower and deeper. Particularly when under pressure or stress, our breathing becomes faster and shallower, which also reduces the amount of oxygen available to the brain and working muscles. Focusing on the breath automatically directs our attention back into the present moment, which causes the stress or anxiety to immediately subside (stress and anxiety only arise from our thoughts being in the future). By intentionally making our breaths slower and deeper, it's possible to induce present-moment focus and up the oxygen levels. Once calm and more present, it's time to shift focus from our breathing (internal focus) back to the task at hand.

Slowly counting the breathing cycle can also help settle the nerves, especially when sitting and waiting to bat next. With eyes closed and breathing through the nose, inhale into chest, diaphragm and then stomach area for the count of four, hold for two, exhale from the stomach, diaphragm and then chest for six, hold for two, and repeat for a few cycles (4-2-6-2).

TRUST, BELIEF, CONFIDENCE

Having a genuine inner experience of trust, belief and/or confidence is a powerful gateway to the zone. Obviously. Which brings me back to one of our simple philosophies, Gary's and mine: the importance of studying the whole book for the exam. The more one studies for an exam, the more trust, belief and/or confidence one takes into that exam room. The more corners you cut, the likelier it is that you will walk in experiencing anxiety, pressure, lack of confidence and doubt. Again, this is obvious. However, it's also a simple fact that although most people who write exams really want to do well, the vast majority still neglect to study the whole book!

Sport is no different. Many people want to do well, to succeed at a level of say eight, to ten out of ten. They say they want this result, but their thoroughness of preparation sits nowhere near these same levels of excellence. The less a player prepares, the lesser are the chances of them being confident, and the more they are going to need mental coaching to get out of the state of anxiety they have got themselves into. (Regarding preparation, if 10/10 constitutes studying the whole book for whatever your 'exam' might be, how would you score your preparation for the important events in your life?)

We knew that the Indian players needed to be fully prepared for any match situation that might arise in the World cup. Gary and Eric would leave no stone unturned in preparing every aspect of the players' skill and game awareness. All I would need to do was instill confidence, remind players that they were ready, that they could trust and believe in their skill, their plans and themselves to deliver the goods, regardless of what Mother Cricket might throw at them.

PLAYING TO STRENGTHS

Another way to remain confident (and deliver success) is to play to one's strengths, as often as possible. This was another pillar of our coaching philosophy. As we plotted against each different opponent, we would give more weight and attention to playing our best game, rather than adapting our game to attack the opponents' weaknesses. Those times when our strength matched up against an opposition's strength, we would stick to our strengths, and accept that the best man or team would win the encounter. Playing to our strengths would ensure that players went into battle with confidence.

One person who really took 'playing to strengths' to heart was the uniquely aggressive Virender Sehwag. His attacking approach provided endless entertainment. There were times where, in the first over of a five-day Test match, he would hit the opening bowler for 6 over the cover area and off the front foot. It also had us scratching our heads on other occasions, such as when opponents placed fielders on the boundary to spinners, whom Sehwag loved attacking. He would try to hit the ball over the fielders' heads, and if he succeeded, he would sometimes try again, in the same over. If he got out, caught on the boundary, he'd simply say to Gary afterwards (with a smile), 'The shot was on.' When Sehwag was at the crease, I made sure to never miss a ball.

A + B = C

Playing a World Cup in India, as with most big events, would require us to manage a great deal of external 'noise' and distraction. An important part of this would be to understand what was in our control and we could act upon, and what was outside of our control and would require attitude management. We've probably all heard the adage 'control the controllables', so this is nothing new. The problem with old adages is that we stop paying heed to them.

When performance specialist Dr Jacques Dallaire, who did some work with the Sydney Thunder team before a Big Bash tournament, shared his take on this concept, I found it to be the most effective one I'd encountered to date. He presented it as a very simple yet powerful performance equation, which I've adapted slightly: A + B = C.

'A' is your A-game, the things that you are good at and that are inside of your control. 'B' are the things that are outside of your control and relates to your attitude towards these things; and the two together add up to 'C', your results.

We would double down on our strengths, and focus on the things that we had control over, specifically skill development, preparation, and smart decision-making. We knew the B-factors would be ever present, such as comments in the press or on social media, playing conditions, opponents' tactics and the expectations of family, friends and fans. I was amazed at how much pressure, often unknowingly, friends put on players, telling them they 'have to win' or 'you must score 100'. We needed to cultivate an awareness of and the right attitude towards these uncontrollables, and to support each other when any of these things did manage to get under someone's skin.

Results are also a B-factor as they are outside of anyone's control, so there is no point expending mental energy on worrying about them. Easier said than done, but already, we had reframed winning the World Cup to 'when we play the final in Mumbai'. And keep things simple: A + B = C.

PRESSURE

Pressure is the one of the biggest mental obstacles to success in sport, yet it is nothing more than a concept in our head; it's not real. Sure, the physiology of pressure is real and can be both felt and measured by increased breathing and heart rate, butterflies in the stomach, fidgeting, mental anguish and secretion of various stress hormones, but the origin of this physiology is nothing more than a concept, a perception. The pressure we feel increases proportionately to the importance we place on the result. If the result is not that important, there is little or no pressure. The more important it is to win (or not lose), the greater the perceived pressure. A World Cup final in Mumbai would represent the most important event in these players' careers, possibly even their lives, and that can only be described as the ultimate degree of pressure. Like with fear, pressure is associated with an event that is going to happen in the future; it is never about something that is happening now.

We decided to work on reducing pressure in the following ways:

- By decreasing the perceived value of the result in the mind of the players (and the coaches).
- By equipping players with the tools and awareness to bring their focus acutely into the present.

- By helping the players to detach their self-worth from the result, or differently put, helping them to have full confidence in who they are as rounded and grounded individuals, entirely separate from the result. Win or lose, they should know that they were and would be okay. This point relates back to the fourth goal Gary and I had for the team when we started out: To help the players become better people.

WANT VERSUS NEED, AND BELIEVING VERSUS KNOWING

There were two more aspects that resonated with a number of players and are worth mentioning here. One of these was differentiating between *wanting* to do well and *needing* to do well. We need air, water and food, and the threat of not having these needs met causes a state of genuine fear and desperation. Such a state is fine in the fight for survival, but not for athletic performance. The desperation and excessive pressure associated with 'needing' a result is likely to lead to panic or choking. Ideally, players should *want* to do well, but shouldn't *need* to.

The other distinction was *believing* versus *knowing*. Belief is a flimsy concept in the head, which can change with new or different information. There was a time when people believed the earth was flat, man could not fly, we could not reach the moon, and so on. When a coach says to the team, 'We've got to believe we can win', I suggest the underlying message that many players subliminally receive is, 'I think many of you, and maybe even I, believe we can't win, so I'm trying to convince us that we can'. Believers in all walks of life are always trying to convince non-believers. In contrast, when you have a genuine conviction that you can win, when you know, there is a much deeper confidence, and no need to try and convince yourself or others. When you know, you know. We wanted players to know we could win the World Cup, and had to figure out how to instill this knowing.

That's when we turned to the learnings from a story that ex-Springbok rugby flyhalf Joel Stransky once told Gary and I. The Springbok (South African) rugby team had qualified for the 1995 Rugby World Cup finals, and were waiting for the other semi-final to see if they would meet England or the New Zealand All-Blacks in the final. During that second semi-final, too nervous to watch the formidable All-Black team in action, Joel and his teammate and lock-forward Mark Andrews were playing pool in the hotel team room. There was only one other man in the room, coach Kitch Christie. He stood about a metre in front of the television watching the entire game, never turning around to interact with Joel or Mark. New Zealand ended up crushing England 45-29, largely thanks to the 6-foot, 5-inch, 120-kilogram man-mountain and winger Jona Lomu literally running over England players to score four tries.

As the final whistle blew, Joel said he found himself turning his attention to coach Christie. He saw Kitch nod his head and mutter quietly to himself, 'We can beat these guys', before turning the television off and casually strolling out of the room. Joel said it was in that moment he knew they could beat New Zealand and win the World Cup. The coach's conviction left Mark feeling the same, and the two of them took that knowing to many of their teammates. (Joel himself would go on to kick a drop-goal in extra time that would see South Africa win that 1995 Rugby World Cup final on home soil, against all odds). There is power in *knowing*.

A PERSONALISED PATHWAY TO THE ZONE

As a result of all this work, players got to design their own detailed map of how to access the zone. In sessions ranging from thirty to about ninety minutes, players took anything from two to six hours to gain real clarity about their unique pathway, beyond it being a concept in their head. Each time a player achieved success in a game or made an error due to a mental distraction (which happened often), unpacking it afterwards added more detail and colour to their unique map, which would eventually include:

- What happens for them when in the zone.
- What constituted a deliberate focus, which included what players would say to themselves, what they wanted to feel, what they needed to focus on, and what trigger movement, if any, they would use to be correctly focused.
- What their unique distractions were on the map of mental errors, what tended to cause these distractions, and what the

common results would be when they succumbed to them. They added to this after every game as the picture became clearer and clearer. Eventually, they would notice that the same mistakes kept repeating themselves, and that no new ones emerged.
- What type of preparation led to the zone, and what tended to obstruct it.
- What tools and tricks could be used to get back onto the right path of thinking, such as asking 'what's important now'; focusing on the breath; creating a trigger movement; saying a phrase like 'watch the ball' for batsmen and 'hit your area' for bowlers; and inducing (helping the body remember) the right feeling, the most common triggers being 'trust' and 'relax' for batsmen, and 'rhythm' or 'smooth' for bowlers. Deliberately standing proud and tall, forcing a smile and singing also worked.

From my perspective, a significant body of mental and emotional preparation was required to set the team and players up for success at the 2011 World Cup. There was little doubt that this Indian team had the skill and talent to win the tournament. But, as with any such event, it would probably be the team that made the smartest decisions in the key (pressure) moments, and was able to fully commit to those decisions that would win, not the most talented team. The 2011 tournament would be no different.

164 | THE BAREFOOT COACH

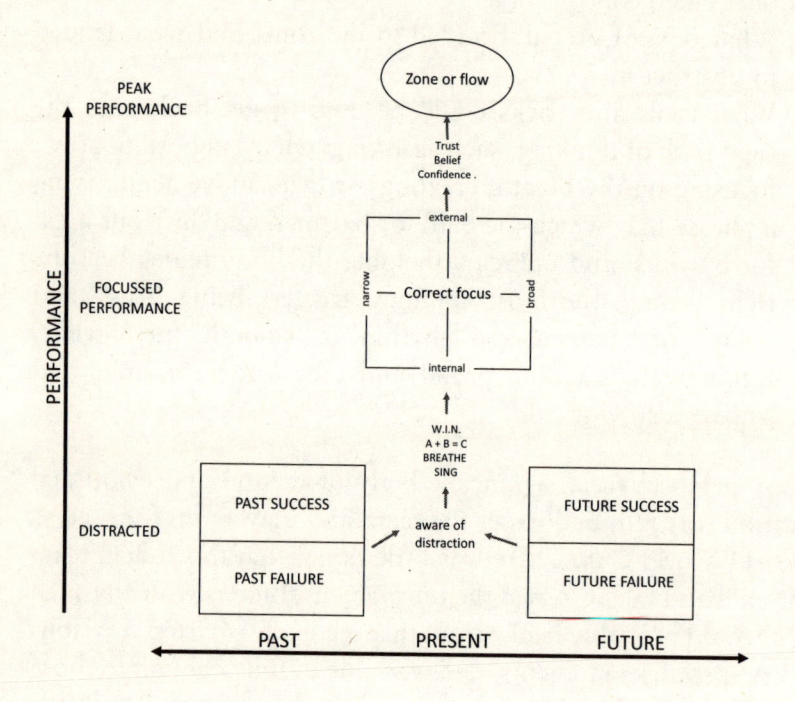

PERFORMANCE (y-axis)
- PEAK PERFORMANCE
- FOCUSSED PERFORMANCE
- DISTRACTED

Zone or flow
↑
Trust
Belief
Confidence

external
narrow — Correct focus — broad
internal

↑
W.I.N.
A + B = C
BREATHE
SING

↑
aware of distraction

| PAST SUCCESS | | FUTURE SUCCESS |
| PAST FAILURE | | FUTURE FAILURE |

PAST — PRESENT — FUTURE

14

THE MYTH OF MENTAL TOUGHNESS

At this juncture, it is worth having a conversation about the concept of 'mental toughness', which is currently the most overused and least understood concept in sports psychology.[1] I neither agree with, nor use the term.

When helping the Indian players to develop better mental resolve and manage their emotions in preparation for the World Cup, we were not attempting to create 'mentally tough' athletes. Because there is no such thing as mental toughness, and even if there was, the idea of striving to be mentally tough is flawed.

THERE'S NO SUCH THING

I contend that mental toughness is like Batman and Superman. We all know them. But they're not real and don't actually exist.

In a review of over thirty published academic papers on mental toughness involving forty-four world-class researchers, it emerged that there is no agreement on the definition of mental toughness.[2] Sport psychologists cannot agree on what mental toughness is. In trying to define this concept, they broke it down into subcomponents like grit, resilience, focus, emotional control, mental control, hardness and so on. Collectively, those thirty-plus papers present as many as seventy-five subcomponents that supposedly make up mental toughness!

Of all the instruments available to measure mental toughness, there are only two that have been validated: The Australian Football Mental Toughness Inventory (AFMTI) and Mental Toughness Q48

(MTQ48). These are the only two instruments that reliably measure what they are supposed to measure.

However, there is no agreement on whether these instruments are relevant for both men and women. There is disagreement about the relevance to different age levels, different experience levels, different levels of competitiveness and, importantly, there is no transfer between sporting codes. Thus, the Australian Football instrument does not necessarily apply to other sports.

Further, when 'mentally tough' players assess themselves, and coaches, who know them well, also assess them, the results are fundamentally different. There isn't even agreement over how players see themselves and how a coach sees those same players. There is also no agreement on whether mental toughness is to do with nurture (something we're taught), or nature (something we are born with).

What becomes patently clear from a review of these academic papers and literature on mental toughness is that sport psychologists, who are supposed to be the experts, cannot define and don't even understand the concept. And yet, as coaches and parents, we continue to use the term and judge players based on it. Players also use it to judge each other and commentators apply it liberally in their descriptions of players.

How then should we ordinary sportspeople interpret the findings and subcategories in those thirty-odd research papers on mental toughness? Let's have a closer look.

The following is what, and who, some of these researchers studied: 160 elite athletes, ten international performers, twelve mentally tough UK cricketers, eight Olympic champions, and thirty-one elite coaches. In other words, what the world's academics are trying to tell us is that they've studied the world's best.

PSYCHO-WHAT?

When we study the best of the best, consider the following as a list of definitions associated with mental toughness: massive belief in self and one's ability; emotional control; clear thinking under pressure; ruthless pursuit of goals; operating well in chaos; not intimidated by others; unaffected by loss and failure; easily spots weakness in opponents; inspirational, popular, influential; and compulsive liar.

I would bet that, until you got to the last point, you were in agreement that this was a pretty accurate list of mental toughness attributes.

However, the list I provided above is not a list of definitions of mental toughness—those are character traits of psychopaths taken from an article on psychopathy.

At this juncture, you'd be perfectly justified in asking why on earth I would include this list of psychopathic traits in a discussion on mental toughness.

What if I told you that the academics who studied mental toughness amongst elite athletes might unknowingly have unearthed their psychopathic traits and prescribed these as characteristics of mental toughness? Barring only one or two, the traits are the same.

Okay, so who are these people, and how many of them are out there?

Psychopaths are born with brain functioning that is different from 'normal' people, and this is not reversible. As luck would have it (for them), these brain differences manifest outwardly in that individual possessing many of those performance assets mentioned earlier—all of which are highly sought-after qualities for success (and leadership), and of so-called mental toughness. This is the reason for so many psychopaths achieving such high levels of success in business, as well as in politics and sport.

Prof. Clive Boddy from Middlesex University suggests that one out of every hundred people is born a psychopath.[3] He suggests that one in twenty managers in corporate America is a psychopath, called a 'corporate psychopath' because they thrive in business environments. In industries like the media, the legal fraternity, finance, banking and politics, Boddy suggests *one in five* top executives or CEOs are in fact psychopaths. Research has not yet been conducted on the prevalence of psychopaths in sport, but do the math.

If this is the first time you've encountered the concept of corporate psychopaths, you may be struggling to join the dots between serial killers and successful businessmen (and athletes). The only difference between a corporate psychopath and Hannibal Lecter (*Silence of the Lambs*) and co. who torture animals as children and end up as jailed serial killers as adults, is their propensity for violence. Illustrating this point, one study at the University of Surrey on thirty-nine high-level British executives compared their psychopathic traits to those of criminals and psychiatric patients.[4] They found that business executives were more likely to be superficially charming, egocentric, insincere and manipulative, and just as likely to be grandiose, exploitative, and lacking in empathy as criminals and psychiatric patients. The criminals only scored higher than these executives on being impulsive and physically aggressive.

If you're still not quite joining the dots, remember Lance Armstrong, the cancer survivor and seven-times Tour de France champion who put both cycling and the fight against cancer on the world map! A study of Armstrong the cyclist will reveal possibly all you need to know about what mental toughness looks like.

This is the same person that the United States Anti-Doping Agency (USADA) called 'the ringleader of the most sophisticated, professionalised and successful doping programme that sport has ever seen'. He cheated, lied and bullied his way to those seven titles, and when threatened with exposure, he covered his tracks, intimidated witnesses and lied to hearing panels and to the world. When the prosecution presented irrefutable evidence of his doping from twenty-six people, including eleven of his own teammates, he still vehemently denied having ever doped. The prosecution went on to suggest that some of the most shocking evidence had to do with Armstrong's vindictive, mendacious and vicious character. One report suggested, 'He comes across less like a cyclist, more like a psychopath.'

Without going too far down this rabbit hole, the following is worth noting: What sport psychologists, coaches, parents and players are prescribing as a model of mental toughness is equally likely to be the success-producing traits of highly successful and highly functional psychopaths. I have worked with a few psychopaths. I've seen the so-called attributes of mental toughness in them, which help deliver results on the field. I have seen how fans, friends and the media adore these people. But I have also seen what it looks like when their mental toughness is unmasked as psychopathic behaviour. They come across as being narcissistic and entirely self-serving, compulsive (and clever) liars, manipulators without any remorse and an inability to take responsibility for their errors. These are not qualities we should encourage as general conditions for performance.[5]

In short, psychologists themselves cannot agree about what mental toughness is. At best they have provided a list of seventy-five subcomponents to describe the concept. There's also a case to suggest that researchers have inadvertently identified the success-producing traits of a sports version of the 'corporate psychopaths', and are prescribing those as a model of mental toughness. Although only a recently detected (and initially confusing) phenomenon, there are already a few papers published and books written on corporate psychopathy, which we might hear more about in the time to come. One final note is that corporate psychopaths exhibit degrees of psychopathy, with some possessing a greater number of psychopathic traits than others, both positive and negative.

MENTAL TOUGHNESS AS A FAILED CONCEPT

The second reason Gary and I were not trying to create mentally tough players relates to the judgement directed at athletes based on this. It's sad that someone is either mentally tough, or not. And if they're not mentally tough, they're 'fragile', 'weak', 'soft', 'they crumble under pressure', 'they can't handle the heat', 'they're insecure', 'they're vulnerable' or 'they're doubting'. That's how we label athletes who make mistakes under pressure.

Here's the rub. Except for out-and-out psychopaths, all other athletes, professional and amateur, make mistakes, often under pressure, and all of these so-called mistakes are frequently labelled as 'weak' and 'soft'. Almost every one of us has doubts and insecurities. I have hardly ever worked with an athlete who is fully confident, secure and ever positive. Sure, I have worked with some who are good at hiding their doubts, but their vulnerabilities and insecurities still gnaw away at them from the inside. They try really hard to protect themselves from the public perception that these normal human fragilities are in fact unforgivable weaknesses. But they all have them. The 'mentally weak' labels we place on those who fall short of our unrealistic expectation of perfection are harsh, unfair and I'd say, uneducated.

I did some of my best *and* least effective mental conditioning work with Gautam Gambhir, the International Test Cricketer of the Year in 2009. I worked with him up until that time, but I had little to do with him being named the world's best cricketer.

Often, when I got onto the Indian team bus, Gautam would invite me to sit next to him. What followed was predictable: 'Paddy, man, I know I just scored 100, but I should have got 200. I mishit too many balls, I struggled in the beginning, I hit the fielder too many times ... It just wasn't good enough. I need to sort things out.' He would be in mental agony about losing his wicket and about needing to fix things.

He was so riddled with insecurities, doubts and vulnerabilities. He was one of the most negative people I have ever worked with. I tried everything I knew to at least try to get him to be a bit more positive, become more optimistic, and to at least get some perspective.

We must have had fifteen sessions on the bus in one year, but I just couldn't help Gautam shift. Until I came across some research that could potentially help me understand why. It was either that I lacked the skill or knowledge to help Gautam (which could have been the case), or there were some lessons to be learned from Martin Seligman's work on positive psychology.

Positive self-talk, being positive, is very important, especially when we want people to 'believe'. It's the 'Yes, we can' attitude that defined President Barack Obama's first presidential election campaign.

However, research suggests that most people sit somewhere on a continuum between being an optimist and being a pessimist, with 100 standing for über-optimistic and 0 for pessimistic. Gautam was definitely wired towards the 'lower' end of the optimism/pessimism scale; let's say his range was from 20 to 40, with 30 being his normal. When he scored 150, he would be disappointed at not scoring 200. And when he got the ICC Test Cricketer of the Year award, he shifted to about 40, but he very soon moved back to his set point at around 30. When he didn't score runs in 2 or 3 consecutive innings, he'd drop down to 20.

No matter what we did, Gautam was negative and pessimistic. In his remarkably honest interview after receiving the ICC award, he said, 'The award does nothing to help overcome my insecurity. I can't help it.' I'm not letting out any of Gautie's secrets here either; he has openly acknowledged his insecurities and doubting mindset.

Using the popular notion of mental toughness, he was one of the 'weakest and mentally most insecure' people I have ever worked with. But at the same time, he was undoubtedly one of the best and most determined, and successful, Test batsmen in the world. Something he would prove, yet again, in the 2011 World Cup final.

So, when we tell people to have positive self-talk—this pillar or subcomponent of mental toughness—it would probably work for about 50 per cent of them, those who are lucky enough to be wired on the optimistic side of the scale.

When a great athlete who also happens to be wired as an eternal optimist has an accident, breaks their body or worse, is paralysed, they might go from being 95 on the scale to about 75. That is their low end. But they're still very high on the 'positive' side of the scale. And as soon as they accept and then reconcile with their situation, they shift back to 90 or 95 on the scale. And those people are the ones who are generally admired for being mentally tough; the eternal optimists. They become the shining light we all have to aspire to, and they are often encouraged onto the public speaking circuit where they share their optimism in an attempt to help others become as positive as they are. Audiences are inspired and motivated, but only temporarily, before the vast majority return to their normal set point, often the very next day.

Trying to engage in positive self-talk for people who naturally have more negative thoughts can be frustrating, and because they often can't get it right, can cause them to further think negatively about themselves.

In Oliver Burkeman's book *The Antidote: Happiness for People Who Can't Stand Positive Thinking*, he suggests taking a radically different stance towards those things most of us spend our lives trying hard to avoid, like failure, negativity and death.[6] He makes a case for learning to enjoy uncertainty, embracing insecurity and becoming familiar with failure. We're often told to 'face your fear', to embrace it rather than run or hide from it. It turns out, we might also benefit from facing and experiencing negative emotions—or, at the very least, by not running quite so hard from them. Fear of failure is one of the world's most prominent negative thoughts. Failure will happen, so why not rather face and embrace it?

After all those sessions of trying to get Gautie to be more 'positive', which never worked, at least not for any length of time, I changed track and got him to try and accept exactly how he felt.

We made it okay to feel frustrated, negative and disappointed. Once these thoughts and feelings were acknowledged, we'd say, 'Okay. So, what do you need to do to get even better?'

Seligman contends that it is possible to learn to be more optimistic about a negative situation; he calls it 'learned optimism'.[7] Let's use the example of a batsman scoring three low scores in a row. An optimistic approach would be to attribute it to external circumstances. 'It was unlucky', rather than the pessimistic approach of turning the mirror inward and blaming yourself by saying, 'I'm not good enough'. Next is to see it as a setback in one small area of your life: 'It's just my batting, but so much else about my game and life is great', rather than an all-encompassing negative perspective of 'I'm a failure'. Finally, and not necessarily in this order, is to see that the failures are temporary. 'This will soon pass and I'll be back to scoring runs', rather than 'I don't know if I'll ever get out of this slump', which is the more permanent worldview of the pessimist.

Because of the way they view problems, pessimists suffer 'poor form' for longer than optimists. In fact, Seligman's work suggests pessimists are eight times more likely to become depressed when bad things happen, they do worse at school, in sport and at their jobs than their talent suggests, have poorer health, shorter lives and rockier relationships. This is a tough pill to swallow, considering that over 50 per cent of people are wired on the pessimist side of the continuum. The good news is that optimism can be learned, by attributing the problem to external factors, seeing it happening in only a small area of your life, and as being temporary.

It's also worth mentioning that a dose of pessimism is healthy, especially in situations where mistakes may have significant consequences. Where optimists will charge ahead with full (sometimes unfounded) confidence and without much considered thought, pessimists will think through everything that can go wrong, take necessary precautions and come up with contingency plans. Pessimism helps by preventing us from taking unnecessary risks or acting recklessly. Any athlete engaging in a dangerous sport needs to have a healthy dose of pessimism. Too much, and they'll never get out of the starting blocks; too little, and they may not reach the finish line. George Bernard Shaw famously said, 'Both optimists and pessimists contribute to society. The optimist invents the aeroplane, the pessimist the parachute.'

Because people are different, the concepts of being mentally tough, positive and optimistic, or of being in control of one's emotions, at least outwardly, are unrealistic for everyone. M.S. Dhoni, as an example, has incredible emotional control. He *never* shows emotion, and he is lauded for that. Just as with being openly optimistic as opposed to being pessimistic, 'having emotional control' is sometimes seen as evidence of a player's mental toughness. But I would go as far as to say, with the greatest respect for MS the man and the cricketer, that it is not emotional control, but lack of access to emotions. MS is not wired as an emotional type. It's almost as if he doesn't have them; a performance-enhancing gift from birth. Imagine taking that trait as the ultimate characteristic of a 'mentally tough' athlete, and then try to prescribe that to someone who is very emotionally wired, like his successor Virat Kohli. Virat uses his visible and overt emotional charge to drive his success, whereas MS's success is facilitated by his lack of emotional charge.

The emotional and mental side of the game does not have generic prescriptions for performance. 'Mental toughness' is perhaps not even a generic drug. It's closer to being a placebo prescribed by coaches, psychologists and academics who don't really appreciate the art, beauty and complexity of working with athletes as individual human beings first, and as high performers second. When the placebo doesn't work, the athlete gets blamed.

Judging athletes who are not 'mentally tough', optimistic and positive, inhibits us from effectively dealing with the legitimate mental side of the game—specifically when instruction-based coaching is the preferred method.

I honestly believe that we should do away with the concept of mental toughness and replace it with something that is more real and relevant to most people. It has to be authentic to the individual and something he or she can relate to. The overwhelming majority of players lack confidence, have insecurities, doubts and vulnerabilities. So do most of us. We're human and this is normal. Let's keep it *real*.

With this in mind, our strategy with the Indian team was not to convince the players of how special and tough they were. The media and fans tried to convince them of that 24/7. Our job was to convince the players that they were actually human, and thus to keep things real. Enclosed in that acknowledgement were relief, understanding of the self, and the tremendous power that flowered in conditions that could otherwise easily see self-proclaimed superstars choke up.

15

INTUITIVE LEADERSHIP

In sport and business, the mantra that is becoming increasingly popular is: 'If you can't measure it, you can't manage it.' This is in part because technology is able to provide the support to facilitate a great deal of measurement.

In certain instances, this approach does have value. For example, with pension funds, you would rather have an algorithm manage them than some random human's greed, fears and whatever other biases might inform his or her judgements and investment decisions. There are just too many variables impacting the value of your portfolio, and in this day and age, there are too many concrete 'big data' sets available to guide investment decisions, to not make use of mathematics as an alternative to human judgement.

In the West, we've been brought up in a world of cause-and-effect. It's quite scientific. In order for something to exist, you need to be able to measure it. And to change anything, you need a measure that proves the new way is better than the old way. It's a very concrete, linear way of operating.

People are, however, not like pension funds, and the measure-to-manage mantra should not be the overarching principle guiding the management of human beings. In the case of coaching, measure-to-manage is a way to optimise one's efficiencies within the realm of the science of coaching. When it comes to the art of coaching—those more abstract human elements such as thoughts, feelings, attitudes and team spirit—we need to hone our ability to lead from our gut or intuition. This means going beyond the stats and trends that are revealed through the scientific approach.

'Knowing' comes from two different parts of our brain. Our thinking brain (neocortex or left brain) which is responsible for analytical, cause-and-effect thinking is more recently evolved, in contrast to our prehistoric brain (limbic or right brain) that is the home of creative thought, art, music, senses and emotions, as well as intuition or instinct. What has been proven is that the instinctive brain is far quicker and 'knows' answers well before the thinking brain does, and sometimes it 'knows better'. Sometimes, the thinking brain cannot actually explain what the instinctive brain knows—like in the example of tennis coach Vic Braden, who knew when a tennis player would double-fault but had no idea how he knew.

Cape Town has the largest population of great white sharks in the world, and no shark nets. Most people who surf there, myself included, spend a lot of time in the water thinking about sharks, but we stay in the water and carry on surfing. Yet, it's happened more times than I can recall that someone *feels* 'something is not right'. You feel spooked, leave the water, and moments later, a great white is spotted. Ancient man relied on this kind of 'knowing', and modern man still has this capability, more than we might realise.

In the East, there is far more acceptance of the intangible, the unseen, and the cyclical nature of life. Someone from the western world could easily dismiss or disregard that as an esoteric, touchy-feely way of thinking. You see western coaches and players do this in the IPL from time to time. But it can be a big error to dismiss someone's intuitions or beliefs and the energy they create.

Intuitive leadership became a cornerstone of mine and Gary's working relationship in India. It wasn't a concept or philosophy we arrived with, but it gradually developed as we worked with the Indian team. The two of us literally spent several hours a day talking about what we needed to do and learn about leadership, life and cricket in our new working environment.

For us, intuitive leadership wasn't an airy-fairy, go-where-the-wind-blows style of management. We planned our team meetings and practice sessions meticulously. We always planned, but once we went into the meeting, we'd sometimes change direction or even let our ideas, plans and strategies go if they didn't feel right.

There were times when we had planned for Gary to hand over a conversation or discussion to me, but as the meeting unfolded, I'd get a sense that it wouldn't be appropriate. Gary would just look over to me, I'd shake my head, and he'd go on. Gary, too, knew.

At other times, Gary might start talking about something that moved into a space where, whether planned or not, I felt moved to add something to what he was saying, and he'd just hand over to me. He would sense it, and he would merely glance at me, and I would continue the conversation as if there was a comma between his sentence and mine.

It was often seamless because we understood each other, and the space in which we both operated, so well. Part of being able to trust our gut or instinct was being clear on what our intentions were, and the philosophies we truly believed in. For example, we were happy to change course as long as it was done to serve the players' and the team's best interests, in that moment. And if that was the intention, then it did not matter much if we had made the right gut-decision or not, as long as it was done for the right reason. The reality is, decisions made from this place were, and are, hardly ever wrong.

With intuitive leadership, you do all the planning but when the rubber hits the road, you allow the feel or the energy in the room to guide where the conversation should go. There were times when we cancelled a meeting or even a training session, because it just didn't feel right to go ahead with it. Intuition or gut-feel informed our interactions with players at times, whether to engage them or not, what to say or not to say, guided by what felt right for the player, in that moment. The right word at the right time could lift a player and make a tangible contribution to their game; the wrong word or the wrong timing could have the opposite effect. Sometimes it's only through intuition that we can 'know'.

Everyone has intuition or gut-feelings. Remember that person you hadn't seen for ages, whom you thought about, and then they called you or bumped into you later that day? Or the time you sensed danger, maybe slowed down your car or changed a course of action, and avoided some potential disaster? Athletes in the zone often know what's going to happen before it does, and they act accordingly. But we do not all listen to our gut or intuition. Has it happened that you knew to say something, or to keep quiet, but you didn't listen, and then afterwards thought, 'I knew I should have said something, or kept quiet?'

I recall a Big Bash League game which was a must-win for Sydney Thunder, when I was moved to give advice to a senior international player who I 'knew' was distracted. As I moved towards him, my thinking brain stopped me with, 'He's an experienced player, he doesn't need your advice, especially when he's about to walk out to bat.' He went out and made the exact mistake I 'knew' that he was going to make. And when he came out, he sat next to me and told me, using literally the same words I had thought, what he should have done. I still kick myself for not having followed my intuition in that key moment, which makes me partly responsible for the player losing his wicket, and potentially for the team losing.

Interestingly, this is one of those coaching errors that, if I kept quiet about it, nobody would ever recognise. It has also happened on a few occasions that Rahul Dravid and I sat next to each other on the sidelines during an IPL game, when the captain made an instinctive field placing or bowling change that was not part of the plan, which had us respond by saying to each other, 'What's he thinking? That's not a smart move.' And on more than a few occasions, the decision paid off and worked. Each time, Rahul and I chuckled, and with a smile said, 'Let's keep that one to ourselves.'

In the example of not speaking to the 'distracted' batsman above, my intuition was felt somewhere in my body and I overruled it in my head. I found that it was also not always possible to hear and heed the wisdom of the (subconscious) intuitive brain, and to really absorb the subtleties in the case of each of the players and gauge the feeling within the team culture.

It might sound silly or trivial, but a few things really impacted my ability to engage with Gary, the players and my work: I couldn't be hung over (two beers were enough to leave their influence the following morning), because that experience in my body would interfere with *feeling*. The same would happen with the caffeine buzz from two cappuccinos in the space of one meeting. Poor diet, lack of sleep, lack of physical activity and stress are other key actors that create 'noise' in the body, that can leave us un-centred and on edge, and can interfere with the body's natural ability to respond to those subtle yet important messages from the external world. The better my physical and mental state, the more in-tune and effective I became.

I'm certainly not a bastion of health and discipline, but I do place a high value on the energy levels and mental clarity that come from being fit and healthy, and sometimes wonder how leaders and coaches with poor physical conditioning manage with the subtle underlying 'noise' from a constant physical and energetic imbalance in their body and mind.

A wise therapist who helps me maintain mind-body balance suggests that 98 per cent of the population walk around with this noise or imbalance and are oblivious to it. They think it's normal to feel like that. Our health is possibly our single greatest asset, yet we spend so much time, money and energy maintaining other assets in our lives. Only when our health falters significantly do we realise its value, and the degree to which we take it for granted. Look after your body like you want it to look after you. As you would know by now, I'm fairly allergic to issuing instructions, but at this point I'd like to offer a strong suggestion. Review your lifestyle choices and find at least one way to make a positive change today.

Back to intuition. In the case of excitement or danger, research shows that intuition causes the sweat glands to open up before the event happens, and well before the mind realises or conceptualises it. Thus, we instinctively know before our minds can explain. It's also important to distinguish the feeling of intuition from the mental chatter in the thinking brain, like when it stopped me from talking to that batsman, or to know the difference between thinking about sharks while in the water versus feeling something is genuinely not right.

It may not be for everyone, but doing regular breathwork, meditation and yoga helped me tune in and practise listening to those subtle and quiet voices of wisdom that sit inside all of us. Once considered too touchy-feely or airy-fairy, more and more athletes and business folk are engaging in these activities because of the tangible benefits they're experiencing. For the linear cause-and-effect thinkers, these pursuits have also been validated through scientific measurement of their benefits. There are a plethora of mindfulness practices that also work in this regard, with apps like *Calm, Headspace, Insight Timer* and others providing simple and very effective tools to tap into our inner knowing that is often drowned out by the 'noise' in our head, the stress and the busyness of daily living.

YUVRAJ AND OUR MAN HUG

In the months leading up to the World Cup, Yuvraj Singh was going through a difficult time. Gary asked me to have a conversation with him after a disruptive incident, because I had a good relationship with him.

I remember when I tuned in for that conversation with Yuvi, I found myself wanting to point out to him where he was wrong, wanting him to see that his behaviour was undermining what the team was trying to achieve. The energy behind this approach was of me being the controlling authority, and Yuvi being the apologetic wrongdoer who needed to change his behaviour. But I couldn't. It was the natural thing to do, but I knew it would be ineffective and counterproductive. I'd be serving my needs, not his.

I sat in my hotel room and went into a contemplative space. What I eventually touched on and then focused on growing, in my heart of hearts, was a real experience of care and compassion for Yuvi. I wanted to support and help him in any way I could, so he could be the best version of himself.

He couldn't have chosen to simply behave the way he did; it wasn't a manifestation of his higher self, or of his true nature. There must have been something going on for him. Through his behaviour, he was reaching out for and seeking something. I had no tangible evidence to prove this was the case, but I knew intuitively that this was the case.

With the energy of caring and compassion having dissolved any need for reprimand, I went to his room with the intention of enquiry, to see how I could help. I had no real plan for what I was going to say or how the conversation was going to unfold. It ended up being a very deep and personal sharing, which Yuvraj was able to enter into.

He later mentioned that he really felt the caring and concern. When I left his room, we gave each other a warm and sincere man hug. We had got to touch on some truths that underline and drive behaviour, yet we never spoke about the incident itself. Touching a deeper foundational place in his being created some shifts in attitude, which would (and did) drive a shift in behaviour.

This happened at around the time Yuvraj was dropped from the Indian Test squad due to a drop in form. In the time that he was away, his goal was to come back and win the World Cup. He personally called 2010 'the worst year of his career', but he did do the necessary work to bounce back and eventually win Player of the Tournament at the World Cup. He did his work and it paid off.

Immediately after the World Cup, Yuvraj was diagnosed with cancer. We had not been aware of his health issues during the tournament. That, too, was a battle he would go on to win.

For me, there is something Shakespearean about Yuvraj's life story over those few months—being dropped, coming back, doing really well, hitting the winning runs against Australia in the quarter-final, being named Player of the Tournament, being diagnosed with cancer, and then overcoming that tremendous obstacle as well.

I cannot help but wonder how different Yuvraj's inspiring story may have been if the Indian team had had a culture where we only managed what we could measure or see, and where intuition was considered to be a relic from yesteryears with no application in a postmodern world.

16

FAILURE: PART ONE

OUT OF THE DUMPS

By the end of 2010, the Indian One Day side was on fire. After convincingly beating New Zealand 3-0 in the third of a five-match home series, we went onto the field to shake hands with the opposition.

Prior to that tour, the New Zealand One Day team had lost 4-0 in a five-match tour to Bangladesh, one of the weaker teams in international cricket at the time. After seven consecutive defeats, which would soon become nine, it was clear that we would be meeting a dejected group of Kiwis as they left the field.

As I shook hands with each player, I observed their energy, body language, and the look in their eyes. Some were not able to make eye contact. They had the energy of 'defeated men' about them, none more so than Kyle Mills, the team's main fast bowler.

His disappointment was so evident that it spilled over to me and I felt it as a pain in the pit of my stomach. I could not help but feel sad for him. He had always been friendly when we met and spoke in the past; he came across as a really good guy. It wasn't pleasant seeing him in such a difficult mental state.

Most of us, at some stage in our lives, get to experience something close to this level of disappointment. It may happen in our professional lives, when we've tried hard to achieve something that is really important to us, only to be confronted with failure. It may happen when we are not hired for a job we really wanted and expected, or have been retrenched from such a job, or when someone else gets the promotion or assignment we desperately wanted and had worked for. Or losing an important deal or contract that we were heavily invested in. It may happen in a romantic relationship or in a marriage, where we feel complete despair through repeatedly failing to resolve conflicts and disagreements. Or it may have to do with our finances, when we just cannot see a way past what seems like insurmountable financial difficulties.

At times like this, the mind has a natural tendency to narrow its focus onto the problem, scrutinising the situation in minute detail. The more we dwell on it, the more closely we see the problem, and the larger it looms. This view of failure can become so all-encompassing that it eventually spills over into all areas of our lives. We take the work problem home, or the marital problem to work. It impacts our social life so that we either don't go out, or we go out and repeatedly indulge in activities or substances that temporarily hide the pain, disappointment or hurt.

The problem clouds our vision such that it blocks any possibility of a solution shining through. Like with Kyle that day, it permeates our physical as well as emotional body and causes us to experience feelings of despair, hopelessness, helplessness, and, eventually, even depression.

Most of us start out by fighting for a solution, and when that doesn't happen, we may find ourselves fighting for survival. When the fight does not deliver the survival or salvation we are seeking, it is replaced by the desire to want to run, to get out, and to get away from it all. In the financial world, this gives rise to thoughts of liquidation, declaring bankruptcy or, in the worst case scenario, to thoughts of suicide. In relationships, it gives rise to thoughts of separation, infidelity or divorce. In our professional lives, soon after furious thoughts of strangling the boss, we begin to consider giving up on trying, or maybe even resigning from the job or retiring from the sport. It's no use, I've had enough, I can't go on…

Actually, this 'letting go' is the beginning of the solution. We stop looking at the problem, we avert our eyes, and for the first time, we are able to see beyond the problem. However, resigning or giving up is not the solution. It is letting go of the focus on the problem that begins to clear space for the solution to emerge. That is the first step.

Albert Einstein famously said, 'We can't solve problems by using the same kind of thinking we used when we created them.'

Later that evening, I met one of the support staff of the New Zealand team in the hotel foyer. I asked how they were doing. 'Bad,' he said. 'So much so, that some of them are even talking about retiring from the game.'

This was hardly surprising. In most professional environments, we would have been very happy to have our opposition in such a low-confidence place, particularly with two games still to play. Professionally, I felt that way, but personally, I could not bring myself to feel so ruthlessly competitive. I'd come to really like some of the New Zealand players. I mentioned to the support staff member that I would really like to have a chat with Kyle, maybe if I saw him in the corridor of the hotel or at the airport, which is usually where we tend to bump into opposition players.

I had hardly finished speaking when Kyle walked down the stairs and straight past me. I took this as a clear indication that the universe was lining things up as I had imagined. Well, at least I decided to believe that this was the case, because it gave me permission to cross professional boundaries and have a conversation with a member of the opposition team, as one human being to another.

I opened with the usual insincere question that people often ask one another: 'How are you doing?' The truth is, of course, that we only ask this question for the sake of sounding friendly or courteous, and are not really interested in the answer. Since everyone else also knows this they, too, oblige with 'Fine, thanks', and then reciprocate the friendly lack of interest with a courteous 'And you?'

Observing Kyle's energy and body language, I think answering my question with 'Fine, thanks' would have been a little too ambitious. He said that he certainly had had better days.

GAINING PERSPECTIVE—IT'S NOT ALL BAD

Once the problem in one area of our life has become so all-encompassing that it's all that the mind can see and it feels like our whole life is under its cloud, it's time to step back and gain perspective.

Not in any way to diminish the nature of the problem, but to see it as only part of our life, and to note that the other parts are actually pretty good, or certainly not as bad.

There are many ways to gain perspective, but it cannot happen without first acknowledging the loss of perspective. What are the areas of your life that are directly affected by the problem, and which areas are not? Bring attention to, and focus on, the areas that are working, such as health, family, finances, opportunities, friendships or relationships that are outside of, or not affected by, the problem. For Kyle, it was his health, his family, friendships, talent, the opportunities he had … the list was long.

Gaining perspective also requires seeing the failure or problem as a temporary setback. 'We have just lost our seventh consecutive cricket match this month, but so much about this New Zealand team is still really good, and so are so many areas of my life', rather than an all-consuming negative perspective of 'We're total failures' or 'I hate this game'.

It happened a long time ago, but I am often reminded of the time when I was fitness trainer of the South African team and Jonty Rhodes was on the brink of being dropped from the Test team. He needed to get runs to stay in the team, and on this particular day, the team also needed him to score to help us stay in the game. Neither was to be, as he was given out lbw for a very low score when the ball was clearly missing the wickets. After the day's play, I noticed Jonty sitting in a corner, very subdued and clearly upset. I had never seen him like this; he was the team's perpetual Energizer bunny. As I sat watching him and wondering what I should do, I noticed him cock his head to the side a little, pause in this strange position for a few moments, and then his entire energy changed. He bounced off his chair and immediately went around the change room picking players up and injecting energy into the team, saying, 'Guys, we're still in this, we can still do it.' Jonty was back.

I asked him about it a little later, and he told me that he was sitting directly under the television set, with the sound turned right down as usual (players do not want to hear commentators), when the news came on. He craned his head to listen to a report on the Bosnian war, and then realised that he couldn't bring himself to sulk about being given out lbw when he had just heard how 8,000 Bosnian men and boys had been killed in one of the largest massacres since the World War II holocaust.

On more than a few occasions, I've shown a cricket team one of the YouTube videos on Team Hoyt, about a father who literally carries his son, who is stricken with cerebral palsy, to complete Ironman triathlete competitions around the world. Father Dick pulls his son Rick in a special boat as he does the 3.8-kilometre ocean swim, carries him on a seat fixed to the front of his bicycle for a 180-kilometre cycle ride and finishes the race by pushing him in a wheelchair during the final 42.2-kilometre run. By 2016, they had competed in 1,130 endurance events, including seven Ironmans and seventy-two marathons, and run 6,011 kilometres across the US in forty-five days. Team Hoyt gives a perspective on dedication and commitment that goes well beyond what is ever asked of a cricketer, or of most coaches, athletes, teachers, and even business leaders for that matter.

THE REALITY OF FAILURE

Let us for a moment take a step back from the conversation with Kyle, to consider failure in sport from a really high-level drone view.

Using 50 runs as a measure of success for top-order international batsmen in 50-over cricket, let's think about how some of the world's top batsmen fare. At the time of writing, world number one Virat Kohli (India) had failed in 61 per cent of all his ODI innings, number one England batsman Joe Root in 63 per cent, South African A.B. de Villiers in 64 per cent, and the top Australian David Warner in 70 per cent. And these are the world's best.

Let's also use points won on first and second serve in tennis to illustrate failure. Breaking an opponent's serve is what wins tennis matches, and saving your own serve is therefore crucial. Having a strong first serve could therefore be considered the most important arrow in one's quiver. At the time of writing, however, world number one Roger Federer is ranked a lowish 18th in the world for career first serve points won on all surfaces (77 per cent). Ivo Karlovic is first. Yeah, me neither ...[1]

Missing one's first serve means additional pressure; there's no third time lucky in tennis. While Roger Federer may be ranked 18th

Meeting our country's president, Nelson Mandela, at Newlands. This time I would not forget to ask the one question I had, to please sign my photograph from the previous time he visited the team.

The photograph Nelson Mandela nearly ruined (see Postscript). You can see above Mandela's head, the scratches from his initial attempt to sign with the pen's dry nib. (He had just come from a local music carnival and he was therefore dressed in a carnival outfit.)

(All the photos here are from Paddy Upton's collection, unless indicated otherwise.)

The Proteas ODI team at Newlands, in 1996. The only support staff back then was Bob Woolmer (coach), Goolam Rajah (manager), Craig Smith (Physio) and me (fitness trainer).

Me doing boxing training with Darryl Cullinan during a tour of India in 1996. Improvising with a batting pad as a punching bag.

Pounding the pavements, putting Herschelle Gibbs, Gazza and Jonty Rhodes through their paces.

During my time as fitness trainer with the Proteas. Meeting the Queen of England prior to a Test match at Headingley, in 1996.

Nearly sixteen years after meeting the Queen, I'm back in England, here with the Proteas support staff on the famous Lord's cricket ground balcony, posing with the newly won World Test Mace (September 2012).

Gary and I arriving in India for the start of our tenure. Me, armed with my surfboard, having heard that there were waves in India, which proved to be the case.

Creating a 'happy team' environment was one of the four goals Gary and I set for the team, and this is evidence of it really happening!

Celebrating winning the 2008 Border-Gavaskar Trophy, having beaten Australia in Kolkata.

The Test team with the 2008 Border-Gavaskar Trophy.

Celebrating a historical day in Test cricket history, in Mohali on October 17, 2008. Earlier that day, Sachin Tendulkar went past Brian Lara's record of 11,953 runs in test cricket to become the player with most runs in the format.

A hillbilly from Rondebosch (Gazza) and me, a barefoot surfer from Houtbay (both suburbs of Cape Town) receiving a traditional Indian welcome.

Sehwag, Sachin and Gambhir at the movie-making day for the Test team, just outside Bangalore.

The Indian support staff formed its own movie-making production company at the movie-making team building exercise. Gazza, Nitin Patel (physio), C.K.M. Dhananjay (analyst), Russell Radhakrishnan (manager), Robin Singh (fielding coach), Ramesh Mane (masseur), and me as 'film director'.

The moment Gazza and I had set as a goal whilst on an aeroplane in March 2008, and which we doubled down on achieving since that breakfast meeting in Dambulla on 24 June 2010, becomes reality! On 2 April 2011, India are crowned ICC World Cup champions for the first time since Kapil Dev's team achieved the same feat in 1983.

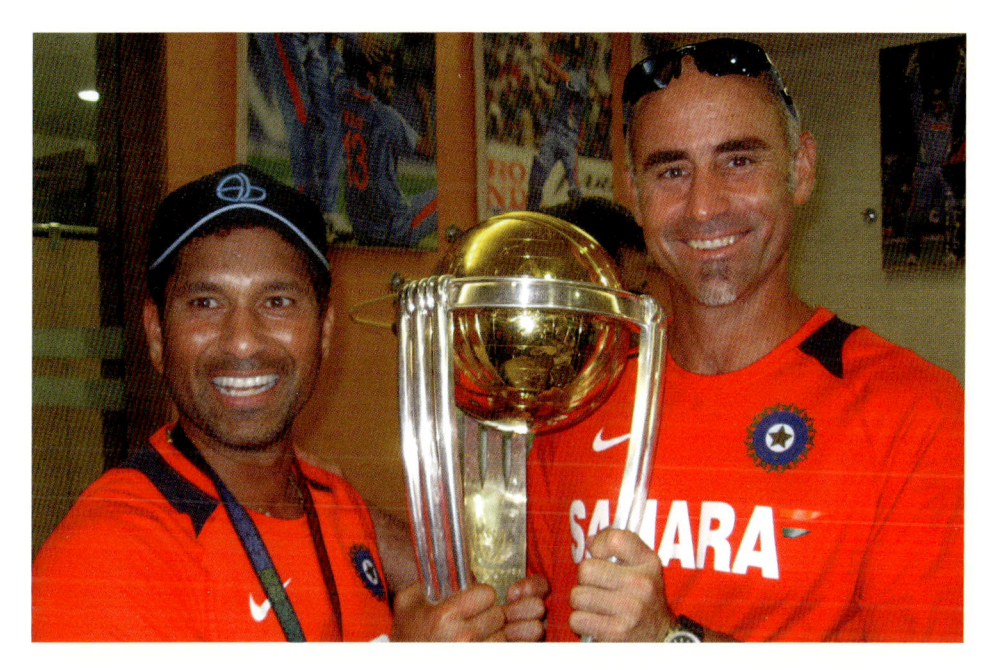

In the Wankhede Stadium (Mumbai) dressing room on 2 April 2011. Sachin and I with the ICC World Cup which we had won that evening.

Eric Simons (bowling coach), me, Gazza and Mike Horn. Four South-Africans and four good friends in the dressing room after winning the World Cup in 2011. This would be our last time in the Indian cricket team dressing room ... and what a way to bow out!

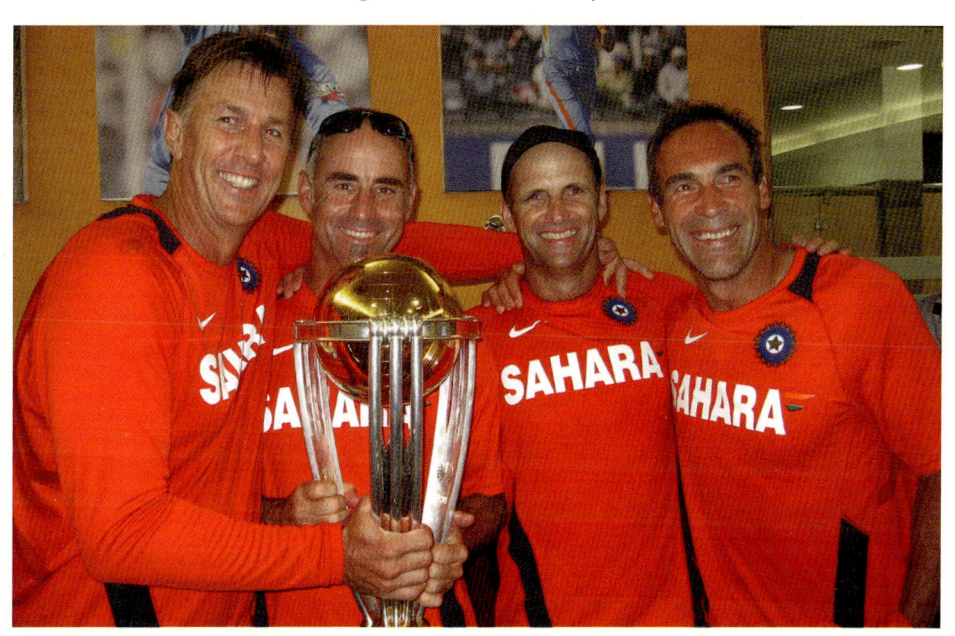

The Proteas in the Lord's dressing room, after securing the world's number one Test ranking by beating England in a Test series, on their own home soil.

Proteas team photo at a Newlands Test match in 2012. Note the eleven support staff members, compared to only four support staff the 1996 photo, also taken at Newlands. Four members feature in both – Gazza, Allan Donald, Jacques Kallis and myself.

The Proteas Test team in Switzerland. Posing under a billboard showing the peak we would climb the very next day.

The Proteas, summiting the first peak of the tour. The next would be to summit the world Test ranking against England, in the UK. Both were successful.

For five consecutive IPL seasons, (three at Rajasthan Royals and two at Delhi Daredevils), I was lucky enough to work as head coach, alongside Zubin Bharucha (team director - who has an amazing cricket brain), and Rahul Dravid (right), in his role as captain in the first two years, and then team mentor for the next three.

As coach of Sydney Thunder. Working alongside Mike Hussey (Mr. Cricket) was a true privilege, both on and off the field.

Sydney Thunder, Big Bash League champions in 2016.

In the dressing room with Sydney Thunder at the MCG in Melbourne, after beating the Melbourne Stars in front of their home crowd, to win the 2016 Big Bash League trophy.

During the 2008 tour of New Zealand, I would take the team fishing on three occasions, twice 'heli-fishing', where we flew in a helicopter some thirty miles out to sea to fish off small remote islands, and this time, off a fishing boat. Here is Rahul Dravid and M.S. Dhoni with the first fish of the day, a small shark. (The shark was immediately released back into the water.)

Between the second and third of those gruelling Test matches in Australia, 2012, a few of us spent four days living on a boat off Port Douglas, fishing for Giant Trevally. Physio Brandon Jackson and I after a double hook-up.

During the 2012 tour to the UK in pursuit of the world number one Test ranking. This is me during the second test. I had a long-standing arrangement to go surfing in the Mentawai islands (off Sumatra) with ten mates. Going on that trip was part of my contract negotiation with Cricket SA. (Nobody ever lies on their death bed wishing they spent more time at the office.)

The first of my two marriages, both to Nicki. This was outside Bangalore in 2006, and the second marriage a few weeks later, at home in Cape Town, in a traditional South African wedding.

My family in Auroville, outside Pondicherry, at the end of a three-week tour around India, where we committed to travel only on third-class buses and trains. This was to give the kids a sense of India outside of five-star hotels. (It remains one of their most fondly remembered holidays.)

in the world for career first serve points won, at the time of writing, he was ranked number one for career second serve points won on all surfaces. It is a fact that points from the second serve are much harder to win, but Roger Federer doesn't allow facts to dictate his story.[2]

For the Rafael Nadal fans reading this, the Spaniard's rankings were 99th (first serve points won) and 2nd (second serve points won). Arguably, the two best players ever to grace the game with their godly presence both 'fail' compared to other pro players when it comes to points won on first serve. They are unmatched when it comes to winning back the advantage with their second serve.

Let's go from tennis's greatest modern rivalry to football's: Lionel Messi and Cristiano Ronaldo. I'm not going to debate which one of these two mercurial players is the greatest ever. But let's assume it is one of them. Between 2008 and 2017, the Ballon d'Or, Europe's greatest individual football prize, had been awarded to only two players: Cristiano Ronaldo (2008, 2013, 2014, 2016, 2017) and Lionel Messi (2009, 2010, 2011, 2012, 2015). Both are strikers, and given their reputation and skill, one would expect them to fulfill their primary function of scoring goals almost faultlessly. Except, they fail quite often.

In an article comparing Messi, Ronaldo and Luis Suarez's 2016 Spanish La Liga performances, this is how the first two players measured up against each other:

RONALDO:
- 27 goals in 28 games
- 178 shots at goal (45.5 per cent on target; 15.2 per cent scored)

MESSI:
- 21 goals in 21 games
- 105 shots at goal (53.3 per cent on target; 20.0 per cent scored)[3]

In effect, we can say that 54.5 per cent of Ronaldo's shots at goal were off target and 84.8 per cent of his strikes were unsuccessful. Messi's radar was out 46.7 per cent of the time, and 80 per cent of his attempts at goal failed. For what it's worth, Suarez had better accuracy and success at goal than both of them (55.7 per cent on target and 24.5 per cent goals scored).

In 2008, when Tiger Woods was still the world's undisputed number one golfer, he only hit 59 per cent of his fairways off the tee. He was ranked a scanty 157th on the PGA tour in that category. He missed his assumed target four times out of every ten attempts. At the same time, Woods was one of the greatest risk-takers and putters in the game. 'Failing' in one area didn't make him a lesser player. As his then caddy, Steve Williams, explained in an interview with New Zealand's *The Dominion Post*: 'When Woods doesn't three-putt over a 72-hole stretch, he will win the tournament 90 per cent of the time—and that's a goal they strive for.'[4] Warts and all.

The list of examples is very long. To mention just one more, at the time of writing, Kobe Bryant has missed more shots than any professional basketballer in history: 14,481. I guess this makes him the game's greatest ever failure?

The rather obvious reality of failure is that it will come to all athletes—it is as inevitable as death. If you play, you will fail, and if you are born, you will die. Yet athletes fear failure, coaches get upset, parents are disappointed, fans find fault and commentators dissect every move in great detail. At the outset of every new season, I give the athletes I am working with a guarantee that they will make mistakes and will fail, imploring them to not worry about what is bound to happen. We then focus all our energies on setting up for success.

IT'S JUST A GAME

Back to Kyle and me, in that hotel in Baroda. I explained to Kyle that in a really tough situation, it is useful to remember that cricket is just a game, and for that matter, so is life. There is no shred of evidence anywhere to suggest that life is meant to be serious, or that we are meant to take ourselves seriously. I wasn't suggesting that one should give up trying just because it is a game. And I certainly do not advocate sitting in the grandstand watching others play. It's just that disappointment and failure are part of the game. They are not problems in themselves, or reasons for giving up on life. On the contrary, failure is a reason to feel alive in the midst of the game of life, even though it feels downright shit.

I regularly point players to a pearl of wisdom from Benjamin Zander, musical director of the Boston Philharmonic Orchestra and a wonderfully transformational leader. In times of stress, he reminds people of his rule number six, which states, 'Don't take yourself so f...ing seriously.' He goes on to add that 'rules one to five all state, refer to rule number six'. It's a good rule.

THIS TOO SHALL PASS

I asked Kyle, 'What, in six months' or a year's time, when you look back on this moment, will you say about it? Take yourself one year ahead of today, and tell me what you would say about this experience?'

I noticed a confused look on Kyle's face as he tried to extract himself from the moment and project into the future. After a few moments, he said the problem would probably be something in the past. He also, somewhat awkwardly, explained that he felt it might not be as bad an experience as he thought now, and that maybe there would be some valuable learning and life experience that came from it.

When the mind sees a problem as permanent or something that will be around for a lot longer than it needs to be, with thoughts like 'this will never work' or 'I'll never get it right', it can lead to unnecessary loss of confidence, esteem, and even to depression. When you're in a pickle, it's useful to remember the Persian adage about the temporary nature of the human condition, expressed in wisdom literature throughout history and across cultures: 'This too shall pass.'

A + B = C

The next thing to do was to assess what parts of the problem Kyle could take responsibility for resolving, and what parts were outside of his control, that he needed to let go of. Remember the performance equation A + B = C? Moving on from failure would require Kyle to understand that he could actually do something about his A-factors, which included planning and practising his best balls, according to his strengths, knowing what fields to set, and to execute that plan as best as possible. He also needed to know what to let go of: the B-factors, the things outside his control, such as how the pitch would play, what the batsman would do, the umpires' decisions, how fans and critics would react, and the results. Much of our stress comes from worrying about the things we have no control over, and this leaves us feeling further out of control or like victims of circumstances. It's important to separate what we can take responsibility for, and what to let go of (and have the right attitude towards). Remembering that our attitude is in our control and thus is an all-important A-factor.

By this stage in our conversation, Kyle had gained some perspective. He could see that this losing streak was only one part in the context of his otherwise good life and that it would soon be a distant memory. He had some clarity around the areas where he could take action and what he needed to let go of. The aim was to leave Kyle feeling more optimistic, energised and empowered to pursue solutions, rather than wallow in the problem and in a state of self-pity. As I had already overstepped the usual professional boundaries with this interaction, we left it at that. From my point of view, Kyle may have been an opponent in the game of cricket, but he was still a compatriot in the game of life.

17

FAILURE: PART TWO

LESSONS FROM KARACHI

Nearly two years prior to this comprehensive beating of New Zealand, Gary Kirsten and I were presented with one of the many opportunities to do our own 'dealing with failure' exercise, courtesy of India's disappointing loss in the 2008 Asia Cup in Karachi.

I recall driving back in the Indian team bus after that game, amidst a rather subdued bunch of players, thinking about how much is written about how to win, comparatively little on 'how to behave once you have won', and virtually nothing on 'how to behave when you lose'. My only reference for this dated back to when my brother beat me in garden cricket. I cried, and my dad told me, 'Be a good loser.' I was still young enough that my mom had to wipe the snot from my nose as I carried on snivelling, but not old enough to understand what my dad meant.

We got back to the hotel at 1 a.m. Gary had a 4 a.m. flight back to South Africa, so he came to my room to see if he could keep me awake until his departure time. And we got to process the loss.

We had both invested almost every one of our waking hours and efforts over the past weeks to setting up a winning environment—made easier by being pretty much hotel-bound in Karachi due to tight security measures. There were no sightseeing or outdoor ventures to distract us. No waves to ride or ocean to fish in.

We had also made sure that despite the air of disappointment in the dressing room immediately afterwards, we remained consistent in our team processes. In this case, it included music being played, consistent behaviour and energy from coaching staff regardless of results, and a team huddle and chat (we didn't normally chat after a game, but this was the last of the tour, and players would be leaving for their homes later that night). It's so easy to bond as a team when you win, but bonding needs to happen in times of loss, too. All sports teams know that winning papers over cracks in strategy and/or culture, and losing exposes them.

There are many inappropriate ways in which individuals or teams manage losses: disintegration, with each person doing their own thing; blaming something or someone outside the team; fixing blame within the team; denial; sulking; taking the result personally, with the accompanying loss of self-esteem; drowning sorrows in a heap of empty beer cans, etc. Fortunately, we managed to avoid all of these.

We started the conversation in that team huddle by asking all players to share one word or sentence about how they felt. The rationale behind this was that emotions are temporary and in order to move on from them, they need expression and acknowledgement. When suppressed too long, they can manifest in physical or mental illness, or 'explode' like the proverbial pressure cooker blowing its lid, with the ensuing damage to relationships or reputations. As each person gave voice to their feelings, I acknowledged them by repeating the words to the group, with 'disappointed', 'gutted' and 'frustrated' being most commonly expressed.

We had all wanted to win with every cell of our bodies, and it hurt that we hadn't. Gary always says, 'It's good that it hurts, it shows that you care.' But it was also important to avoid getting stuck in the loss and attaching oneself to it. A small but important point here is that different people process disappointment and loss differently. Same as handling pressure. For example, extroverts tend to talk more when they are nervous, introverts tend to talk less, jokers joke more and serious people get more serious.

In one T20 team I coached, there was one player who was very funny and engaging, the kind of person who brings good camaraderie to a change room regardless of results. He went fairly quiet and almost disengaged from the team for a period of a few games, at a time when we were struggling and wanted his enthusiasm. When I asked if anything was bothering him, he reluctantly told me that after one particular loss a few games back, he was being his usual jovial self when one of the club's senior administrators happened to walk into the change room. The man scowled at him, telling him that it was not appropriate to behave like that after a loss, and questioned his commitment by asking whether he actually cared. That one throwaway comment poured cold water on his enthusiasm and led to him suppressing his natural and authentic way of being. (I immediately invited his full personality back into the room—which brought him relief, but it still took some time for him to bounce back.)

REVIEW: WHEN YOU LOSE, DON'T LOSE THE LESSON

At the team meeting, we reflected on the loss and the tour as a whole, and expressed our gratitude to the players and the management, specifically for their commitment and efforts in preparation and training. While seeking lessons and areas for improvement, there were two places we looked: at what had worked (success), and what could work better next time (errors or failure).

One of the best ways to learn, grow confidence and build team culture is to focus on what worked, and to do this by asking team members to point out what others had done well. Particularly after a loss, or in fact after any game, this is a great place to begin the review process. When coaches and players give feedback on what worked, it's best to focus on effort and intensity rather than results. This constitutes a process focus, on the things we can control, rather than a result focus, on that which we cannot. Gary's favourite adage is: If you give everything of yourself in your preparation and in the heat of battle, then that is all we can ask. Giving your best and losing is better than cutting corners and winning—we know that giving your best will make winning happen far more often. And don't be misled by the saying, 'Winning is a habit'; it's not. Winning is a result; one that follows the habit of planning smarter and working harder than the other guys.

When it comes to learning from errors or failure, the departure point is to acknowledge the errors and accept without judgement that something did not work as planned. 'We lost 3 wickets in the first 6 overs. We know this is not an ideal start, but it happened.' Next, rather than unpack the error, explore what the solution would be for the next time that same situation arises, answering the question, 'Next time, what would you do differently?'.

Whilst we advocated addressing errors by focusing on solutions for the future, there are times where there is power in players acknowledging and owning their errors, specifically owning their errors in the thinking that might have preceded a technical or tactical error.

This owning of errors cannot be not done in the form of a demure or pessimistic self-flagellation, but rather as a courageous and empowering act of taking responsibility. It takes courage on the part of players, and maturity on the part of the team leadership to hold space for this honesty, and to not judge, criticise or hold it against players. I have not met many teams that get this right, and those that do, have been quite incredible to work with. It starts with the leaders and senior players having the courage to model this when they make a mistake. If leaders don't own up to their mistakes, there's almost zero chance that other team members will.

By this stage, most players in the Indian team had learned to use the word 'I' in owning errors: 'I could have prepared better', 'I made a mistake', 'I could have given more', and so on. It's much easier to say 'you' or 'we' when losing, like 'We need to train harder', 'We need to take responsibility', 'We need to be more honest with ourselves', etc. This absolves each person of the responsibility of having to actually do that, compared to taking responsibility and using the word 'I', as in 'I need to train harder' or 'I need to be more honest with myself'. This is one of the places where there is, and needs to be, an 'I' in team. My own personal mantra is, 'If you f... up, front up, then fix up.'

Finally, the one learning that many people neglect is what the opponents did well. Our competitive ego does not like to acknowledge that someone else was good, especially if we have just been beaten by them. Nonetheless, this remains a rich source of learning for those open to mining the opportunity it offers.

PLAN TO IMPROVE

Having extracted some of the lessons from the past, it's good to let the past go and look to the future, asking, where do we go from here? What does each individual and the team need to do to be even better prepared for the next game? There were some good ideas that emerged in that short team huddle after the game in Karachi, but we did not spend much time on the discussion as players and staff were still caught up in the emotion of the loss.

It might be worth reiterating the importance of having athletes actively contribute their ideas in the planning phase, and to state plans and solutions in terms of what you want to do, avoiding stating what you don't want to do.

GROW (SHOW) CHARACTER

It's in the tough times, when we are under pressure or stress, when the world has dished up lemons, that our character is truly defined. How we pass these tests is often how we will be remembered in life. As Gary says, the pressure of Test match cricket reveals more about the character of a player than about their skill.

So often, in the world of sport and business, it happens that a person gets defined by others, or defines themselves based on some measure of their success—runs scored, wickets taken, deals clinched, shares held or the size of their bank balance. This view of success, however, is only an alluring trap.

Simply put, for the performer, it is a trap that defines you exclusively by what you do or what you have, as opposed to who you were being as a person while you were doing that which brought success or led to failure. Who you are and what you do (and the results of this doing) are different. We can cheat to win, as much as we can remain principled in loss.

Who are you when your title is not 'cricketer', 'coach', 'CEO', 'manager', or 'sir/ma'am', and when you are simply in the process of being someone's son or daughter, father, brother, friend or a fellow human? Who are you when you encounter a complete stranger, maybe the person who is serving your food in a restaurant, checking your groceries at the supermarket, or opening a door for you in the hotel? Who are you being through success or failure, or when no one is watching? When standing alone in your room, in your underwear and in front of the mirror, who looks back at you?

In the world of international sport, both measures count—what you have achieved, and who you are as a person. A good question might be, 'How do you want to be remembered when you retire from your current career? What would you want people to say about you, such as your teammates/colleagues, your competitors, your family, your friends, and anyone who is important to you or who might look up to you as a role model? What legacy do you want to leave behind?' Once that is answered, ask yourself, if you retired today, how would you be remembered in relation to your ideal legacy? (If you followed this thought-exercise with some intent, consider asking yourself, 'What can I do in the next few days or weeks to move closer to the person I ideally want to be remembered as? How can I move even closer to living my ideal legacy, now?')

As Gary's 4 a.m. departure loomed closer, he and I referred back to this very exercise which we had done when starting out with the Indian team and which revealed some key things that we still needed to focus on. Although we started working on these in March 2008, defining how we would like to be remembered as coaches remained part of our armoury right up to the day India won the World Cup on 2 April 2011.

I think now that what my dad meant when he told me to be a good loser was to not change as a person based on winning or losing. Regardless of results, I should remain the same good person I was born to be.

THE SEVEN HABITS OF HIGHLY EFFECTIVE LOSERS

A summary of these two chapters on failure could well be read as 'The seven habits of highly effective losers'. A suggested pathway to optimally navigating the losses and failures that pave the journey through all of sport, relationships and life, includes:

- Gaining perspective: See the loss or failure as happening in only a limited area within the context of your whole life. You might also want to see it in the context of people who are far worse off than yourself. Remember, too, that it's just a game, and if even that doesn't work, apply rule number six.
- Expecting and accepting failure: It happens, and is an integral part of learning, and of life.
- Knowing that this too shall pass: Realise the temporary nature of the problem.

- Controlling the controllables: Take action when you are able to, and when things are outside of your control, cultivate the appropriate attitude towards these uncontrollables.
- Reviewing to learn: Acknowledge and express emotions. When they've subsided, it's time to take lessons from what worked, what didn't work, and possibly from what others might have got more right than yourself. Then let go of the past.
- Planning to improve: Focus on the next opportunity, planning how to be even better next time—ideally engaging players in this exercise.
- Growing character: Win or lose, be the same (good) person. Your results do not determine your value as a person, your words and actions (in winning and losing) do.

A TASTE OF THINGS TO COME

At that time, I wasn't to know that these lessons in losing would be put to the test in my future role as head coach of various T20 teams. As happens in the game of T20 cricket, I would be presented the chance to benefit from some heroic wins and some gut-wrenching losses—not just in games, but in entire tournaments.

18

RIDING THE WAVES OF FEAR

For over a decade, I have coached others—specifically business leaders and professional athletes—to manage their naturally occurring fear while continuing to execute with excellence. This was an important aspect of India's mental preparation for the World Cup, and about two years into our stint with the Indian team, I was pushed to walk my talk.

As a passionate surfer, I am aware that, regardless of ability, two feelings that nearly every surfer experiences are *stoke* and *fear*. Fear is much the same in every aspect of life. Stoke is surfer-talk for that elusive peak experience of being fully in the zone, or in flow, or experiencing temporary enlightenment. It's what every athlete seeks.

Like many professional athletes, surfers, too, will admit to having experienced the latter, but not the former. Surfers aside, every one of us has and probably will still metaphorically paddle out in conditions that stretch us beyond our level of competence or comfort. Maybe it's about paddling into the unknown, into dangerous or challenging conditions, submerged rocks, sharks, difficult entry or exit points, or simply, metaphorical waves that are bigger or gnarlier than we have previously experienced. We all know that feeling of fear or nervousness.

Between cricket tours and on a short visit back to my home in Cape Town, I woke up to a very early morning WhatsApp message from a mate: 'Platboom (translated from Afrikaans as "Flat Tree" which is a remote surfbreak in the Cape Point nature reserve) will be firing and being mid-week, we might have it to ourselves.'

We arrived just after first light and after an hour's drive, to find challenging conditions, including water temperature of about 11 degrees Celsius, a thick seaweed forest to paddle through, and waves more than twice my standing height breaking powerfully across a shallow rock slab. This same place had claimed a surfer's life a few months earlier. I stood in the empty parking lot, staring out to sea, shitting myself.

I was doing what I loved, in an unfamiliar but stunning environment, with excellent waves ... and I was scared. My fear kicked in at the sight of the double-overhead waves breaking on the shallow rock slab, and kept gnawing away as I pulled on my wetsuit, booties and hood to protect myself from the cold. It intensified when we crossed from dry land into the water, and I'm not sure if my heart rate rose because of the paddle, the cold water or the nerves. My heart felt like it was in my throat as I sat above that rock slab waiting for my wave, knowing that if I started in the wrong position or messed up on the take-off, I would suffer.

As the first set of waves approached and pitched as it hit the slab below me, my heart rate rocketed. I was in the right position, I even picked my wave, but then I chickened out and let it go by. I watched and listened to it crash down, leaving tumultuous water in its wake. I imagined myself, the air knocked out of my lungs in the fall, being held underwater in a kelp forest with my board that could hit me at any time, and not too far off, a rock that had already claimed one life.

As I was justifying not taking off to myself, my mate Grant asked, 'Where's your commitment?'

As India's mental conditioning coach, I got to work with players who experienced anxiety when waiting to go into bat, which intensified when they crossed the boundary and peaked as the bowler ran in to bowl. They learned to feel the fear, treat it as a friend and take it with them into battle. With their heart rates rocketing in the high 180s, they still needed to get into strong positions, have good footwork and a clear mind despite the fast bowler looming over them—threatening to get them out, humiliate them or hurt them. I had had similar conversations with business people in the lead up to a big deal, a crucial presentation or a change of careers.

Admittedly, the difference is that the business person could only have their pride or wallet hurt; the batsman (and me in this case) also faced potential physical harm.

I admitted to Grant that I was scared. Good start. It's normal and okay to be scared. I was able to accept fear as my friend. A few years earlier, I would have tried to pretend that I was not scared. Thinking it was a problem, or worried that my mates would call me 'soft', I would have tried to hide it or make it go away.

THE WAVERING EDGE OF RISK

We all have our *edge of fear*. It does not matter so much what we fear or where our edge is, but rather, where we operate in relation to it. To deliver upon our fullest potential in life requires us to bring all of who we are to whatever it is we're doing. And one of the deciding factors for how much of ourselves we bring to any situation is *fear*. We truly live, learn and feel the stoke in life when we operate at, or just beyond, our edge of fear.

Most people operate short of their edge, living in the 'comfort zone' of low risk. They will be safe and their lives pretty okay, maybe quietly despairing, but they will never deliver on their potential or feel fully alive. You won't get injured, embarrassed or fail if you don't try—spectators don't fail.

I would not fail or get hurt if I let the waves pass under me. But life for those in the risk-free 'avoidance zone' is stagnant, idle and filled with procrastination.

In his profound spiritual guide, *The Way of the Superior Man*, David Deida suggests that males avoid living fully by over-indulging in television/the Internet, alcohol and ejaculation, and females in excessive shopping, eating and socialising.[1] One can add social media, smartphones and recreational gaming to this list of activities.

Then there are others who operate well beyond their edge of fear, in the 'over-stressed zone'. These people take on stress unnecessarily and render themselves unable to appreciate the moment, the process or even their lives. Always pushing to be more and better, they tend to be over-competitive and can become easily frustrated when things don't go the way they want. These are the surfers and other extreme athletes who constantly push themselves, which also makes them prone to accidents and death. Their equivalents in the business world are workaholics, exercise-aholics and serial risk-takers/gamblers.

Many of the cricketers who operate in this zone do so due to their insecurities and doubts, or a perceived lack of something that leads them into over-strive, seeking to become victorious even over their own sense of lack. They never succeed because the lack remains, so they push even harder, only to still feel the lack.

Maybe it's a bit harsh, but I sometimes call this the 'bullshit zone'. Filled with bravado or aggressive masculinity, such a person's fragile ego—even if outwardly confident—not only prevents them from acknowledging fear, but also holds them back from living fully, performing fully and having authentic relationships. I speak of this zone from personal experience.

GARY KIRSTEN AND FEAR

Despite the received wisdom that 'acknowledging fear helps you manage it, while denying fear helps it manage you', it remains commonplace to hide it in most performance environments, particularly amongst male sport jocks.

For the better part of his career, Gary Kirsten battled his fears. After eleven years of international cricket, he made them public when he said:

> For so much of my career, I was over-critical and extremely judgmental of myself. I was not satisfied with who I was or what I had to offer. I lacked confidence in being the 'authentic' Gary Kirsten, so I was constantly striving to prove myself. I wanted to play better shots, to look more comfortable against the short ball, to look better technically. My career was a constant battle against the odds and against my limitations.
>
> Make no mistake, my self-doubt gave me the determination to succeed and continue to prove myself to people. However, when I stopped trying to prove myself, and faced and dealt with my fear and insecurities, I not only had the most successful season of my career, but I was able to surrender my constant struggle. In fact, most areas of my life worked so much better.

Acknowledging and working with vulnerability and fear is a greater leadership and performance strength than the old model of avoiding or denying this human condition. Respect to Gary and to the way he incorporated this personal experience into his armoury as a cricket coach.

You may want to define your edge of fear and where you are operating in relation to it. According to novelist Tom Robbins, 'It is from the wavering edge of risk that the sweetest honey of freedom drips.'

PLATBOOM. FEAR. CHECK!

Fear acknowledged, I went into my body to feel how it felt inside. My breathing was shallow and faster than usual. I felt my heartbeat in my chest and heard it in my ears. Most of all, I felt those familiar butterflies in my stomach. I checked where else in my body fear may be manifesting. Clenched teeth, a screwed up forehead, tensed up shoulders, twitching muscles, bowels that needed emptying, fidgeting, yawning and so on.

One often yawns in the lead-up to a big moment, whether you're a surfer waiting for your next heat in a competition, or a batsman waiting to bat next. It's not due to the lack of sleep the night before a big event. It's simply because anxiety makes your breathing shallow, which in turn leaves you oxygen-deprived. The body intelligence then kicks in to bring on a yawn, which is nothing more than your body forcing you to take a deep breath. Don't judge the yawn. Be assured that even if you didn't get enough sleep, the adrenalin during competition or whatever that important moment might be, will totally override the lack of rest.

The above-mentioned body check-in process is guaranteed to reduce anxiety or fear, often significantly. The reason being that fear is a direct result of thinking about something that may go wrong *in the future*. You are here *now*, and your mind is in the future—the gap in time is where fear or anxiety arises. The process of focusing on what is happening in the body draws the attention from the future and directs it into the present. The fear or anxiety subsides. *You cannot simultaneously be fully present and feel fear.*

Not yet possessing the mind control of an enlightened yogi, I continued to feel anxious. I gave myself a quick reminder then, that fear is a friend because it triggers adrenaline, which would sharpen my reaction time, unlock the maximum strength available to my muscles, sharpen my eyesight, and in case of an accident, it would help my blood clot quicker and also increase my pain threshold—essentially placing all survival instincts on red alert. Shark attack victims speak of clear thinking and the absence of pain. Shun Jujimoto helped Japan to an Olympic gold by competing on the rings with a broken kneecap (which then dislocated when he landed). Graeme Smith couldn't brush his teeth or tie his shoelaces due to the pain of a broken hand, but still went to bat in an attempt to save a Test match against Australia. Adrenaline can be a marvel 'drug' when called upon.

Elite batsmen often find that someone bowling at 120 kilometres per hour in the nets appears faster than one who is bowling at 140 kilometres per hour in a game in front of 40,000 people. Adrenalin speeding up the body and focusing the mind also has the effect of slowing down, whatever happens 'out there'. Once at the optimal level of anxiety and adrenaline, surfing whatever your 'big wave' might be, everything happens in slow motion—leaving you hyper-aware of every nuance of the environment, your position and your movements.

When this happens, the stoke is maximised. In cricket, think of Virat Kohli and A.B. de Villiers entering that zone of near immortality when batting, or a champion boxer who ducks and weaves his opponent's punches like he knows where they're coming from before the punch is even thrown. This is where genius manifests.

However, too much fear or pressure can have the opposite effect, paralysing the mind, overly narrowing the focus of attention, and tightening the body. Take the batsman who struggles to nail the shots in a match although he readily pulls them off in practice, the bowler who holds the ball too tightly and can't release it with optimal accuracy or speed, and the golfer who rushes his swing. When a surfer attempts a big wave, too much fear may cause them to chicken out, not make the drop, or if they do, everything happens so fast, with reduced control and awareness, they can only hope that things work out all right.

Two common forms of mental meltdown under pressure are panic and choking, which might look the same, but are different. Panic comes from lack of thinking, and generally happens to someone when they encounter a new (and stressful) situation they have seldom or never encountered before. They literally don't know what to do and so their thinking shuts down.

Choking comes from over-thinking. It happens to people who are experienced, and who go too much into their own heads and thus out of the zone, often with their thoughts focused on the future and not in the present moment. Choking and being stuck in the thinking brain block access to instinct, which is where the actual 'knowing' resides.

DON'T SAY DON'T

When Gary and I were coaching the Proteas, A.B. de Villiers was hit on the head by a bouncer whilst batting in the nets. Being hit on the head was a rare occurrence for him. He said that before the net session, he had been *worried* about getting hit, admitting that he felt he would get stuck on the back foot and would not move well. It is not surprising that what he was worried about, and thus subconsciously preparing for, actually happened. The error in technique was clearly visible, yet it had nothing to do with his technique.

Whatever memory you choose to bring to the front of your mind immediately before you get into a situation, it prepares you for the best possible chance of that outcome happening.

If a surfer fears wiping out, like I was, the image of wiping out is automatically brought to your conscious and subconscious mind, preparing for that very eventuality. In the moment of take-off, where thinking is absent and instinct takes over, you will have readied your body with muscle memories of how to wipe out. The same happens to a golfer who thinks, 'Don't hit the ball in the water'; a tennis player who thinks, 'Don't double fault'; a batsman who thinks, 'Don't flash at the wide one'; or a bowler who thinks 'Don't bowl short'. It even happens when your partner says to you, 'Don't forget to get milk on the way home.' We all know what happens next. It's the same as if I tell you now, 'Don't think of a dancing monkey. Especially not one wearing red polka dot underpants.' Pause here for ten seconds, and try and not think of that dancing monkey, especially not in those polka dot underpants.

The mind does not hear 'don't'. It only conjures up the image of hitting the golf ball in the water, the second serve into the net, flashing at the wide one, dragging the ball short, forgetting the milk, and of that dancing monkey in his funny undies.

So, when strategising, focus on what you *do* need to do, eliciting the mind-body memory of a successful execution, which at least sets up a better chance of it happening. Like hitting that golf ball into the middle of the fairway, the tennis serve into top left, leaving the wide ball or pitching just back of a length if you're that bowler. Think of anything that would be really cool to think about in that moment, and the monkey has less chance of featuring.

FEAR ACKNOWLEDGED. WHAT NOW?

Back at Platboom, I admitted to being fearful, embraced fear as my friend, checked where I felt it in my body, and also checked my ego to confirm that I really wanted to be doing this, for me. Now it was time to check my strategy.

Remember the equation A + B = C? I needed to check what my A-factor was, the things that I had control over: My position in the line-up, paddling in strongly, knowing what sort of take-off this particular wave required, and visualising a successful take-off. I also had a strategy for 'failure', which was to take a full breath, hold it, relax and roll with the punches.

The B-factor that I did not have control over was what the wave would do. If I wiped out, I knew I would be at the mercy of the water. My strategy was to cover my head with my arms to prevent potential contact between my skull and my board or the shallow rock. I reminded myself that my board would surface before me, due to its buoyancy, so my leash would guide me as to where 'up' was. (Anyone who has wiped out on a decent-size wave, especially in cold dark water and a seaweed forest, will know it's not possible to identify which way is up and which way is down, so there's no point in trying to swim for the surface.)

Fear (and pressure) often causes the mind to become distracted by the impending object of that fear, whether it is losing or being injured. A good way to regain focus is by answering the question, 'What's important *now*?'

FEAR AND GOD

Once you have done everything within your control to prepare yourself for a successful execution, it's time to stop thinking and let your instincts take over. Or more accurately, brain activity needs to shift from the planning and slow-to-process-things 'thinking' brain (pre-frontal cortex) to the much faster processing instinctive (limbic) brain, where all the hours and hours of instinctive or automated muscle memory is stored from practice and visualisation. At least, that's the theory. For now, know that truly trusting your preparation, planning and skill is a key part in allowing your thinking brain to hand control over to your instinctive brain. That's why as a batsman, Gary Kirsten told himself to 'believe', so as to trigger the deep-seated belief in his skill, preparation and game plan.

When it comes to techniques to let go of thinking about the outcome (the future), religious and spiritual people may have an advantage. If this is you, then it's likely you will consider your talent to be a God-given gift, and you will know that once you've done everything in your power to set up for success, it's time to hand the responsibility for the result back to God, or whoever your chosen higher power might be. Truly letting go of any attachment to the result and surrendering the outcome will help free your mind from the anxiety caused by trying to force success or avoid failure at some point in the future. Relinquishing the result allows the athlete to focus all their attention in the present moment and on the process designed to deliver the desired outcome. After all, God willing, all will work out as it is meant to. This process of letting go has delivered profound successes for some of the more religious or spiritual (and nervous) athletes I've worked with. It is what led Gary Kirsten, overnight, from the brink of being dropped, to his record-breaking 275 runs against England, in Durban in 1999.

On that day in Platboom, I got to take off on some of the biggest and best waves of my life, and I extended my perceived edge of 'fear of big waves'. I also learned what it felt like to take some of the heaviest wipe-outs of my life. And they were not as bad as I had thought they would be—the fear of them was worse.

What I did get wrong was that I stopped thinking before the experience was complete. Exhausted after an epic session at this unfamiliar spot, I exited the water at the same place I had entered it (well, so I thought), only to find myself getting washed across the rocks thanks to the rise in tide and increase in swell size and thus, the changed conditions. I had not thought through nor checked the exit strategy, and in hindsight, I probably did not leave myself with enough energy to get out of the water safely had a strong rip or bigger seas developed.

This is true of mountaineers, too. Approximately 80 per cent of mountaineers who die on the mountain die on the way down (only 15 per cent of the 212 mountaineers who died on Mt Everest between 1921 and 2006 died on the way up).[2] People plan to get to the top of their mountain, but not how to safely return after their moment of glory has passed. I learned this lesson the hard way.

19

THE ZONE OF DEATH, THE NORTH POLE AND THE WORLD CUP

It was amazing to see. It was a week before the start of the ICC World Cup in 2011, and I sensed that it was probably the very first time that Sachin Tendulkar would have someone to look up to. Mostly, everyone looked up to him.

Then Mike Horn entered the room. He is a humble South African and a friend from my university days, who is considerably more acclaimed outside his country than within. He speaks English with a strong, unpretentious Afrikaans accent, overflows with enthusiasm for life, and personifies courage, mental strength and a sense of adventure that is beyond the comprehension of most people on earth. He epitomises the triumph of the human spirit over the most daunting odds.

When he was twenty-eight, Mike found himself bored with routine life. His story began then. He threw a 'leaving party' and gave away his house, car and other possessions, all except the clothes he could fit into his backpack. His first stop was Switzerland, where he found himself struggling to make ends meet, first as a dishwasher in an old hotel, then as a ski instructor and river/canyon guide. Having completed some pretty advanced military training in South Africa, he decided to hitchhike to Israel to see if he could make ends meet a little better in the Israeli Army.

But he never made it out of Switzerland. The first car he thumbed down dropped him off in the next village where he found a good river to ride on his hydro-speed (basically, a body board with handles), met the woman he was later to marry, and moved into the home he still lives in today. Well, for some of the time.

From there, his story moves as far away from the 'house, dog, two kids and white picket fence' as can be imagined. Except that he did have two beautiful daughters who are very much part of the life he has created for himself and his family. Sadly, his wife passed away a few years ago from breast cancer.

As I'm writing this, Mike is recognised as probably the world's greatest modern-day adventurer having accomplished a remarkable list of world-firsts. After crossing the South American Andes on foot, he swam the 7,000 kilometres of the Amazon River from source to mouth using his hydro-speed as transport. He travelled alone with only a backpack for survival, hunting baby crocodiles and monkeys for food, before reaching the mouth of the river after six long months.

Mike next set out to reach the North Pole in mid-winter. For sixty consecutive days, he walked and swam twenty hours a day in total darkness. Till today, there are only two people in history who have succeeded in doing this: Mike and his teammate, Børge Ousland.

After that, with expedition Latitude Zero, Mike circumnavigated the world around the equator. Alone and without any motorised transport, he sailed, cycled, walked and paddled for nineteen months and covered over 40,000 kilometres, including a world record solo crossing of the Atlantic Ocean.

His greatest feat, possibly, was circumnavigating the Arctic Circle; a trip that most would never dream of and which those who knew said was impossible. Once again travelling solo and without any motorised transport, Mike pulled a 200-kilogram sled for two years and three months, covering over 20,000 kilometres over two Arctic winters in some of the harshest conditions known to man.

To date, Mike has climbed four of the 8,000-metre-plus mountains without ever using high altitude porters or supplementary oxygen. He has also covered the 7,000 kilometres to the South Pole and back, walking alone.

In 2001, Mike was awarded the Laureus Alternative Sportsman of the Year award, and in 2007, he was inducted as a member of the Laureus World Sports Academy.

In February 2010, I knew Mike was on his yacht somewhere near the Andaman Islands, on one of his around-the-world expeditions, at the time when the Indian Test team was scheduled to play against South Africa in Kolkata. I asked him if he would sail 1,300 kilometres across the Bay of Bengal to spend two nights with the team. (1,300 kilometres might sound like a long way to travel for a short visit, but Mike was on a 100,000-kilometre expedition and so this trip would have been like you and I walking down the street to visit a friend.) The guys loved Mike's visit so much that they asked if we could get him back for the World Cup, which we did. He joined us for the week leading up to the tournament.

A key piece in our preparation was dealing with the perceived pressure of playing the World Cup on home soil, and then the final in Mumbai. For the players, that was the ceiling of pressure. However, when Mike speaks, you get a totally different perspective of what pressure can be.

As coaching staff, we did everything within our means to prepare the players for all that was about to come their way. But even a week before the World Cup started, and until the Indian players listened to Mike speak, they had thought their pressure meters were redlining. The same with pain: playing with a dislocated finger, or being bruised or getting hit on the inside of the thigh, or getting hit in the ribs a few times—that was the kind of pain the batsmen had to endure. They got a new perspective when listening to Mike talking about his journey down a river, going through rapids and over waterfalls with a broken kneecap, and of amputating the tip of his own finger due to frostbite.

On 10 February 2011, Mike had the first of two conversations with the World Cup squad, relating some of the biggest pressure situations he had ever experienced.

I. INTO THE ZONE OF DEATH

As a kid, Mike dreamt of being the first person to circumnavigate the world, the first person to get to the North Pole in winter, the first person to walk the 7,000 kilometres to the South Pole and back, and of becoming the best climber in the world.

'I found out very quickly that the complexity of my dreams meant that I had to stay simple,' Mike said. 'The simpler I became, the easier I could make my dreams a reality. When you make everything in your life so complex and difficult, the dream that you set out to reach becomes unreachable. I stayed simple in every little thing that I did. All my approaches and all my training were to better myself to reach my complex dreams. I wanted to better my life and know more about myself. I wanted to increase my knowledge and my physical power, my core power, my inner strength, my psychological attitude to overcome all these little obstacles. If I don't train and better myself, how can I have confidence in myself when I get out there and go where nobody else goes?'

Mike spoke of the moment he reached his very first major summit. 'I realised my dream was completely wrong. Reaching the summit should never, ever have been my dream. When I reached my first summit, stood and looked down the mountain, I realised, Mike, as a kid, your dream was to stand here. But now that you're here, how the hell do you get down?'

This experience changed the way Mike perceived and approached challenges. The way down became part of his dream. For the Indian cricket team, being selected for the World Cup was like reaching the summit. Winning it would be like making it out alive.

THERE IS NO SECOND INNINGS

At an altitude of 8,000 metres, you have 7 per cent oxygen, compared to 21 per cent at sea level. Mountain climbers call this the 'death zone' because there is insufficient oxygen to sustain human life.

'When I "go out to bat" on those summits,' Mike said, 'I don't lose credibility and faith in myself. I just lose my life. There is no second innings in what I do. That's where commitment comes in. Commitment means that your will to win must be bigger than your fear of losing. If you're afraid of losing, you'll never win.

'When I stand at the bottom of the mountain and look up and say, "Wow—this doesn't feel right," it's just because I'm afraid of losing.'

To Mike, commitment is a way of dealing with pressure. The fear of losing creates pressure. By overriding that fear with the will to win, one decreases the relevance of pressure as a by-product of fear.

'Guys, if you can transform the power of the mind, which we all can do, when you make that will to win bigger than the fear to lose, you get rid of a lot of pressure that you yourself put on your shoulders. It's up to you,' he told the team.

THESE ARE NOT UNREASONABLE EXPECTATIONS

Having the will to win is one thing. Knowing that you are capable of winning is a different ball game altogether. By now, Mike had discussed with the players the fact that they were good enough to have been selected. He had told them that their will to win had to be bigger than their fear of losing if they were to have any chance of winning the World Cup. If the players' selection and their attitude towards winning were legitimate, there was no reason for them to lack confidence in their ability to make it to the summit of the mountain *and* make it back alive.

'People ask a lot of you because you can give a lot. I don't think people are asking things of you that you are not capable of delivering on. People don't ask stuff of me that I cannot do. I tell them what I can do; I show to them what I can do, and then I do it. If you think people (the Indian public) are asking more from you than what you can produce, you're self-pressurising your own mind. Your mind plays games with you, thinking that they are asking too much of you. But they're actually just asking what they know you can produce,' Mike said.

Self-doubt is, however, a natural human condition, and whether one is standing at the bottom of a mountain or on the eve of playing in a World Cup final, it is worth having a good look at oneself.

'When I stand at the bottom of the mountain, I look very carefully at myself. I write down a couple of bullet points on myself. What do I think about myself? What are my strong points? What is my strongest characteristic? Then, I try to write an A4 page full of positivity. On another page, I write all the things that I think aren't so great about me—reasons why I shouldn't climb. Then I go out and train and better my negatives. Then I start focusing on getting to the summit. The moment I start climbing is the moment I know that I can assume all the pressure and responsibilities of getting to the summit and back.'

THE 'NEGATIVES' IS AN ATTITUDE; NOT CIRCUMSTANCES

In the Indian team, as discussed earlier, we had an approach of playing to our strengths. Going out and bettering our 'negatives', as Mike called them, wasn't really our thing.

Sensing that Mike was on about something different, Gary asked what sort of negatives he'd had to overcome, and the answer had nothing to do with Mike's physical attributes and skills.

'Negativity usually lies within your attitude,' he replied. 'It's your attitude to what you are going to do. It's the energy you put into what you want to do. That, and not my climbing skill, is where I have to battle the negatives. Using my ice axe, I can pull myself up twenty times with one arm. That's not my problem. I can put that ice axe exactly where I want it. But my attitude at the beginning of the climb, and the energy that I put into training, and how I feel about myself, is where I found my most negative points.'

Again, Gary asked how Mike had overcome those negatives.

'I focused on what I must do to climb. I said no to a lot of things that I would have said yes to in the past. I improved my physical core strength and my training abilities, and I felt better about myself. I'm focusing on everything that I should do to become the best climber in the world. Get rid of the baggage!

'We drag baggage around that influences us so negatively that we cannot perform. And that puts pressure on you. You are only pressurised by what is negative.

'Imagine your head is a garden and you plant flowers in this garden. You're not going to plant weeds in your garden, are you? You're going to plant flowers, and you want your garden to stay clean. So, this bullshit of thinking positive doesn't exist. In the end, you must keep the negative away from you instead of thinking that you should be thinking positive all the time.

'When I go through these big crevices and these big chunks of ice keep falling everywhere, and every step is a step into the unknown, it's like you guys being a little bit lost on the cricket pitch. You don't know where the next "negative" is going to come from. In that situation, you can only do what you know you can do. And that is the only positive thing you have—your abilities. The negative influences are all around you: the chirps (sledging), the bowlers peppering you with short balls and body shots. None of these negative influences should in any way affect the way you do what you know you can and should do. Focus on what you can do and control.'

Eric Simons, the Indian bowling coach, then asked what many of the players were thinking. Here was this forty-four-year-old man who could do twenty one-armed pull-ups hanging from his ice axe. Was the key to his mental resolve not his extraordinary physique?

'No! It's not about being able to pull yourself up twenty times. It's about wanting to pull yourself up once.'

PREPARING FOR THE UNKNOWN

Most of Mike's feats are world-firsts. He enters places and conditions where no person has ever set foot before, or, if they did, didn't survive—his are discoveries of the unknown.

For many of the Indian players, the pressure they would experience during the World Cup—the hype, the local expectations and the politics—would be unlike anything they had ever had to endure.

Knowing this, one of the players asked Mike how he prepared himself before entering these unknown worlds.

'Imagination,' was the unexpected answer. 'I strongly believe in mental preparation. I prepare through imagination. Just before I go to climb these mountains, when I am sitting at home, I look at books and at photos I have taken. I set them out on a table. You can use pictures of shots you have played or of places you have played at. I then look at these photos and imagine, in my head, what those conditions are going to be like.

'Forget that you are here, and imagine walking into a specific cricket stadium with your bat under your arm. Then imagine your stance and the bowler running up. Can you hear the crowd? What is the smell? What is the temperature? Your knowledge of the conditions becomes the most stable thing in your life. You prepare for that.'

Pointing at a picture of him on one of his summits, Mike said, 'Before actually being in this unknown situation, I knew exactly what it smelled like. I knew exactly how cold it was. I knew exactly what my mental attitude was. And the outcome of that expedition was positive. It's like having scored three centuries at the venue before getting there for the first time.'

'Mental preparation prior to climbing is taking what you know, enforcing what you know into your body and then stepping out with that positive knowledge to face the next ball. That's how I prepare myself. I take my best moment, my moment of glory. And I take that proverbial cricket bat out and I'm just going to play another shot that I have already played before in my life. It's not something new. Although it's six grades more difficult, it's just another mountain I'm climbing. I'm simplifying the complexity. I'm using just another movement to climb another mountain.'

PREPARING TO SURVIVE

When climbers enter the death zone, that part of the climb with just 7 per cent oxygen in the air, their minds no longer function normally. Mike explained that he could make no rational decisions when he was in the final push towards a summit.

'All you want to do is to sit down and die. I count on my survival instinct to come back alive. You want to survive. That's the mental preparation I do. The moment I'm on that final ridge and 8,300 metres of altitude, you cannot think logically. You know one thing, and that is to not sit down when you get to the top. Because the moment you sit down is the moment you will never stand up again.'

Besides the mental pressures, the human body also starts shutting down in the death zone, and the only thing that keeps a climber from falling is his ice axe and two spikes in his mountain shoes going into the ice.

'With 7 per cent oxygen, it will take you over an hour to walk less than twenty metres. One movement becomes sixty breaths of air just to have enough oxygen go to your muscles. And then your brain tells your foot to move and it's not moving. When I experienced that on Makalu, it was the weirdest thing, but it was also the moment when I knew that I was well-prepared. Mentally, I was doing exactly what I wanted to be doing up there. That's how it's supposed to be. When you're up there, seeing the planes flying lower than you, you know you're high. When I reached the summit, I took a picture and realised that wasn't the moment to take out the bottle of champagne, because we were only halfway there. We still had to get down.'

Mike then asked each of the players whether it was their dream to play cricket for India. It's an obvious answer, he said. 'But being here is not the end of your dream, it's the start, the place to work from. If your dream was getting here, then your dream is over. The moment we reach our dreams, that's actually where everything starts. There is nothing wrong with saying representing India at a World Cup is what you wanted from your life, and nothing more. There's nothing wrong with that. But then you shouldn't be here. Because you're taking the place of someone who might do it better than you, or me, or all of us.'

REGAINING PERSPECTIVE

Once, standing on a summit, with his mind not working properly, Mike decided to walk to the edge of the mountain. The summit itself was the size of a kitchen table. Standing on the edge, Mike looked down.

'My mind told me to walk, so I was walking. Then I told myself to stop, but I was still walking. There was no connection between what my mind wanted to do and what my body functions were doing. I lost it all. There was a lack of oxygen to my muscles. So, I nearly went over the edge of the mountain. I stood there, only just understanding that I was standing at a place where we humans cannot live. But down there, where we left from, we can live. The world below, the place we call earth, feeds us all. Mother Earth keeps us alive. Standing on the edge, I realised that the world that keeps us alive is actually not as big as I thought it was, because, moments earlier, I had climbed out of the living space of a human being. At base camp, I could breathe. But at those 8,000 metres I climbed in thirty hours, I couldn't live. The world is like an onion, I thought. Pull away one onion leaf, and we're all gone; the best cricket players, the best rugby players, the best adventurers, the greatest Bollywood stars and the greatest musicians, everything, gone. That's what made me humble. I was where people cannot go. I was where people cannot live. And when you look down from way up there, people who are supposedly great actually are very small.

'That was the greatest moment of my life. The moment I realised how insignificant I was. I just wanted to play a bigger role. That is what I encourage you to do—play a bigger role.'

For Mike, that realisation also drove home the importance of teamwork, especially in an environment where man's insignificance was accentuated. To the Indian team, he then offered a metaphor that would stay with us for the rest of the World Cup.

'You work as a team to achieve your ultimate dream of winning this World Cup. When you walk out onto the field of play, you shouldn't feel as if you've got the pressure of the whole of India sitting on your shoulders. They are walking out there with you, holding your hand in support.'

PULLING UP THE WEAKEST LINK

While knowing that sitting and falling asleep are the two biggest taboos once you reach a summit, Mike and one of his fellow climbers once did exactly that.

'When I woke up, my friend Jean Troillet was asleep right next to me. Twenty metres after I started walking down, which took me half an hour, I looked back and saw Jean still sitting fast asleep. With hardly enough power to get down myself, I went back and told him we had to go. He stood up and said, "Leave me here."

'I forced him to wake up. And he followed me along this ridge. When I turned back, he was standing behind me. We were still not really speaking to each other until we got to an ice fold that was going down, where we had to face the mountain with our backs to the void. And I thought Jean should go first. All of a sudden, I forgot about me. My focus was on him. I said, Jean, you should go first. Because if I'm down there, I'll never be able to come back up to help you.

'And I think that is what a team is all about. If you can take what I say and adapt it to your team, then I seriously believe you will be the ones most equipped to bring the World Cup back home. And you're at home, so it's not too far to carry, is it?

'But you have to help each other. If you're strong, bring those weaker ones up. But if the weaker ones bring you down, there's that Rubicon; a point of no return. You'll never be able to get back up again.'

CLIMBING WITHOUT OXYGEN

Not sure whether all the players understood the enormity of Mike's achievement, Gary asked him to elaborate on the part he 'humbly didn't mention': the fact that very few climbers climb these peaks without using supplementary oxygen.

'Gary, what people don't understand is that we all get put in the same bag. You can count people climbing without oxygen on one hand. The rest of the guys use supplementary oxygen. Climbing to 8,000 metres with oxygen and with porters carrying your oxygen cylinders is like climbing a 6,000-metre peak. I feel very strongly that when you're using supplementary oxygen, you're cheating the mountain. You're bringing the level of the mountain down to 6,000 metres when, in actual fact, it's 8,000 metres high. To be able to go out there and climb these summits without oxygen is a way of proving to the people who climb with oxygen that humans can climb without it. I'm not fitter or stronger than anybody else. The difference is the psychological power that differentiates one guy from the other. You can be the most talented climber or cricketer in the world, but if you do not have that psychological advantage of believing in yourself, then you're useless, because, actually, you can't apply your knowledge to the mountain. You're cheating it. And the truth is, you can only feel pressure if you are not well enough prepared. So you try to cheat your way out of reality.'

WOULD I PICK YOU FOR MY EXPEDITION TEAM?

Mike asked the players to privately answer to themselves whether they would get picked if he had to select a summit team from among them.

'Do you think I'll choose all of you? Only you can answer that question, because it depends on your preparation, motivation, mindset, on what your contribution to the team is. How many of you are going to use oxygen to get to the top of the mountain, and how many of you are going to climb without oxygen?

'If we can climb without oxygen together, we'll all reach the summit. But if there is one guy who climbs with oxygen, then our team is as strong as our weakest link. That is what we cannot afford to have in this World Cup. We have an ideal situation today where you guys are prepared, talented, and you have home-ground advantage. But who, today, is ready to go into this World Cup to be a climber without oxygen? In other words, fully committed? It's important that we all know.'

One by one, Mike asked the players whether they would climb this summit without oxygen. The answer, one after the other, was yes.

'Now, that "yes" commits you to the cause.'

In the way we spoke in the months leading up to the World Cup, the team had already committed itself to playing in the final. That was the cause. As a way of managing pressure, it had seemed sensible to use the phrase 'play in the final' rather than 'win the final'. But now that the rubber was about to hit the road, was it perhaps time to shift to a higher gear?

Mike recalled his expedition from six months earlier. 'One of the climbers turned around when he was ten metres short of the summit. He'd worked his whole life to get within ten metres of the summit. And he stopped. Why didn't he go to the summit?' Mike said, sounding slightly perplexed still.

'I went to him on the way down, and I was trying to converse with him. But the conversation didn't really make sense. That's when I realised that he was not mentally prepared to go all the way. How many of you are going to turn around ten metres from winning the World Cup? Maybe we won't know until we are there. But I'll tell you that when the pressure is on, saying "no" to it is not always the easiest solution. When you feel like turning around ten metres from the summit, don't think of reasons why you can't reach the top, but reasons why you can. That is when you need to grab the bull by its balls a little bit and squeeze. You all have the mental and physical power and the will to be here. Take up your individual responsibilities, because your individual responsibility is not to look for excuses but to execute solutions and to find the positives when things are going wrong, so that you can make it right.'

II. CONQUERING THE NORTH POLE

On the second night of Mike's visit, he asked whether the individuals sitting around him were actually a team. Somehow, he was not convinced that they bonded or behaved as a team. He suggested that some of the players may already have excuses ready in the event of India not winning the World Cup, perhaps as a conscious or unconscious strategy of dealing with pressure.

'It is easy to look for excuses as to why you didn't make it. Making excuses is the easy way of washing your mind and your conscience.

Sometimes people think of excuses even before they start playing, because if they lose, the pressure is off. Losing is a way of releasing pressure, because then you are not involved in the race anymore. It's an easy way out.

'In the World Cup, once you reach the quarters, semis and finals, the pressure is going to be there. So, what do you do about that? The pressure on you is partly self-inflicted. Other people inflict pressure too, and then there is the pressure that individuals within the team inflict on each other.

'From that perspective, my honest observation is that we're not a team yet. I might be wrong. If we can become a true team, the pressure that all of you as individuals carry will get offloaded and distributed through all of you. That means we won't count on one person to win this thing, whether he's a batsman or a bowler. Because that pressure becomes so much on that one person who has to carry the burden that, in the end, he doesn't want to take all that pressure. So what does he do? He looks for excuses to offload this pressure and walks away. If we can take all the pressure and put equal amounts of it on all our shoulders, then that's how we're going to become a team and win the World Cup.'

A FAMILY OF 'FOES'

Mike used his North Pole expedition in 2006 to illustrate the power of true teamwork. More people have walked on the moon than individuals who reached the North Pole in mid-winter. Many have tried and failed. Only two succeeded: Mike Horn and the Norwegian explorer Børge Ousland.

'We're standing on the edge of the Arctic Ocean, on the last piece of land before you step away from it, navigating yourself on floating ice and moving on top of the ocean. It's the middle of the winter. The sun sits south of the equator, and its rays go past the North Pole. We're attempting the unknown in perpetual darkness. There is no light in the Pole.

'And the guy standing next to me, I didn't really like. And he didn't really like me either. But we had one goal in common: he and I together, otherwise isolated from the rest of the world, wanted to be the first people to reach the North Pole in the winter, in constant darkness, without dogs or motorised transportation. We hardly ever spoke. Perhaps three words a day. But I lived with this guy, I slept next to this guy, I ate with this guy. This guy never moved out of my space and I never moved out of his. But that's what we needed. To eventually understand that we needed each other to get to the Pole was to become one in what we were doing.'

He said the Indian team and players were in a similar situation. Although there were people around them all the time, they were, in truth, isolated for the World Cup. We were not even allowed to leave our hotel for anything besides training sessions and matches. But the isolation served a purpose—it was what needed to happen for the team to become the best in the world.

'You don't win the second prize at a World Cup, guys. You lose the first prize. If you think it's okay to make the quarter-finals or the semi-finals, you shouldn't be here. If you don't reach for the top, you're not even going to hit the bottom of the mountain.'

RELIEVING PRESSURE ONE STROKE AT A TIME

Mike and Børge weren't always walking on ice. At times, they also had to swim in arctic water, not able to see a metre in front of them. Mike recalled those conditions.

'The ice had just broken up, we had to put on our dry suits. It's less than minus forty degrees Celsius, and you swim in the darkness where you cannot even see where you're going. I don't know whether I have given more commitment to anything in my life than when I had to get into sub-zero waters in absolute darkness. Five or six times a day, I jumped into the Arctic Ocean at minus forty, knowing that I might never again get out. But the more often I did it, the easier it became. The easier it became, the more relaxed I was and the less pressure I felt. The first time, I can tell you, I was just standing in front of the ice breaking up, quickly putting on this dry suit over my boots and everything, and the pressure at that moment was amazing. *But ...* that is what I was there for! Getting across to the other side was not a problem, that would follow later. My focus was here and now, and it was exhilarating.'

Navigating local expectations under extreme pressure was something the Indian team discussed quite often. We knew they were going to be under pressure, but again, Mike stressed that the pressure was justified, and that these players had been picked exactly because they could perform under demanding circumstances.

'While you will experience pressure in the qualifiers, I don't think it should influence what you do at all,' said Mike. 'Because you are the best team in the world, you can qualify for the play-offs, and you should only start feeling the pressure later in the tournament. If you're going to allow yourself to experience peak pressure early on (in the tournament), what's going to happen? It's going to crack you up before you reach the end. Here's the thing. If we can have the pressure build up towards the end, allowing it grow slowly and at the same time *distributing the pressure between you*, then we've got a good chance of making it.'

At the time, we didn't necessarily understand what Mike meant. But as we'll discuss in the following chapter on the World Cup, the distribution of pressure between the individual players happened quite naturally. Yuvraj Singh played the game of his life against Australia in the quarters. Knowing that, M.S. Dhoni took the yoke of pressure from Yuvi in the final and, together with Gautam Gambhir, carried much of the burden on behalf of the team.

WE ARE A TEAM, REGARDLESS ...

While walking on ice, Børge fell through. Mike used his camera's flash to see what was happening, taking a picture in the process; one that leaves him emotional to this day.

As he shared the story with the Indian team, Mike said, 'This is a guy I don't like. The ice has just broken. He's fallen into the ice. His mouth is wide open, and his eyes ... he's got one will: the will to survive.

'But before we left, we'd had a short discussion. We said if you're in the shit, I'm not going to help you. If I'm in the shit, you're not going to help me. Let me die. That was the deal we had.

'Then I saw this guy going into the water, and you have to understand that this is ice. You cannot lift your legs. It's not only that you cannot lift your leg; it's that you get pulled down because of the resistance of the ice against your body. When I saw him go into the water, I knew I was going to go into the water as well if I got close to him.

'I was going to turn my back, and I was going to walk away and hope that he was going to get out of it by himself. But as I was taking that picture with my camera, using the flash, I knew that Børge needed me. I knew that this guy that I by now had grown to not like but to accept, needed my help. In that moment, he reached the point of no return. He was on his way down. The easiest thing I could have done was to turn my back and let him sort it out by himself. But I didn't.

'I pushed my sled closer to him. We had this long line that pulled the sled. I unhooked it from me, and through the sled, pushed the line to him. He got hold of it, and then, all of a sudden, I realised that I had given him my lifeline. Everything in this sled was there to keep *me* alive. Everything I had to keep me alive, I had just sacrificed to get Børge out of there. My will to pull him out must now be bigger than his will to drown. The tug of war started. As he got pulled down by the ice, I got pulled to the edge. He was slowly but surely pulling me into the ice. But that will of mine, of wanting to survive and reach the Pole, needed him. I honestly and sincerely needed this man who was drowning. And he needed me at that moment. I managed to pull him out.

'We didn't become better friends. We didn't speak many more words. But he came in next to me two or three hours later, and said, "You know what, Mike, I'm not here to thank you. Doesn't mean I like you more. But I want you to know that if ever something goes wrong for you, I'll be there for you."'

Whether the Indian players had the same sort of commitment among themselves was a question only they could answer, Mike said.

'Do you have that same feeling of commitment of saying: I'll be there for you? I'll put everything on the line for you to pull you out of this difficult situation, because alone you are not going to make it? That's a team, and that's what made the two of us a winning team, and why we are the only two people in the world to have ever completed that expedition.'

UNDER PRESSURE

On 23 March 2006, Mike Horn and Børge Ousland completed the first ever winter expedition to the North Pole. A journey many had thought was impossible, and others thought was suicidal.

'Every time I look at footage or pictures from the moment we reached the North Pole, I can still feel that unique moment of achievement that only two guys in the world have experienced. For you, winning the World Cup will make you experience something that only one team in the world can achieve'.

At this point, somewhat unexpectedly, Mike turned up the heat. He showed the players a picture of a man who had lost his toes due to frostbite.

'What we (extreme athletes) do is not a joke anymore. We are serious about this. Guys who don't take it seriously end up with no toes and possibly, no life. So, I've got a question for you: Are you a joker? Or are you serious? If you are a joker, you shouldn't be here. You have to understand the importance of your role. You don't want to end up like that. That's pressure! If you lose focus, you lose your life. *That* is pressure!

'You'll have very little time to make the right decision when somebody bowls at you. Don't let your eyes freeze up. Be prepared.'

GAZZA'S ON FIRE

The team meeting with Mike was about to adjourn when Gary started speaking. He clearly had fire in his belly, and what he was about to say would change the nature of our conversations within the team until India would go on to win the World Cup six weeks later.

As mentioned earlier, we had changed our language after the Dambulla experience in 2010. Our conversations and plans were prefaced by 'when we *play* in the final of the World Cup'. But then Mike came along, and this is what Gary said to the players:

> We had a discussion with Mike two days ago, and we were talking about how we are going to map out this World Cup. I recall myself saying that we weren't going to talk about winning the World Cup anymore. But Mike's blown that out of the water, and we're talking a lot about winning the World Cup.
>
> Certainly, what comes to mind for me, is that a lot of time there might be two ways of handling pressure. We know there are going to be pressure situations. The first part of the tournament probably won't (cause that much pressure). We'll go through (to the play-offs) and then the pressure and expectations will grow, especially on you

guys. A lot of the time, we just say that we'll give our best; there's nothing more we can say. That's what it's about. Giving our best.

I get a sense from what Mike is saying to us, and from the analogies that I'm picking up here, that giving your best is bullshit. Because that's the cop-out. 'We didn't win, but at least we gave our best …'

We have to go win this thing. Every one of us has got to believe so deep and so intensely that we are going to win this thing. Every one of us! And Mike talks a lot about the weak link. Are there guys out here that just say, 'We'll give it our best shot'? You have worked out a way to make excuses and how not to win.

I've said to you guys many times before: We have the team to win this tournament. And we can either go and say we'll give it our best shot, or we can say we are going to f….ing go win this thing. Every one of us has to get it so deep inside here, that every time one of your teammates walks past you, he can feel it.

It's all very well we are talking now; six weeks before we get to the final. We need to constantly remind ourselves that we are going to win this thing. Everyone is going to take on the responsibility for the pressure there is going to be. We're not going to rely on our mate to take on the pressure. We will take it on when it is *that* situation and it is *that* day. I need to make this play for this team, and I will take on the responsibility—because this team needs me today. I'm not just going to nick off or hit one straight in the air, or top-edge on a soft delivery and let someone else go take the responsibility. I'm not going to let a guy at number six come in and make the runs that I should have made. I'm not going to let another guy take the over where we have to defend 5 or 6 runs, because I cocked up the over before.

We can win this thing. We've got the team. There is absolutely no doubt we've got the team. We've got time on our hands. We've got to believe it. Every one of us has to believe it deep down.

Gary's impromptu speech led to a whole new conversation between him, Mike and the players. To bring you into the team room, I'm not going to paraphrase what happened next:

Mike: *You can only be disappointed if you really believe*. I don't want to be disappointed, because then I'm a failure. The quality of your life only comes from what you put into it. The more you put into it, into the team, the higher your quality. *You can only get what you give*. It's important that you guys understand that things don't always go easy and right.

Gary, in your career, was there ever a moment where you felt you were a failure? We don't like speaking about failure as such, but was there ever such a moment where you felt I couldn't do it?

Gary: Yes. I was part of the South African team in the 1999 World Cup. We should have won the World Cup, and when I look back on that, I look back on that with regret. It is something that lives with me with the deepest regret, because we should have won the tournament. We had a real opportunity and it would have been a massive highlight in my life, and we didn't. And that disappointment lives with me. There is nothing I can do about it now.

Mike: Will winning this World Cup be a highlight of your life?

Gary: It will be awesome. It will be one of the most awesome things I have ever been part of. And this team can do it.

Mike to Sachin: Will it be a highlight of your career?

Sachin: It would.

Mike: For who will it not be a highlight?

(No hands go up)

Mike: I think we have two answers that are pretty straightforward. I can certainly tell you it will be a highlight of my life. I've done a lot. I don't speak a lot about what I've done. It will definitely be a highlight of my life, because we are all here together to not walk out with second prize. We want to walk out with the cup. In most of the cases where I was not successful, it was because I was not well-prepared. That was the only conclusion to all my unsuccessful stories, of which there were only two in my career of twenty years. Only twice did I call defeat. And both times I sat down, and it was my own personal mistake. I didn't point fingers at anybody. I could only point fingers at myself.

Paddy: You can actually only point half a finger at yourself.

Mike: Well, yes. This one is off.

Gary: Yesterday, when chatting to one or two of the guys about it, Mike said that when the will to win is greater than the fear of losing, you are going to make it.

Mike: Don't worry about losing, guys. Losing takes care of itself. Get that will to win. Shit, hey, it's a great feeling. Putting that national flag on that pole ...

Gary: That's a great point. Losing takes care of itself. We don't have to have a strategy to lose. It will take care of itself.

Mike: Losing takes care of itself. Just get that will to win.

Gary: We just need that will to win.

Mike: My father always told me that if you worry about worrying, you die. If you don't worry, you still die. So, why worry? Why worry about stuff that we shouldn't be worried about?

20

THE WORLD CUP: COMETH THE HOUR, COMETH THE TEAM

As the day of the first game arrived, we were largely satisfied that everything humanly possible had been done to prepare the Indian team for the challenges that lay ahead, including that:

- After three years of ingraining it, we were clear on what T.E.A.M. India meant and how to execute on being a Team of Excellent Entertainers, with the right Attitude and Maturity, both on- and off-the-field.
- We would manage our minds better than all opponents, especially in those key moments of a game when smart decisions and accurate execution change its course.
- Mike Horn's lessons of spreading the load of pressure, delaying the intensity of its onset for the play-offs, climbing without oxygen, supporting our teammates, having the will to win and more, were freshly etched in our minds.
- We had the requisite skill, game plans and home ground advantage.

We were only a handful of weeks away from World Cup glory, for the first time in twenty-seven years.

WE HAVE LIFT-OFF

On 19 February 2011, a solid team effort handed us our first World Cup victory as we beat Bangladesh by 87 runs. Virender Sehwag contributed a mammoth 175 off 140 balls, and Virat Kohli scored 100 not out.

Since we had six Group B matches before all the play-off sides would be decided, we didn't really mind the tied result against England in our second outing. I hadn't been involved in many tied ODIs, and I must say it was exciting. We set them a target of 339 and took a lot of confidence from the batting performances of Sachin Tendulkar (120), Gautam Gambhir (51) and Yuvraj Singh (58). England captain Andrew Strauss started their innings with willow fever, knocking 158 off 145 balls. At the end of their 49th over, England still needed 14 runs to win. With 4 balls remaining, Ajmal Shahzad hit a 6 off Munaf Patel, leaving Graeme Swann to score 2 runs from the final delivery moments later. He had to settle for a single and only the fourth tied match in World Cup history.

In the next match, against Ireland, Yuvraj delivered his first of four Man of the Match performances at the World Cup. He claimed 5 wickets and added 50 not out to India's chase of 208. On 9 March, he followed that up with another half century and another Man of the Match trophy against the Netherlands, with India chasing 190 and winning by 5 wickets.

THANK GOODNESS! WE LOST ...

Our fifth match was against South Africa. Even though the World Cup was being played in India, the Proteas were touted as one of the favourites to win the tournament. The South African eleven we faced in Nagpur included Graeme Smith, Hashim Amla, Jacques Kallis, A.B. de Villiers, J.P. Duminy, Faf du Plessis, Morné Morkel, and the devastatingly good Dale Steyn.

India batted first, and whilst Steyn bagged a fifer, he did so only after our top three of Sehwag (73), Tendulkar (111) and Gambhir (69) had got us off to a great start.

And then we lost.

Although I must admit that we were probably looking for a silver lining to make us feel better about losing, Gary and I, at the time, were quite 'happy' with this outcome. We thought there would be a good chance of India meeting South Africa in the play-offs later, should they get through. The fact that the Proteas beat us would see them coming into this potential play-off game as favourites, with India as the underdogs against a team that had already beaten them. Being expected to win had not yet worked for South Africa in a big tournament and would see them coming in at a mental disadvantage. And being underdogs would be a mental advantage for India, as it would mean less pressure and expectation. (New Zealand eventually beat South Africa in the quarters, so the match never took place.)

But at the back of their minds, South Africa would have known that although they had won, chasing India's 297 thanks to that Tendulkar 111, they had been in a massively commanding position after 40 overs, at 220 for 3, before limping across the line 7 wickets down and with only 2 balls to spare. They must have expected to win far more easily, and we had expected to be beaten more comprehensively. But they were visibly rattled as the winning line drew nearer. This game, and the areas that emerged as needing some fine-tuning, would prove to be a very useful learning experience for India, and the loss lowered expectations of us.

In our last group-stage match, we beat the Windies by 80 runs—a confidence-boosting result that was by no small measure led by Yuvraj Singh, who scored his first ODI century in more than two years. This was his third Man of the Match performance at the World Cup, and his best was yet to come.

Any concerns that we might still have had about the team's unity and commitment to winning the World Cup were dissolved during a team meeting the day before we played Australia in the quarter-finals.

Gary and I really wanted the players to take ownership of the processes. In preparation for the meeting, I wrote a question on the board: *What's really important for tomorrow's game?* The team came into the room, we asked them the question, and then all of the support staff, including Gary and me, left the room while the players discussed it among themselves. They were told that when they were done, they were free to leave, and nobody was going to ask them to report back.

Gary, Eric Simons and I had a conversation down the corridor, expecting the players to come out after fifteen minutes or so. But it was a full fifty-five minutes before they walked out of the room. We could see in their body language and energy, in the way they carried themselves as they filed out the meeting room, that they were ready. We never asked them what they had discussed—we wanted them to take ownership. And they did.

YUVRAJ: CONQUERING EVEREST WITHOUT OXYGEN

While no one was aware of the cancerous tumour in Yuvraj's lung at that stage, he had been dropped from the Test team six months before the World Cup tournament. This was a blow to him, even though he retained his place in the One Day side.

Part of what might have contributed to him being dropped was the suggestion that he may have been somewhat caught up in his celebrity status as a cricketing star.

During those months, whilst in the ODI team and outside of the Test team, Yuvi and I had several individual sessions in which we delved into and talked through his game and various aspects of life. During that time, he developed a personal goal, more of a dream actually, one which he visualised day after day after day until 'that day' came. Well, sort of. He visualised and dreamt of scoring the World Cup winning runs in Mumbai, and interestingly, each time he dreamed that it would be against Australia.

Australia, in the meantime, seemed to be on course to win their third consecutive World Cup. And although Yuvi envisioned us playing them in the final of the 2011 tournament, our destinies ended up colliding in the quarter-finals.

Ricky Ponting led a strong Australian side in his 46th World Cup match, and he showed his class and experience by scoring 104 in their innings against India. Bar a half century by Brad Haddin, Ponting didn't receive much support from his top- and middle-order batsmen, but they still set us a respectable target of 261. As with almost every knock-out match, the pressure was palpable at the start of the game and turned up another notch at the change of innings and as we prepared to chase down the Australian total. We were 261 runs away from being another step closer to the final we had been preparing for, for so long.

Sachin and Gautam scored fifties, but we had a few shaky moments with the bat. When MS lost his wicket for 7 runs, we were 5 down on 187, still needing 74 off 12 overs. That's when Yuvi went into top gear. He and Suresh Raina never allowed the required run rate to climb above 6.2 per over. Yuvi took his singles, found the boundary when he could, and with every run added on the scoreboard, we could feel the pressure easing in the Indian change room.

Then, after facing 3 dot balls in the 48th over, Yuvi cut Brett Lee's fourth ball to the boundary to clinch victory and a ticket to the semi-finals. As the ball raced to the boundary, Yuvi ran down the pitch, and as it crossed the ropes, he fell to his knees, raised his arms aloft, and celebrated reaching his Everest (57 not out). He had fulfilled his dream of scoring the winning runs against Australia. Not quite in the final, but pretty close.

Australia probably needed just one more wicket to put them in the driver's seat. But as MS said afterwards: 'We needed 70-odd runs and had our last batting pair out. There was pressure, and it was about handling it.'

It reminded me of what Mike Horn had said to the players a few weeks earlier: 'If you're going to allow yourself to experience peak pressure early on (in the tournament), what's going to happen? It's going to crack you up before you reach the end. Here's the thing. If we can have the pressure to build up towards the end, allowing it to grow slowly and at the same time *distributing the pressure between you*, then we've got a good chance of making it.'

Yuvi was named Man of the Match for the fourth time in the tournament, and this time for a mature performance under extraordinary pressure. When he walked into the press conference a short while later, he was met with loud applause from local and international media. 'For the first time in my life there have been claps in a press conference. This is a special moment for me, guys,' he said, visibly humbled by the experience.

Yuvi climbed his Everest against Australia. *That* was his final. In our semi-final against Pakistan, he got out for a golden duck. But he'd already earned himself the Player of the Tournament award after doing what he had dreamt of doing against Ponting's men. The award was a testament to the hard work he had put in during the preceding months. Gary and I merely helped him gain perspective when he went through a difficult time. Accepting responsibility for himself and the team was something he did on his own.

The cancerous tumour in Yuvi's lung was discovered shortly after the tournament. Here was a man who truly conquered Everest without using supplementary oxygen.

SEMI-FINALS: THIS MEANS WAR

The India-Pakistan semi-final would be played under enormous political pressure. If we lost, Pakistan would play the final in Mumbai, at a time when Indo-Pakistan relations were still at an all-time low after the Mumbai terrorist attacks of 2008.

These attacks were later pinned on an Islamic terrorist organisation based in Pakistan. One of its main targets had been the iconic Taj Mahal Hotel, where we had been due to stay for the match against England as part of the 2008 India-England series. The ODI series was immediately called off (the Test series, in which Rahul Dravid revived his career, went ahead), many of the English players were sent home, the Indian players went back to their homes, and I headed off to the Mantra Surf ashram in Mulki (just outside Mangalore) to hang out and surf with my friends at Surfing Swami's.

Memories of the Mumbai attacks were still fresh and there was repair work still being done at the Taj Hotel when we stayed there during the World Cup. And the winner of our semi-final would be staying at the very same hotel for the final.

For most Indians, and also the BCCI and the Indian government, it was almost unthinkable that the Pakistan team would go to Mumbai. There is no question that the organisers did not want this match to happen. Pakistan had not played in India since the terrorist attacks, and for the World Cup, they were deliberately placed in Sri Lanka for all their group matches and in Bangladesh for their quarter-final.

A World Cup semi-final is pressure enough, and to this was added significant and far-reaching political pressure for India to win.

We played Pakistan in Mohali on 30 March 2011, in front of a packed stadium, with the Indian and Pakistan prime ministers up front. We posted the same score of 260 that Australia had set us in the quarters, and with the exception of Sachin, who scored 85, none of our batsmen scored 50 or more.

This time, our bowlers took the pressure on them, with all five—Zahir Khan, Ashish Nehra, Munaf Patel and the two Singhs (Yuvraj and Harbhajan)—taking 2 wickets each. Pakistan was bowled out on the second last ball of their innings, still 29 runs short.

And thank goodness for that. The victory, and India's advance to the finals in Mumbai, was celebrated by both jubilant fans and relieved politicians. 'India at war' was a metaphor we had used in the Indian team, but we wouldn't have wanted to be the cause of an actual military confrontation between neighbouring countries!

THE NIGHT BEFORE THE FINAL

As mental coach, I was offered the opportunity to deliver the final team talk on the night before we played Sri Lanka in the World Cup final.

In the months leading up to the World Cup, Gary and I had already been setting up team meetings and team routines in such a way that everything would be familiar to the players by the time we reached the final. In my mind, I just had to inject that final dose of enthusiasm the team needed to successfully cross the rope one more time. I was ready for my Al Pacino moment.

As it turned out, my speech turned out to be *nothing* like that! The feeling in the team meeting room on the eve of the final was a lovely combination of focused and relaxed. Gary touched upon some key strategic points of playing against each of the Sri Lankan players (whose game we all knew very well), as well as how the wicket at Mumbai's Wankhede stadium would play, the nuances of the outfield, and how loud the crowd gets at the venue. Fielders would have to watch the captain, bowler and wicketkeeper closely and at all times, as it would be impossible to hear them shouting to get their attention.

The players were already in the final in their heads. I could see that. And so, my entire speech came down to this: 'This final is like a Bollywood movie. We know exactly what our scripts are. We have the best actors. We are completely prepared for our roles. Tomorrow, we only need to go out and perform those roles, to do what we know to do. And we *will* cross the line.'

The speech was over in less than a minute, and it was delivered with a calm and deep conviction. Nothing more needed to be said.

THE FINAL: COMETH THE HOUR, COMETH THE MAN

M.S. Dhoni, as anyone who has followed his career would know, is the kind of man who comes into his own in high pressure situations.

On the eve of the World Cup final, MS had a lot of pressure riding on him. Up until then, he had only scored 150 runs in the tournament, with 34 being his highest contribution.

In an impromptu speech during one of Mike Horn's presentations, Gary had stressed the importance of playing for the team and taking responsibility when 'that situation' and 'that day' arrived. Although MS didn't show any external concern about his drop in batting form, he would have known that, as a batsman, he hadn't yet carried the yoke of pressure for the team.

The final would provide him with the opportunity to set things straight.

Sri Lanka went in to bat first, scoring 274 for 6 in their 50 overs; a really competitive score for a final.

Virender Sehwag was out lbw for a duck in the second ball of our innings, and Sachin would soon depart after a quick 18 runs off 14 balls. Yuvraj was to come in at 5, and Dhoni at 6.

The most significant moment of that final, if not of the entire World Cup, was when an out-of-form Dhoni decided to bat ahead of Yuvraj. Although Yuvraj was a clear favourite for the Player of the Tournament by then, he had for all practical purposes already played his final against Australia. He had literally been vomiting in the change room before the final—whether it was because of nerves or the illness we weren't aware of then, I don't know.

MS just knew within himself that he was the man for the high pressure situation. We were 31 for 2, and with Sehwag and Sachin having got out, we seemed to be in trouble. Sehwag was the team's most destructive batsman, and Tendulkar the most experienced and most loved. But, in reality, India's best players under pressure were Gambhir and Dhoni.

I will always remember that moment, that small gesture, which signalled (at least to me) that the World Cup was coming to India. We were 2 wickets down, with Kohli and Gambhir at the crease. Dhoni always waits inside the dressing room before going to bat; he never sits outside. I was sitting next to Gary and Eric Simons in the players' viewing area when we heard a tap on the window behind us. It was Dhoni. He looked at Gary and pointed to himself, signalling, 'I'm next in.' Whether that small gesture was a statement or a question addressed to his coach, I don't know. But Gary simply nodded his approval. And I smiled. Cometh the hour, cometh the man.

When Kohli got out and Dhoni walked down the stairs at the Wankhede with India on 114 for 3 and needing 161 for victory, I said to Gary, 'MS is going out there to fetch us the trophy.'

Gambhir's amazing match-anchoring innings of 97 runs in that final is not nearly as much spoken about as Dhoni's 91 not out off 79 balls. But Gambhir was the guy who steered the innings from the start and held things together. Gambhir was the Gary Kirsten of the Indian side, the nitty-gritty grafter batting alongside the usually destructive Sehwag. That was the hallmark of his career. Mr Reliable, whom Gary fondly called 'The Rock'; Sehwag was the Destroyer. But on 'that day' and in 'that situation', India needed Mahendra Singh Dhoni from Jharkhand.

With Yuvraj on 21 at the non-striker's end, MS famously launched a full-pitched Kulasekara delivery into the dark Mumbai sky, and it sailed across the boundary for a 6 that transported the Wankhede stadium and a billion Indian fans into a state of rapture. That Dhoni 6, and Yuvraj Singh whooping with extended arms at the non-striker's end as the ball disappeared into the crowds, will forever be etched in the memory of Indian fans who witnessed the moment. Victory with ten balls to spare would bring the trophy back home after an absence of nearly three decades, and would deliver the promise a number of Indian players had made to Sachin Tendulkar—to add the final and elusive trophy to his illustrious career: a World Cup.

2011 WORLD CUP FINAL: SCORECARD

SRI LANKA

W.U. Tharanga	c Sehwag b Khan	2 (20)
T.M. Dilshan	b Harbhajan Singh	33 (49)
K.C. Sangakkara	c Dhoni b Yuvraj Singh	48 (67)
D.P.M.D. Jayawardene	not out	103 (88)
T.T. Samaraweera	lbw b Yuvraj Singh	21 (34)
C.K. Kapugedera	c Raina b Khan	1 (5)
K.M.D.N. Kulasekara	run out (Dhoni)	32 (30)
N.L.T.C. Perera	not out	22 (9)
Extras		12
TOTAL (50 overs; RR: 5.48)		**274/6**

Did not bat: S.L. Malinga, S. Randiv, M. Muralitharan

Fall of wickets: 1-17, 2-60, 3-122, 4-179, 5-182, 6-248.

BOWLING (Overs, Maidens, Runs, Wickets): Z. Khan (10-3-60-2); S. Sreesanth (8-0-52-0); M.M. Patel (9-0-41-0); Harbhajan Singh (10-0-50-1); Yuvraj Singh (10-0-49-2); S.R. Tendulkar (2-0-12-0); V. Kohli (1-0-6-0).

INDIA

V. Sehwag	lbw b Malinga	0 (2)
S.R. Tendulkar	b Sangakkara b Malinga	18 (14)
G. Gambhir	b Perera	97 (122)
V. Kohli	c & b Dilshan	35 (88)
M.S. Dhoni	not out	91 (79)
Yuvraj Singh	not out	21 (24)
Extras		15
TOTAL (48.2 overs; RR: 5.73)		**277/4**

Did not bat: S.K. Raina, Harbhajan Singh, Z. Khan, M.M. Patel, S. Sreesanth

Fall of wickets: 1-0, 2-31, 3-114, 4-223.

BOWLING: S.L. Malinga (9-0-42-2); K.M.D.N. Kulasekara (8.2-0-64-0); N.L.T.C. Perera (9-0-55-1); S. Randiv (9-0-43-0); T.M. Dilshan (5-0-27-1); M. Muralitharan (8-0-39-0).

INDIA WON BY 6 RUNS
MAN OF THE MATCH: M.S. Dhoni
PLAYER OF THE TOURNAMENT: Yuvraj Singh

THE MORNING AFTER

I still think about the morning after the World Cup final. There hadn't been a day in ten months when we didn't talk about or try to figure out how we'd get to that moment. Then, we got there, we won, and after much celebration, the sun rose over the boats anchored off the Gateway of India outside the Taj Mahal Hotel in Mumbai. It was a beautiful morning, yet I felt a cloud hanging over my head. I remember the feeling still, the sum of four overarching emotions: the throbbing of a hangover, the fuzzy-headedness of euphoria, the lightness of relief and a sinking feeling of emptiness.

The hangover came from the same place all of them do. Euphoria needs no explanation, especially when I reflected on the first sixty seconds after that 6, to the incredible rush of emotion, and to those next few minutes, as the realisation sank in. Relief? Still to this day as a coach, one of the main feelings associated with winning for me is relief. All our planning, training and preparation are about setting ourselves up with the best chance of winning. I always say that winning should not come as a surprise—it's what we work towards—so for me, winning is a relief. As for emptiness, it came along with the question, 'What now?' Up until MS hit the winning runs, my days had meaning. We were preparing for the ascent—and the descent. Or so we thought. Suddenly, the journey was over. For all of us. For Gary and me, it was the end of three amazing years with the team.

Rafael Nadal has spoken of the concept of 'getting back to zero'. When he wins a tennis tournament on a Sunday, he is back at the gym at 5.30 the following morning to complete a strenuous cardio session before his trainer arrives. When he's on a high (say, +5) after a victory, he needs to get himself back to zero. When he has lost, he needs to get himself from -3, back to zero. It's about resetting his mind and body for whatever the next challenge might be.

We never did that, and India went on to have a poor run after the World Cup, including a winless streak of seven ODIs between June and August 2011. Maybe one reason was that we didn't get together and celebrate the journey as a team because we were always surrounded by others or attending functions in a frenzied 36 hours before we all parted ways. There was no reset button pressed and no re-focus on what the next goal might be. We had only ever planned to get to the top of the mountain.

On a deeper level, experiencing the blues after achieving gold is not an uncommon occurrence in sport, and it even has a name: 'Post-Olympic Depression Syndrome'.[1]

Shortly before the end of the 2016 Rio Olympic Games, Prof. Scott Goldman, the director of the Performance Psychology Centre at the University of Michigan, described this 'under-recovery' after a big event. 'Think about the rollercoaster ride prior to the Olympics, and just how fast and hectic that mad dash is,' Goldman says. 'This ninety-mile-per-hour or hundred-mile-per-hour ride comes to a screeching halt the second the Olympics are over. ... (The athletes) are just exhausted; it was such an onslaught to their system. And when it's all said and done, they're just physiologically depleted, as well as psychologically.'

The experience, according to Goldman, is not that different from the drops we all feel after major milestones, such as getting married or giving birth. But in the case of Olympic athletes, some find themselves at such a loss they can't stop the slide—and wind up in a state of clinical depression.

An antidote to these post-podium blues is having another goal to work towards. I suppose coming second is sometimes easier, because you can immediately focus on trying to win next time. Winning can be difficult, especially if that's what you've focused all your energy and attention on. There is nothing to wake up to or work on the following day.

In hindsight, I think part of the immediate 'depression' I experienced was from the unconscious realisation that the victory also signalled the end of Gary and my three-year adventure with the Indian cricket team; one that had started with a hillbilly from Rondebosch and a barefoot surfer from Houtbay getting on an aeroplane and dreaming up some lofty goals. At least three of them had been achieved by 2 April 2011.

I've since been asked whether Gary and I achieved the fourth goal we set when we first joined team India, the one we never publicly mentioned, to 'help players become better people'. In all honesty, it's difficult to say, or even measure this. If I had the opportunity again,

I would re-word that goal to something like 'creating an environment that enables players to learn, grow and become their best self (as athletes and as people)'. This implies unshackling and encouraging players to fully, freely and authentically express all of their unique talents and personalities in becoming the best version of themselves. Our time with Team India was not so much about helping players to become better people or about us doing something to them, but rather about creating a fertile environment for them to flourish by themselves and thus deliver on their own highest potential (as cricketers and as human beings).

The journey was now over, and that gloomy feeling I had the morning after the final really got me to understand, at a deeper level, what is really meant by the saying, 'Life is a journey, not a destination.'

As an African who experienced the beauty, grace and passion of a journey passing through India, I conclude this chapter with a Sān perspective on life, quoting from Van der Post:

'This pattern is not limited to "birth, copulation, death". It is one of birth, procreation, death, and rebirth. All together, they make of life, not a dead-end valley, but an eternal *here* and *now*.'

INTERLUDE

My journey as a head coach has been a bit like that of an unlikely 400-metre athlete. I have had to overcome and disregard the opinions of people who believed my running style wasn't suited for a 400-metre sprint. In the world of cricket, it was safe to have me cover shorter distances—the fitness guy, the mental coach, the strategic leadership coach, but never the quarter-miler who covers every metre, turn and straight.

Yet, my research from outside of sport clearly indicated where leadership trends and philosophy were headed. And although I wasn't sure when and exactly how I, or sport for that matter, was going to get there, I knew I had to keep Forrest Gumping—running and running until I hit that coordinate where my predictions and the changing landscape of leadership intercepted.

There are those who regard the mental game and the coaching thereof as a specific discipline covering part of the track but not all of it. From what I've seen in the world of professional sports, a high percentage of mental errors or mental factors inhibiting performance arise from within the environment itself (for which the leadership is responsible). Players frequently complain about over-training, not training in the way that suits their game best, not having a voice, being over-dictated to or criticised, the fear of failure or fear of being reprimanded for failing, being asked to do things which do not match with their strengths, lacking clarity on their roles, poor communication, being negatively affected by cliques, lack of honesty… the list goes on. All these create mental noise and distract athletes from achieving the heights available to them.

Removing prohibiting environmental factors and creating an environment where people can grow and flourish fall beyond the job description and realm of influence of the mental conditioning coach or team psychologist. However, underestimating or delegating those responsibilities would be like a 400-metre athlete cutting corners and being surprised about being disqualified after 'completing' the home stretch. If anything, the head coach *is* the catalyst for mental conditioning.

My convictions about the role of the head coach or executive leader really started taking shape in 2003, when I did my study about leadership in cricket. Very little of what I learned was new in the world of leadership—cutting-edge business was far ahead of sports in terms of people management. I merely tried to transfer those ideas to cricket, and I was convinced that the Proteas would become unbeatable if Cricket South Africa (CSA) started implementing those principles before the rest of the world adopted them as the norm. I predicted that the competitive advantage would be available for two to three years, before other countries would catch on. I wrote a letter to CSA about this, but there was no response from any significant administrator.

I did, however, receive a positive reply from one of the board members, the banking entrepreneur Paul Harris. He invited me to his beautiful Ellerman House in Bantry Bay to discuss these ideas, which were in keeping with best practice in business environments and which he had long implemented as CEO of the FirstRand banking group. Cricket, however, was not there yet, and the door I was hoping would open for me remained closed. Asking coaches to loosen the grip on their power base, to set their own agenda aside, to let go of what had brought them the success they had achieved thus far and to collaborate with athletes, listening to players' views and even allowing players' agendas to prevail, was a leap too far.

Prior to the phone call from Gary Kirsten to join him in India in 2008, I had been working as an executive coach and leadership consultant in my own business. During this time, I had also started doing private sessions with some of South Africa's top cricketers, most notably Jacques Kallis, Graeme Smith and Gary Kirsten.

By the time Jacques and I started working together, it had been more than a year since the colossus of South African cricket had scored a century. His run drought coincided with the death of his father and a relationship that didn't work out—all external factors. We began talking and working through these things together. By his own account, our conversations restored clarity to his thinking, something that had been missing for a long time.

When there are things on and off the field that trouble a player, the runs tend to dry up. When they have to play, they think only of that run drought and they become trapped in a cycle. All Jacques needed was to take a step back so that he could gain perspective and clarity about himself, his life and his batting. When you come back after that, you have a new way of thinking and a new perspective on the future that is accompanied by peace of mind. Jacques scored centuries in five consecutive Test matches immediately afterwards.

In other cases, as also with Jacques, I would listen to players listing obstacles that were holding them back, and when I asked them whether they'd spoken about these things to their coaches, they would almost always answer in the negative. As mentioned before, roughly 80 per cent of the issues players have to deal with are off-field and/or related to the team environment, but they don't feel comfortable talking to their coach about these 'noises' deafening them in their working environment. I tried to help the players identify and silence the noises that were within our control, but I couldn't change the environment in which they had to perform.

Except for Gary Kirsten and one or two others, very few of the players I 'mentally coached' had an 'aha moment' during our conversations that would change them on a fundamental level. But something was working. People started categorising me as a mental conditioning coach. Slowly but surely, this opened the door into cricket for me. And through cricket, doors into other sports were opened. It was, however, 'safe' to use me in that limited capacity where I couldn't really rock the boat. In cricket's eyes, I was still a 200-metre athlete or a useful member of the 4x100-metre relay team. Gary invited me to India in the mental conditioning and strategic leadership roles, to which we added another 100 metres, the fitness role.

All the while, I knew much of the stuff that I was doing would eventually become the responsibility of the head coach, who would have to create and sustain a team culture where the environment served as the mental conditioner. It was obvious that the motivation would have to come from the leaders, often the head coach or some combination of coach, captain and/or senior players, depending on where the power and influence lay. Alongside mental distractions arising in athletes' personal lives and within the team culture, the two biggest on-field obstacles to success are the fear of failure and pressure. Senior leaders would have to work to eliminate these, more so than the mental conditioner or team psychologist. It is the team leadership's responsibility to create an environment that is largely free of obstacles and where performance flows freely.

When Gary was asked to coach the Indian team, he had asked me to come along 'to do for the Indian players what you did for us'. During the early part of our time in India, I did a lot of one-on-one sessions with the players, as I had done in South Africa, but for the first time, it was with the full support and sanction of the head coach.

The one-on-one sessions were at the players' request, but the more Gary and I worked on the team culture, the less the players asked for these sessions. In fact, most of my one-on-one sessions were with Gary, discussing how best to create the kind of team environment we believed would deliver maximum learning, growth and, ultimately, performance. The culture we tried to create was one where the environment could serve as the 'mental conditioner', and the more purposefully we dealt with impeding factors, the less influential they were in our environment.

During this time, Rahul Dravid was the first person to regard the so-called 'mental work' I did with the players as arrows that belonged in a head coach's quiver. It was he who first appreciated my unorthodox style as appropriate for the '400-metre athlete' that I was to become. When the Rajasthan Royals needed a head coach in 2012, it was Rahul who called me up and said, 'Run, Forrest, run!'

Looking back, I was right about the changes in the leadership (and coaching landscape), but very wrong about the predicted timelines that I had presented to Cricket South Africa in 2003. The concept of 'athlete-centred coaching' is fairly well-known in most sports and countries today, with a Google search of 'player- or athlete-centred coaching' bringing up over 385,000 hits in 2018. In 2003, there would have been less than 50.

In January 2018, I ran a coaching masterclass for twenty-five coaches of junior representative cricket teams in Australia. When I asked who had heard the term 'player-centered coaching', not one hand went up in the room. This is probably an extreme example of coaches not being up-to-date, but still, I'd say more team sport coaches have not undertaken the shift than have. Because of this slowness to update their coaching software to a modern-day knowledge-era coaching approach, they left a lane open for me on that 400-metre track.

At the time of writing, I have been a T20 head coach for twelve tournaments, spanning five teams across three leagues: the Indian Premier League, the Australian Big Bash League and the Pakistan Super League. I am more convinced than ever before that 'mental conditioning' is not a vacancy that needs to be filled by an individual on your management staff. Mental conditioning is a result of an authentic, athlete-centred approach to leadership where the head coach does everything in his or her power to create an environment that frees up athletes to learn and grow, both as people and as athletes, and be given the responsibility required for them to perform to their fullest potential. It's about serving the player's development needs more than serving the coach's agenda.

Sure, at times players could do with some mental conditioning with an expert in the field, but it should ideally be to take their game to the next level, to break new ground or create new levels of consistency, rather than to try and reconcile problems within the environment so that they can merely get back to feeling okay and normal. As mental coach, I ended up doing far too much of this problem-fixing work with professional athletes.

In fact, I'd go so far as to say that many teams and their corresponding performances might benefit more from coaches receiving good leadership support, than from players receiving mental skills coaching. Both, however, would be ideal.

Part 3

LIFE IS BUT A JOURNEY

21

HARNESSING COLLECTIVE INTELLIGENCE

'So, I understand you're not really a cricket coach' is not on the list of the most desirable remarks to hear when being interviewed for the position of head coach of an elite cricket side. Well, I ticked that box, back in 2012.

Rahul Dravid had asked me to put my name in the hat to coach the Rajasthan Royals (RR) in the IPL. Just like Gary in India three years prior, I had no experience of coaching a cricket team. That remark—or concern perhaps—from Sir Clive Woodward, who was on the panel that interviewed me, was justified. Especially if one considers the shape of the Royals at the time.

After winning the inaugural tournament in 2008, Rajasthan had ended up near the bottom of the league from 2009 to 2012. Also, the owners gave the management, with Rahul as captain, a little over 50 per cent of the salary budget allowed by the IPL for players. Forced to employ a very smart auction strategy to get emerging stars, Rajasthan ended up with the youngest, cheapest team of underdogs. They were the least capped side and had the least number of superstars. They seemingly reserved the right to occupy the bottom part of the table. Incidentally, this salary restriction did lead to Rahul, team director Zubin Bharucha and their team of analysts becoming some of the smartest talent scouts and list managers in the game.

And there I was, being interviewed for the vacant position of salvage master.

'Yes, you're right, Sir Clive. I'm not really a cricket coach,' I replied.

'So tell me,' he continued, 'you're probably going to get a batting coach, a bowling coach, and maybe a fielding coach to bring in the expertise that *you* don't bring to the team. I'm just interested in how you see that dynamic working, if you're going to be the head coach, but you're going to bring in people who are senior to you in the coaching world? How are you going to manage that?'

'Well, there won't be a problem,' I said. 'If you give me the job, I want no batting coach, no bowling coach, no fielding coach, and no fitness trainer. I want no experts on the staff.'

Silence.

Perplexed, somebody on the interview panel, I don't recall who, asked: 'What ... what do you mean?'

Sir Clive had coached the England rugby team to glory in the 2003 Rugby World Cup, and before being appointed as director of elite performance for the British Olympic Association in 2006, he had coached the British and Irish Lions rugby team when they toured New Zealand in 2005. Sir Clive had then famously picked forty-four players and twenty-eight support staff that included an ex-referee, ten coaches, a legal advisor and a head of media relations. 'I want no experts on my staff' wasn't exactly what he, or most people, expected to hear from an interviewee who himself had never coached an elite side before.

'Well,' I said, 'you are going to give me twenty-five players from five different countries who have played under about twenty different coaches and twenty different captains in this year alone, each with their own ideas of how to play T20 cricket. Collectively, the players will have over a thousand matches in experience. And *that* is the expertise I'm going to use to build the campaign.'

I contend that in the current knowledge era, a team of athletes in sport (or employees in a business) collectively will possess more intelligence than any two or three 'experienced' coaches (or business executives) combined. The challenge and the *art* of leadership is for these leaders to unearth, employ and maximise the extent of the intelligence that sits within that group.

I have often joked that I was appointed only because of the impression I made on Rajasthan's chief bean counter—my philosophy of no additional coaches or expert consultants was totally in keeping with their budgetary constraints. In all honesty, though, I owe a tremendous gratitude to Rahul Dravid; not only in this instance, but also when Zubin Bharucha, Panish Shetty and I later joined him at the Delhi Daredevils.

As I write this, I can't help marvelling at the synchronicity of, and feeling the gratitude for, starting out this 'coaching' chapter of my life working first with Gary Kirsten, then Rahul Dravid. The very words I've used to describe Gary as a cricketer and a person could be copy-pasted to describe 'The Wall'. The humble and unassuming Rahul was in India what Gary was in South Africa—with half a billion more fans.

Many would say the Australian version of these two is probably Mike Hussey, a man of sound character and much-loved individual fondly known as Mr Cricket for how he did everything right, on and off the field. You guessed it, I went on to be head coach of the Australian Big Bash League team, Sydney Thunder, working closely with Mike for four years while he was captain and then list manager. It's been a gift and a privilege to have worked with these consummate professionals, from whom I've acquired lifetimes of knowledge. They're all ordinary men (we all start out that way) who are as deliberate about their cricket professionalism as they are about living a life of sound values and moral fibre. In this way, they are great teachers and role models to me (and millions of others), although none of them would see themselves like that.

In my three years with the Indian cricket team, Rahul and I had grown to understand each other's thinking, and I appreciated his acknowledgement of the work he saw I was doing behind the scenes, especially with Gary. When Rajasthan was looking for someone to facilitate the team and create a cohesive team environment, Rahul dialled my number. He convinced the owners to put me on a shortlist of four coaches, three of them with previous experience, and from there, it was up to me. He believed that between him, Shane Watson, Zubin, Panish and the team, they already had the cricketing expertise. My approach of creating an empowering team culture and harnessing a group's collective intelligence was to complement that.

We've probably all heard the overly evangelised corporate mantra: 'Don't bring me problems. Bring me solutions.' In his book *Originals*, Wharton Professor of Psychology Adam Grant questions this approach:

> (David) Hofmann is one of the world's prominent authorities on creating organisational cultures that detect, correct, and prevent errors. After the space shuttle *Columbia* exploded upon entry into the atmosphere in 2003, Hofmann's research was instrumental in assessing and documenting improvements in NASA's safety culture. ... Hofmann found that a culture that focuses too heavily on solutions becomes a culture of advocacy, dampening inquiry. If you're always expected to have an answer ready, you'll arrive at meetings with your diagnoses complete, missing out on the chance to learn from a broad range of perspectives.[1]

Grant contrasts this with a jury at (an American) courtroom trial, where all twelve members get to hear the entire case and then all engage in the same debate—whether the defendant is innocent or guilty. Hoffmann goes on to say that '... organisational life doesn't work like a courtroom. It is more like sitting through a twelve-hour trial where each juror hears only one hour of testimony, and no two jurors listen to the same hour. When every member of a group has different information, inquiry needs to precede advocacy—which means you have to raise problems before pursuing solutions. To make sure problems get raised, leaders need mechanisms for unearthing dissenters.'

No one person can ever be expected to have all the answers. In an instruction-based environment, the coach is assumed to be the expert, the task of finding solutions is centralised in him or his team of analysts, and the intellectual power of the playing group is neither valued nor extracted. Even on the other side of the spectrum—abdication—a similar locking out of collective intelligence can happen when individuals are encouraged to enter team meetings with ready-made answers invented in isolation, rather than with an open and inquisitive mind. Inquiry, not solutions, is the key to *real* coaching, and not only because it brings to the fore a wealth of knowledge, but because it empowers individuals, which, in turn, strengthens the side.

It stimulates individuals to think, to challenge personal assumptions, and to broaden their horizons of possibilities in an environment where it is okay to say, 'I don't know, but I'm really interested to hear what your thinking is.'

As with the Indian national team under Gary, this was also our belief at the Royals. Rules (and consequences for breaking them), dress codes, pre- and post-match meetings, and what happened at practice or training were all decided via player inputs. We formed a 'brains-trust' comprising key senior players, and at least one player of mid-level experience and one junior player who showed an interest in leadership. This group would be involved in key strategic decision-making, including how we would run selection meetings. The entire team discussed in detail how we would react to teammates who made mistakes, as well as how we wanted to conduct ourselves after losing and winning games. Our responses needed to reflect the true nature of the team we wanted to be and the culture we hoped to uphold, which we made explicit at the beginning of the season.

Players were asked to carefully consider whether they wanted to be the type of person who verbally abuses opponents to unsettle them, or not. Bowlers were asked, when under pressure, maybe after being hit for consecutive boundaries, what they wanted from the captain and fielders who were in close proximity to them. It was fascinating to hear which players wanted clear instructions from the captain, who wanted just a word of encouragement, and who wanted to be left alone unless they actually called for advice. There were senior campaigners with over a decade of experience of playing for their country who preferred instruction, and uncapped nineteen-year-olds who wanted to be left alone to make their own decisions.

We did the same with batsmen, asking them to share with teammates what they wanted when the pressure was on. What emerged from these conversations with both batsmen and bowlers was that, under pressure, 1) it is not possible to accurately predict what different players want, and 2) if you use an approach that they don't want, it actually adds pressure. If you want to know what someone wants, ask them!

When someone made an on-field mistake, especially when fielding, players wanted support and encouragement, and to not be shouted at or have others make any negative gestures, like head-shaking, arm-waving or the like. Everyone agreed to this. We would be humble in victory and balanced in our response to loss, and would follow the same post-match routines, like having music in the dressing room, regardless of the result.

We acknowledged that some players were likely to (unconsciously) err on discipline or agreed behaviours at some stage of the tournament, even if only marginally, which would most likely happen when he was under pressure or stress. I posed the question: 'Is there anyone here who feels that he would deliberately choose to break our team guidelines or ethos?' No hands went up. Next I asked, 'Do any of you think that, especially if you find yourself under pressure, maybe after a string of poor results, a fight with your girlfriend/wife, or if you don't get selected when you think you should be, that you might find yourself behaving in a way that goes against what we have just discussed?' Almost every hand in the room (slowly) went up. Finally, the most important question was, 'If this happens to be you, what would you like from your teammates and/or coaching staff? How do you want us to deal with this situation?'

Interestingly, having done this exercise with more than a handful of teams, nobody has yet said they wanted to be reprimanded or punished. Players from all countries, of all ages and all levels of experience, almost always wanted the same two things.

Firstly, they wanted to be reminded of what had been agreed to, and have it pointed out that their behaviour was in divergence. And secondly, they wanted the person who approached them with this feedback to check in with them and ask how they were doing. If they were behaving differently, which would not be a conscious choice, they probably needed some form of support. What was often mentioned was that they would prefer this approach to be made by their closest friend, someone in the team who they hoped would have their back. When this was first mentioned, I immediately asked players to move to sit next to the person who they felt knew them the best, and asked them to have a conversation about how they could support each other over the season, especially in the tough times. Since then, I regularly employ a buddy-coaching system in teams, with friends supporting or peer-coaching each other; strangers get to do the same, and thus get to know each other better.

Another exercise I do at the beginning of a season is to ask players to write down their own personal goals—everything they want to achieve for themselves. The exercise is totally confidential, and players are encouraged to be fully self-focused. I don't agree with the adage 'there is no I in team'. A team consists of a bunch of individuals—I's—who each need to pull their own weight, in the same direction the team is headed.

Next, I ask them to write down what the team wants from them in each of their roles, as batsman and/or bowler, fielder and teammate.

Even though many teams preach a 'team first' attitude and maintain that the team is more important than the individual, it's not realistic to expect people to subjugate themselves for the group, at least not all the time. Individual needs and team needs should both be considered, mainly because that's how it comes naturally to most people anyway.

The players were encouraged to compare these two lists and actively pursue those areas where the two were aligned: their own needs and what the team required of them. There would always be areas of conflicting needs. Such as when a batsman wants to score X number of runs in the season, but the team wants them to play attacking cricket and thus potentially sacrifice their wicket; or where a bowler wants to take wickets and thus to bowl attackingly when the team needs them to defend, or in sports like football, rugby or hockey, where a player wants to score X number of goals in the season, but the team needs them to pass the ball to someone who might be in a better position to score.

In these instances, I'd ask players to consider what decision they would ideally want to make when the conflict arose. In doing so, players were asked to project to the end of the season or even the end of their career, to look back from that vantage point and ask, 'What decision would I most want to have taken? What is the best advice I can give myself?' This helps them recognise that whatever decision they make, whether it's to serve themselves or serve the team, will have consequences.

Personally, I don't instruct people on what decision to make, but encourage them to make the smartest one; one that has the most positive long-term consequences. Most people will make their own decision anyway, but this exercise brings the selfish option into the light of awareness.

These are just some examples of how we harnessed collective intelligence at the Royals, and which I would continue expanding upon with each new team I coached. These, and other approaches to fast track team bonding and co-create team culture and team strategy, are vital in 'temporary teams' of this nature and that only exists for six to eight weeks of the year, and is increasingly the case in todays' business context. I share them not so much to tell you what we did, but hopefully to spark ideas about what you could possibly do in your environment and context.

The virtue of this philosophy is beautifully illustrated by the growth of our youngest and oldest players on the squad: Sanju Samson (eighteen at the time) and Pravin Tambe (forty-one).

COMETH THE STEYN REMOVER, COMETH THE TEENAGER

In 2013, when asked what the Royals stood for, Zubin Bharucha, our team director, said: 'At the Royals, we've always believed, from the start, that it is about the youngsters. It is all about the promotion of Indian youngsters. Sanju is without a doubt the most exciting youngster in the IPL this season.' Raghu Iyer, CEO of the Royals, mirrored this sentiment. 'Rahul (Dravid) just had to look at him (Samson) once in the net, and knew we had to sign him.'

Sanju is a wicketkeeper batsman from Thiruvananthapuram, Kerala. Rahul knew that by signing him, and others like him, to create a young, unknown team, we'd have to go the extra mile to get the best out of each one, for they would be in a position they'd never been in before—the 'Big Leagues'.

I knew just enough about India to know that in every IPL team, there are a small number of superstars. There is a longer list of youngsters or less experienced players who have to be in the playing XI. I also knew that those young players, especially in India and especially a few years back, were more likely to withdraw than flourish in the shadow of the senior players. Most times, these youngsters were (or would adopt a position of being) quiet, shy, withdrawn and over-awed, and the would-be outspoken ones knew it wasn't their place to speak while they were still 'juniors'. I knew they wouldn't talk much. Junior Indian players generally do not talk in team meetings, although this is slowly changing.

Getting these younger players to feel comfortable and able to express themselves, both on and off the field, and to feel that they were genuinely important and valued cogs in the team was one way for us to gain a competitive advantage over other teams. We had more youngsters than most, so it was something of an imperative. (I believe this as an advantage still available to most teams today, in sport and in business.)

We decided that we would not have a video analyst studying the opposition and presenting the analysis in a pre-game meeting. (The players had the opportunity to engage our analyst on an individual basis and in their own time). Instead, the opponents' names would be written up on a board and we would sit as a team and talk about them—and everyone was invited to talk. When discussing a young Indian player from Mumbai who was going to play against us, we knew for example that another young Mumbai-based player in our team would have played against him, year in and year out, since their under-13 days. This young player, who hadn't even played a game for us, knew that player way better than Rahul Dravid, Shane Watson and I did. He knew him better than the video analyst did. So this player would be regarded as the expert in the team at that moment. (At school sport level, it's likely in almost every instance that players know their opponents better than any of their coaches do, by virtue of playing against them through the different age groups.)

The team and I let him know that, there and then, he was the most important person in the room. 'You know more about this player that any one of us do. Share with us what you know.' And once he'd done sharing, I would remind him that when that player came out to bat and the team came together in a huddle, he should run drinks onto the field and remind captain Rahul of this information. It was going to be busy and crazy at that moment, so he'd have to remind the rest of us what we needed to know about the new batsman.

We got young players talking, acknowledging the really valuable intellectual contributions they had to make. Our aim was to integrate these youngsters into our team better than other IPL teams may be doing with theirs. One of the other ways in which we accomplished this was to get different players to lead the team talk immediately before going out to field. I would always start with one of the younger players, and make sure that everyone got a chance over the season. This also provided us with a few funny moments. When the fielding team comes together in the usual pre-innings huddle, the TV director would have dangling 'spider cams' swooping down the field, zooming in on the captain talking. The camera would zoom in on Rahul standing with his mouth shut, listening, while someone other than our captain was actually leading the conversation; sometimes it was an unknown teenager from Kerala, one of the few Indian states where cricket is not the most popular sport.

Another benefit of this culture is that thinking players become confident players in an environment where their contributions—both asking and sharing—are valued. Sanju was promoted to number 3 in only his second match for RR, playing against Royal Challengers Bangalore (RCB). We had to chase down 172, and in doing so, Sanju became the youngest player in IPL history to score a half century, smashing 64 off 41 balls. He was later named the most promising player in the IPL of 2013. However, one of my fondest memories of him comes from the season after that, against Sunrisers Hyderabad.

We had an 8 p.m. start on a fast bouncy wicket that swung quite a bit, especially at night. And Sunrisers had a certain Dale Steyn in their bowling attack. At the time, he was the world's number one bowler. We knew they were going to give Dale at least two overs up front, with another over or two at the end of the innings. Our main batsmen were Shane Watson and Ajinkye Rahane, and we didn't want both of them to be exposed to twelve of Steyn's devastating out-swingers on that pitch so early in the innings. Rahane and Karun Nair opened the batting for us, and whoever came in at three had to be stable, but also somewhat expendable; someone who could survive Dale if we lost a wicket in the South African's first spell with the ball, saving Watson to attack the rest of the bowling. Enter Sanju Samson, who had lost his wicket to Dale twice in the previous season. On this occasion, my direct words to him were to 'survive Dale Steyn' if a duel should ensue.

At the change of innings, as the Royals were preparing to chase down the Sunrisers' score of 134 for 9 on a very lively wicket, I realised that I had never spoken to Sanju about his strategy against Dale. I generally don't speak to players about their strategy shortly before they go in to bat, but this was an unusual situation since I wasn't sure whether we should expose the nineteen-year-old to this kind of pressure. Well, that's what I thought.

I went to him with a clear idea in my head of what was required. 'Surviving Dale' would mean playing with a defensive mindset, ideally by standing deep in the crease, giving himself as much time as possible to see the ball, and then looking to play off the front-foot, and to either defend or leave the full-outswingers that Dale would predictably bowl. As usual, I approached Sanju with a question, hoping he would share my thinking. 'If you get in early, what's your strategy against Dale?'

His response stumped me. He first assured me, 'Don't worry coach, I've got this one.' I couldn't help but respond with a smile (I'd already developed a very good relationship with Sanju). He continued, 'I know he is a great bowler, but I also know he is going to pitch the ball full against me and try to swing me out. Everybody knows Steyn pitches it full. He will have his mid-on and mid-off up. So, I think if I stand this far (indicating about fifty centimetres with his hands) outside of my crease, I can counter Dale's swing, get him on the half volley, and hit him back over his head. If I hit him for 6, he may well bounce me with the next ball, in which case I'll pull or hook him for another boundary.' Taken aback, I thought a silent and rather drawn out, 'O ... kay'.

Sanju, at the time, was one of the few under-19 Indians I had seen who could play the fast short-pitched ball really well. In our discussions as a team, we always spoke about not worrying about failing, but rather to focus on setting oneself up for the best chance to succeed and then going for it. For Sanju, the shot back over Dale's head and the hook shot were obvious counter strategies. And there I was, about to ask him to play defensive, although our theme for that season was 'Smart and Attacking'. I never gave Sanju my advice, but he did preach my own teaching right back to me that night. The environment we had created shaped him to chase success even under enormous pressure.

Sure enough, Rahane lost his wicket to Bhuvneshwar Kumar on the third ball of the innings. In came Sanju, with Dale to open his spell in the second over. Both bowler and batsman attacked each other, with Dale drawing first blood by beating Sanju's outside edge with one of his trademark devastating out-swingers, before Sanju reciprocated by hitting the very next delivery for 4 over mid-wicket.

Dale was about to start his second over of the innings. Sanju was facing, and as Dale started his run-up, Sanju moved to about half a metre outside of his crease. I looked at Dravid. I looked at Watson. We smiled. We all knew what was coming. Dale pitched the ball full and straight at a recorded 146.6 kilometres per hour. With a steely look in his eyes and a commanding presence, Sanju hit him straight back over his head for a 6 of 78 metres. He ended up scoring just 16, and Sunrisers won the match by 32 runs. But on that night, we celebrated a young man who had no fear of failure and the courage to attack the best in the game. He would go on to become the youngest player to score 1,000 runs in the IPL.

'WHAT WAS DRAVID THINKING?'

It was shortly after sunrise in Mumbai when Pravin Tambe, affectionately known as PT, arrived at the Maidan, the cradle of Indian cricket. This was where he had learned his craft. But with his lifelong dream of representing Mumbai in a first-class match realistically beyond his reach, this forty-year-old leg-spin-bowler now coached at a local academy in the mornings before leaving for his day job, where he had to be in at 10 a.m.

PT grew up playing for the Parsee Cyclists Sports Club, founded in 1905 and now housed in one of many similar military-style tents pitched all over the Maidan. These are clubhouses, dressing rooms, and whatever they need to be for the hundreds of children who spend their days there, playing 'leather ball'. The pitches are as flat as they get, which explains why Mumbai produces so many 'wristy batsmen', as Tambe calls them. As a child, he dreamt of becoming a fast bowler, but these pitches would have none of it. He became a useful leg-spinner, but never proved to be much more than a hindrance for reasonably skilled batsmen. Nevertheless, he was unlucky to have missed out on the opportunity to play at least some first-class cricket.

As early preparations and planning for the 2013 IPL season began, PT got a final shot at making it to the big leagues. Rahul, Zubin and coach-cum-talent-scout Monty Desai decided to hold one or two trials for potential players. Their player budget was painfully minute, but India has never had a lack of talented cricketers who would leap at any opportunity to play representative cricket. Monty brought PT with him, and they immediately liked his variation and control. Also, he had more than twenty years' experience, which could prove vital on and off the pitch for a team building its identity around youngsters. As an unknown, uncapped player, he would also come cheap. He was affordable, the franchise had nothing to lose, and there was some talent to work with. So Rahul signed him for the IPL.

I remember arriving in India and reading a newspaper headline in Jaipur: 'What was Dravid thinking?'. He has signed on a semi-skilled, forty-one-year-old leg-spinner over some of India's most promising young players. We would play him in just one match during the IPL, in Mumbai, in front of his home crowd. PT went for 38 in his 4 overs, and it was there for everyone to see why we didn't pick him again. He was good in the nets, but better players got hold of him, so it was a risk playing him.

Even though we narrowly lost that match in the Wankhede Stadium against the Mumbai Indians, we had already qualified for the play-off rounds beforehand; a massive step forward for the IPL's perennial wooden-spooners. As a team, we felt that we hadn't really lost a game that season. Yes, we had been outplayed at times, but in none of our losses did we back down from the fight or hand the victory to our opponents.

The Mumbai defeat was, however, the beginning of one of the most difficult phases in my life as a coach, although it ended up strengthening my belief in a system of shared ownership and the importance of maintaining that culture.

We woke up the following morning with three of our players having been arrested for spot-fixing: S. Sreesanth, Ajit Chandila and Ankeet Chavan. We were meant to be a dream team playing for the same cause, fighting together. And all of that was shattered in a moment. The players were arrested in their hotel rooms shortly after 4 a.m.; Chandila and Chavan from the team hotel, and Sreesanth from a nearby hotel. The reason for this—a little-known fact—is that twenty-four hours earlier, Sreesanth had been sacked from the

Royals squad and sent home for poor behaviour. He was one of two players who were (non-publicly) sacked mid-tournament from one of the T20 teams I coached. A player-centred and empowering environment does not mean a wishy-washy one without discipline and clear boundaries. It's just that they are set in consultation and full agreement with players. Neither of the sacked players was surprised, nor resisted being sent home; they knew they deserved it.

The reason for Sreesanth's repeated poor behaviour, which amongst other things included blurting out in front of the team that Rahul Dravid and I could go and f...k ourselves in response for dropping him, now made sense. In Mumbai, as had seemingly happened previously that season, we had left him out of a game where alternative arrangements were in place for his performance. We had also dropped Chandila for that Mumbai game, and so these two apparently needed to enroll a third person to meet their fixing arrangements. That someone was Ankeet.

I remember how tough the arrests were on PT. He had made his IPL debut the night before and woke up to the news that one of his dearest teammates, Ankeet, had been arrested for cheating. There is something almost childlike and naïve, yet beautifully pure, about the way PT carries his soul. The ultimate team player, upbeat, ever-learning ... and then, broken after learning of a friend's brokenness. 'I played with Ankeet in club matches,' he said in an interview. 'When I signed with Rajasthan Royals, I grew very fond of him in the four or five weeks we were together. When we were off the field, we were together. I am shocked. If he was in trouble, he never said a word to me. I wanted to cry when I heard this. We were bonded together like brothers.' PT was unsuccessfully fighting back tears, almost blaming himself for not becoming intuitively aware of Ankeet's impending tribulations.

We went through a period of deep soul-searching that included rediscovering the joys and laughter that had bonded us together as a team before our squad was involuntarily reduced by three people. With a broken team and just three days out from the elimination play-offs, we sent our cricket kits to Delhi, but as a team we went in the other direction—heading to a private hotel just outside Jaipur in Rajasthan. On the first day there, I facilitated conversations about how the players really felt about the match-fixing and our three teammates currently in jail. Some foreign players wanted to go home there and then for fear that they might end up in an Indian jail, thanks to some careless and unfounded comments on social media. For example, a rumour was posted on Twitter about large sums of money having been discovered in Australian fast bowler Shaun Tait's hotel room, which was totally untrue but scared the shit out of him, and others. It was fascinating to see how different people responded under this type of pressure, which was way more consequential than losing a game or getting out for a duck.

Players were asked, encouraged and even pushed to speak about what they were feeling, to get it all out without any restrictions or fear of being judged. This took some time, as the common and hardwired practice, particularly in male sporting environments, is to put on the tough-guy, cowboys-don't-cry mask of stoicism and pretend that everything is, or will be, okay. They did begin to speak up, though, after initial hesitation. One by one, they opened up and articulated their feelings, which ranged from frustration, anger and disappointment to fear, and some tears. They were courageous in their honesty and vulnerability, and in this they were led by two people in particular.

One was Rahul Dravid, who is sufficiently secure within himself as a person to speak his mind openly, even in front of younger Indian players, who tend to idolise him. Any show of vulnerability by a leader is a sign of security and strength, which Rahul has no shortage of. The other was Shane Watson, who, for a period of time, was vilified in the Australian media for not being a team man. Having worked with Shane for six seasons, this continues to amaze me.

The thing that people don't see about Shane from the stadium seats, or on their couch watching or reading about this fierce competitor on the field, is that he is a sensitive, caring, thoughtful person, who is an amazing team man thanks to these nurturing qualities. He does not fit the mould of the tough beer-swilling Aussie bloke. Sure, in his younger days, Shane needed a fight to get the best out of himself and so often picked confrontations with opponents. He still needs that fight, but he has realised and openly acknowledges that he doesn't want to be the kind of person who picks fights for his own benefit; he has more respect for himself and his opponents and so finds better ways today. In the difficult time the team found itself in, his caring and sensitivity towards what his teammates were going through, and his openness in sharing his own concerns in that situation, helped illuminate a dark space. Rahul's and Shane's courage and honesty gave others permission to be honest themselves. If these two had acted tough, what chance do you think there would have been for any other players opening up?

The following morning, I set about arranging a full day of wacky and fun activities. I broke up the team into groups of about six and had them make five-minute movie trailers, film funny fashion shoots with clothes from the hotel souvenir store, build human pyramids in the swimming pool, have spoof bodybuilding contests, make music, and just having good old-fashioned fun with plenty of laughter. That evening we had a fancy dress dinner and awards evening where each team got to show off their movies, fashion shoots, and various other activities from the day. The previous day's tears of anguish and fear transformed into tears of laughter, in abundance!

When we flew into Delhi the day before the play-offs, despite having not picked up a cricket bat for two days, we were ready. Brad Hodge made a promise to Pravin Tambe that he'd bat us into the semi-finals, even if it was the last thing he ever did. Coming in at seven, he did just that against the Sunrisers in the Elimination Final, scoring 54 (5 sixes, 2 fours) off 29 balls. We went on to lose the semi-final to Mumbai (the eventual IPL champions) on the second-last ball of the game, but Shane Watson was named the IPL's Most Valuable Player, and by competing in the semis, we qualified for the Champions League later that year in India.

And that is when Pravin Tambe flowered, in an environment where the harnessing of collective intelligence became one of the team's biggest competitive advantages.

CRICKET BALLS ARE EXPENSIVE

The Champions League, played between the top domestic teams from each of the major cricket-playing nations, required of us to cut our squad down from twenty-five to fifteen players. As we went through the names during selection, we realised we didn't have a primary spinner; our two main spinners were in jail. All our round robin games would be at home, and in 2013, the Jaipur wicket was hard, bouncy, and didn't turn at all, so we could probably get by without a spinner in the CL squad. Hypothetically, if we reached the play-offs, we might need one in places like Delhi. But as the underdogs (again), we had to be realistic, especially given the constraints we had on the size of our squad. But in the end, we decided to pick Pravin. It was unlikely he would play a game, but we agreed he would give our batsmen good practice playing spin in the nets.

The squad came together with only six days to prepare for the first match in the League. I knew nothing about leg-spin, and we didn't have a leg-spin or even a spin coach for that matter. But one thing about Pravin could prove really useful: He's a very modest guy.

We trained in Jaipur, where the facilities were fantastic. Except for one thing. There was a quadrangle of buildings just beyond the boundary, and in the middle of that quadrangle was a derelict swimming pool with rainwater, about knee high. While batting in the nets, any 6 hit in that direction would have the ball ricochet off one of the walls, into the swimming pool, and it would be ruined.

I recalled that during IPL practice, Pravin would get quite upset about being hit into the pool, because a ball is valuable, at the time costing about Rs 7,500 or US$110. That gave me an idea. I went to him during our first training session and told him, 'PT, for the next six days, you are mainly going to bowl to our five most destructive batsmen: Watson, Hodge, Faulkner, Binny and Rahane. I'm going to tell them to hit you into the swimming pool with every single ball that you bowl. But, PT, please, do us a favour. Those balls are expensive—do your best not to get hit into the pool.' I felt almost guilty of cruelty when PT responded with a timid and almost nervous, 'Okay sir, I'll try my best.' (No matter how many times I ask him to call me Paddy, five years later he still calls me 'sir'. He's just too respectful not to.)

I then asked the batsmen to attack every ball that PT bowled, and to hit him into the pool. The convention with net practice is that the new batsman replaces the previous one, and the bowler just keeps bowling. This was going to be slightly different. Each time one of the batsmen came out of the nets, I asked him to immediately go and have a conversation with PT about what balls were easy to hit, and more importantly, what balls were difficult to hit. They spoke about speed, the length and line of his leg-spin, googlies, top-spin and flippers, as well about using the width of the bowling crease from where he released the ball. They had been asked to be very specific in their feedback to him.

From about half-way through the second practice, at least one of those five guys was standing next to and talking to Pravin all the time. Brad Hodge was particularly good with taking PT under his wing. By the time we came to select the team for the second game, Shane Watson said, 'You know what? I can't hit PT out of the net anymore. He's figured out how to keep batsmen quiet. I think we should pick him.'

This in a Champions League game, on a Jaipur wicket that had plenty of grass for fast bowlers but would offer no turn at all for spinners. Rahane and Hodge were in that selection meeting, and echoed Watson's sentiments; they couldn't hit him either. So, we picked him, the forty-one-year-old, 'over-the-hill', part-time leg-spinner, whose only appearance in the cricket media to date was under the headline: 'What was Dravid thinking?' I must admit that I was more than a little concerned that we were setting him up for failure, especially as the wicket would not offer any assistance and he would be bowling to some of the best T20 batsmen in the world.

We picked him again for the third match, and the fourth, and after winning all our four round robin games, we picked him for the semi-final, and for the final. He got Man of the Match in two of the five games he played, taking 12 wickets in 119 balls against the best batsmen in the world. Of those 119 balls, over half of which were on a wicket that did not turn at all, he was hit for only three 4s and no 6s. He received a nomination for Player of the Tournament, and he won the Golden Wicket award for the highest wicket-taker. He also had the best tournament average runs per wickets taken (Ave), best strike rate (SR), and best runs per over economy (Econ). Here is a list of the top five bowlers at the 2013 Champions League, and below that, our bowling stats from the final, where all our bowlers went for more than ten to the over, except for PT.

Pravin Tambe was an ordinary performer who, in seven days, was built into a champion by his peers. That is what I mean by harnessing

Player	Team	Wkts	Inns	Ave	SR	Econ	BBI	4WI
Pravin Tambe	Rajasthan Royals	12	5	6.50	9.50	4.10	4/15	1
Sunil Narine	Trinidad and Tobago	11	5	7.81	10.90	4.30	4/9	1
Ian Butler	Otago	8	5	19.37	13.6	8.53	3/21	0
Dwayne Bravo	Chennai Super Kings	7	5	17.42	13.0	8.04	3/26	0
Marchant de Lange	Titans	7	4	18.14	12.85	8.46	3/13	0

Player	Overs	Runs	Wkts	Econ
Faulkner	4	46	1	11.50
Watson	3	30	1	10.00
Shukla	4	49	1	12.25
Cooper	4	40	1	10.00
Tambe	4	19	2	4.75
Binny	1	16	0	16.00

the collective intelligence of the group. I'm not dissing the value of expertise, but I am arguing that traditional coaching methods do not necessarily mine the spaces where much of the expertise in a team resides.

Harnessing the collective intelligence of a team is not just a strategic imperative for teams that want to play smartly and develop thinking players. I have also found it to be a path towards lasting contentment and better results in cricket, business and life.

In our pre-game talks, the Australians in the team explained how to bowl to or bat against fellow Australian teammates playing in opposing IPL teams. The South Africans would compare some of their country's strategies and tactics with those of Indians, New Zealanders, Australians and Bangladeshis. Players freely shared their secrets, sometimes teaching an IPL teammate how to add a switch-hit or slower ball leg-break to their game. Compatriots today, they would be fierce competitors on the international stage tomorrow. And that's beautiful.

One fascinating example of this is from the time when I was coaching Sydney Thunder in the 2015-16 Big Bash League. Australian all-rounder Shane Watson had been struggling with form to the extent that he had retired from Test cricket earlier that year, and by the time he arrived at the Big Bash, he had been dropped from the Australian ODI and T20 teams. The runs seemed to have dried up and his international career was being written off. At one of the first net sessions, whilst he was batting, South African all-rounder Jacques Kallis came to me and said he had been watching Shane bat in international games for some time now, and that he thought he knew both what his problem was, and how to help him fix it. His question to me was how he felt Shane might react to this, given that the two of them had been arch rivals on the international stage, with both bat and ball, for well over a decade. Knowing both players well, I encouraged Jacques to speak directly to Shane.

Twenty minutes and a short conversation later, Jacques Kallis was throwing balls to long-time rival Shane Watson in the nets, coaching him around a specific aspect of his balance and stance. This continued for the next few weeks. The result was that Shane regained his form of old, helped Sydney Thunder win their first Big Bash title in that same season, and went on to regain his place for the T20 World Cup in April 2016. Fierce rivals for nearly thirteen years, then teammates, and this happened during a one-off seven-week season!

The game cannot but advance with such sharing of knowledge. That, and the huge number of T20 games that provide abundant opportunities for trying out new innovations, gaining experience and honing game plans; all under pressure, in front of 40,000 fans and millions of TV viewers.

Another stand-out for me has been the pleasure of witnessing the friendships formed between international cricketers. Before the advent of the IPL, these same players may have only conversed through sledging and abusing each other on the field. Today, it's commonplace to walk into the dining room during a lunch interval at a Test match and see players from opposing teams catching up over a meal. I've been in a Proteas change room where the entire Australian team joined the Proteas players to knock back more than a few beers. After a gruelling English series in 2012, the South African and English teams shared stories, a few laughs, beers and Veuve Clicquot immediately after the awards ceremony.

The popularity of the IPL with owners, sponsors, players and the public has seen sister T20 leagues sprouting in other countries. Cricket has mostly woken up to the fact that the game is no longer located in the sports industry, but in the entertainment industry, competing with PlayStation, Netflix, cinemas, concerts and festivals for bums on stadium seats, bar stools and living-room couches. Some Test nations are finding themselves competing with the lucrative T20 circuit for the loyalty of their top players. T20 cricket is not just about entertainment and money, but also innovation, excitement and camaraderie, and that's what is taking this format to new levels. And it's here to stay. Like the once-ignored PT in the 2013 Champions League, it, too, will dominate. Its ability to harness the collective intelligence and inputs of players, broadcasters, administrators, players' associations and the ICC will determine the degree to which Test cricket and ODIs become casualties in the process.

22

PERSONAL MASTERY

Stepping back more than a decade to 2004, Gary Kirsten was Cricket South Africa's high performance manager, tasked with helping prepare a group of high-potential cricketers who had been earmarked as next in line to play for the country. Gary asked me to have about five sessions with each player, working specifically on their mental game.

I asked the players to arrive at each session with the specific topic they wanted to discuss or gain clarity on. They brought questions about preparation, pressure, fear, concentration, some longer-term career goals, and how to reconcile their personal and professional lives.

One of the players would almost always bring questions about life, wanting to discuss things like spirituality, personal mastery, humility and ego, and how ego and its need for competitiveness plays out in professional sport and life. We spoke about transcending ego towards various forms of personal mastery. We didn't talk much cricket. It was his decision and I went with it.

I hadn't seen him play much, but some commentators of the game said he probably wouldn't make it as a batsman, mainly because he had a flawed technique, which apparently he was resistant to changing.

At the final session with each player, we spent time wrapping up, checking that the main topics or concerns had been addressed, and spoke about 'where to next' in their cricket careers, with clarity on what was required to get there.

This particular player arrived at the last session and said he only had one question, which was, 'If I pursue my spiritual path as the main priority in my life, do you think it will negatively impact my cricket career?'

It was a great question. I really liked this player, and I really wanted to help him. I remember searching for an answer that might add clarity and value. My answer, which I remember offering him with some disappointment in myself, was, 'I really don't know.'

He said he wasn't sure either, but was very clear that personal mastery (my term, not his) and his personal spiritual path (his term) remained a priority for him, and that he would pursue it even if it compromised his career. He would still keep working hard on his game, because he wanted to do well, but it was not a need.

The player's name is Hashim Amla. He did not change his technique; he went on to play for South Africa, and then went further to become the world's number one ranked batsman in both Test and ODI cricket. At the time of writing, he remains the fastest cricketer in history to reach 2,000, 3,000, 4,000, 5,000, 6,000 and recently, 7,000 runs in ODIs. To this day, his personal life journey remains a priority—while travelling to international matches in the team bus, he can be seen reading his spiritual texts.

Hashim makes a good case for the value of personal mastery as a vehicle that strongly underpins and drives professional mastery to greater heights of success. It has not only taken him to those heights, but sustained him there for long periods of time.

As a believer in the infinite potential of people, I must admit that few professional cricketers live their lives and manage their careers in the holisitic way Hashim does. I'd hazard a guess the same applies in other team sports, too, and in workplaces. More people are (mis) guided by the trappings of the ego, fame and celebrityhood, than not—and self-awareness may well be the only antidote to this.

IN THE SHADOWS OF THE LIMELIGHT

As global T20 tournaments move cricket further into the entertainment industry, the limelight shines more brightly on the entertainers. Cricketers are increasingly enjoying more money, glitz, glamour and exposure than ever before; a situation that seems mirrored in almost all professional sports today. It's fun and exciting, but are emerging athletic stars sufficiently prepared for what might be lurking in the shadows of this limelight?

The obvious shadows—long known to those in positions of prominence and brought to us by the media—include a pub or nightclub brawl, driving fast and/or over the alcohol limit, sexual indiscretions, dodgy business liaisons, drug abuse, excessive drinking, and match- or spot-fixing. These shadows are often trawled by (social) media vultures stooping to create or scrape up some dirt on players for whatever reason. Some high-flying celebrities feel they are above the law, invincible and somehow immortal, which provides fertile ground for such indiscretions to occur. A decade ago, many of these incidents may have been excused by an admiring policeman or traffic officer, or covered up behind a lawyer's closed door. Social media has changed that. Little happens in the public space around a celebrity that is not captured on a phone or security camera, or reported on one of the social platforms.

There are less obvious dangers lurking in the shadows, ones that slowly envelop the unaware. Like models, actors and high-flyers, sport stars are easily seduced into needing to look good, into defining themselves and their happiness by their fame, money and results. Scoring runs and taking wickets make the cricketer feel happy and self-confident. Basking in success, he may go out and socialise, and finds it easy to be nice to his partner, family, friends and fans. The sport-watching public judges him positively; people ask for his autograph, praise him in the print media and on TV; he gains likes and followers on social media; corporates and individuals sponsor his gear, grant him privileges and send him gifts. The fans' emotions are attached to the results of their hero or favourite team; each plays off the success of the other.

When these same athletes fail or hit low form, they might find themselves feeling low, to the extent that their inner contentment and sense of self-worth are attached to their results. They may feel deflated and unenthusiastic; their self-confidence takes a blow. Touring athletes are more likely to stay in their hotel room, sulking, and are more likely to be grumpy with other people. Journalists and commentators start criticising them, which sometimes leaves the critics feeling a bit better about themselves. But the fans get restless. They blame the athletes or teams for having failed in their responsibility to make their 'supporters' happy.

Often, celebrities buy into the image of fame that fans and the media create for them. They begin to see themselves as a superstar, a brand, and a celebrity, confusing being a special talent with being a special person. After all, fans and sponsors treat them as 'special' people. Gradually, they become more alienated from themselves, losing touch of who they authentically are. They begin to see themselves as superior to ordinary mortals, not only better at the skill that made them famous, but also better and more important as people. They become dependent on their popularity, and surround themselves with people who feed their inflated self-image. Needing to be with others or out in public, they struggle when they are alone, uneasy in their own company.

At the same time, they become incapable of nurturing genuine relationships. According to renowned spiritual teacher Eckhart Tolle, a relationship where there is a sense of 'me being the important one around here' can never be genuine. During the good times, friends flock. Sadly, many are 'false friends' or 'name-droppers'. According to Tolle, when these people seek out their hero, often unbeknown to themselves, they are not actually interested in the star, but rather in enhancing their own identity and sense of self-worth. They believe that through knowing a celebrity, they become more, better and complete in the eyes of others.[1]

When things are going well, these 'relationships' work for the stars as they find themselves surrounded by people who fuel their celebrity status. But in tough times, when they are struggling with injury, low form, being dropped, or retirement—times when friends are important—the celebrity may find few, if any, around. These false friends cannot have their needs met through a falling star, so they move off to nurture their associations with the next fashionable celebrity. Attached as they are to celebrityhood, the players find their loneliness deepening and when results can no longer boost their fickle self-confidence, made worse by lack of genuine friends, what follows is a deep-set alienation from their authentic self. There seems to be nowhere to turn to.

In his book *Silence of the Heart,* David Frith wrote that cricket is the sport with the highest suicide rate in the world, with South Africa being the country with the highest rate. When Frith's book was first published, one in every twenty-four of South Africa's Test cricketers who died, had died by their own hand. Additionally, cricket's divorce rate is apparently second only to Hollywood's. Underlying these facts are possibly far more widespread symptoms of unhappiness—the unseen and creeping emptiness, loneliness, depression and substance abuse that many celebrities and retired professional athletes are affected by. Anyone who is involved in high-level sport would know someone who is struggling with one or more of these.[2]

In an article on cricket suicides, a well-known English county cricketer related his experience of contemplating suicide to Michael Atherton: 'I bottled everything up; I didn't feel as though I could talk to anyone. I had nowhere to go, nowhere to turn. I felt like I was in a big black hole and there was no way out.'[3]

Celebrities from the music, film, business and sport world have long reported higher than average incidences of depression and substance abuse, which are known to be associated with loneliness and/or a lack of connectedness with others—the feeling of being all alone in the world and of having to fend for oneself. The advent of social media has made this celebrity trap of loneliness, disconnectedness and discontent available to everyone with a smartphone. Today's social media platforms provide everyone with abundant opportunities to live the discrepancy between a publicly portrayed life and their felt reality.

As in Paulo Coelho's book *The Winner Stands Alone,* rock stars, models, actors and sport stars at some point will touch the inner emptiness that accompanies an over-focus on results, power, status, glamour, material success and looking good.[4] The growing discontentment drives the celebrity to find happiness by trying to become even more successful, make more money, acquire more expensive possessions, get more likes or followers, improve their looks, or indulge in more alcohol, sex or drugs. Smartphone screens and gaming are becoming increasingly popular escape mechanisms for this held-in grief, even if they only temporarily quell the problem.

Sad are yesterday's heroes whose only solace is to regurgitate stories of their glory days, surrounded by lonely souls at the bar counter, or around the barbecue or the blackjack table. Former England captain and psychotherapist Mike Brearley warns ex-cricketers not to be lured or 'prostituted' into jobs that use them to fulfill the star-struck desires of others.[5] He also cautions those who choose to move into the caravan of entertainment, as after-dinner speakers and so on, suggesting that a player risks compromising his integrity in some situations; there are even times when the temptation is to subtly denigrate one's own earlier career. Most current players probably don't want to hear this, or disregard it if they do. Why shouldn't they? They're styling at the moment. Or maybe they have touched the emptiness, but there is little or no safe space in the sport to admit it, and thus address it. A few well-known cricketers, and athletes from other sports, have had their careers interrupted by depression, whether due to hereditary or environmental factors, we'll never really know.

Whose job is it anyway to prepare emerging stars for the possibility of being blinded by the limelight of stardom?

The reality is that many people actually push them even further into the limelight, with coaches sometimes prepared to turn a blind eye to questionable behaviour, as long as they are winning, agents who are far more interested in putting athletes on billboards and driving their celebrity status even higher, and false friends who help prop up shallow relationships.

A few lucky athletes may have a close friend or a courageous coach, agent or partner who calls them out on acting like a superstar, even though this person risks being excommunicated for saying what the athlete does not want to hear.

Should the responsibility lie with the sport bodies, team owners, athlete managers, coaches or the athletes themselves? Nike is reputed to have lost between five and twelve billion dollars as a result of the Tiger Woods scandal, and to date have already withdrawn sponsorships from Lance Armstrong (doping), Kobe Bryant (alleged sexual assault), Oscar Pistorius (murder) and at least six others.[6] I wonder whether sponsors might look to 'insure' their endorsement by insisting on (and paying for) some form of mentorship. In the absence of this guidance, and blinded by the limelight, athletes update their social media status, post the selfie and head for the party.

But it's not all doom and gloom. There are also happy endings. As the external world dispenses discontentment, it also gives birth to a more conscious world; one where the outward search for fame, money, success or vice is balanced by the pursuit of inner contentment. Those who look *out there*, dream. Those who look *inside*, awaken.

This shift is already happening. Hashim Amla is a fine example. He has seemingly little interest in pursuing fame or money. Neither these nor cricket are his God. His self-worth and contentment are largely independent of on-field results. The more praise that is heaped on him, the more he thanks and diverts it to others. Apart from relentlessly practising to become a better cricketer, he spends much of his time reinforcing his values and strength of character—*growing himself as a person*. Mike Horn, mentioned earlier for his work with both the Indian and South African teams, is clear on this: 'Developing talent is not enough. Every day you have to do something to better yourself as a person. This will not only allow you to handle success, but will allow it to keep growing.'

Hopefully, sport and its athletes will learn from fallen celebrities as well as from genuine role models. Former England captain Michael Atherton advises cricketers to 'avoid the grasping claws of celebrity if at all possible, because it will chew you up and spit you out when you are at your most vulnerable'.[7] Developing strength of character and living according to one's own (not others') values and expectations is critical to sustaining successful performance and successful living.

PERSONAL MASTERY AND COACHING

In developing our stars of tomorrow, hopefully, sporting bodies, team owners, sport agents, sponsors and even players themselves will act more responsibly by shining the light of awareness on the trappings of stardom (read, 'ego'). It starts early. Kids who have a special talent should not be treated as special kids, as this sets them up for failure later in life, both on and off the field. Treat them as ordinary kids who are lucky to have a special talent. Parents and school teachers/coaches also need to strike a healthier balance between achieving results and developing healthy self-esteem independent of these results. The funny thing is, the less attached one becomes to winning, the more likely it will happen.

In their study on 'servant leadership', researchers from Eastern Washington University found that coaches who emphasise values like trust, inclusion, humility and service—as opposed to 'winning-at-all-cost' behaviours—were most successful at coaching teams to victory.[8]

At the heart of this paradigm shift in behaviour sits the coach's ability to develop athletes as rounded human beings. Sharon Stoll and Jennifer Beller, two of the world's foremost academics in the field of sports education and development, offer the following perspective:

> We must reconsider how the win-at-all-costs attitude that permeates virtually every aspect of our athletic programmes affects the moral character and development of participants. While teaching the will to win does not have to be eliminated, coaches, athletic administrators, and others in sport leadership positions must re-evaluate their philosophy regarding the importance of winning as it relates to character development, particularly when the participants are children and young adults.[9]

Often driven by parents and/or coaches, some current win-at-all-costs practices serve to teach kids that 'in order to get ahead in life, it's okay to cheat, lie or manipulate'. These include promoting or condoning the use of performance-enhancing drugs, particularly the use of anabolic steroids at schoolboy level, fudging birth certificates so older kids can make age-group teams, encouraging kids in contact sports to maim opponents or to 'take them out', and any other form of bending rules or compromising sportsmanship in the name of winning.

As coaches, regardless of it being at the school or elite level, it is our primary function to create an environment that supports players on their path towards a lifetime of success, both on the sports field and in the game of life. This is not a job to be delegated to a sports psychologist or a mental conditioning coach.

Neil Powell, head coach of the World Series Champion South African sevens rugby team, has the following mantra guiding his thinking and behaviour: 'If I improve you as a player, but not as a person, I have failed you as a coach and mentor.' One of the most successful sports teams in modern history, the (New Zealand) All Blacks rugby team, has a similar mantra: 'Better people make better All Blacks.'

It has been said that after coaching his team in the college football national championship game, Amos Alonzo Stagg was asked, 'What do you think of your team?' He responded, 'I won't know how good a job I did for twenty years. That's when we'll see how my boys turned out.' He knew that his greatest victory as a coach of young people had very little to do with a scoreboard and much more to do with the impact he would have on the rest of their lives.

Anyone with the desire to learn, grow, improve or extract the richness that life has to offer would benefit from embracing this path towards becoming better and better versions of themselves—not only as players, but as coaches as well.

I would go as far as to say it should be a prerequisite for leaders, coaches, teachers and parents, and for anyone who is instrumental in the nurturing, growth and development of others. Like any instrument, fine-tuning is required. Personal mastery does this. It's a journey of refining and aligning our inner and outer worlds. It's about gaining deeper awareness of our purpose or calling as leaders and coaches, of *why* we are doing what we are doing, and *what* we are hoping to achieve in the world through this work. It's about constantly refining our values, beliefs, attitudes and intentions, aligning these with the way we live our lives and lead others.

Like the unseen foundations of a building, it provides the foundation from which to project to great heights. The further one advances along the path of personal mastery, the more effective, respected and valued you will likely become as a person, and in whatever role you happen to engage in your community. Without this strong foundation, the heights of success can be undermined by misguided intention, compromised values, questionable character or maybe just a lack of awareness, sending once successful sports- or business people tumbling back down to earth.

I recommend being intentional about self-mastery, about actively embracing the journey, which is certainly not always smooth, nor comfortable, but one that is immensely rewarding. In a world where computers, technology and artificial intelligence will increasingly dominate all that can be automated, 'being human' will become increasingly valued and rewarded. We short-change ourselves, our lives and others whom we intentionally or unintentionally impact if we don't continuously improve ourselves. Whether you're an athlete or an employee in an organisation, don't wait for your coach or boss to pave your road towards self-mastery; map it out for yourself and stay on the path.

Below is a continuum along which this journey progresses, following on from what was covered at the beginning of the book. It's not about absolutes, about being one way or the other, but rather about a journey towards increasing degrees of mastery in more and more areas of our lives.

PERSONAL MASTERY IS A JOURNEY

- From focusing on improving only what we *do*, to actively fine-tuning who we are *being* when we are doing what we are doing. From primarily focusing on building our professional muscle and know-how, to additionally building our emotional, social and spiritual competence.
- From the importance of looking good and gaining confidence by impressing others, to looking inwardly to build our self-esteem, grounded by our own inner substance, strength of character and moral fibre (living more from the inside out than the outside in).
- From taking on societies' values or living up to other people's expectations, to living authentically according to our own values, and in so doing, adding value to society.
- From trying to be liked, to being the likeable person we already are.
- From thinking we have the answers, or needing to be seen to have the answers, to knowing and openly accepting that we have much to learn (Socrates' definition of wisdom).
- From covering up mistakes, weaknesses and vulnerabilities, to embracing and owning these normal human conditions, while still remaining self-confident.
- From our behaviour being dictated by unconscious and self-serving ego drivers, to awareness of these, then choosing words and actions more intentionally and consciously as we serve more abundantly.
- From being a 'taker' or 'people pleaser' to authentically being

a 'giver', energiser and/or servant-leader, thus experiencing the true joy and reward of this other-orientation.
- From being reactive to being proactive; such as from blaming others when things go wrong to taking responsibility for our play, or from waiting to be told what to do to taking responsibility for what needs to be done.

Personal mastery is this and more. It's a never-ending journey, bringing difficulty and reward, clarity and confusion, but also a deeper, fuller and more rewarding experience of life.

23

SELF-AWARENESS: A JOURNEY OF UNINTENDED CONSEQUENCES

The Western Australia Cricket Association (WACA) ground in Perth is a notoriously difficult venue for visiting sides to play at. The wicket is extra fast and bouncy, the crowd can be hostile, and the verbal abuse visiting players have to endure, especially from the cheap seats, remains an unfriendly experience, to say the least, even when one arrives prepared for whatever chirps and chants the locals will employ to enforce their home ground advantage.

As coach of the Sydney Thunder team in the Australian Big Bash League, I specially remember a red-bearded fellow who seemed to have a thirst for both beer and abusing our players when we played the Perth Scorchers on new year's day, 2015. We batted first and posted a defendable score of 179 for 3. When we returned to field, Red Beard led an army of spectators who used explicit language to remind the players where Sydney Thunder had ended their first three seasons: at the bottom of the league.

Our response on the field gave Red Beard and Co. very little to work with, though. After 10 overs, we had Perth with their backs against the wall on 64 for 4, needing probably only 1 more wicket to seal the game. On the first ball of the 11th over, Jacques Kallis delivered a perfectly executed bouncer to Sam Whiteman, who skied the ball to Nathan Hauritz, fielding at deep square leg. It was a perfect scenario: Whiteman handed us the opportunity we were looking for, and in Nathan we had a seasoned international player who would shortly complete the regulation catch we needed to secure a vital away victory.

It was not to be. Nathan dropped the catch, and Red Beard ripped into him.

I sat thinking, 'Shit, shit, shit'. It was difficult not to react with disappointment. But I made sure not to show any negative gesture or emotion, which would only have added to the pressure. While I was focusing on managing my own reaction, Dirk Nannes, a veteran international cricketer in our team who was sitting out injured, immediately picked up a bottle and rushed off towards Nathan, saying, 'Our mate's going to need some support.'

In that split second, I went from a sense of disappointment to overwhelming pride and gratitude. Dirk's response brought to life the concept of teamwork and selflessly backing your mate when he needs it. In that moment, I knew the team was on the right track.

But was I?

When it really mattered, my first inner reaction was disappointment at a player's mistake and the possible implication thereof—losing and not advancing in the competition. Yes, I didn't show any emotion, but I knew what I was thinking, and it wasn't about the player and what he must have felt like when he made an elementary error, at a crucial stage of an important match, in front of a hostile crowd. It was about me and my ego, specifically how Nathan's dropped catch could affect my reputation as coach of a winning versus a losing team. In contrast, Dirk didn't think; he instinctively did what he knew was right—the moment was about Nathan and not about Nathan's dropped catch.

After winning the Big Bash trophy that season, Dirk's gesture remained one of the season's highlights for me. It reminded me of another story about responding to failure, told about Tom Watson Jr., a former CEO of IBM. During Watson's tenure, a company junior vice president made some decisions that ended up costing the company millions of dollars. When this employee was summoned to Watson's office, he apparently had his letter of resignation ready, saying, 'I suppose after that set of mistakes you will be wanting to fire me.' Watson replied, 'Not at all, young man; we have just spent a couple of million dollars educating you.'

Had I reacted when Nathan dropped the catch, I would have compromised our team culture and my credibility as a proponent of player-centered coaching, of supporting players as people ahead of their performance. What I felt and what I preached were at odds with each other in that moment.

These small (and sometimes not so small) gestures, in moments of pressure, often reflect the pulse of your team. These are also the moments when coaches are truly tested, and on that occasion, I only got a 50 per cent pass mark. Had Dirk not set a better example, I might not even have become aware of my own failings.

The late Bill O'Brien, CEO of Hanover Insurance, summarised his most fundamental insight from leading transformational change in his own company, saying, 'The success of an intervention depends on the interior condition of the intervener.'[1] Differently put, who the person was being when they were delivering the intervention is way more important than the content they are delivering. It's what Tendulkar was referring to when he said that the impact he had on people would be remembered long after they forgot his results on the field. Who he was being as a person was more impactful on others and longer lasting than what he did as a batsman.

THE IMPORTANCE OF SELF-AWARENESS

In coach Clive Woodward's build-up to the 2003 Rugby World Cup victory with the England team, he acknowledged that '... for two years I had been making some fundamental errors in player selection.'[2] It took a visit to the Royal Marines for this error to be made explicit by some of their senior officers. They told him, somewhat hesitantly, 'There are men in your squad whom we wouldn't go into battle with.' Woodward instinctively knew this, but had not put his finger on the problem. Some of the players were 'energy sappers', people whose behaviour and words tended to undermine or break down others, and the team energy. This is especially problematic when under pressure and when the team really needs to pull together. It had nothing to do with skill; it was about attitude. The Marines would not go into battle with people who would moan, complain or have a negative impact on others. The opposite of these people are 'energisers', players whose attitudes, words and behaviour uplift and boost the team.

I sometimes refer to the team 'bank account', and ask players to carefully consider their words and actions, and whether they are adding to the bank account, growing it (being 'givers'), or whether they are taking away from it ('takers'). The size of the bank account determines the size of the storm the team can weather. A great example is how the Rajasthan Royals team of 2013 was able to go from being in total disarray from the spot-fixing scandal and having three players jailed, to winning a crucial knockout game just three days later.

It's important to know that everything you do or say, even the things you choose to not do or say, will have an impact on others. For example, if someone makes a mistake (which incidentally means the person did not deliberately err; it was a mistake), you could shout, reprimand, ignore, support, give feedback or ask questions. Each of these actions will have a different impact on the person, their confidence and the learning outcome. It's important then to consider what impact you ideally want to have, and choose your words and actions accordingly. Few team members will deliberately choose to be 'takers'; it's more likely that they lack awareness of the extent to which their behaviour negatively impacts others, like those few players in Clive Woodward's rugby team.

Self-awareness has been described as the single most important quality in a leader. I'd contend it's not dissimilar for athletes, parents and anyone else who is in a position to influence others, for better or worse. Awareness is the first step towards managing both ideal and non-ideal behavioural tendencies, especially those that come to the surface in the heat of the moment. For example, awareness alerts us to the presence of irritation, frustration, disappointment or anger, which tends to drive inappropriate or reactive behaviour. Awareness allows one to choose a response more intentionally, such as offering a word of encouragement or an act of compassion even when you don't 'feel' it, or knowing when to keep quiet, walk away or take a deep breath.

Without this awareness and fine-tuning, we run the risk of our efforts being random, and thus confusing others with whom we engage. We also run the risk of saying or doing things that could undermine relationships of trust, credibility and respect, or of succumbing to the common human fallibility of acting out unconscious egoistic behaviour, which sees our smaller self or ego serving its own selfish needs, wants and desires, at the expense of the people whom we're supposed to be serving. It is also at the expense of one's full potential.

Embarking on this invaluable and critical inner journey to self-awareness is an important step towards mastering leadership, performance and life. Author Jim Collins suggests that the answer to becoming a great leader (a Level-5 leader, as he puts it) lies in the inner development of a person.[3] Daniel Goleman, author of *Emotional Intelligence*, maintains that self-awareness is at the core of emotional intelligence.[4]

WHOM ARE YOU SERVING?

One of the primary aims of leadership, coaching and managing is to grow both people and performance, ideally by serving others' interests over those of the leader or coach. Leadership effectiveness is reduced when leaders place their own interests first.

One of the ways to check whether your focus is on growing others, and if you are placing their interests above yours, is to ask yourself, 'What is my intention?' This is the deliberate pursuit of self-awareness, and it was what Gary Kirsten and I attempted when we contemplated whether to talk to the Indian team immediately after the disappointing opening match in the Sri Lankan ODI series that we discussed earlier.

When I make presentations, coach teams, and even as I'm writing this chapter, there is a part of me that wants to look good and have people think that I am good at what I do. This is about me serving myself, or more accurately, my ego and its need to look good.

There's another part of me that has a deep desire to serve others with the best of my knowledge and experience, hoping that in some way I can add value to other people's lives. It's not so important that I do in fact add value; what is more important is that I offer my best and with the best intention, knowing that I certainly don't know it all, but some of what I know might be useful.

From my experience of doing both, I'm convinced that operating with the intention of serving others *authentically* works way better, for others and for myself. When serving others is the coaching philosophy—and behaviour—one ascribes to, being aware of one's internal self is vital, since we all have the tendency to drift (back) towards a place where it's about us. When things are going well, we want to receive the credit. When things are not going well, we look for scapegoats.

Self-awareness doesn't lead to the elimination of this 'me first' tendency, but to the illumination thereof when it does occur. While I intentionally made the decision not to show any negative (or overly enthusiastic) reactions during matches, the Perth experience—the dropped catch, my inner reaction to it, and Dirk's response—served as a sporadic, unforeseen, yet powerful moment of self-reflection that shaped me for the better.

THE UNINTENDED CONSEQUENCES OF OUR ACTIONS

The following is a brief story I wrote and posted on a blog, which, to be truthful, I only did because I had not posted anything for some time, not because I thought it was a particularly valuable reflection. How wrong I turned out to be.

> After a few very cold and rainy Cape Town winter days, the clouds parted and the sun only just re-emerged, offering me a small gap to run a Houtbay mountain trail.
>
> As I arrived at one of my favourite spots, there was already a car, all covered in outdoor adventure gear logos. Moments later, the owner emerged from the path, dressed in the showiest of trail running gear, but without a drop of sweat. He told me, 'It's not worth it, the path is too wet and slippery'.
>
> Bummer, I thought. But I was dressed and ready, so I thought I would at least go and check just how slippery it was. As I headed up, I could see the slide marks where the other guy had tried to make his way up to the contour path. I saw where the footsteps ended, and my ego decided to get further than my predecessor had. No more than twenty metres further and around the very next bend, the soil changed from clay to red mountain soil, which was wet but not at all slippery.
>
> I continued to have one of the most awesome runs I've ever had in those mountains, surrounded by every little ravine and crevasse bubbling with the joys of recent rains as nature brimmed fresh from a three-day-long cold shower (and some light snow).

I pondered the times when I had given up on a person, a project, a relationship or a venture. I'm all for not flogging a dead horse, not going down on a sinking (relation)ship or throwing too much good money after bad. But I wonder how many times we bail on our trail, give up on an idea or person or stop trying when success or contentment lies only a few slippery steps ahead, just around the next corner?

I shared this story and reflection when I got home that afternoon, and then went on with my life.

The next morning, I found the following comment below the blog post. I read it in my local coffee shop, with tears streaming down my cheeks.

Blog: A STORY OF PERSEVERANCE

Date: 10 July 2014

User comment: Wow Paddy, you have inspired me ENORMOUSLY. I considered ending my own life on 16 June 2014 (Freedom Day) after 'giving up' on life and my AMAZING family (wife and two sons!) due to my own financial greed that 'backfired', I truly believed that I was worth more to them dead than alive! How evil and misguided I was ... this fantastic article has truly given me a new perspective on my current difficulties. THANK YOU. Please keep writing. Much love, DaveH, Joburg

Everything you say or do, however unintentional or inconsequential it may be in your own mind, has an impact on the world. Sometimes you see that impact and sometimes you don't. Your actions are weighed. Your influence is felt. Who you are, what you say, and what you do matters greatly.

24

THE PROTEAS IN SWITZERLAND

By beating the England One Day side by 80 runs on 28 August 2012, the Proteas became the first international cricket team in history to be ranked number one in all three formats of the game at the same time.

Achieving this 'Triple Crown' was one of the goals the team had set for itself when Gary was appointed head coach in June 2011. I joined him as team performance director—a new title for a position with similar responsibilities to those I had with the Indian side.

The journey started at the Arabella Golf Estate just outside Hermanus in the Western Cape, which was the venue for our first official engagement with the Proteas. We spent three days discussing where the team wanted to go, how we would get there, and most importantly, working on our golf. Having just taken the Indian team to the World Cup championship and the world's number one Test ranking, Gary told the Proteas that he did not have the silver bullet. If anyone there was expecting to hear how Gary intended to take the team to the top of the world, they were in for a disappointment.

In terms of goals, the team decided that they 'wanted to get to the top of the mountain' (meaning, to be the top team in all three formats of the game, Test cricket, ODI and T20). After lengthy discussions on how we would get there, Gary summarised the session, explaining that we would all build the metaphorical bus that would take us to the top, that every person would need to help navigate, and that everyone would have a chance to drive when their time came—whether that meant scoring runs, taking wickets, supporting teammates or contributing in meetings. Whatever it took to keep the bus moving onward and upward.

Some parts of the journey would be planned, and some parts we'd need to figure out in the moment. We acknowledged that there would be unforeseen twists, turns and obstacles, and it might happen that one or two people would want to go in a different direction. If this happened too often, that person would need to get off the bus so the rest could continue.

I took a big risk, calling a session where WAGS (wives and girlfriends) were invited into a conversation where we discussed what it was like for players and their partners, with the men being away from home for so long (up to nine months a year), what their challenges were, and what requests each had of their partner. Anyone who travels for business or sport will know the difficulties it places on relationships, especially how disruptive the first few days at home can be. A grumpy partner offloading daily frustrations over the phone and whilst they're on tour can have a disruptive effect on the players' mental and emotional preparation, especially when the males try to offer rational solutions to problems, forgetting the value of listening with their mouths closed.

The conversation in that hour was fascinating, heated and led to both valuable clarifications as well as more than one argument. One of the players had a partner who was critical but honest in the meeting, and when they got back to their hotel room afterwards, he told her that if she ever brought the subject up again or spoke like that in front of the team, she could pack her bags and leave. If I had the choice to do it all over again, I'd suggest spending that hour on the golf driving range. Much safer.

In July 2012, en route to England, where South Africa would successfully compete for the number one ranking in Test and One Day cricket, the team stopped over in Switzerland for an unconventional training camp. Gary believed that one couldn't simulate the pressure and intensity of Test cricket in warm-up matches, since the former was more a test of mental resolve than of skill. So, to prepare for what was to be a gruelling eleven-week series between the two strongest international outfits at the time, we stepped away from cricket and into a world that Gary and I knew would challenge the players mentally and physically at levels they had never previously endured.

Our host? Mike Horn, who had been instrumental in India's final World Cup preparations a year earlier.

At the time, Mike had a training camp in the Swiss Alps, which was almost exclusively used to train young explorers from every continent, whom he took to the most distant and extreme corners of the world, teaching them about both surviving in, and caring for, the environment. As an old university friend of mine, he agreed to take a break from his four-year journey around the world, to host us at his training base.

Day 1 saw the team driving around the Alps in seven of the latest generation E-cell and F-cell Mercedes-Benz cars, which run on electricity and water and produce zero carbon emissions. Having had a good look around the region, we shifted our mode of transport to mountain bikes. During a two-hour ride, we soon discovered there is no flat terrain in the Alps, something we would learn again and again over the next few days.

While a few players went over their handlebars and donated skin to the gravel tracks, none were badly injured. A fair bit of that skin was mine, after which I made an important note to self: 'Next time, *don't try and keep up with Mike on the downhills*.' Alviro Petersen came hurtling down a steep and narrow road to find a closed boom gate across his path. Unable to stop, he narrowly made it through a tiny gap between a fence and a concrete pillar and then went tumbling head-over-heels as Gary held his breath and prayed he would not be too badly injured. Luckily, he escaped with only a sprained wrist and a little less skin than he started out with.

We would later learn that this 'reckless' approach to preparing for a Test series in England was heavily criticised in the media, but Gary didn't really mind the injuries (and we had the blessing of Cricket South Africa)—he just wanted the players to reach England sufficiently unharmed, to play Test cricket. We knew what the players would gain in terms of personal growth if they emerged safely on the other side of what Mike was to put them through. Initially it was about coping mentally with the gruelling experience, but there were times when physical survival also came into the reckoning. I had arrived a day early to work out the activities with Mike, and right away I knew we'd be going well beyond the edge of the envelope.

The evening after the drive and bike ride, Mike had us all riveted with his stories and slideshows of expeditions. As we listened, concepts like dreaming big, preparing excellently, seeing the solution on the other side of obstacles, never giving up, committing to decisions and respecting your teammate took on entirely new dimensions for all of us.

The next day was an opportunity to visit Mike's training grounds. Kitted up in snow boots, Gore-Tex pants and jackets, gloves and beanies, snow rackets and ski poles, we headed for a three-hour hike through snow to summit a 3,300-metre peak. This would entail a rope climb, traversing an ice field with crevasses, and a steep and exhausting push for the summit on a clear day, with temperatures near zero and in deep snow. Not quite your average cricket-playing conditions.

When we were met with a steep rope descent and then an unsupported (not-strapped-in) short walk across a narrow divide with a snow field on one side and a steep drop-off on the other, three players and two of the support staff could not muster the courage to do it. We respected their decision, and the rest of us proceeded with caution. Once on the snow field, we were roped together in two eight-man teams, which wasn't done as a team-building exercise. It was to keep us alive should one of us slip and fall into a crevasse, one of many glacial cracks scattered across the ice field, all of which were deep and concealed from the naked eye by a shallow layer of snow. Mike gave us all a lesson in how to stop someone from disappearing after a fall.

Among the many memorable moments from that experience, one stands out. When Hashim Amla couldn't progress beyond a certain point on the glacier, or so he said, Graeme Smith literally picked him up and carried him to the next point—a moment we all recalled during the first Test at The Oval when Hashim returned the favour, scoring 311 not out in our victory of an innings and 12 runs over the English. At the time of writing, this is still the highest score by a South African in Test cricket.

We reached the peak, exhausted and exhilarated. So small was the area, with sheer cliffs over 500 metres high on two of the sides, that not many players rose from a kneeling or sitting position. Standing up, in the wind, with so many people on such a small surface, was just too risky. On the walk back down from the peak to the cable station, Mike routed the party down the ski slope, so that we had another killer of an uphill climb to finish before we sat down, completely exhausted, for a well-earned lunch.

In the cable car on the way back down, we were entertained by a terrified Jacques Kallis, who has a genuine fear of heights, and who was on a journey well beyond his edge of fear. A truck filled with mountain bikes met us upon arrival at the base station. Mike pointed to a mountain opposite the one we had just summitted, and said, 'We're cycling over that mountain back to the hotel.' No one believed him, and Graeme Smith actually laughed at the absurdity of it. The peak loomed some 750 metres above us, and there were no contoured paths leading up—it was a straight climb. Mike hopped on his bike and headed straight up, shouting, 'Follow me!' Joke over.

The next ninety minutes saw players using every swear word in the book, until they were too exhausted to swear—and there was still some way to climb. For seven kilometres, we climbed; never once did the gravel path level out. Not once!

I have never been so physically exhausted in my life. But I was in Mike Horn territory, so I refused to get off my bike, refused to rest and refused to walk. I found reserves that I never knew I had. The method to Mike's madness wasn't lost on anyone.

A.B. de Villiers later said that he was beyond exhausted, and that he pushed harder than he had ever done before. He now knew he could do more than he had believed he could. Another player said, 'I've had enough being the best I can be. It's time to be better than that.' Cramps struck three players on the way. Jacko, our ultra-marathon-running physiotherapist, stretched the muscles out, helped the players back on their bikes, and the slog continued. Marchant de Lange, a giant of a man at 2.01 metres, battled cramps for nearly three hours, but refused to give up, and didn't. On the way up, about three kilometres or forty-five minutes away from the summit, Gary's bike got a puncture that we could not repair. Mike gave Gary his bike, and then proceeded to carry Gary's bike to the summit.

From the top, which came as a massive relief, a descent of about 900 metres lay ahead of us, and some fourteen kilometres. We were all looking forward to cruising downhill. It was not to be. We carried our bikes for the better part of the first two kilometres, down terrain too treacherous to cycle. Larger men like Graeme Smith and Jacques Kallis found this particularly daunting, but they never backed out.

It is too much for my limited writing ability to describe what it was like to cycle down a Swiss Alpine mountain, through virgin forests, along tracks forged by cattle during their higher-altitude summer living, accompanied by teammates encouraging one another through sometimes steep or technically challenging terrain. It was spectacular; a true privilege to experience. Mike did it all on foot, still carrying Gary's bike.

The locally brewed beer tasted particularly good that evening.

After a fitful sleep, we woke in time for a 7 a.m. departure, to go canyoning. The team would walk, swim and in places be forced to cliff jump or rope descend a glacial river, which was essentially melted snow.

Players and management were all kitted out in 5 mm thick neoprene wetsuits, specialised river-walking boots, full length protective overalls over wetsuits, waist harnesses, life jackets and helmets. Once we entered the steep and narrow ravine, we spent the next two hours bum-sliding down slippery, moss-covered waterfalls, jumping into natural plunge pools from heights between three and eleven metres, and sliding down a flying-fox pulley system that was the only safe way to descend a twenty-five metre waterfall. Most, if not all of us, were shivering, a combination of operating out of our comfort zones and spending hours in just above freezing glacial water.

'Man of the Match' went to Jacques Kallis, who again was asked to overcome his fear of heights to complete the flying fox and an eight-metre jump into a small rock pool. Jacques often compared his experience of batting under pressure to that of a duck swimming on water—he might appear calm on the surface, but he is paddling like mad below where nobody can see his anxieties. As he emerged at the bottom of the flying fox, Jacques was as terrified as I've ever seen him, visibly shaking and repeatedly exclaiming, 'I can't believe I did that! I can't believe I did that …'

After a full-on, high-energy forty-eight hours, players were given the afternoon to rest or take a leisurely stroll around the quaint village of Château-d'Œx. It was impressive to see seven men opt for a ten-kilometre run instead, along the river, while another five decided to go on a 'leisurely' mountain bike ride with Mike, which ended up being a gruelling three-hour and thirty-eight kilometre round trip to the famous Swiss town of Gstaad.

The evening saw us travelling to a traditional high-altitude cheese-making cottage, where host Pipo opened his 'home' to us for a lesson in Swiss cheese-making-and-eating culture.

Mike gave another of his impromptu talks; this time, sharing stories of preparation for his 7,000-kilometre solo journey body-boarding down the Amazon River. Of the many lessons, this time we heard about making critical decisions and committing fully without any second-guessing, that if dreams don't scare you, they're not big enough, that bettering yourself every day is not negotiable for someone wanting to live life fully, and that saying you will do something is not enough; it's the action that counts.

Despite one or two players suggesting a chilled final morning to conclude a wonderful Swiss adventure, Mike and Gary had other ideas. At 7 a.m, Mike took us through the famous 'church run', which was up a never-ending flight of stairs to the top of the village church, down the other side, and then back up a steep hill to our hotel. We then hopped back onto the bikes, with most of us letting out a little 'ouch!' as bruised bums from the previous day hit saddles.

Again, Mike showed us a loop of the village, ending with an ascent of the steepest road it had on offer. Now that he had familiarised us with these two routes, players and management were divided into four teams, and the gun went off for three laps of the church run, followed by three laps of the mountain bike route. That half-hour power race was a fitting way to end our four days in the Swiss Alps, Mike Horn-style.

I led a forty-five minute debrief of the experience, along with Gary and Mike. One cannot be guaranteed victory in cricket, but one can do everything possible to set up for the best chance of victory. There is no doubt that the time spent at the training camp was a massive success from many perspectives, and would go a long way to preparing us for success in the upcoming Test series against England. What emerged from the debrief, amongst other things, was that we had definitely taken our unique team culture to new heights; each person had learned more about themselves, specifically how they could go well beyond what they perceived as their physical and mental boundaries; we realised that physical boundaries of exhaustion and pain are actually mental boundaries and that the body can endure way longer than we think. Everyone got invaluable lessons and insights into performing at the top of their game. Lessons that we hoped would pay dividends as we moved into an important season of cricket.

MARK BOUCHER

The tour of England was to be Mark Boucher's final 'expedition' as an international cricketer. When Gary was appointed head coach of the Proteas, Mark's spot in the Test side had been under threat for a while, and the end of his career loomed large after he was left out of the 2011 World Cup squad.

Mark and Corrie van Zyl, Gary's predecessor, didn't have a natural rapport at the time. But on Gary's request, Corrie—who had moved up the managerial ranks at CSA—agreed to let him manage Mark's exit from international cricket. Creating and managing exit strategies was something we had done for a number of senior players in India.

Gary said to Mark: 'Why don't we set a date, to give you clarity on the whole thing? I want to see you go out on a high. Please don't wait for someone else to tell you that you're finished. You deserve better than that.'

This understanding from his former teammate and now coach was exactly what Mark needed to end his illustrious career on his terms. He said he had one more year in him, and since the dream of winning a World Cup was now beyond his reach, he would at least want to end his career by contributing to the Proteas becoming the number one ranked Test side in the world. So, England 2012 it was. In Mark's words: 'The England tour was the perfect scenario: the world number one (England) playing the world number two—effectively a World Test Championship.'[1]

It was with this sense of purpose and gratitude that Mark set foot in Switzerland. Being a tough-as-nails character himself, he formed an immediate bond with Mike. When everybody else went to bed at night, Mark stuck around, absorbing as much of Mike Horn as he possibly could. He studied Mike's every move, internalised his every word and, in his mind, transferred this newfound knowledge and inspiration to the Test arena, where he would soon conquer his final summit as an international cricketer.

It was not to be. Unknowingly, the Mike Horn experience was preparing Mark for a life beyond cricket and for a challenge beyond any that the sport had ever thrown at him.

On 9 July 2012, Mark's career was ended by a freak eye injury during a warm-up match against Somerset. An Imran Tahir delivery clipped a bail off the stumps into Mark's left eye. Mark held his hand over his eye while being walked off the field by our physio Jacko, and once in the change room, he lay down on the physio bed for Dr Moosajee, our manager-cum-doctor, to have a look. I made the mistake of standing with them as Mark took his hand away. He had what looked like thick mucus on his cheek, with a strange black stripe running through it. When I realised I was looking at the white of his eye, his cornea, and in it, his pupil streaking down his cheek, my stomach turned and I went cold. It was bad.

In his autobiography, Mark credits Mike for the impact he had on all of us at the time. First, for his significant contribution to the Proteas beating England 2-0 in a three-test series to become the world's number one Test team. 'Several times during the series I saw a player rise to the occasion and produce a critical performance to win a key moment. I thought of Mike every time.'

But Mike's lasting influence would be on Mark himself. Doctors anticipated that his eye's process of recovery would take more than two years. 'I didn't care,' said Mark. 'I could survive that. I would do whatever I had to do in order to regain some sight. I kept hearing the voice of Mike Horn in the back of my head. Calm, determined, prepared, self-belief. Fortunately, I had my self-talk to fall back on.'

At the time of writing this, Mark has made as near-perfect a recovery as possible. Besides dedicating much of his time to the fight against rhino poaching, he has also established himself as a formidable cricket coach, leading the Pretoria-based franchise, the Titans.

While he didn't get to end his playing career in the way he and Gary had anticipated, the team's last and lasting memory of Mark Boucher in action in national colours is still befitting of the man and his career: while summiting the Swiss Alps, Mark was right in front, in the snow—wearing just a Proteas T-shirt.

The Proteas won the first Test match at The Oval in London, and Hashim Amla became the first South African to score a Test triple century, scoring 311. We drew the second Test at Headingley, which I never watched a single ball of. I had a long standing arrangement with a bunch of friends to spend ten days on a yacht, surfing the Mentawai Islands off Sumatra. When I signed my contract with the Proteas, going on this trip in the middle of the England series was part of the deal. I returned in time for the third Test at the iconic Lord's stadium, which South Africa won, again thanks to a Hashim Amla century. The victory secured the number one spot in the ICC World Test ranking, and Mike Horn was with us to celebrate a journey that had begun on the slopes of the Swiss Alps six weeks earlier.

HAVING THE COURAGE TO SUFFER

In Switzerland, we had experienced frequent moments of extreme fear, but by relying on Mike, his brother Martin, and on each other, not a single one of those moments turned out to be insurmountable, whether it was Hashim being carried by Graeme on a glacier, or Jacques jumping off a cliff. Being real with each other was way more important than being tough. When those five people genuinely did not want to risk stepping onto that precarious ledge, no one badgered them.

In the South African team, we put a premium on being authentic and genuine. We regularly emphasised humility and sincerity. Such an environment discourages one from having a big ego.

On the second morning of the third and final Test against England at Lord's, for example, in the on-field huddle moments before going out to start the day's play, Graeme asked the team how they felt. A.B. de Villiers responded by saying that he was feeling nervous.

For a coach, this was a wonderful moment, because here was someone acknowledging in front of the whole team that he was jittery. There was something very real and sincere about the revelation. The truth, of course, is that if someone is not nervous before a Lord's Test match day, he's probably not paying attention.

Once a senior player like A.B. de Villiers had admitted that his nerves were on edge, a few of the younger ones followed by saying that they, too, were feeling anxious. When you acknowledge that you're nervous, the nervousness actually decreases. And it's okay to feel like that. The point is to accept it, and then ask the question: Okay, so what's most important to focus on?

Nerves can narrow or distract focus, and they also serve as a reminder to make sure the focus is on the right things—those that will give us the best possible chance of success; whether you're about to summit a mountain or the world's cricket rankings.

If Graeme or AB had simply said: 'Come on, guys, let's grab the bull by the horns and take these guys down,' they would have simply increased the nervousness because their bravado would have been a means of denying its existence. Nerves are like emotions; they need to be acknowledged in order to be managed. Either that, or they manage you.

In the teams I worked with, openly acknowledging nervousness, amongst all other naturally occurring thoughts and emotions associated with high pressure international cricket, was most encouraged and rewarded. Acting tough and pretending that these emotions don't exist, was not.

In *Man's Search For Meaning*, Viktor Frankl's moving memoir of his time in Nazi concentration camps during World War II, he recalls the countless times he had to help fellow prisoners find meaning in their lives with the aim of creating hope and therefore reasons to stay alive; to fight illness or resist suicide. In some cases, it was to remind someone of a child he adored who was waiting for him in a foreign country (someone to stay alive for), or a scientific paper that still needed to be completed (something to stay alive for).[2]

Finding meaning and hope did not lead the prisoners to deny or turn a blind eye to the suffering they had to endure—it merely gave them a reason to live through and beyond those. In doing so, Frankl wrote, one tried to keep moments of weakness and furtive tears to a minimum. 'But there was no need to be ashamed of tears, for tears bore witness that a man had the greatest of courage, the courage to suffer.'

25

ALPHA LEADERS

When the South African cricket team departed for a three-Test-match tour of Australia in November 2012, we had one goal. Win the series and retain our position as the number one ranked Test team in the world. Lose the series, and we would lose the ranking to Australia. And it might take as much as a year before being in a similar position to regain it. My job as team performance director was, amongst other things, to assist Gary and the players with plotting the psychological battle.

The Australian team would predictably come hard at us. Attacking with bat and ball, they would hustle us in the field and they had enough players who would engage in the sledging and verbal abuse that the team was well known for.

Barring a few, the South African team did not have players who were naturally aggressive and, man for man, it was unlikely we would be able to meet and match fire with fire. This situation led us to draw on our knowledge and experience of how some of Africa's largest animals engaged in their own psychological battles.

In the African bush, it's particularly useful to know the difference between a charge and a mock charge. For example, when an elephant pins its ears back, lowers it head, curls its trunk downwards and charges, your only chance of survival is to be in a vehicle capable of out-running it. If its ears are flared out sideways, it trumpets wildly with trunk raised and charges while kicking up a dust storm, it's best to stand your ground and make yourself look as large as possible, maybe by raising your arms. It's important to not retreat, nor to advance. This is a mock charge amounting to little more than loud noise, stomping of hooves and posturing to try and scare you off (okay, and maybe have you soil your underwear).

The Australian team we would be facing were a shadow of the great team of the early 2000s, but they were likely to come at us with the same aggressive approach. We felt they did not have the skill to match the charge we expected from them; it was more likely to resemble a mock charge. As in the African bush, our strategy was to stand our ground, to not back down, but also to not charge back at them. We expected things to be tough, grinding and confrontational, and we needed the same courage and resolve as would be required to withstand an elephant's mock charge. We would absorb their initial onslaught, like a boxer backed against the ropes with gloves up and protecting his face, we would allow our opponent to throw repeated non-knockout blows, until they eventually became exhausted. We would bide our time, waiting for the right time to attack.

The tour got off to a bad start for the Proteas, with J.P. Duminy tearing his Achilles tendon whilst playing a gentle touch rugby match at the end of day 1 of the first Test match. The Australians amassed 565 for 5 with the bat, with in-form Michael Clarke scoring an unbeaten 259. It was his third Test double century that year, and he would go on to score another in the very next match. Thanks mainly to rain interruptions, South Africa managed to hold out for what is known as a losing-draw (meaning Australia had the upper hand and were unlucky to not win).

The second Test didn't go much better. Opening bowler Vernon Philander fell sick the night before the match and had to be replaced, and if this wasn't enough, all-rounder Jacques Kallis injured his hamstring in only the fourth over on day 1. Unable to bowl for the rest of the match and unable to run properly, he would only bat low down the order.

Against this depleted South African bowling attack, Australia batted first, scoring 550 at an attacking rate of more than 5 runs per over, including another Michael Clarke double century.

A funny moment came from this pasting. Morné Morkel told us how, that evening as he knelt down to say his usual daily prayer, he started with 'Dear Lord, thank you for this day ...' And then paused mid-prayer and continued, 'Actually Lord, I'd like to take that back ...'

South Africa replied with 388 at a pedestrian scoring rate of 3 runs per over. Eventually set 430 runs to win in approximately 150 overs, we got off to a bad start and found ourselves at 45 for 4. We ended the fourth of five days at 77 for 4, scoring at a rate of just 1.5 runs per over and needing a further 353 runs for victory. Using the boxing analogy for those who do not understand Test cricket, if we were that boxer, at this point, both our eyes would have been almost swollen shut, our face would have been marked by cuts and bleeding, and we would probably have been knocked to the ground and survived about five count-outs. We were one or two punches away from being out cold.

It was at lunch on the fifth day that I gained some insight on how to potentially gain a psychological edge. All we had to do was, well, nothing.

Clarke, the Australian captain at the time, was visibly frustrated with his team's inability to break through the dogged defensiveness of A.B. de Villiers and debutant Faf du Plessis. They were literally defending every ball bowled to them, even balls that could easily be hit to the boundary given the incredibly attacking field placing.

I could see that Clarke was engaging in the verbal abuse that the Australian team was well known for at the time, but that his focus had now shifted to his own teammates.

At the tea interval, I was walking towards the dressing room behind the Australian team, which had just spent a wicket-less session in the field, when Clarke blurted out at the top of his voice, 'How the f…k are we meant to get wickets when you bowl such soft f…g crap!'

This was a public attack on a small group of his teammates, delivered within earshot of not only his full team, but also everyone in the South African change room. It was another outburst in a fairly long line of abuse I had heard him deliver to, or about, his teammates, including abusing the twelfth man for taking what he felt was too long to bring drinks onto the field for him whilst batting.

Clarke's tendency to undermine his own team had come to our attention on the very first morning of the first Test match. The

Australian coach Mickey Arthur, who was an ex-South Africa coach, and Proteas captain Graeme Smith were talking when Mickey told Graeme how captain Clarke kept putting pressure on him to get rid of ex-captain, Australian icon and teammate Ricky Ponting, who was nearing the end of his playing career. It was rather strange to have a coach share such information with the opposing captain, and it was one of the early signs that all was probably not well in the Australian camp.

Pulling off possibly one of the greatest defensive efforts in Test cricket, and in keeping with our plan to 'stand our ground' in the face of attack, Faf du Plessis and A.B. de Villiers batted for a total of 596 deliveries (nearly 100 overs) between them, effectively more than a full day's play, scoring only 143 runs! Their marathon session also genuinely exhausted the opposition. In fact, two of the Australian bowlers threw so many punches that they would not recover sufficiently in time for the third Test match.

The two teams had a week to lick their wounds and recover before starting the third and final Test match in Perth. A few South African players headed off to play golf, others to a beachside resort, and four of us to Port Douglas in far North Queensland, where we spent three days on a live-on-board charter, fishing for Giant Trevally (GT's). Our skipper, Damien Collett, certainly knew his stuff, and got us into some really good fish (all of which were released).

Going on to the third Test, we reinforced our psychological plan, which was to wait for the right moment to strike. Already the Australian team were tiring, they had lost two bowlers from the last encounter, and some of the psychological blows that we wanted to drive into the opposition were being delivered from within their own ranks. However, readying our battle-weary troops for another fight would require resolute leadership from captain Graeme Smith and coach Gary Kirsten. They needed to create as healthy and supportive an environment as possible, one that would get the best out of the by now exhausted players. They would have to get them to play for each other and for a cause greater than themselves, in the face of what had been a relentless onslaught.

Going into this final Test match at the WACA in Perth, Ricky Ponting announced his retirement. And again, it did not start well for South Africa, who batted first and slumped to 75 for 6 just after lunch on day 1. Thanks again to Faf du Plessis, they managed to scrape their way to 225.

Day 2 would turn out to be moving day. Australia were bowled out for 163, and on the afternoon of day 2, after twelve gruelling days of Australia attacking and South Africa holding its ground, the Australian team ran out of punches to throw. Sensing their moment had come, Graeme Smith and Hashim Amla attacked for the first time in the series, and attacked hard, scoring 230 runs in one session at a rate of over 6 runs per over. Amla went on to score 196, Smith 84, and A.B. de Villiers 169, to set Australia a target of 632. The game was over on day 4, with Australia bowled out, over 300 runs short of victory.

To be honest, when South Africa devised the strategy of standing ground against the metaphorical mock charge, to sit back against the ropes and absorb punches, I don't think any of us were expecting to take such a sustained beating, for almost twelve days, before an opportunity presented itself for a counter-attack. Towards the end of the second Test, and after day 1 of the third, there were moments when I feared that our plan could backfire badly.

In hindsight, I don't believe the players or the team as a unit would have been able to withstand the onslaught had it not been for very strong, courageous and caring leadership from Smith and Kirsten in particular. If we were not a happy team, or if the team environment and culture was not very strong and secure, cracks would have developed and the team would have fragmented and succumbed well before our chance came on the afternoon of day twelve. Faf du Plessis would not have selflessly defended 24 balls in that second Test, with his score on 98, 2 runs away from the amazing personal milestone of scoring a century on Test debut.

This was the experience that prompted me to explore in finer detail the concept of alpha leadership and its impact on others.

ALPHA LEADERS: TOP DOGS WHO RALLY OR RUIN TEAMS

'Man's greatest strength is his gentleness. It's the weak (leaders) who are cruel.'[1]

Throughout this next section, I speak of alpha leaders, which in literature is most commonly referred to as 'alpha male' behaviour. Although some literature refers to alpha males and alpha females, I think it is more accurate to speak about alpha leadership, which has typical and largely gender-neutral behavioural traits, whether exhibited by a male or female leader. That said, so as to avoid the fence-sitting often associated with being too politically correct, I'll also stick my neck out and say that when it comes to unhealthy alpha leadership, males are more often guilty than females.

As mentioned before, research suggests that 74 to 84 per cent of people who voluntarily resign from their jobs cite their manager and the way the manager treats them as the main reasons for doing so.[2] These disgruntled employees move on in search of a better working environment. Most professional cricketers are selected into their position and are not so lucky. If they have a lousy 'boss', they can't resign mid-season to go to another team like their corporate counterparts can. Conversely, most people who are happy in their team or workplace are likely to have a coach, captain or boss they respect and who is a likeable person. After all, the leaders set the culture and tone for most performance environments.

In professional sport and big business, it is most likely that a successful leader will be a combination of dynamic, driven, strategic, confident, intelligent, opinionated, result-oriented and dominant. These are qualities of the proverbial alpha leader, who is often given, or assumes, a leadership role.

Not all alpha leaders are the same. It is too general a term to define this class of animal. On one end of the scale, some are awesome to work with; towards the middle of the scale, some might deliver success, might be nice to learn from but are not nice to work with; and at the other end, there are those that might well deliver results, but are downright awful and soul-destroying to be around.

When alpha leaders walk into a room, they are noticed, they have presence. When in a group, they will naturally lead and others will follow.

Characteristic of the really good ones is that they believe deeply in themselves and thus are secure, self-confident and have strong opinions. They are highly intelligent and are able to see the big picture, are able to find solutions, and can see further into the future than most. They take action and make the difficult decisions. They have high expectations of themselves and of others. They motivate people to produce results, and lead from the front. They are good communicators who speak slowly and clearly, and have a good sense of humour. They have high energy levels, are hugely productive, and are not scared to work long hours. They have sound morals and ethics, and live a principled life. They revel under pressure, with others looking to them for leadership in times of chaos and difficulty.

Ex-Proteas captain Graeme Smith produced more match-winning performances in the fourth innings of Test matches than most in the game, when batting was most difficult and his team needed him most. Ex-India captain M.S. Dhoni was in poor form leading up to the World Cup final in India in 2011. With India on 114 for 3 and needing 275 to win the final, he moved himself ahead of in-form Yuvraj Singh. He walked out to bat, taking the responsibility on his shoulders, and returned from the crease with 91 not out and the World Cup trophy.

The above are some of the healthy characteristic of alpha leaders. The more a leader exhibits these qualities, the more he will be respected and followed, the healthier the team environment will be, and the more they are likely to produce sustainable results. There is little surprise that coaches like Gary Kirsten, Stephen Fleming, Rahul Dravid and Trevor Beyliss are respected by most cricketers today, and that they lead happy teams that have enjoyed success.

Like heads and tails on a coin, there is another side to these 'healthy' alpha leaders. Too much self-confidence can flip over into arrogance, creating closed-minded know-it-alls who talk but do not listen. They rarely admit to being wrong and will cut down anyone who disagrees with them. Many of us have been around that leader who is so full of his own ideas that he does all the talking and answers his own questions without giving anyone else the chance to do so. In this way, alpha leaders become what I refer to as 'unhealthy' versions of the same animal.

The alpha leaders' high expectations can lead to them being constantly dissatisfied if things aren't perfect—which they seldom are. They will constantly find flaws in others and will harp on the mistakes they make. There are sport coaches who regularly rant and rave after their team has delivered a performance that is below the coach's expectations—even though, in any given season, this will naturally happen. They harp on the error each time a mistake is made, whether it's a catch dropped, a below-par bowling spell or dismissal through a poor shot. Some captains openly berate their players' errors on the field of play, whilst managing to overlook their own errors.

Unhealthy alpha leaders are overly critical and do not appreciate a job well done. Their habit of highlighting the negative and overlooking the positive is demotivating for others.

The desire to produce results can be over-amplified, causing the unhealthy alpha leader to become impatient and demanding. Getting the job done right becomes more important than relationships, as they readily explode at someone who is a bit late with a report, who doesn't follow their often-rushed and incomplete instructions, or who does not bowl to the field that is set for them. For them, someone's child being sick or a grandmother dying is no reason not to get the job done on time. Many a young fast bowler is bowled into the ground for the sake of a trophy and the coach looking good, even though it puts the bowler at risk of suffering a stress fracture and missing six months of cricket.

Alpha leaders are often (outwardly) unemotional and are highly judgmental of others who show emotions. A cricketer who shows emotion may be labelled as weak or soft. Yet, when angry, the alpha leader may well display this anger, without seeing it as an emotional outburst. Also, his humour tends towards sarcasm and is often at the expense of others. In some professional team sporting environments, dissing, putting down or trashing teammates is a popular source of humour, which, whilst funny, does cause some emotional hurt. But, of course, in this type of environment, hurt cannot be shown because it would be called soft and would invite even more abuse. So, players act tough to hide their hurt, which is neither healthy nor sustainable. They laugh to hide their real reaction, and then return the diss.

Unhealthy alpha leaders will convince themselves that it is okay to compromise on morals and ethics if it helps them achieve their own selfish needs.

Younger and older alpha males may act differently. A younger (teenage) male will often be good-looking, physically strong, and will look to dominate others through their physicality—conquering males by intimidation, a physical fighting or dominating them on the sports field and conquering females through sexual conquests, as they 'hunt' them in night clubs and pubs. Older alphas (male and female) will evolve to dominate others psychologically and emotionally rather than physically, exercising power over others in their professional capacity, hiring, firing and directing them in business or sport environments. Older alpha males will still seek to dominate females sexually, just as alpha females may use sex to dominate. Although it's said that while alpha females might use sex to dominate, many still want the male to take the dominant role when they enter the bedroom.

Thus, not all alpha leaders are the same, nor do they have the same impact on others. Below, I summarise the impact of two types of alpha leaders, healthy and unhealthy.

HEALTHY ALPHA LEADERS

Healthy alpha leaders will exhibit positive characteristics most of the time and will succumb far less often to the negative or unhealthy ones mentioned above. I suggest that they can be best recognised by their impact on others around them, rather than by the traditional measure of the results they produce. A healthy alpha will be surrounded by subordinates and team members who are mostly happy, who respect and like them, and who warm up to them most of the time. Such a team will probably produce better results than more skilled teams, because players have a sense of playing for something greater than just themselves. There is a sense of unity and loyalty towards the team or the company.

During the 2012 New Year's Test against Sri Lanka, Jacques Kallis was not out on 183 at the tea interval. When captain Graeme Smith asked if the team should declare at tea or after he reached 200, Jacques answered, 'Don't consider my score, make whatever decision is best for the team.'

Faf du Plessis defending 24 consecutive deliveries with his score on 98 on Test debut might well have been an early sign of the success and followership he enjoys as the current South African captain.

A healthy alpha will most likely place high demands on others, but they will experience it as being fair, and might even feel cared for.

Graeme Smith was an alpha leader. He asked a lot of his players and did not accept mediocrity. He was a strong leader with a good presence, and people listened when he spoke. Especially towards the end of his tenure as Proteas captain, he listened to others, he was sensitive to what they may be going through, he asked how people were doing, and waited for the answer. He was both respected and well-liked, and led a happy team. When a sports team has a healthy alpha leader, other alphas in the team will almost always take the lead and themselves adopt more of the healthy characteristics. Graeme Smith's leadership, which by his own admission was not always healthy in the earlier part of his tenure as national captain, went a long way in keeping the Proteas united and resolute against the Australian onslaught for twelve consecutive Test match days.

Healthy alpha males treat women with respect and forge healthy relationships with them. They are comfortable in a woman's company, find it easy to make conversation, and are comfortable with silence. They do not need to impress.

UNHEALTHY ALPHA LEADERS

These people display more of the negative tendencies. The more regularly they display them, the less healthy their leadership and the team culture they create is likely to be. And the people who suffer the most are those around them. Particularly in the corporate environment, unhealthy alphas may deliver good financial results because they are intelligent, hard-working, strategic thinkers, excellent implementers and hard disciplinarians. But they achieve these results at the expense of others, often using these others as 'resources' that are there to achieve their own selfish or egotistical needs.

When sports teams take them on as administrators, coaches, captains or senior players, they use their position to serve their own needs and aspirations, to appear better or stronger than others in the team, to increase their public profile, and grow their income. Their position of authority allows them to use disciplinary measures as the stick to control others.

The environment under this leader is likely to be one where people are focused on looking after themselves, as they go into survival mode, whilst seeking to use the situation for their own gain or development. People may still work hard, not for the team's cause, but their own.

In cricket, one would find a culture of players selfishly looking after their own performance, looking for a 'not out' rather than sacrifice their wicket for the team. Bowlers might bowl defensively to look after their figures when the team needs them to attack, or to attack and chase wickets for themselves when the team needs them to defend. In an unhealthy environment, there will be very little backing of a teammate who is struggling; few will notice, some won't care, and others will actually be happy, as it takes the limelight or pressure off them. (Some of these things might also happen in healthy teams, but not as a permanent feature.)

In an organisation, in the shadow of an unhealthy alpha, some employees will do just enough to be seen to be doing their job, working at maybe 50 per cent of their capability, while other, more ambitious employees will use the time to learn as much as they can, accumulate as many contacts as possible, with their CVs out there. Again, there will be little loyalty towards the leader or the organisation.

Thing is, it is unlikely that such leaders will care much or be overtly aware of other people's responses to them. Their entire focus will be on themselves and on the things that matter to them; it will be more about their own results and the bottom line than about people.

A sports team with an unhealthy alpha leader inadvertently permits other alphas in the team to also be unhealthy. A toxic environment is likely to ensue, along with infighting and the emergence of rivalry between alphas. There will be jostling for power, disciplinary problems might well arise, and eventually team results will suffer. During his tenure as vice-captain, Clarke had a much publicised physical confrontation in the Australian dressing room with teammate Simon Katich. Three months after the Test series described above and under the same captain and coach, four Australian players (Shane Watson, Mitchell Johnson, James Pattinson and Usman Khawaja) were sent home from a tour of India for not submitting a homework assignment to the coach. Clarke was reported to have publicly called teammate and ex-vice-captain Shane Watson a 'tumour' that could lead to cancer in the team. Some of his teammates suggested the reverse was more the case.

Under an unhealthy alpha leader, a team with highly talented individuals might do well for a while, even for a few seasons, while really good players are at the top of their game, but this will not last, and when things do start to unravel and go wrong, it could take years to rectify the culture of selfishness, backstabbing and infighting.

There are teams that project an image of a bunch of tough guys, hardcore alpha males, the put-on-your-warrior-outfit blokes. When your leaders are stereotypical blokes, they endorse stereotypical 'blokeness' as being fine and acceptable, and things like sensitivity, emotion, caring or vulnerability as being weak or soft.

Australian all-rounder Shane Watson was in the Rajasthan Royals team when I first joined them. Until that point, he was one player in international cricket I couldn't quite put my finger on. I could figure out the broad strokes of most players' personalities and find ways to work with them. But not Watto. It took me only one day on the same team to get him. Unlike the image often projected of him—the image I had mistakenly taken to be true—Shane is a very sensitive, very caring, very thoughtful and a very gentle man.

At the time of writing, I had worked with Shane in the same T20 team for six competitions, in India and Australia. He is one of the best team players I have ever worked with. He is as engaging and attentive to senior players as he is to young and inexperienced players, regardless of nationality. He brings beautiful, nurturing, empathetic, caring qualities to the team *when he is able to be himself*. But if he's in one of those alpha environments where these traits are judged as being weak, he can't bring these things to the party and the team doesn't get the full value he has to offer.

I wonder how many other sensitive, caring, empathetic, thoughtful males have had these wonderful yet gentle qualities subdued under an unhealthy alpha or an old school, hardcore, tough-guy leader. I'm certainly not knocking being tough, but tough works best when balanced with gentle or other-oriented qualities such as caring, empathy or self-awareness.

A genuine alpha is secure and does not need to prove anything to anyone. In some cases, and this is more so with males, an unhealthy alpha might in fact not be a genuine alpha, but a wannabe alpha whose posturing, bullying and generally unhealthy ego-driven behaviour is used as a mask for his personal insecurities. This is where one might witness the cruelty of the weak leader.

Unhealthy alphas are less likely to feel concern for the well-being of teammates or others, unless of course they have something to gain from the others' well-being. In the case of the unhealthy alpha male, he is more likely to be a womaniser, chasing women for the sake of conquering, whilst harbouring a lack of respect for them. He is more prone to trying to impress women through his behaviour and stories, or by buying things for them. He will seek out the 'trophy girl' or best-looking girl to impress others, as much or maybe even more than for the quality of the relationship. In seeking validation, he will often need to tell others of his sexual exploits.

Both healthy and unhealthy alphas have a strong focus on themselves. The fundamental difference, I believe, is in their wiring around things like compassion, empathy, caring, concern and similar 'other-person oriented' traits. In the example earlier of the Proteas in Australia, both Graeme Smith and Gary Kirsten were sensitive to the difficulties of others and had compassion. They were genuinely concerned about the well-being of the players, and also of the players' partners and families. These characteristics would almost certainly have prevented either from acting out as an unhealthy alpha and thus having any negative impact on the team.

Traits such as caring, compassion, empathy and thoughtfulness, which I suggest are characteristic of healthy alphas and antidotes for unhealthy alpha behaviour, are generally accepted to be 'feminine energies' since, whether by nurture or nature, they tend to manifest more often in females. As a result, it's less likely for a female to be an unhealthy alpha leader.

Alpha leaders are not boxed into one way of being, into healthy or unhealthy; rather, they have the ability to shift along the continuum from degrees of healthy to unhealthy. With coaching, awareness and/or a good reason and willingness to change, an unhealthy alpha can shift towards operating in a healthier manner. Similarly, a healthy alpha who develops greed, a hunger for power, or becomes caught up in his own success, can (often unconsciously) shift towards operating in a more unhealthy fashion. As discussed in previous chapters, self-awareness and personal mastery helps underpin and sustain healthy alpha leadership and avert its unhealthy manifestations.

WARRIOR, SOLDIER OR COWARD

I have spoken about alpha leaders, but there is another lens through which to view high performers, especially those who participate in contact or combat sports: the lens of the warrior.

Almost any athlete in a combat sport, whether team or individual, wants to ideally access their 'warrior mode' in competition. The warrior is an ancient archetype, standing for someone who has a clear purpose and mission, is loyal to causes greater than themselves, and in combat is strong, decisive, disciplined, detached, unemotional, focused and clinical in the execution of their task. They do combat in the proverbial 'zone' or flow. They can overcome pain and setbacks, as they master their body and mind. Almost all martial arts have these characteristics at the core of their ethos.

At the peak of his career, a fired-up Dale Steyn epitomised warrior mode when he had the bit between his teeth and smelled opposition blood. Think Bruce Lee, Julius Caesar, Richard the Lionheart, William Wallace, Mr Miyagi in the *Karate Kid* and the Samurai Warriors. A rugby team with all fifteen players in warrior mode, as can be seen in the eyes of the All Blacks during their famous pre-game haka, is a sight to behold and an ominous prospect for any opposition.

Like unhealthy alphas, throughout history we have encountered unhealthy warriors, either those who are fired up with too much warrior energy, or too little.

Lacking warrior energy in a combat situation, one might encounter the coward, cry baby or mommy's boy, epitomised by Commodus in the movie *Gladiator*, the cowardly Prince of Rome who arrived only after the war had finished, and who was filled with jealousy of the true warrior, Maximus. Lacking backbone, cowards seek comfort, safety and ease, they back down or run away from conflict, are pushovers, have a low tolerance for pain, and tend to complain about rather than resolve problems. They also tend to be people-pleasers.

When the volume is turned too high on warrior energy, one might encounter the bully or sadist, or the soldier who kills for the sake of killing. Think Johnny Lawrence and his trainer, sensei John Kreese in the *Karate Kid* movies.

This unhealthy 'warrior' compromises values, ethics and the spirit of combat in order to win or injure, like Mike Tyson when he bit

Holyfield's ear, and rugby players who gouge an opponent's eye. They are so consumed with winning, they can ignore others, family and even their own health, they lack discipline and are overly aggressive and even abusive. It becomes all about them, as they serve their own rather than a greater cause.

Especially in contact sports, competitors will often provoke opponents to push them out of warrior mode, either to instill fear and get them to back down, or to get them over-charged, to 'see red', to 'snap', and make the game-changing errors that follow. In the 2006 soccer World Cup final, Italian Marco Materazzi insulted Frenchman Zinedine Zidane's sister, to which Zidane infamously responded by head-butting him in the chest, and got sent off as a result. Italy went on to won the final 2-1.

The (questionable) practice of verbal abuse or sledging in cricket is an attempt to break players' focus, to get them to retreat and doubt themselves (turn the volume down on warrior mode), or turn the volume too high, getting them out of their zone so that they make retaliatory mistakes. Zidane admitted: 'If you look at the fourteen red cards I had in my career, twelve of them were a result of provocation. This isn't justification, this isn't an excuse, but my passion, temper and blood made me react.'[3]

There is debate about whether engaging in sledging (chirping) or verbal abuse is within the spirit of the so-called 'gentleman's game' of cricket. The best advice I've ever heard on the subject came from the late Hylton Ackerman senior, fondly known as Dutchman, a former South African cricketer and one of the best cricket brains I've ever had the privilege of working with. (He was coach for the three years I captained the Western Province under-23 team.) He said, 'In order to chirp a fellow cricketer, you need to earn the right to do so. And when you've earned the right, you don't need to chirp.'

Some disruptive comments are funny or clever, others are abusive and insulting. The latter, in particular, might work to disrupt an opponent in the moment of play. There is, however, another and longer-lasting impact, which is on the type of person you will be remembered as. A true warrior would not engage in such behaviour, only a coward posturing as a bully or a real bully would do so. The likes of Rahul Dravid, Gary Kirsten, Michael Hussey, V.V.S. Laxman and Hashim Amla never abused an opponent; they had too much respect for themselves and their opponents.

The focused, combative and confrontational energy of the warrior mode that athletes access in the heat of battle requires de-rolling after the game. This mode is not suited for public spaces, family homes or social environments. When players do not come down from this testosterone-fuelled mode, when the beers and war-cries continue in the dressing room, players run the risk of even the smallest spark triggering the fight that sits just below the surface. We've all read of the post-match nightclub or pub brawl, or the domestic violence that happens on the night of a game. Soldiers involved in long-term conflict often find it very difficult to de-role and integrate back home, into general society and family life.

Coaches and captains, especially in contact sports and/or after emotionally charged games, should take time to bring players and the team energy back down, and connect players with the friend, family man, role model, good-guy aspects of their personality. Warrior mode is only desirable on the field of play, in training, and maybe when there's a genuine threat to your or your family's safety. The true martial artist or warrior has enduring self-esteem, discipline and respect, and will only engage in physical confrontation as a necessary last resort.

ALPHA LEADERS: A STORY OF CARING, COMPASSION AND EMPATHY

Healthy and unhealthy leaders have an impact on culture and people. In teams where leaders have the 'care-factor', the impact is often fondly remembered.

In 2013, the Rajasthan Royals beat the Chennai Super Kings to progress to their first ever Champions League T20 cricket final. On that same semi-final night, the Royals demonstrated something quite extraordinary, something that had me unexpectedly choked up with emotion when I spoke about it at the next day's team meeting.

The extraordinary thing was not the comprehensive and clinical manner in which we defeated the superstar-laden Chennai team (they had ten internationally-capped players in their team; we had three). It was not that the win secured us our first-ever CLT20 final placing, nor that it recorded the Royals' thirteenth consecutive win at our home, the Sawai Man Singh Stadium in Jaipur.

For me, as the team's head coach, it was something else that was remarkable. In the 17th over of Chennai's second-innings chase, as the game was heading towards a nerve-wracking finish, two of our fielders collided in an attempt to save 1 run (the team had already agreed to put their bodies on the line to save a run). The 1 run was saved, but it left Shane Watson dazed from a nasty collision with Brad Hodge's knee. Brad did not get up. He was carried off the field wincing in pain, clearly suffering from more than just a bruise.

3 overs later, the Royals' fighting spirit prevailed over the Super Kings to win them a place in the 2013 CLT20 final. The on-field celebration was, well, hardly a celebration, but a rather muted, 'Okay cool, we won'. After every game, the Royals had a deliberate 'humble-in-the-result' attitude, not getting over-excited by victory nor depressed by failure. But this stifled celebration was not normal.

In the privacy of our change room, we were visibly more depressed than after any defeat. There was not one whoop of celebration, no high fives, no music. This somewhat bizarre situation saw players sitting in silence and others quietly staring into their post-match plates of food. Off to the side, Brad Hodge lay on his back, ice-pack strapped to his knee, still writhing in pain. We were later to learn that his knee ligaments were badly damaged.

Each player made his way past Brad, some offering quiet words, others just putting a sympathetic hand on his leg, chest or head. Shane Watson sat in his usual chair and seemed to be fighting back tears. It had been an accident, but he felt responsible. It was his head that had hit Brad's knee.

Attempts to lift Shane's spirits were fruitless. I was not surprised by this. Watto epitomised the Royals' team spirit—he placed the team's needs ahead of his own, and he was hurting for Brad.

After an hour in the change room and not one single beer or glass of champagne later, the team headed for the team bus. Brad had left much earlier for an MRI scan at the local hospital. We drove back in a silence characteristic of a defeated team—the bus driver must have thought he was transporting the Chennai team.

En route to the hotel, I got a phone call. It was Brad. He had already returned to the hotel. He was calling to request the team to meet in the team room immediately upon our arrival, which would be about 1 a.m. This was a bit strange because we usually steered away from team meetings after a game.

Back in the team room, we waited while Brad slowly made his way to join us. He would have had no idea that the mood in the team was still somewhat subdued. He hobbled into the room on a set of crutches, to what I can only describe as a hero's welcome. He pulled us into a huddle and then proceeded to deliver a powerful and moving off-the-cuff speech. He enthusiastically congratulated the team on a 'tremendous win' and went on to tell us how excited he was about our 'truly magnificent performance'. He congratulated the match-winning efforts of Rahul Shukla (he had removed Dhoni early in his innings) and (man-of-the-match) Pravin Tambe, and he hailed the Royals' campaign in the Champions League as a 'lion's effort'. To conclude, he invited the whole team to celebrate an 'awesome victory'—a celebration that had been stifled since victory was sealed. Brad's talk gave permission for, and lifted the lid on, the celebration that the team so richly deserved.

As I walked back to my room at 1:30 a.m., I was filled with emotion and a sense of pride. Rajasthan Royals was a team that spent only seven weeks of the year together. A team that consisted of senior international cricketers from different countries as well as lesser known and uncapped Indian players, with ages ranging from eighteen to forty-two. It was a team that only months earlier had had their hearts ripped out by three teammates being jailed for spot-fixing.

In the two hours after beating Chennai, I had seen the team discover for itself that sharing the sadness of a teammate who had been injured in battle was more important than winning the second biggest game in its six-year existence.

This was the epitome of 'team' spirit; the impact of leaders who, above all else, care more for their teammates than any consequential externalities that could make or break their careers as professional cricketers. When people talk of a care-factor in a team, that is what it looks like.

26

THE PAINFUL LOSSES

The pain of losing, coupled with the desire to not want to repeat the experience, often drives us to learn more diligently and comprehensively from failure than from success. Some of my biggest lessons came from painful failures, as happened with the sex dossier blunder. Two other career failures stand out in particular, and to be honest, part of me would rather omit them from this book.

One happened to the Rajasthan Royals team en route to the IPL finals for the second consecutive year during my stint as head coach, in 2014. In order to qualify, the team needed to win only one of its last three games. Such was the strength of our position that even if we lost all three, the only way we wouldn't qualify was if a struggling Mumbai Indians went on to win five of their remaining matches. This situation left the Royals' owners, fans and players confident of making another play-off. But we lost our next two games, and Mumbai went on a four-game winning streak. The two teams met in the last game of the season, and between them, there was only one slot available in the play-offs. RR batted first and scored a very respectable 189 in the allotted 20 overs. We had a superior tournament run rate and had won one more game than Mumbai, so they would need to beat us, and they would need to do so by crossing our score within 14.3 overs. A near impossibility.

After a relentless assault of boundaries and more than their fair share of luck, Mumbai found themselves on 188 after 14.2 overs, needing 2 to win off the final ball to qualify ahead of us. That ball saw Mumbai batsman Ambati Rayudu getting run out attempting the second run. At 14.3 overs, scores were tied, leaving most Royals' players and fans celebrating qualification (Mumbai had not passed our score by the required 14.3 over mark). But the game was not over. A lengthy period of confusion followed as each team tried to understand the run rate equation. Match officials eventually confirmed that for Mumbai to qualify with a better run rate, they needed 4 runs off the very next ball. There was a new batsman on strike, Mumbai's number 7, and our bowler was the experienced Australian James Faulkner. The fourth ball of that fourteenth over was a knee-high full toss directed at the new batsman's legs, which he sent sailing across the ropes for 6. In that moment, and as Mumbai sealed a miraculous finals birth ahead of us, I knew I'd have some serious dealing with failure to navigate. Not only the team's, but also my own!

In the hours that followed, the players, owners, fans and I were gutted, devastated, bewildered. I didn't know where to turn, what to say, or even how to lift Faulkner and the players' spirits. I felt sorry for the owners and fans, and wanted to apologise because I felt so responsible, but couldn't find suitable words other than 'sorry'. This apologetic state also gave rise to an old pattern of thinking, that 'I'm not good enough'. It left me lacking confidence when I really needed to be strong for others. I was also so preoccupied with questioning all that had happened, in my head, that I paid little attention and gave very little support to the players I was employed to serve. I failed the team as a leader in the dark hours that followed that loss.

The next few days continued to be horrible, made worse by learning that that one ball meant the owners missed out on nearly two million US dollars as a result of not qualifying for play-offs, and I later realised that I had missed out on a 20,000-dollar bonus. The players packed their bags and went their individual ways, not knowing who would still be in the team when we next met, ten months later. What also followed was months of investigations by owners and management into what went wrong and what changes needed to be made. The difference between this happening versus not, was one ball.

Whilst it took a number of days for me to process the disappointment, one saving grace was that I had no regrets. Even though we had been in a strong position, we had never become complacent or cut any corners in preparation. Had we done so, I would not have been able to sleep at night, following that freakish loss.

This horrible experience did however deliver an incredibly rich lesson in how to (and how not to) manage myself, and others, after a really disappointing tournament loss. I would get to draw on it two years later, in Dubai.

Fast forward to February 2016. I was coach of the Lahore Qalandars. After coming fifth out of five teams in season one of the Pakistan Super League, we found ourselves needing to win the last game to qualify for play-offs in season two. In a low-scoring game, with Karachi Kings chasing 156 to win, we needed to defend 28 off the last 2 overs, and 14 runs off the last. The first 4 deliveries of the final over went for 4 runs, leaving 2 deliveries to defend 10 to win and thus qualify. West Indian batsman Kieron Pollard, who had enjoyed very little success that season, chose that moment to sweetly time 2 consecutive balls over the ropes for consecutive sixes! It would be our second successive bottom of the log finish, and another very bitter pill to swallow. The owners had extended themselves to support the team in every conceivable way, and were understandably devastated. We all were.

Drawing on the experience of the loss two years earlier at the IPL, I was able to suspend the level to which I felt sorry for myself, and to channel my energy towards supporting the players in dealing with the loss. That evening, we all met in the team room and discussed our feelings and experiences of the season. As it turned out, we had failed on the field, but had created a very special team culture in a very short space of time, which saw players pull together strongly rather than fragment in the wake of the demoralising loss. Great cultures make it easier to weather stormy seas. Also, it's in difficult times that coaches and leaders get tested. Dealing with victory is easy.

Another aspect about losing that I'm moved to mention relates to something the ex-Proteas all-rounder and highly experienced coach Eric Simons speaks about: that 'as coaches, we are hired when we are not ready, and then fired when we are'. Those who know him, will know that Eric has a profound depth of knowledge and wisdom regarding coaching, and life.

Maybe it's human nature, but we tend to scrutinise losing more than winning. The only upside is that when losing hurts enough to motivate deep, thorough and honest learning, it leaves the 'loser' as a real winner when it comes to lessons learned and experiences gained.

I found myself well prepared and confident, the most I had been ahead of a season as head coach, leading into season three with the Lahore Qalandars in the Pakistan Super League. After two bottom-of-the-log finishes in ostensibly a brand new tournament, pretty much all, including the smallest of errors and cracks, had been exposed and resolved. We now had the right players and support staff on board, understood how to manage most of the players, and what strategy suited the team and the tournament. Three months out, with much of the preparation already complete, the decision was taken to fire the old and bring in new coaching staff. This was when I really got to understand what Eric meant when he said about coaches, 'that we are fired when we are most ready'. (The team went to end sixth out of six in that third season.)

Being fired was another form of failure that I would now get to navigate (it was my first time being fired), especially as I had felt so ready and on track to lead the team into season three. Once I learned that the decision was made and set in stone, the first thing was to accept it. Which I did. I understand how professional coaching works. Lose often enough; get fired. It's simple. Next was how to respond.

Being fired is a blow to the professional ego, and however I chose to spin it to myself, it still hurt. So, I decided to write a letter to the decision-makers, who were all successful businessmen in their own right but new to owning T20 cricket teams.

I wrote about the problems that we inherited in season one, how we had remedied many of these ahead of season two. Following that last ball loss in season two, I detailed the areas we had further improved upon, including listing some difficult yet key leadership decisions, which very few knew were required, and that I was best placed to make. With good people, good systems, a very stable and happy team culture, all that was now required were the all-important runs and wickets—which we knew would come, and we had clear plans for how to get them.

Finally, I highlighted the well-known phenomenon that a team will initially regress in terms of its development when there is any significant change in key leadership positions. This team was nearing the peak of its upward curve and was in a strong position to launch from the lessons of the first two seasons. Three months away from the tournament was possibly not the best time to change course from a 'mature' team entering the 'performance' phase; there was a risk of it going back to a 'growing' team in a 'building' phase. After two years of changes associated with growth and building, if the team did badly in the third, it would require possibly another two years of rebuilding with the new leadership.

Rightly or wrongly, I never did send that letter. Partly because I knew that some of it was written with the need to point out in what ways the decision was wrong, and where I was right. This was my ego speaking; it needed to fight back after the upset of being fired. But the decision had been made, it was outside my control, and could not be changed. I needed to accept it, wish the new coaching staff well and continue to support the owners and players (who had always been good to me throughout those two years, and still are). My previous experience of a painful loss (with the Rajasthan Royals in 2014) had helped equip me to follow the seventh habit of highly successful losers: to grow, and show character in loss.

Losing is inevitable, and it hurts. What's important is to work diligently, smartly and tirelessly to stave it off. When it does come, accept it, knowing that your character will often be defined by how you manage it. Be courageous, get back up, learn, refocus, grow, and go again.

27

NO 'ZEN SHIT'

There's a phrase to describe an issue that is too important to ignore, but sufficiently unpleasant that people shy away from mentioning it. They call it the elephant in the room. Well, in this case, it turned out to be more of a rhino than an elephant, as it was a vet committed to fighting rhino poaching who allowed me to confront the single most important question hanging over the Proteas—how to deal with choking.

Citing family reasons, Gary Kirsten had resigned his position as head coach of the Proteas in May 2013, a year before the end of his contract. I stayed on as team performance director, mainly to help with the transition. Seven months into his tenure, Gary's replacement, Russell Domingo, would be taking the team to an ICC event for his first time: the T20 World Cup in Bangladesh. And nobody in the team set-up—neither the players, nor the coaching staff, the media, the players' families—needed reminding that choking was an issue for the South African cricket team.

Our preparation for the World Cup kicked off with a two-day camp at an Eastern Cape game reserve where we were treated to a wonderful mix of bush hospitality, stunning landscapes, close encounters with big game, an array of fascinating guest speakers and our own internal workshops. I was scheduled to lead a morning session on the mental aspects of playing in a World Cup. Although I had already planned my session, something happened the night before that had me going back to the drawing board. We heard an ordinary man give an extraordinary speech.

Doctor Will Fowlds is a vet, a fine profession but hardly a rarity. Even his specialist expertise in treating game animals is relatively common in a country like South Africa where the safari industry is so well developed. But what he said had me thinking about a different calibre of individual entirely, people like Nelson Mandela, Mother Teresa, Mahatma Gandhi, Martin Luther King Jr., William Wallace (from the movie *Braveheart*) and Maximus (from *Gladiator*). None of these people needed to be motivated by a coach before going to their personal 'World Cup', the critical moment in their lives. They did not need to get their mind right for performance. They were not impaired by setbacks or tempted to give up in the face of extreme adversity. They did not choke. Quite the opposite. Crisis situations saw them at their best. When the pressure was ramped up, they prevailed. I found myself wondering what it was about these people that gave them this ability. What lessons might there be in their lives for a team of cricketers? How was it possible to acquire at least some of their clarity, resolve and unwavering focus?

Dr Fowlds is no trained orator, no regular on the motivational speaker circuit. But what he told us that evening was unforgettable; not just his story, but what it told us about him, his passion for being a vet, and something much more fundamental.

Dr Fowlds shared with the Proteas a story about two rhinos that had been poached for their horns in the very same game reserve where we were staying. Both animals suffered horrendous disfigurement and were barely alive when he got there. He showed us pictures of their hacked faces, which depicted the gruesome reality of poaching. Their names were Thandi and Themba, and we felt his pain as he described day after day of desperate treatment and care-fighting to nurse these noble animals to life. We were riveted, listening to him. And then he showed video footage of Themba drowning, too physically weak to clamber free from a shallow waterhole, twenty-four days after the callous attack (see video link in the 'References').[1] Dr Fowlds spoke openly of his heartache, of these animals' struggles against human cruelty and the reality of poaching. As he shared his story, I sat with tears streaming down my face, aware of many other Proteas crying around me. Dr Fowlds described the day of Themba's death as one of the worst of his life. As one man in a small team fighting against a multi-billion-dollar poaching and smuggling racket, he pledged that he would win the battle against rhino poaching someday; that 'the poachers will only win over my dead body'.

In *Braveheart*, William Wallace cried freedom as he was about to be decapitated. And Nelson Mandela famously served an ideal for which he was prepared to die. In his defence statement at the 1964 Rivonia trial, Mandela famously stated, 'I have fought against white domination, and I have fought against black domination. I have cherished the ideal of a democratic and free society in which all persons will live together in harmony with equal opportunities. It is an ideal which I hope to live for, and to see realised. But my Lord, if need be, it is an ideal for which I am prepared to die.' He would spend a total of twenty-seven years in jail for his cause.

Dr Fowlds appeared on the surface to be an ordinary man, yet he was accomplishing extraordinary things in his world. His efforts were having a significant impact against poaching. His story moved the room like I have seldom witnessed, and this was a room packed with individuals who had sat through countless presentations by the good and the great.

It is tempting to suggest that Dr Fowlds's message to the Proteas was about what can be achieved through commitment, dedication, self-belief, focus, determination, the will to win, and similar traits that most performance experts and motivational speakers routinely advocate. If we studied the ways of Mandela, Gandhi, Mother Teresa, King Jr. and other icons, we would know that they demonstrated these traits in abundance.

Here's the rub. I wasn't convinced of the relevance or even importance of trying to instill these traits in the Proteas cricketers in their pursuit of T20 World Cup success.

The traits that we observe when we study successful people are not necessarily what makes them successful. It's almost like observing winners standing on the podium and then concluding that standing there makes them winners. The podium position and the observable performance traits are a result of something that came before, something that came from deep within the individual, and which then manifested itself to the outside world as dedication and commitment and the podium finish that followed. To focus on the traits of a winner is to miss what makes a winner.

If we look deeper, we find that Mandela, and so many other inspirational people, had experiences in life that led to them becoming deeply connected to a purpose or a cause that extended well beyond themselves. Dr Fowlds is connected to protecting animals, that is his cause, driving him to counter the most savage rhino poaching crisis in history. The cause is the centre of focus for all these truly special individuals, placed ahead of personal comfort, ahead of looking good, or of reward, and even ahead of their personal safety.

Plugged in as they were to this greater life purpose/calling/cause, call it what you will, there was no need for anyone to coach them around motivation, goal-setting, positive self-talk, affirmations, self-belief, dedication and commitment. These so-called key performance factors flowed naturally and in abundance, emanating from a source deep within, like a broken hydrant gushing with water. They didn't need approval or applause, nor did they baulk at criticism or repeated failures. They were not in it for name, fame or fortune.

ASK NOT 'WHAT', BUT 'WHY'

The following morning, after an early game drive where we were lucky enough to see rhinos in the reserve, still enjoying the protection of Dr Fowlds and his team, I was scheduled to discuss the aspect of mental preparation for our World Cup campaign. Inspired by the talk the night before, I decided to cover not *what* we needed to do to win the World Cup, but *why* we wanted to win it.

I wanted the players to explore if there was potentially a greater purpose or calling that could serve as their deep internal driver. I wanted to ask questions they might never have been asked before, to try to tease out something I believed could be the most powerful motivator of all.

It was a crisp autumn morning as we gathered outdoors, surrounded by the sounds and smells of the African bush. I started the session by referring to Dr Fowlds and the remarkable impact he was having in the world. If he was able to accomplish this without the fame, fortune and celebrity enjoyed by the cricketers in our squad, what might be possible for us? Were we doing justice to the potential impact each player had as an international cricketer in a sports-crazy country?

I asked the players to contemplate whether there could be a reason or a higher purpose for being born with the talent they were gifted at birth, and for the opportunity to represent their country at a World Cup. Although a slightly obscure question, I knew that nine of the fifteen-man squad were men of faith, either Christian or Muslim, so they would have a natural reference point to this higher purpose. The players thought about it and then shared their views in pairs. No one answer was agreed upon, but as planned, it got them thinking.

Next, I asked who the players had to thank for where they were today; to whom did they owe a debt of gratitude. I asked them to write this down, so that they got to really 'sense' the feeling of gratitude. Apart from gratitude being an ancient practice across all cultures and religions, feelings of gratitude have been shown to reduce negative emotions and increase positive emotions such as feeling energised, alert and enthusiastic.[2] The mere act of giving thanks can have a remarkable impact on a person's well-being, leaving them more agreeable, happy and less narcissistic compared with less grateful people.[3] Modern neuroscience supports this theory, affirming that gratitude causes dopamine and serotonin to be released in the brain, which activates our 'bliss' centre and averts loneliness and depression. Literally, the more often we do the gratitude exercise, the happier we get, and the easier it becomes to find contentment.

Discussing the first question and then adding the feelings of gratitude saw the team energy become increasingly sincere and connected. When the time was right, I asked the next question I had up my sleeve: 'So, *why* do you want to do well at the World Cup?'

This was met with silence, even some blank stares. I let the silence hang.

Author Simon Sinek suggests that most organisations and leaders focus primarily on *what* they want (in our case, win the World Cup), then decide *how* they will do it (with good on-field strategy), and that's where they stop.[4] *What* we want to do, and *how* we do it comes from our thinking brain, which is where language comes from. But this is not the part of the brain that drives our behaviour.

Why we do what we do, emanates from our deeper and more primal limbic brain, which does not have language. Our deeper 'knowing', our 'gut feel', comes from this place where our *why* sits, which is the purpose, cause or belief that inspires us to do what we do. Dr Fowlds, Mandela and all the others I mentioned were all wired to and driven from this place. All of us have it, this well of inspiration that sits deep within our being, but not all draw from it. Yet, it's there, waiting.

If at least some of the cricketers could identify and plug into this greater purpose, they might find that motivation, focus, resilience, calm under pressure, freedom of expression, etc. would flow in abundance. Possibly, this deeper drive might prevail over the shallow and more self-oriented thoughts related to fear of failure, anxiety or pressure that arise in the superficial thinking brain.

For these Proteas cricketers, there was a direct link between wanting to do well (their *what*) and how they ended up playing (their *how*) in World Cup games. Too much focus on wanting to win (and overcome the choker label) caused overthinking in the pressure moments, which led to basic errors in thinking and thus execution. It was a self-fulfilling anxiety. By definition, this was 'choking'. The overthinking brain dominates the limbic brain, shutting down access to the all-important instinctive knowledge acquired from thousands of hours of training, practicing and playing.

If you're not one of the 43-odd million who have already watched Sinek's TED talk, 'How great leaders inspire action', I would suggest doing so. It's only eighteen minutes long, and if that sounds like too much, there's a good five-minute summary of the talk on YouTube.[5]

Not just for these World Cup cricketers, for everyone in a professional pursuit, it is worth asking not only *what* you want and *how* to get whatever your World Cup might be, but also *why* you want it. You might want to get rich, make a team, get a great job, be the first to hold a particular record. But these are all results, not motives. This is your *what* answer. The more important question is *why* you want it.

Guiding the exploration of w*hy* they wanted to do well at the World Cup, I suggested that players focus on the positive impact they could have on others, whether it was family, friends, society, the environment, the game of cricket, their country, or whatever else it might be.

Most of this team had already listened to Mike Horn, and possibly some other speaker-adventurers, and thus would know that almost every extreme adventurer who goes beyond what was previously thought to be humanly possible, does so for a cause greater than himself or herself. Waterman Chris Bertish paddled solo for 120 days and 7,500 kilometres across the Atlantic Ocean on a stand-up paddleboard to raise funds for Operation Smile and The Lunchbox fund. Mike Horn circumnavigated the world and some of the most extreme parts of the planet to raise environmental awareness. Lewis Pugh swims in Arctic oceans to raise ocean awareness, and Sir Ranulph 'Ran' Fiennes has adventured to raise over US$20 million for six different charities.

When the going gets tough for these and other extreme adventurers, way tougher than any World Cup situation could ever be, when it may appear far easier and safer to quit, they don't. Bertish said after his incredible Atlantic crossing: 'There were so many life-threatening situations (…) But here's the thing—your "why" has to be so powerful that you can call on it at any particular time to be able to get you through and overcome any obstacle or challenge that comes your way (…) your why has to become so powerful, emotionally, that no matter what challenge you have, you can use it as a leveraging tool to get you through anything.'[6]

Extreme athletes are able to tap into this greater cause, focusing their efforts on something beyond themselves, their *why*, and so they press on. There is something profound in this understanding.

Building on this, I concluded that finding a meaning beyond themselves would have players shift their mindset completely; instead of being self-focused, defined by what is received, won or taken, the emphasis would shift to giving, sharing, providing. The latter is a potent motivator and performance enhancer, the former runs a significantly higher risk of inhibiting performance.

According to Dr Alex Pattakos, who has written about the work of neurologist, psychiatrist and holocaust survivor Viktor Frankl, finding meaning comes from being a 'giver', suspending what we want and desire for ourselves, and from sensing the impact of our work on others. He adds that a feeling of meaningfulness at work is one of the most potent ways to increase productivity, engagement and performance.[7]

Pattakos goes on to say that seeking happiness, on the other hand, is associated with being a 'taker', someone who focuses on what they want to get from others or from their own achievement. Elaborating on one of Frankl's key principles, *don't work against yourself,* he says, 'We should avoid becoming so obsessed with or fixated on a result that we actually work against the desired result. This happens especially when the stakes are high and our success is essential, causing an over-focus on the results rather than the process.'

This is precisely what had happened, more than once, with the Proteas (and other teams) at World Cup events. In essence, this is what happens when a team chokes.

In the room that morning was a group of men who were familiar with both the concept and experience of choking, a mental hijack from over-thinking, which happens when we place too much importance on a result. The more important we perceive the result to be, the greater is the pressure. And the more we focus on the result, the likelier it is that we will take our eye off the all-important (present-moment) process that holds out the best possible chance of achieving the result. Choking and failure are an obvious result.

As each player sat in his own quiet space and wrote down his thoughts, there was a profound silence, no fidgeting or talking or glancing at cell phones. Almost to a man, they were deeply engaged as they wrote or attempted to explore this new concept of a greater meaning or purpose to their lives.

When the majority had completed the exercise, I asked if anyone was willing to share their experience of the process, or even what they had written down. Some players opened up and shared their thoughts without restraint. Such was their sincerity that midway through, one of them had the courage to openly weep. The exercise had touched something deep inside, triggering some measure of an existential crisis, which can happen when an individual questions the meaning, purpose or value of their life. I had not anticipated this when I planned the session, and it was clear from their reactions, that neither had the players.

Frankl suggests that most humans live with an inner 'emptiness', with a 'crisis of meaning', whether they are aware of it or not. As mentioned earlier, the feeling of inner emptiness can be exacerbated in the case of celebrities and sports stars. According to Frankl, this will not disappear through the pervasive modern-day pursuits of *power* (fame, success, fortune) or *pleasure*, although many do try.

In their book *Stealing Fire*, Steven Kotler and Jamie Wheal estimate that people currently spend US$4 trillion per year (twice the GDP of Russia) on trying to find a happier mental space, seeking ways to get out of their head by reaching for alcohol, pornography, gambling, smoking, drugs, social media, TV games, or any of the other distractions that they hope will make them feel better about themselves. Over-eating, over-working, over-exercising and over-shopping are also culprits. All this, to avoid the reality of how people actually feel.[8]

Frankl also suggests that where there is a crisis, there is an opportunity. Hence, a crisis of meaning is also a call for meaning—in our personal lives and in our work. According to him, it is *meaning* that sustains us throughout our lives, no matter how little or how much power and pleasure come our way, no matter how much success or failure. *Meaning* sustains us as we face the challenges of everyday life in our relationships, at work, and with society as a whole.

The conversation that day, in the African bush, was about the players recognising and expressing gratitude for the talent they were born with, and for the opportunity to represent their country at a World Cup. Parking the discussion of *how* we might win the trophy, we thought about *why* players wanted to win it, hoping to plug into that deeper part of our psyche that drives behaviour and from which motivation and inspiration naturally flow.

Finally, we looked to identify others whom we could serve in those pressure moments, when the stakes were high and the game was on the line, the critical times when we were required to remain focused and on-task. How might we become 'givers' rather than 'takers'? Like those extreme adventurers who all had a greater purpose than themselves and who did not choke in the big moments, what deeper motive might we be serving?

Of all the team workshops I've led, that was a special one. In a conversation that transcended sport, fame, winning and even losing, the Proteas shared as seldom before, speaking with candour, honesty and intimacy. It was unforgettable.

But the rough rule of sport is that it is a rough business, and highs are often followed by lows and unexpected twists.

The players broke for coffee and got ready for the next session. Head coach Russell Domingo was ready to lead a discussion focusing on T20 cricket strategy. Once everyone was seated in the lecture room, Russell started his session by turning the flipchart paper to reveal three words in bold and in his handwriting, covering the full extent of the chart. It read, 'NO ZEN SHIT'. He then stated quite plainly that the World Cup would be won by playing better cricket than the opposition, and that we would spend the rest of the camp figuring out the *what* and *how* to achieve this. The *why*, well, that was just Zen shit.

As with India in 2011, there was little doubt in my mind that this South African team had the talent to win the 2014 T20 World Cup. Still, experience taught me that it would probably not be the most talented team, but the team that made the smartest decisions in the key pressure moments, *and was able to fully commit to those decisions*, that would win. 'Zen shit' is only 'zen shit' when it isn't fully understood or appreciated. It's not exclusionary to the *how* of cricket. The *why* enhances it.

The Proteas went on to get knocked out by India in the semi-finals of that World Cup. After having done what I could to assist Russell Domingo to settle into his position post Kirsten's departure, it was time to move on.

To extract its full value from sport and from life's delightful and frustrating journey requires more than just setting goals and then honing technique, tactics and strategy to achieve them. It requires more than addressing the so-called 80 per cent of the game that is played in the mind. It also goes beyond understanding your *why* and then plugging into a greater purpose and meaning, while serving a cause greater than yourself. One needs more than talent, the right attitude and gratitude, and more than dedication and commitment to perfect practice. Some of the most useful tools to pack for the journey include an open mind, wisdom to know that we don't know it all, and the courage to keep unlearning and learning. That's why life's a journey, not a destination.

28

OUT OF THE BOX

After exiting my role as performance director of the Proteas, I would continue as head coach of teams in the Indian Premier League, the Australian Big Bash League and the Pakistan Super League. Each of these teams had forward-thinking owners or management, and for the first time since publishing my research findings in 2003, I had the full freedom to innovate.

My continued search for what the best were doing in other sports and industries led me to the Chelsea Football Club's Stamford Bridge for a premier Sport Performance Summit in November 2014. In a world where science and technology had dominated sports performance enhancement for over two decades, many believed that culture was emerging as the new differentiator. In keeping with this, then England rugby coach Stuart Lancaster delivered the opening keynote on the importance of culture. He had inherited a team that had been dogged by on-field and off-field indiscretions, and had recently suffered a quarterfinal knockout in the 2011 World Cup. At the time, it was the worst result for a sole host nation in the tournament's history.

Lancaster discussed some novel ways he used to set about rebuilding the team culture, which he suggested needed to happen before focusing on winning rugby matches. Similar to Peter Drucker's claim about culture eating strategy for breakfast, Lancaster argued that culture needed to precede strategy.

Later that day, I would share a stage with Ric Charlesworth—medical doctor, politician, international athlete, international coach,

Hall of Famer and multiple times Coach of the Year. I was a daunted lightweight in comparison, as we debated ways to get the best out of athletes and teams. One of Ric's adages was to 'trouble the comfortable and comfort the troubled', and I made a case for happy players translating to success.

One of the keynote presenters whose path would cross with mine and who would influence my coaching, was Dr Andy Walshe, director of the Red Bull High Performance Centre in Los Angeles (LA). His presentation expounded on Red Bull Stratos, a daring and record-breaking project that saw Felix Baumgartner skydive from a height of nearly 39 kilometres and reach a speed of 1,357 kilometres per hour on descent.

I had about an hour to kill after the conference before flying home to South Africa. As delegates filled the pub across the road from Stamford Bridge, I noticed an unoccupied seat next to Andy. What transpired was me leaving that seat well over an hour later, and well over the one beer I had popped in to have. How I made my flight I have no idea, but that conversation led to me visiting Andy at the Red Bull Centre in Los Angeles on two occasions. Some of the innovative and out-of-the-box thinking I was exposed to in LA would prove useful in times to come.

LIGHTS. CAMERAS. EXIT YOUR COMFORT ZONE!

On one of these visits, I was one of 120-odd sport performance delegates from around the world to have received an invitation to attend 'Glimpses'. We had been given no information, other than being told to arrive at the Red Bull Headquarters at a certain time on a certain date; we could leave two days later. That was it. Although ostensibly a 'sports performance conference', there were *no* sport speakers.

Entry to the opening function was through one of three passages, with no indication as to where they led. One of these took delegates to a three-metre high platform where an instructor explained how to leap and safely back-flop onto an inflatable mattress that would break their fall. There was no other way down, so regardless of whether people were wearing suits or cocktail dresses, they had to jump!

The second entrance was via a fancy dress wardrobe where people were given alternative clothing items which they had to wear for the duration of the function. The third, which I was led to, saw us sitting at a makeshift restaurant table on a stage, and in front of cameras projecting onto a big screen, we had to enact a short play with 'waiters' who were from an improvisation theatre (acting) company.

Most events of this nature start by trying to make people comfortable; this one quite intentionally did the opposite.

For the next two days, we listened to an array of presentations, ranging from insights into the mind of a notorious computer hacker, to a medical doctor who expounded on the use of ayahuasca, a hallucinogenic spiritual medicine used by indigenous people of the Amazon basin, to Indian schoolchildren who had invented a simple, cheap and effective water purification system from waste and stones. In between presentations were short spectacles from an improvisation theatre troupe. I resolved to take some of this alternative thinking (and the science behind it) back into cricket. Admittedly, I did so with some trepidation—players might think I'd gone nuts.

Some years prior, I had led the India cricket team through an afternoon of making movies. The team had arrived at an undisclosed venue to find a full theatrical wardrobe of (men's and women's) clothing, all sorts of plastic weapons, plus movie-making equipment such as cameras, tripods, clapboards, lights and a crane. Cricket met pseudo-Bollywood as players were grouped into three theatre companies, each tasked with making a five-minute movie of their choice, which needed to include an original soundtrack, as well as a fight, sorrow, humour and a love scene! And yes, *all* the movies met *all* these requirements. Some years later, I would do the same activity with the Sydney Thunder team in Australia.

I had also taken the Proteas, the South African national team, through an evening of improvisation (Improv) theatre like in the TV series *Whose Line Is It Anyway* (for those who remember). Only the players and management were present. I would go on to do the same with the Sydney Thunder, with the understanding that the rules of improvisation theatre are highly relevant for sport performance, teamwork and life.

Some of the rules of Improv require that participants need to focus on what is happening right now, remaining fully present to the people and the environment around them. They need to accept and say 'yes' to whatever happens. It's about relaxing, having fun, playing the game and fully expressing yourself to create something special as a group. There are no failures or mistakes, only opportunities.

The things that are required to be not done include worrying, about what happened in the past, what will happen in the future and judging or rejecting an event or what someone does or says. Ego is one of the biggest obstacles to success in Improv, specifically with its need to look good, its worry about making a mistake and/or concern about what others think.

Although I only employed Improv as a once-off event with these teams, I believe regularly doing it can help athletes train to be in the zone, deal with stressful situations, overcome ego and manage their fear of failure. During competition, when the game situation deviates from the plan, which happens more often than not in most team sports, it really is all about improvising.

IN HOLLYWOOD, THE STARS ALIGN

Whilst in Los Angeles for the Glimpses event, I met up with newly-appointed Sydney Thunder general manager Nick Cummins, to be interviewed for the position of head coach. This was Nick's first job in cricket, and he had inherited a team that had lost twenty-one out of the twenty-two games in the first three seasons of that tournament. It wasn't just the results; the team also suffered from poor culture and environment. One team member said in a recorded interview, 'The whole joint was in chaos. Everyone was saying, "don't go to Sydney Thunder, it's the worst experience, it's a poor franchise, poorly run, poorly coached".'

During the recent IPL in India, I had already met up for an 'interview' with newly-appointed Thunder captain, Mike Hussey. He said that it was a difficult decision at the back-end of his career to leave his home in Perth to join a struggling Thunder team, but the challenge excited him. The main driver for him was the opportunity to help build a sustainably successful team and organisation from the ground up. He saw the potential more than the risk. After sharing our philosophy on coaching and leading teams, I left Mike's Mumbai hotel room excited about the prospect. It's difficult to find a better person in the game, or a more consummate professional to be able to work alongside. The next step would be to convince Nick to hire me for the Australian Big Bash.

So, there we were, the new Sydney Thunder GM who was from Melbourne and had never worked in cricket, interviewing an inexperienced head coach from South Africa, and doing so in Hollywood. To the casual observer, it could easily have been the scene for a comedy movie—or a horror movie, if you were a Sydney Thunder fan.

Nick's vision was to be 'the people's team' as far as fans were concerned, and 'to be the club of choice' for players and backroom staff. We were aligned in our philosophies, on the importance of getting good people and building a great culture, and of brave, innovative and out-of-the-box thinking. Not out-of-the-box for the sake of it, but in applying common sense, practical and relevant solutions ahead of a traditional and 'because-that's-the-way-it's-always-been-done' approach to elite performance.

Building a great culture would mean getting the right people on board with the right attitude towards the club and the team. That's easier said than done when you're building a club or franchise up from the bottom of the pit.

First, some tough decisions had to be made. Specifically, what to do about two players who took up two of the eighteen allocated spaces in the team, but who would not play many games due to their national duties.

At the time, David Warner was one of the top ten T20 batsmen in the world, and Michael Clarke held the 'second most important job in Australia', as the national cricket captain. The path we plotted for the team did not include them, which meant Nick, a 'nobody' in Australian cricket, would need to release two very big somebodies from a failing club squad. Whilst it was the smart call, for many it was an unpopular one. In the years that followed, Nick would lead remarkable turnarounds of this and another struggling organisation, which would include making some very brave decisions in the face of entrenched thinking. Warner ended up 'retiring' from the Big Bash despite having a year left on his contract, which neither he or his manager realised at the time. And Clarke went with a promise to never return. Leadership is about doing the right thing that is best for the medium- to long-term prospects of the organisation; it's not about doing the popular thing.

On that day in LA, given the opportunity to work alongside Mike, and aligned with Nick's vision, values and courage, I said 'yes' to the job. The only thing missing was a movie director shouting, 'Cut!' as Nick and I finished acting out the scene.

To turn Thunder around, we needed to do things very differently. We could not rely on results in that first season, so we needed to build a club that would attract the right players and would somehow draw fans. The way Mike Hussey and, in the following season, Shane Watson, would remain on the field after every game we played, home or away, win or lose, signing autographs until the last fan had left the ground, went a long way to accomplishing the latter.

For the next four years, every member of the Thunder squad followed their lead without having to be asked. More than once, after the floodlights were out in the stadium and well after midnight, Shane Watson would still be out there signing autographs by the light of some die-hard fan's cellphone torch.

WHEN YOU THINK YOU'RE DONE, THERE'S MORE

I started with the team, far away from the nets and training ground, at an indoor aquatic centre. Award-winning big-wave surfer Mark Mathews, of *Bra Boys* and *Facing Fear* fame, had an intimate conversation with the team about fear and riding waves upwards of fifteen metres high, sometimes in shark-infested waters. We related his stories to our competitive environment, as Mark discussed the nerves on the days leading up to when the monster swell was due to arrive; the value of thorough preparation; the calm focus required as the wave neared; and of needing to be totally committed and being in the zone or flow from the moment of take-off. He also spoke about wiping out and shared the techniques he used to remain calm whilst being held underwater for long periods of time, as the ocean tried to violently separate limb from body. Surviving underwater is almost all in the mind, because the body can survive that time period without oxygen, even if the limbs are dislocated and broken during the ordeal (this would happen to Mark some months after this talk). It required one to remain calm in the face of the body's natural panic response to apparent lack of oxygen.

I'd planned for the players to more than just hear about these survival techniques in stressful situations. A qualified free-dive instructor followed Mark, explaining the mechanics of optimal breathing, using every part of the lungs, which most people seldom do, as well as the physiology of oxygen starvation. After a period without oxygen, the body triggers reflexes such as compulsive swallowing and contractions in the solar plexus. This in turn triggers a natural panic reaction in the mind: 'I'm gonna die. I *need* oxygen.' These reflexes are not caused by a shortage of oxygen, as is commonly believed, but by high levels of carbon dioxide in the blood. Diving physiology suggests that when the first swallow or contraction is experienced, the body still has about 50 per cent of its oxygen stores available, meaning however much time passed from the breath hold to the first swallow or spasm, that same amount of time is still available without another breath. But the feeling of panic is compounded by each swallow and stomach contraction becoming more powerful than the last, and occurring at shorter and shorter intervals. Managing the mind becomes correspondingly more and more challenging.

After practising some breathing and relaxation techniques, we all got into the pool, and under strict partner and instructor supervision, we tested our maximal underwater breath-hold time. Most players managed between twenty-five to fifty seconds. Within the space of thirty minutes of implementing some of the mental focus and relaxation techniques, every player recorded an underwater time of over one minute, many over two minutes, and a handful over three minutes. Andrew McDonald was the last to surface after three minutes and fifty-five seconds. We all doubled or tripled our time, not by increasing oxygen or carbon dioxide management, but by gaining control over our minds. This would hopefully prove valuable when the pressure was really on in key moments, enabling players to remain calm when natural panic reflexes kicked in.

When I met him again a year later, Sydney Thunder all-rounder Chris Green remarked that those two hours had a lasting and significantly positive impact on his game, teaching him the value of breathing and focus in key moments of performance. He continues to use a breathing technique before each ball he bowls.

(Important: Holding your breath underwater can lead to shallow water blackout and drowning, without any warning. One moment you're holding your breath, the next you pass out, sink to the bottom of the pool, and drown. Hyperventilating before going underwater places you at the greatest risk. Do not try this exercise without qualified supervision, not even in the bath. If you must, do it out of water so you can't drown, and lying down, so you don't fall and hurt yourself if you hold long enough to pass out.)

KEEPING IT REAL

When I started coaching Thunder, my personal goal, which I have never shared until now, was that once players retired, they would look back on their time at the club as the best experience of their entire career. And as their time in this team might only be six weeks in a twenty-year career, their experience would need to be significantly more inspiring, empowering and enlightening than in any other cricket environment. I knew this was an audacious goal and realistically it might never actually transpire. But this would not stop me from trying everything I could to deliver such an experience for the players.

Mike Hussey and I planned to empower players and to find exciting and creative ways to harness the collective intelligence of the team. For example, when planning for games, the players themselves would do almost all of the talking, sharing their views on opponents, playing conditions, and on how to best build a strategy that would suit each individual in the team. Players would discuss plan A, B and C. Mike and I would arrive with questions, not answers.

Post-match reviews would take a similar shape, with players sharing their experience of how the game had unfolded for them, which included sharing how they got things right and where they got things wrong, owning their errors and suggesting what they could do to get it right the next time.

At the outset of the season, players had already acknowledged that 80 per cent to 95 per cent of the errors they made were errors in their own thinking. They also owned up to not sharing these errors with their coach, mainly for fear of judgment. Armed with this insight, we had agreed that if we were going to take our individual and collective game to the next level, we needed to find ways to address this part of our game.

Mike and our two internationals at the time, South African Jacques Kallis and England captain Eoin Morgan, took it upon themselves to be true leaders in this respect. When they erred in a game, they would openly own it in the team meeting, sharing the error in thinking, plus the solution in terms of what they would do when next in that same situation. Vulnerability, honesty and courage to own mistakes were acknowledged, encouraged and even prized in this environment. We did not strive to be tough or strong, but rather to be real.

My years as a mental coach had alerted me to the handful or more of the problems that players commonly experience in a team environment, as well as the fact that they are reluctant to address many of these directly with their coach. I raised this with the players, asserting that if they had an ongoing problem in the team environment, and especially if they departed at the end of the season with that same problem still bothering them, it would be their own fault. If something was not working optimally, they were to bring that concern to me, or if really not comfortable doing this, they should ask someone else to bring it to me. I committed to doing whatever it took to alleviate the obstacle, within and even outside of reason. And I would do just that, aware of the value of happy players when it came to delivering results.

Most training sessions were optional, including what players chose to work on in training. This meant each player taking responsibility for his game and deciding the best way to prepare according to his own game plans and preferences. Each of the players was treated differently, in a way that suited them best. (I disagree with the adage 'treat everyone the same'—people's needs are just too divergent). This was based on the understanding that everyone has a natural motivational flow, and all that is required is to create an environment that aligns with each person's natural flow. Players would then be motivated without someone having to do or say something motivational.

I maintain that if I need to motivate a player on game day at this level of performance, it probably means that I have failed in my job. When a motivator gives his speech, I contend that the message behind it is often, 'I don't think you're motivated, so let me try and do it for you.' Instinctively, players might well receive this subliminal message that the coach thinks they are not motivated, which in itself is a negative message that can undermine their confidence. As coaches, we often live for those Hollywood moments. That's the ego speaking. Remember my hopes of delivering an Al Pacino-like motivational speech in India the night before the World Cup final? To this day, I'm grateful that the Indian team had a healthy environment, and it wasn't egos that dictated behaviour.

Back in Sydney, as with the Rajasthan Royals, a brains-trust comprising senior and junior players was appointed by the team to decide the details of game strategy, team culture, rules and team processes, as well as the playing eleven. Selection in cricket is very subjective—it's a matter of opinion whether one batsman or bowler is more suited to play than another. I'm acutely aware of the gripes players often have with team selection, both about the choices made and about explanations given by the coach or captain to the player not selected. Players ask for honest reasons for non-selection and they want to know what they need to work on. In an attempt to circumvent this common problem, we announced that selection meetings were open for all to attend. If the group was discussing selection of a player who happened to be present, that player was welcome to stay and hear what was being said. It was a risk, but if this was going to be the players' team, then we believed they should be allowed to participate in every aspect. Very few players took up the offer, saying that if the process was going to be as transparent as that, they would trust the decision I delivered to them post the meeting.

Despite being a 'losing' team, we did not wish to compromise on values or how we played the game in the pursuit of winning. We would not adopt a 'winning-at-all-costs' approach. For example, despite sledging being common practice at this level of play, we would not engage in this practice. We would not chase a short-term win if it was likely to lead to any form of longer-term loss, in this case, compromising sportsmanship and the respect of fellow cricketers.

After we had settled on this understanding of how the team would be run, the newly appointed assistant coach for the fourth season of the BBL (and my first as coach), ex-Australia Test opening batsman Phil Jaques, asked what was required of him. I requested that he prepare as he normally would, especially for post-match debriefs and pre-match strategy meetings, which is traditionally where coaches do most of the talking. For each topic under discussion, the players would speak first and only afterwards should Phil, or any other of the coaches, add any insights that they might have missed.

After the eighth and last match of the season, Phil remarked that despite his best thinking throughout the season, he never once spoke in a team meeting. 'I'm blown away. The players covered everything I wanted to say. *Every* time. I never expected that.' As coaches, we think we need to speak, and often think we have the answers. As Phil learned, this is not always true.

In the last game of that season, Thunder needed to defend 23 runs off the final over against Sydney Sixers to end a respectable fifth out of eight teams. The bowler choked badly and served up some very hittable deliveries for the batsman to help himself to the required target. As a result, we ended seventh. This was the only time in ten years of coaching that I could not manage my own emotions, and had to leave the dugout to watch and vent from the dressing room. Both the bowler and I choked in our roles that evening.

INSPIRED BY GREATNESS. WELL, SORT OF ...

After ten months in their separate teams and countries, and after a few changes to the squad, the Thunder players assembled in early December for the fifth edition of the Big Bash League, my second as coach. We were scheduled to kick off the first morning of the week-long pre-season with a four-hour workshop. I was dressed somewhat uncharacteristically in a smart suit, both demonstrating and explaining that we would be taking things a lot more seriously this season. I opened my lengthy PowerPoint presentation with a slide of Mount Everest, explaining that we would spend the next four hours discussing the rules, values and strategies that would take us to the top of our Everest. Already I noticed some confusion (players hadn't seen me dressed in a suit before), and an air of resignation: 'a four-hour workshop, you can't be serious'.

After setting the scene, I announced a special guest speaker. He was none other than Sir Edmund Hillary, who, along with Tenzing Norgay, was the first man ever to summit Mt Everest. He was ushered in, and with the aid of a climbing pole, descended the stairs of the lecture hall, dressed in full mountain climbing gear, snow overalls, climbing backpack, ropes and snow shoes, his head and face covered with a high-altitude oxygen mask. He received muffled applause; apparently, some of the younger players didn't know who Hillary was. Somewhat unrecognisable and probably equally uncomfortable, he proceeded to deliver his motivational speech with the face mask still on. After a while, clearly over-heating inside the mask that was meant for snow and not Sydney in summer, he removed it to reveal that Sir Edmund … was actually Mike Hussey.

The laughter soon wore off and turned back into frowns as we picked up where we had left off, to continue the workshop now that Mike was with us. Moments into it, a malfunction occurred somewhere between my computer and the projector, which left Mike and me blundering around and rather incompetently attempting to fix it.

The players' embarrassment was palpable. Mike eventually burst out with a frustrated call for help, which was the cue for the stage doors to open behind us, and for boxes and racks of movie-making outfits, wigs and accessories to be wheeled in, along with movie cameras and tripods. To much relief and laugher, the dreaded four-hour workshop transformed into a movie-making extravaganza like the one I had done with Team India.

Pat Cummins went on to be much at home playing James Bond, Chris Green turned heads as a cheerleader in a wig and miniskirt, Jacques Kallis delivered an award-winning fight scene in a toilet, and Shane Watson put his song-writing, singing and guitar-playing skills to misuse in delivering a hilariously original soundtrack.

The event was capped by an evening at Fox Studios for our very own Golden Globe Awards ceremony. In their film première theatre, popcorn and all, we watched the three movies plus behind-the-scenes footage. Rather than the Golden Globe Awards, it turned out to be the Golden Box Awards, for the trophies were abdominal guards that had been sprayed with gold paint and imprinted with the name of the award and recipient. The cricket would start the next day.

Towards the back-end of that season, Thunder were mid-ladder. To qualify for the play-offs, we needed to win our final game and also needed the results of other games to go our way. That's when we chose to have our own, adapted version of Glimpses, and what transpired was for some a life-changing event.

With the help of a small network of connected people, we assembled fifteen A-list athletes from seven different sports to spend a morning with the Thunder squad. The invitation had promised 'glimpses into greatness, via multi-disciplinary sharing and learning amongst the world's best'. There would be no recording devices and no autographs or photographs. This would be for the athletes only.

At Glimpses in Los Angeles, I had seen the benefit of going outside the box in search for new learning. Earlier that same year, I had done some mental coaching with South African World Tour surfer Jordy Smith, who was in pursuit of the world title. It seemed that surfing was not engaging with some of the things that other sports had already discovered. Prompted by Glimpses, I invited the world's number one fast bowler at the time, Dale Steyn, South African captain Graeme Smith, and ex-Springbok rugby captain Corné Krige to join us for a mountain trail run in Cape Town, followed by two hours of conversation. Aimed at assisting Jordy, who could ask any questions he wanted, the discussion revolved around what it takes in these different sports to get to the top of the global game. Not only what it takes, but also what challenges each athlete had faced in their pursuit. Jordy's coach at the time, ex-World Tour surfer Jarrad Howse, was also present.

Top athletes almost always find themselves surrounded by fans, competitors, recording devices and/or someone connected to the media. Because of this, they are compelled to audit and edit what they say, not knowing how it might come back to them or get used by others. Even within the same sport and in the same dressing room, peer sharing is often limited because teammates today could be competitors tomorrow. Many, particularly top male athletes, spend the majority of their professional lives pretending to be strong, in control and on top of their game, on and off the field. Their answers to interviews, fans' questions and most public conversations are mostly safe and superficial—they're vanilla. Whilst they often mask these experiences very well, they battle the exact same worries, concerns, vulnerabilities, insecurities and emotional turmoil as you and I do.

They might differ with regard to sporting talent, but not when it comes to matters of the heart. Sitting at my friend Paolo's house in Sandy Bay, overlooking the Atlantic Ocean after an amazing trail run, I listened as Dale, Graeme, Corné and Jordy spoke with remarkable honesty and opened up to one another.

It was that experience that prompted the decision to do it on a grand scale in Sydney. The event started with about ninety minutes of indoor cricket. Visiting athletes played alongside Thunder players as the teams competed against each other. They also got to bat and bowl in the nets against the likes of Shane Watson, Mike Hussey and Jacques Kallis. Prior to the event, I had spoken to the Thunder players and a few of the guest athletes, asking what topics they most wanted to discuss. Three common themes emerged from these conversations: (1) fear, (2) managing the big moment, and (3) off-field distractions and their impact on performance and the players' lives in general.

Like the trail run with Jordy, playing cricket helped people connect and get comfortable with each other before delving deeper into conversation. For each topic, three pre-selected athletes were allocated up to ten minutes to share their most significant story relating to that subject, after which the audience was invited to add their experiences or ask a question. Shane Watson kicked off and spoke about how the death of fellow cricketer Phil Hughes (from being hit on the head by a bouncer) had created a fear in him that significantly affected his mind and performance for over a year. He shared his fears openly, and also how he eventually managed to overcome them through some mental training he did in the United States. Corporal Mark Donaldson spoke about how he managed his fear under intense and prolonged enemy gunfire. He was Australia's first-ever Victoria Cross recipient for (military) bravery for repeatedly drawing enemy fire onto himself to save his fellow soldiers. Mark Mathews spoke next, on fear and big-wave surfing, as he sat on stage with his arm in a sling, recovering from a severely dislocated and broken shoulder from a very recent wipe-out in Hawaii on a massive wave that nearly claimed his life.

Moving to the next topic, 'the big moment', Mike Hussey started by telling us how nervous he was each time he went out to bat for Australia, and how he often questioned whether he was good enough or worthy of his position. This questioning of worthiness is not unique at the highest level of sport, but admitting to it is fairly unique. Mike was followed by Jessica Watson, who at the age of sixteen had sailed solo around the world, and then by Rugby League star Greg Inglis, who gave insights into how he approached and prevailed in big moments, for which he was well-known and respected, having already won two grand finals, a Clive Churchill Medal and the Golden Boot Award.

The third topic, relating to off-field distractions, was kicked off by Jacques Kallis. His mother had died when he was very young, and he and his sister, Janine, were brought up by their father, Henry, who never dated another woman. Jacques was very close to him and spoke about how his father's death in 2003 impacted him personally and as a cricketer. Among other things, he had gone fourteen months without scoring a century at first class or international level. I had known Jacques for twenty years, worked with him for over a decade, and had been his mental coach at the time of that run-drought in 2003. It was amazing to hear him share his journey and pain with such honesty, with a room full of strangers. His story was followed by a drawn-out and empathetic silence.

Australian Rules footballer Heath Shaw spoke next of how he had dealt with being suspended for indiscretions on two occasions in his career, and how, for a period of time, he had conducted himself in a way that he was not particularly proud of. He also shared what he did to help rectify this and to bring his career back on track. He was followed by Sam Burgess, who was a dual code international, representing England in both Rugby League and Rugby Union. Sam had been publicly criticised by a teammate before being selected for the 2015 Rugby World Cup squad, and then got blamed by some part of the media for England's 'humiliating' exit from the tournament (which coach Stuart Lancaster had referred to at the London conference mentioned earlier). It was heart-wrenching to hear what this experience was like from Sam's personal perspective.

Other athletes in the audience included World Tour surfers Ace Buchan, Kai Otten and coach Jarrad Howse, Rugby League's John Sutton and coach Madge Maguire, big-wave surfer and mixed martial arts fighter Richie Vas, and Australian Football League's Stephen Coniglio, Callan Ward and Phil Davis.

Jarrad Howse, Mark Mathews, Ace Buchan and Mark Donaldson went on to join the team in the change room after some of the games that followed, and Mark Mathews and Jarrad promised that if we made the final, they would fly down to watch us (they were good for their word). In the ensuing months, more than a few players reported that the session had a significant impact on their careers and lives.

Thunder went on to qualify for the play-offs, convincingly winning the semi-final against Adelaide Strikers, who were clear log leaders, having won seven of their eight games up to that point, and progressed to meet Melbourne Stars in the final. I've often said that T20 games are won by the team whose big players fire on the day, and this was certainly the case for Thunder, with Usman Khawaja earning Man of The Match for his 104 in the semi-final and again for scoring a match-winning 70 in the final. Four days later, the Sydney Thunder women's team would go on to clinch the inaugural WBBL title. This trophy-double was a very fitting reward for the vision and work of Nick Cummins and Mike Hussey who, two years earlier, had taken on the challenge of raising the club from the dead.

COACHING THE COACHES

I will not fall into the trap I caution against, of claiming the championship win as a coach. I have long maintained and still do, that results are a woefully incomplete measure of how good a coach is. Let's take a real-life example of three championship winning teams from three different leagues: One of them had a way bigger budget than the rest, which they used to buy top players who went on to find great form in the tournament. The second was a team of averagely talented players, backed by an amazing team environment that helped bring the best out of them. And the third was a team of talented individuals, plagued with selfish performances, infighting, cliques, unsporting win-at-all-costs behaviour, with some senior players openly disregarding their coach's worth. All three recorded winning results, so using the traditional measure, could one say that all three coaches were equally skilled? And what about a team of underdogs, maybe from the small club or remote school, which doesn't win too often against bigger teams? It's very possible that there is an amazing coach in that team who inspires and gets the best out of each individual, but how will we know or measure this?

Football (soccer) currently boasts some of the more extreme examples of this result-oriented measuring, with coaches at the professional level being hired and fired within months. This is not about a coach failing; it's an administrative failing. If you hire a coach whom you need to fire within a short space of time, you have hired badly.

Using winning as the primary measure of success is not only short-sighted, but it also creates wide-ranging problems, particularly among younger athletes. The consequences of an over-focus on winning include anxiety, stress, pressure, decreased enjoyment, lack of confidence, excessive fear of failure, unethical and unsporting conduct, doping, and kids prematurely giving up the game. According to the National Alliance for Youth Sports, of the 40 million kids who start playing sport at school in the United States, around 70 per cent stop playing organised sports by the age of thirteen because 'it's just not fun anymore'.[1] A win-at-all-costs attitude and the associated over-coaching, reprimands and tantrums, parents living vicariously through their kids, and schools and clubs fuelling their organisational ego through results are significant contributors to this 70 per cent dropout rate.

Sport has far more to offer than a podium finish: fun, learning, skill acquisition, decision-making, character development, teamwork, friendship, sportsmanship, and many other important sport and life skills. In an ideal world, I'd suggest coaches should be measured and rewarded based on these metrics, as much as on winning. When it comes to coach education and accreditation, in addition to learning how to teach technical skills and game strategy, I'd suggest coaches should be receiving an equal amount of coaching, support and regular feedback around people management and the associated 'soft skills'. In this ideal world, sports captains would also receive comprehensive leadership-specific coaching and support. Currently, captains and coaches in professional and international cricket receive very little leadership mentoring or coaching, if any.

IT'S JUST A GAME

The year after being crowned Big Bash champions, Sydney Thunder lost the first four games of the season, in large part due to injury and lack of form, with our main two power batsmen scoring a mere 28 runs between them in those four games. But the team stayed in the fight and won the next three games, including one where we needed 5 off the last ball to win, to which Eoin Morgan responded by sending the final delivery back over the bowler's head for 6 and victory. We arrived to play the final game against Adelaide Strikers at our home ground in Sydney Olympic Park. I had full confidence and trust that we were as prepared as possible and would complete the four-game winning streak required to qualify for play-offs. But life sometimes has other plans, and this game would deliver a strange twist, and a new life.

As the team joined the huddle to begin the warm-up about an hour before play, news came that England international James Vince's pregnant partner had gone into labour and was experiencing complications back in England. He was in the car in the stadium carpark, speaking to his partner's family on Skype, and would probably miss the warm-up. The umpires were not prepared to deviate from the rules: since his name had been announced in the playing eleven, he could not be replaced. With five minutes to game-time, James emerged from the car, got dressed and went out to field despite his partner still being in a precarious situation, and despite full permission to stay off the field and in communication with home. James was very new to the team, having only joined us twelve days and three games earlier. His commitment to the team was unwavering, and the players' concern for his situation was equally palpable.

I did wonder about players possibly using this 'distraction' as an excuse or mental cop-out to avoid the clear and present pressure of a must-win game. Much of the concern was genuine as Thunder was a very caring team. Regular reports were sent on to James during the fielding innings and each time it was 'no change to the situation, things are not worse, but not better'.

During the change of innings and five minutes before he was due to open the innings, a message reached the dressing room: 'Congrats, Vincie! You're the father to a healthy baby daughter, and your partner is healthy and safe.'

A few thoughts occurred to me as the team received the news with huge relief and congratulations. The first was pride; how this team had embraced a newcomer as their own, and felt free to express real caring and compassion. It also brought home the reality that cricket was just a game in relation to the significance of human life. Another thought was to have a word in James's ear about navigating the first few deliveries, given his state of mind. I stopped myself, thinking that he was an international cricketer and would know what to do. I dropped the ball in that moment by not following through. James made the very error I had intuited, which he acknowledged soon afterwards: 'I should have given myself a few balls to settle at the wicket.' I failed James and the team in that one key moment. Had we won that game convincingly, we stood to qualifiy for the semi-finals, but we lost and came eighth and last.

The following season, after playing only six games and spending three weeks with the Sydney Thunder team, England wicketkeeper-batsman Jos Buttler, who had played for ten different professional teams up to that point in his career, tweeted of his experience: 'One of the best TEAM environments I have been a part of. Great blokes, great set-up.'

Jos's tweet reminded me of a speech Rahul Dravid gave after the final game of his twenty-three-year-long professional career. Rajasthan Royals had been unbeaten in the 2013 Champions League tournament until losing in the final to the Mumbai Indians at the Wankhede Stadium on that night. Dravid spoke to us in our change room, whilst only metres away, the Mumbai team were singing, dancing and celebrating a well-deserved victory. He gathered the Royals into a tight huddle, said his thank yous, and told us what a privilege it was for him to end his career in such an amazing team environment, with such good people.

His concluding words still ring in my ears: 'If I had the choice of ending my career in the winning Champions League team next door, or in this losing Royals dressing room, I'd choose this a hundred times over.' To Rahul Dravid, one of the wisest, most grounded and respected men in the game, winning was not everything.

POSTSCRIPT

Madiba's sleeve

When it became known that I was writing this book, people asked me the obvious question: 'What is it about?'

Like those thirty-second elevator pitches taught in business schools, the question forced me to contemplate the essence of the message I hoped to convey in these pages.

I could have said it's about the 'changing landscape of leadership'. But without diving into detail, this answer merely leads to follow-up questions: 'In what context or industry?' and 'How is the landscape of leadership changing?' So, no, it's not that.

Is it an autobiography? No, not really. I'm a wannabe surfer who loves fishing. I'm not as interested in cricket as I am in building, or attempting to build, extraordinary team cultures in high-performance environments.

Is the book about mental coaching or mental toughness? Absolutely not. Just as sport science couldn't sustain its reputation as the silver bullet to high performance it was made out to be in the 1990s and early 2000s, mental conditioning in isolation, or as a narrowly defined concept in a textbook, doesn't offer a complete or satisfactory answer to what it takes for an athlete to summit his or her Everest.

Is this a how-to guide for coaches or leaders? Honestly, I've learned more about people, relationships and coaching from the things I did wrong. So, in some ways, this book is a 'how-*not*-to guide'. But therein resides a clue to the message I hoped to convey to my readers—coaches, athletes, parents, teachers, even business and political leaders.

On leadership and Socrates, Karl Popper wrote:

> It is not unlikely that (Socrates) demanded (...) that the best should rule, which would have meant, in his view, the wisest (...). And we should realise that, if he demanded that the wisest men should rule, he clearly stressed that he did not mean the learned men; in fact, he was sceptical of all professional learnedness, whether it was that of the philosophers of the past or of the learned men of his own generation, the Sophists. The wisdom he meant was of a different kind. It was simply the realisation: how little do I know! (...) The true teacher can prove himself only by exhibiting that self-criticism (...). 'Whatever authority I may have rests solely upon my knowing how little I know.' (...) Socrates had stressed that he was not wise; that he was not in the possession of truth, but that he was a searcher, an inquirer, a lover of truth. This, he explained, is expressed by the word 'philosopher', i.e., the lover of wisdom, and the seeker for it, as opposed to 'Sophist', i.e., the professionally wise man.[1]

People do not follow leaders for the sake of seeing them lead. There is no joy in seeing the back of someone's head. But what about looking someone in the eye? People follow leaders to grow and improve, trusting that the leader will help them realise their full potential and achieve their goals. When the leader is someone who doesn't have all the answers—which is always the case, knowingly or unknowingly—it requires a fundamental shift in attitude to leadership and relationships in order for them to remain impactful and relevant in the lives of those they lead.

It requires wisdom and humility in the Socratic sense. It requires getting off your high horse of all-knowingness and moving into the neighbourhood with your fellow man. In the words of G.K. Chesterton:

> I admit that your explanation explains a great deal; but what a great deal it leaves out! Are there no other stories in the world except yours; and are all men busy with your business? (...) How much larger your life would be if your self could become smaller in it; if you could really look at other men with common curiosity and

pleasure. (...) You would break out of this tiny and tawdry theatre in which your own little pot is always being played, and you would find yourself under a freer sky, in a street full of splendid strangers.[2]

Under this freer sky—one where we care to learn from and more about each other—leaders go from trying or wanting to be the expert to becoming the teacher who facilitates growth through ceaseless inquiry beyond themselves. It's about being authentic. Cosmetic makeovers don't last.

When an athlete or a coach goes onto the field, in front of a camera or to a public function, they generally put their best foot forward. So do we when we meet our new employer, start a new relationship or meet our significant other's parents for the first time. Politicians do it all the time when making public appearances. They don their public persona and try to create an impression that they care for the people and are the right candidate to vote for.

It's easy to put your best foot forward and look good. But who are we being in our private moments when away from scrutinising eyes—when our true character gets to shine through?

There are few things more telling than how we treat the 'little' people when no one is watching; people like the restaurant or hotel breakfast waiter, the team bus driver, the most junior athlete in the team, or the fifty-first autograph hunter of the day.

During an IPL tournament, I watched Rahul Dravid thank the bus driver for each journey between the hotel and the practice ground. I watched Shane Watson sign autographs for more than an hour after the Big Bash League game was over, remaining until the last Sydney Thunder fan left, which was after midnight, and after the floodlights had been turned off. And this, at an away game and long after the press had gone home. Coach Eric Simons always asks the bus driver's name and then daily greets and thanks him by name. (Some players, after a six-week cricket tour, don't even know what the driver looked like.)

Being the recipient of such generosity of spirit will stay with me forever. And it is in this context that I am reminded of one other private moment, out of the public eye, when the great Nelson Mandela nearly ruined a treasured photograph of mine.

The story began a while earlier, in 1996, when, as a member of the South African Cricket team management, I first got to meet Madiba (the name by which Mandela is popularly known in South Africa). I had planned to ask him two questions. And then, as he moved into my space, I became enveloped by an indescribable presence and a powerful stillness overcame me. Video footage showed that we spoke for a brief few moments—but to this day, I have no recollection of the experience, and I have no idea what he said to me or what I said to him. I don't think I asked my planned questions.

The team then posed for a photo with Madiba, with him still in the colourful outfit he was wearing when he attended the Cape Carnival earlier in the day. This was the treasured photo, developed from film, that Madiba himself was to nearly ruin.

A year later, we got to meet him again at the Newlands Cricket Ground before playing an international match. This time, I had a question I would not forget to ask. I wanted him to sign the treasured photo from our last meeting. Because he was on a tight schedule, he told his security officer, Rory Steyn, to have me meet him at his presidential car on his way out of the stadium. I waited, equipped with my photo, a pen, and excitement.

As it happened, he was ushered hastily past me and into his car. They were about to pull away when he saw me and beckoned the driver to stop. He opened the car door and invited me to sit next to him. When he began to sign, the inkless nib only managed to scratch the photograph. It was one of those gold-ink pens that need pressure on the nib for it to retract into the pen, which then causes ink to be released from the cartridge. I mentioned he should put pressure on the nib, which he did, resulting in the whole cartridge of ink splattering all over the photo. Damn! I should have tested the pen. Damn! My photo was ruined.

Without a moment's thought, the president of our country immediately wiped the photo clean with his trademark Madiba shirtsleeve. He wiped it before the ink could dry, cleaning the photo and ruining his shirt with a permanent ink stain.

I thought, 'Oh no, his shirt is ruined.'

He said, 'Thank goodness, your photo is not ruined!'

He asked for another pen, signed, and apologised for nearly ruining my photo. It was just us in his car, the president of a country and a lowly fitness trainer, in private and with no cameras to look good for. In those few moments, I knew why Nelson Mandela will be remembered in a thousand years' time as one of the greatest men to have walked our planet.

P.S: Thinking about it now, I realise that's one way to tell you what this book is about. It's is not about rolling up one's sleeves. In leadership, that is expected. It's about mastering the self as an instrument of leadership; quietening the ego in the service of a cause greater than oneself. It's about helping athletes gain clarity by doing whatever it takes to wipe those ink stains away. Even if it means ruining your sleeve.

ACKNOWLEDGEMENTS

Much of what I share in this book is courtesy of the opportunities gifted to me by others. In acknowledging these people, there are many who are unmentioned, to whom I remain indebted. Thank you…

Mom, first, for your unwavering love and support. Dad, for your ever calm, level-headed and immensely patient way. You seldom gave me the answers I sought as a child. Instead, you asked me questions and led me to find my own answers, even if it was frustrating for the impatient kid I was. It was only much later that I realised your 'coaching' approach was the foundation of my career.

Professor Tim Noakes, for over two decades of mentoring, and for guiding me to question the status quo and push boundaries in search of new and better ways, while remaining scientifically rigorous in the process. As a giant in the academic world, you epitomise courage and humility.

The late Professor Mike van Oudtshoorn, who created and brought to Cape Town the first-ever two-year masters' degree in business coaching. The learning you ignited in those two years continues to light the way for my career.

The late Bob Woolmer and Hansie Cronje, for opening the door for me as the first full-time fitness trainer in international cricket.

Gazza (Gary Kirsten), for inviting me to join you in coaching the Indian national team, and for your trust, support, friendship and those thousands of hours of conversation.

Rahul Dravid, for your pivotal role in my first appointment as a head coach in professional cricket, in the IPL. Over and above sharing your vast cricket knowledge during our five T20 seasons together, your everyday conduct taught me volumes about humility, personal values and equanimity.

Mike Hussey and Nick Cummins, for the opportunity to coach Sydney Thunder for four years, and for your ongoing trust and support in this role, and Shawn Bradstreet, for being an amazing assistant coach and friend.

To all of the cricket support staff, from assistant coaches to the real workhorses—the logistics managers and physiotherapists—for all of your tireless and often thankless work to keep the players happy and our team's ship afloat.

Karthika V.K., my publisher, for believing in me and saying 'yes' before seeing a word of this manuscript, and then for your amazing edit. Marco Botha, for your clarity, insight, and guidance with the structure and flow of the manuscript. Without your contribution, I would not have got here.

Nicki, my wife, my daughter Lila-Rose and the boys, Janoah and Ben, for being a beautiful family, for keeping us so together for the past thirteen years and holding the space for a decade of my travelling the cricket world for up to seven or eight months a year. Especially Nicki: During my absence, you were required to be mom and dad, wife, homemaker, urban farmer, teacher, friend, daughter, sister, aunt and support to so many. You did all this, like a Trojan, which allowed me to do what I did. Thank you, sincerely.

To you the reader, thanks for offering your precious time to read this book. My hope is that you will find at least some insights here that will add lasting value to your life.

Paddy

REFERENCES

1. **SEARCHING FOR THE AUTHENTIC GARY KIRSTEN**
   1. Peter Senge, *The Fifth Discipline* (Doubleday, 2006)

2. **COACHING. NO, NOT COACHING. *COACHING*.**
   1. T. Olsen, J. Engelbrecht, H. Kwangwari, C. Gimenez, F. Human, L. Nyere, F. Hendricks, Stellenbosch University Business School MBA Leadership study; Original interviews:
      - C. Morris, Anatomy of a Leader (Interview) (01 November 2016)
      - M. Hussey, Anatomy of a Leader (Interview) (29 October 2016)
      - S. Rana, Anatomy of a Leader (Interview) (23 October 2016)
      - N. Cummins, Anatomy of a Leader (Interview) (26 October 2016)
   2. Professor M. Ewing, Dr. J. Newton, T. Altschwager, Deakin University, Faculty of Business and Law, 'Servant leadership in temporary teams: Tensions and Solutions', *working paper, 2019*'
   3. R.K. Greenleaf, *Servant Leadership: A Journey into the Nature of Legitimate Power and Greatness*, (Paulist Press, New York, 1977)
   4. M. Sousa & D. van Dierendonck, 'Servant Leadership and the Effect of the Interaction Between Humility, Action, and Hierarchical Power on Follower Engagement', *Journal of Business Ethics* (2017)
   5. Micah Rieke, Jon Hammermeister and Matthew Chase, Matthew, 'Servant Leadership In Sport: A New Paradigm For Effective Coach Behavior', *Physical Education, Health and Recreation Faculty Publications, Paper 3*, (2008)

3. **THE CHANGING LANDSCAPE OF LEADERSHIP**
   1. Richard Rohr, *The Divine Dance: The Trinity and Your Transformation*, (SPCK Publishing, London, 2016)

2. David Bodanis, *E = mc²: A Biography of the World's Most Famous Equation* (Pan Books, London, 2000) pp. 47-49
3. Martin E. P. Seligman, *Flourish: A Visionary New Understanding of Happiness and Well-being* (Free Press, New York 2012)
4. Ibid.
5. John Whitmore, *Coaching for performance: GROWing people, performance and purpose* (3rd ed.), (Naperville, USA: Nicholas Brealey, London 2002)
6. Karl Popper, *The Open Society and Its Enemies; Volume One: The Spell of Plato*, (Routledge, New York, 1945) pp. 136, 138, 140, 143
7. David Kolb, *Experiential learning: Experience as the source of learning and development* (Vol. 1) (Prentice-Hall, Englewood Cliffs, NJ, 1984)
8. W.T. Gallwey, *The Inner Game of Tennis: The Classic Guide to the Mental Side of Peak Performance* (Random House, New York, 1997)
9. D.P. Hemery, *Sporting Excellence: What Makes A Champion?* (Harper Collins Willow, London, 1991)

4. ARRIVING IN INDIA

1. Chris Smith, 'India Is Nike's Only Hope at the 2015 Cricket World Cup', *Forbes,* 21 Feb 2015, https://www.forbes.com/sites/chrissmith/2015/02/21/india-is-nikes-only-hope-at-the-cricket-world-cup/#20910afc3f75 (Accessed 7 November 2017).
2. *Deccan Chronicle.* 2018. 'Team India captain Virat Kohli's brand value higher than Lionel Messi in Forbes list', Deccan Chronicle, 27 Oct 2017, https://www.deccanchronicle.com/sports/cricket/271017/india-cricket-team-captain-virat-kohli-beats-lionel-messi-as-the-most-valuable-brand.html (Accessed 7 November 2017).

5. PLAYING TO STRENGTHS

1. Marcus Buckingham and Donald Clifton, *Now, Discover Your Strengths* (The Free Press, New York, 2001)
2. Malcolm Gladwell, *Outliers: The story of success* (Back Bay Books, New York, 2011)
3. K. Anders Ericsson, Ralf Th. Krampe, Clemens Tesch-romer, 'The role of deliberate practice in the acquisition of expert performance', *Psychological Review* 100 (3):363-406, (1993)
4. Justin Durandt, Ziyaad Parker, Herman Masimla, Mike Lambert, 'Rugby-playing history at the national U13 level and subsequent

participation at the national U16 and U18 rugby tournaments', *South African Journal of Sports Medicine* (2011)
5. Marcus Buckingham and Donald Clifton (2001)
6. Martin E. P. Seligman, *Flourish: A Visionary New Understanding of Happiness and Well-being* (Free Press, New York 2012)

6. INDIA AT WAR

1. T.H. White, *The Once and Future King* (Collins, London, 1958)

7. SHED THE BLAZER AND TIE

1. Sam Dangremond, 'How the Blazer Gots Its Name', http://www.townandcountrymag.com/style/fashion-trends/a3314/the-history-of-the-blazer/ June 17, 2015 (Accessed 9 November 2017)
2. Malcolm Gladwell, B*link: The Power of Thinking Without Thinking*, (Penguin Books, New York, 2005) pp. 48-52, 67-68

9. CHARACTER AND VALUES

1. Jon Saraceno, 'Tyson: My Whole Life Has Been a Waste', https://usatoday30.usatoday.com/sports/boxing/2005-06-02-tyson-saraceno_x.htm June 2, 2005, (Last accessed 29 January 2018)
2. 'Steve Smith: I hope I can earn forgiveness' https://www.wisden.com/stories/news-stories/steve-smith-ball-tampering-press-conference March 29, 2018 (Last accessed 6 April 2018)
3. Rolf Ulrich, Harrison G. PopeJr, Léa Cléret, Andrea Petróczi, Tamás Nepusz, Jay Schaffer, Gen Kanayama, R. Dawn Comstock, Perikles Simon, 'Doping in Two Elite Athletics Competitions Assessed by Randomized-Response Surveys', *Sports Medicine*, January 2018, Volume 48, Issue 1, pp 211–219

10. EGO: THE BATTLE WITHIN

1. Eckhart Tolle, *A New Earth: Awakening to Your Life's Purpose.* (Penguin Books, New York, 2005)

14. THE MYTH OF MENTAL TOUGHNESS

1. D. Connaughton, R. Wadey, S. Hanton, G. Jones, 'The development and maintenance of mental toughness: perceptions of elite

performers', *Journal of Sports Science* (2002) https://www.ncbi.nlm.nih.gov/pubmed/17852671
2. Ibid.
3. Clive Boddy, *Corporate Psychopaths: Organizational Destroyers* (Palgrave Macmillan, UK, 2011)
4. Belinda Jane Board and Katarina Fritzon, 'Disordered Personalities at Work', *Psychology, Crime and Law*, Volume 11, 2005—Issue 1, https://www.tandfonline.com/doi/abs/10.1080/10683160310001634304
5. A more detailed commentary on psychopaths in sport can be found on my blog, at www.paddyupton.com
6. Oliver Burkeman, *The Antidote: Happiness for People Who Can't Stand Positive Thinking*, (Farrar, Straus and Giroux, New York, 2012)
7. Martin E. P. Seligman, *Flourish: A Visionary New Understanding of Happiness and Well-being* (Free Press, New York 2012)

16. FAILURE: PART ONE

1. *Career 1st Serve Points Won On All Surfaces From All Countries.* http://www.atpworldtour.com/en/stats/1st-serve-points-won, (Accessed: 15 December 2017)
2. *Career 2nd Serve Points Won On All Surfaces From All Countries.* http://www.atpworldtour.com/en/stats/2nd-serve-points-won/all/all/all/, (Accessed: 15 December 2017)
3. Lluis Mascaro, *The 10 Differences Between Messi, Suarez & Ronaldo*, https://www.sport-english.com/en/news/barca/the-differences-data-between-messi-suarez-ronaldo-4963124 , March 9, 2016 (Accessed: 15 December 2017)
4. *Tiger Woods' Greatest Hits.* http://www.stuff.co.nz/sport/732649/Tiger-Woods-greatest-hits, *The Dominion Post*, January 31, 2009, (Accessed: 15 December 2017)

18. RIDING THE WAVES OF FEAR

1. David Deida, *The Way of the Superior Man: A Spiritual Guide to Mastering the Challenges of Women, Work, and Sexual Desire*, (Austin: Plexus, 1997)
2. P.G. Firth, H. Zheng, J.S. Windsor, A.I. Sutherland, C.H. Imray, G.W. Moore, J.L. Semple, R.C. Roach, R.A. Salisbury, 'Mortality on Mount

Everest, 1921–2006: descriptive study', *British Medical Journal*, December 2008, https://www.ncbi.nlm.nih.gov/pubmed/19074222

20. THE WORLD CUP: COMETH THE HOUR, COMETH THE TEAM

1. *John Florio, Ouisie Shapiro, The Dark Side of Going for Gold*, https://www.theatlantic.com/health/archive/2016/08/post-olympic-depression/496244/, August 18, 2016 (Accessed 10 January 2018).

21. HARNESSING COLLECTIVE INTELLIGENCE

1. Adam Grant, *Originals: How non-conformist change the world*, (Penguin Books, New York, 2017) pp. 198.

22. PERSONAL MASTERY

1. Eckhart Tolle, *A New Earth: Awakening to Your Life's Purpose.* (Penguin Books, New York, 2005)
2. David Frith, *Silence of the Heart: Cricket Suicides* (Mainstream Digital, Edinburgh, 2011)
3. Michael Atherton, 'When the glamour disappears', 28 Septmber 2003, http://www.telegraph.co.uk/sport/cricket/2422234/When-the-glamour-disappears.html (Accessed: 3 October 2017)
4. Paulo Coelho, *The Winner Stands Alone,* (HarperCollins Publishers, New York, 2010)
5. David Frith, *Silence of the Heart: Cricket Suicides* (Mainstream Digital, Edinburgh, 2011)
6. 'Tiger Woods scandal cost shareholders up to $12 billion', https://www.reuters.com/article/us-golf-woods-shareholders/tiger-woods-scandal-cost-shareholders-up-to-12-billion-idUSTRE5BS38I20091229, 30 December 2009 (Accessed: 28 February 2018)
7. Michael Atherton, 'When the glamour disappears', 28 Septmber 2003, http://www.telegraph.co.uk/sport/cricket/2422234/When-the-glamour-disappears.html (Accessed: 3 October 2017)
8. Micah Rieke, Jon Hammermeister and Matthew Chase, Matthew, 'Servant Leadership In Sport: A New Paradigm For Effective Coach Behavior', *Physical Education, Health and Recreation Faculty Publications*, Paper 3, (2008) EWU Commons http://dc.ewu.edu/pehr_fac/3
9. Sharon Stoll and Jennifer Beller (2000) 'Do Sports Build Character?' in John R. Gerdy, ed., *Sports in School: The Future of An Institution*, (Teachers College Press, New York, 2000) pp. 18-31.

23. SELF-AWARENESS: A JOURNEY OF UNINTENDED CONSEQUENCES

1. C. Otto Scharmer, 'Uncovering the blind spot of leadership' *Leader to Leader*, (Volume 2008, Issue 47. Pages: 2-64. Winter 2008)https://doi.org/10.1002/ltl.269
2. Clive Woodward, *Winning!* (Hodder, London, 2005) pp. 233-241
3. Jim Collins, *Good to Great: Why Some Companies Make the Leap... and Others Don't*, (HarperBusiness, New York, 2001)
4. Daniel Goleman, *Emotional Intelligence: Why It Matters More Than IQ*, (Bantam Books, New York, 2005)

24. THE PROTEAS IN SWITZERLAND

1. Mark Boucher and Neil Manthorp, *Bouch: Through my Eyes*, (Jonathan Ball Publishers, Cape Town, 2013) pp. 232, 236, 241, 247
2. Viktor Frankl, *Man's Search For Meaning*, (London: Rider Books, London, 2008) pp. 84, 86, 87

25. ALPHA LEADERS

1. These are my words, but taken from a number of quotes that are similar
2. Tom Rath, *StrengthsFinder* 2.0. (Gallup Press, 2007)
3. Matt Pomroy, 'Zinedine Zidane', https://www.esquireme.com/culture/zinedine-zidane, 4 August 2015 (Accessed: 28 February 2018)

27. NO ZEN SHIT

1. A tribute to Dr Fowlds and Themba, https://www.youtube.com/watch?v=GpaEWIQOURA
2. Michael E. McCullough, Robert A. Emmons & Jo-Ann Tsang, 'The Grateful Disposition: A Conceptual and Empirical Topography' *Journal of Personality and Social Psychology*, 2002, Vol. 82, No. 1, 112–127
3. Philip C. Watkins, Kathrane Woodward, Tamara Stone, Russell L. Kolts, 'Gratitude and happiness: Development of a measure of gratitude, and relationships with subjective well-being', *Social Behavior and Personality: An International Journal* 31(5):431-451, January 2003
4. Simon Sinek, *Start With Why. How Great Leaders Inspire Everyone to Take Action*, (Penguin Portfolio, New York, 2009)

5. Simon Sinek, 'How great leaders inspire action', https://www.youtube.com/watch?v=qp0HIF3SfI4 and https://www.youtube.com/watch?v=IPYeCltXpxw (shorter version)
6. *Extreme, Sustainable Philanthropy: Chris Bertish Paddles Across the Atlantic*, https://www.operationsmile.org/blog/extreme-sustainable-philanthropy-chris-bertish-paddles-across-atlantic
7. Alex Pattakos, *Prisoners of Our Thoughts: Viktor Frankl's Principles for Discovering Meaning in Life and Work*, (Berrett-Koehler, San Francisco, 2008)
8. Steven Kotler and Jamie Wheal, *Stealing Fire: How Silicon Valley, the Navy SEALs, and Maverick Scientists Are Revolutionizing the Way We Live and Work*, (HarperCollins, New York, 2017)

28. OUT OF THE BOX

1. Julianna W. Miner, 'Why 70 percent of kids quit sports by age 13' June 1, 2016 https://www.washingtonpost.com/news/parenting/wp/2016/06/01/why-70-percent-of-kids-quit-sports-by-age-13/?noredirect=on&utm_term=.50287d4d9cce

POST SCRIPT: MADIBA'S SLEEVE

1. Karl Popper, *The Open Society and Its Enemies; Volume One: The Spell of Plato*, (Routledge, New York, 1945) pp. 136, 138, 140, 143
2. G.K. Chesterton, *Orthodoxy* (originally published 1908)

INDEX

abdicating, 29
Ackerman, Hylton, 313
Adelaide Strikers, 347, 349
advising or suggestion, 28
Agassi, André, 91
Akram, Wasim, 115
Algie, Rowan, 133–135
Al Pacino moment, 234
alpha leaders/alpha leadership, 303
    are unemotional and judgmental of others, 306
    definition of, 304
    features of, 304–305
    healthy, 307–308, 311, 314
    high expectations of, advantage of, 305–306
    unhealthy, 306, 308–312, 314
    warrior, soldier or coward, 312–314
    younger and older alpha males, 307
Amazon River, 294
Amir, Mohammad, 119
Amla, Hashim, 21, 24, 96, 115, 229, 271, 276, 291, 297, 303, 314
ancient mythology, 78
A New Earth (Eckhart Tolle), 125
Anthem (Leonard Cohen), 48
anxiety subsides, 202
Armstrong, Lance, 22, 116, 119, 168, 275
arrogance, 55, 69, 124, 153–154, 305
Arthur, Mickey, 302
Artscape Theatre, 5
Arugam Bay, 142
Asia Cup series
    2008, 191
    2010, 141, 147
Asif, Mohammed, 119
Atherton, Michael, 274, 276

athlete(s), 171, 353
    -centered coaching, 40–42, 244
    choices all the time, 114
    extreme, 328
    focus on coach, 152
    mentally tough, 165
    of non-servant coaches, 32
    top, 344
    winning as primary source of success, 348
Attention Deficit Disorder (ADD), 66
Australia, 55, 79
Australian Big Bash League, 30, 178, 245, 251, 268, 281–282, 332, 336–337, 349
    2015 series, 87
Australian cricket team, 114–115
    sandpaper on ball use by Cameron Bancroft against South Africa, 115
Australian Football Mental Toughness Inventory (AFMTI), 165
Australian tour of 1997, 2
autocratic coaching style, 33
Azharuddin, Mohammed, 119

ball sandpapering, 116
ball-tampering, 115–117
Bancroft, Cameron, 115–116
Barnes, David, 6
Baumgartner, Felix, 333
belief/believing, 157, 160–161
Beller, Jennifer, 277
Benzinger, Katherine, 65
Bernie Madoff, 116
Bertish, Chris, 328
Beyliss, Trevor, 305
Bhagavad Gita, 113
Bharucha, Zubin, 249–250, 256, 260

Bible, 113
big data, 19, 175
Binny, 265, 267
biomechanics, 19, 38
Blink (Malcolm Gladwell), 91–92
Bob Jones Award, 114
Boddy, Clive, 167
body intelligence, 202
Bond, James, 343
Border-Gavaskar trophy, 83–84
bosses, 34, 37–39, 130
Boucher, Mark, 1, 16, 295–297
Bowden, Billy, 84
Boxing Day Test, Durban, 15
Braden, Vic, 92, 176
Brandvlei Correctional Centre, 11
Braveheart movie, 323–324
Bravo, Dwayne, 267
Brearley, Mike, 275
British Olympic Association, 250
British rugby team, 250
Bryant, Kobe, 188, 275
Buchan, Ace, 346–347
Buddha, 22
building phase of team, 321
bullshit zone, 201
Burgess, Sam, 346
Butler, Ian, 267
Buttler, Jos, 350
Butt, Salman, 22, 128

Caddick, Andy, 16
Caesar, Julius, 312
Calm app, 180
Cambodia, 3
Cape Carnival, 354
Cape Town's Central Business District (CBD), 4
Cassidy, Michael, 139
celebritydom, 21
Champions League (CL), 264–266, 269, 350
Chandila, Ajit, 261–263
Chappell, Greg, 25, 55–56, 99, 103, 114
Charlesworth, Ric, 332–333
Chavan, Ankeet, 261, 263

Chennai, 63, 85, 110–111
Chennai Super Kings, 267, 314–315
Chesterton, G.K., 352–353
Chinnaswamy Stadium, Bangalore, 111
choking, 203–204
Christie, Kitch, 161
Clarke, Michael, 300–302, 309, 336–337
coach/coaches, 1, 18–20, 24–27, 30, 34, 39, 43–44, 46–47, 53–55, 60–61, 63, 69, 73–75, 78, 86, 88–90, 92, 95, 97, 104, 106, 117, 127, 130, 136–137, 139–140, 148–153, 155, 159–161, 166, 168, 173, 175–176, 186, 188, 195–196, 199, 202, 214, 234, 236, 238, 241–245, 249–251, 257, 259, 261, 265, 275, 277, 279, 281–283, 285, 288, 295, 297, 302, 304–306, 308–309, 313–314, 319, 322–325, 331–333, 336, 339–342, 346, 351
believe in autocratic coaching style, 33
buddy-, 254
caretaker, 55
catalyst for growth, 36
-centered approach, 29, 40
challenges faced by, 33
ego among, 128
feedback on what worked, 193
frustrated, 28
magnetism, 42
modern-day requirement of, 29
need players who are mentally tough, 48
non-servant leader, 32
non-thinking players, responsible to create, 45
old-school sports, 38
peer-, 254
preferences and players needs, discrepancy between, 49
required to understand athlete or players thinking, 41
responsibility for in-competition decision-making, 38

role of, 36
servant leader, 33
specialist or technical, 38
coaching, concept of, 17–18, 26–34,
    55–56, 91, 120, 143
    about right technique, 96
    athlete-centered coaching, 40–42
    chasing a light beam, 35–36
    the coaches, 347–348
    collaborative style, 40–42, 46
    errors, 178
    executive, 17, 19–20
    functions of, 58
    is mystery, 57
    manuals, importance of, 96
    measure-to-manage, 175
    mental skills, 245
    methodology of
        external *vs* internal focus, 42–48
        instruction *vs* collaboration,
            40–42
        performance *vs* personal focus,
            48–50
    peer-, 254
    traditional way of, 88
Coaching for Performance (Sir John
    Whitmore), 41
collaboration-based coaching, 40–42
collective intelligence, 256, 268
Collett, Damien, 302
Collins, Jim, 285
Columbia space shuttle, 252
Commins, Donne, 5
Commonwealth Bank Series against
    Australia (2008), 144
computer and video analysis programme,
    39
concentration, definition of, 152
confidence, 16, 59, 71, 124, 129, 133,
    151, 154, 160, 172–173, 184, 189
    193, 201, 211–212, 229–230, 279,
    284, 318, 341, 348–349
    over, 47, 153
    players, 131, 145
    playing to strengths, 157–159
    self-, 33, 68, 272–273, 305

Coniglio, Stephen, 347
conscious mind, 204
conventional swing, 115
Cooper, 267
cooperation, 60, 122, 150
corporate psychopaths, concept of,
    167, 169
corporate psychopathy, 169
courage, 23, 68, 81, 117, 155, 194,
    208, 260, 264, 291, 297–300, 329,
    331, 337, 340
creating
    non-thinking players, 45
    thinking players, 44
cricket balls, 264–268
Cricket South Africa (CSA), 242, 295
crisis of meaning, 330
Cronjé, Hansie, 1–3, 19, 22, 98, 116,
    119
Cummins, Nick, 335–336, 347
Cummins, Pat, 343

Dallaire, Jacques, 158
Dambulla (Sri Lanka), 101–102, 141–
    143, 155, 224
Davis, Phil, 347
Debbie, Kirsten, 150–151
de Lange, Marchant, 267
Delhi Daredevils, 251
    depression, 239
        among celebrities, 274
Desai, Monty, 261
de Villiers, A.B. (nickname Mr 360), 76,
    150, 186, 203–204, 229, 292,
    297–298, 301–302
de Villiers, Jean, 155
Dev, Kapil, 54
Dhoni, Mahendra Singh (MS), 56, 61,
    73–74, 83, 99, 101, 103–104, 135,
    145–147, 173, 222, 231–232,
    234–238, 305, 316
diet, 19, 77, 138, 178
Dilshan, T.M., 237
diving physiology, 338
Domingo, Russell, 322, 331
Donald, Allan, 1, 28

Donaldson, Mark, 345, 347
Dravid, Rahul ('The Wall'), 24, 56, 59, 79, 86, 103–104, 111–113, 115, 137, 178, 233, 244, 249, 251, 256–257, 260–264, 266, 305, 313, 350, 353
dream life, 1, 4
Drucker, Peter, 332
Duminy, J.P., 141, 229, 300
du Plessis, Faf, 96, 135, 229, 301–303, 307
du Plessis, Morné, 8
Dylan, Bob, 72

Eastern Washington University (EWU), 32, 277
edge of fear, 200–202
ego, 4, 9, 20, 24, 42, 61, 133–134, 139–140, 205, 270–271, 276, 279, 282, 285–286, 297, 348, 355
   among coaches, 130
   as an asset or good thing, 135
   competitive, 194
   -dominance, 145
   -driven behaviour, 310–311
   drives us to fight things in life, 127
   fragile, 201
      as obstacle in success, 335
   professional, 320
      as self-serving, 127
Einstein, Albert, 36, 113, 184
Elysium, 78
E = mc2: A Biography of the World's Most Famous Equation (David Bodanis), 36
Emotional Intelligence (Daniel Goleman), 285
employee, reasons for leaving job, 37
England cricket team, 20, 90, 103–105, 160–161, 186, 206, 233, 276, 288–290, 294–297, 340, 350
Enron, 112, 116
Ewing, Mike, 30
executive coach/coaching/leadership, 17, 19–20, 29–30, 137, 241–242
experiential learning cycle, 44

external coaching focus, 42–48
extra fielder, 107
extrapolation, 77

failure or error
   methods to address, 131
   reality of, 186–187
false friends, 273
Faulkner, James, 74, 265, 267, 318
FC Barcelona, 54
fear, 198–202, 205–207
Federer, Roger, 54, 150, 186–187
Fiennes, Ranulph 'Ran', 328
fitness analysis, 19
Fleming, Stephen, 305
focus
   definition of, 152
   external, 151–152
   internal, 151–152, 156
   on breathe, 156–157
   past *vs* future, 153
   present-moment, 156
football (soccer), 5, 7, 46, 130, 152, 313, 348
   bully, 133–135
Forbes, 37, 54
Fowlds, Will, 323–325, 327
Frankl, Viktor, 328–330
freedom, 4, 120–121, 202, 324, 332
full-pitched delivery, 47, 73, 96, 106, 236
future-oriented
   people, 154
   pessimists, 154

gaining perspective, 184–186
Gallup, 37, 64, 68, 70
Gambhir, Gautam, 91–97, 104, 112, 145, 147, 169–172, 222, 229, 231, 235–237
Ganguly, Sourav, 56, 103
Gates, Bill, 118
Gavaskar, Sunil, 24, 53
Giant Trevally (GT's), 302
Gibbs, 16
Gladiator movie, 78, 312, 323

Golden Globe Awards, 343
Goldman, Scott, 239
golf-coaching programme, 39
Green, Chris, 338, 343
Greenleaf, Robert, 31
grow (show) character, 195–196

Haddin, Brad, 231
Haier, Richard, 65
Hannibal Lecter *(Silence of the Lambs)*, 167
hard knocks, 4–11
Harris, Paul, 242
Hauritz, Nathan, 281–283
Headspace app, 180
Hemery, David, 48
hierarchical approach of traditional coaching, 47
highly effective losers, seven habits of, 196–197
Hillary, Edmund, 343
Hodge, Brad, 264–266, 315–316
Hofmann, David, 252
Holyfield, 313
honesty, 24, 102, 131, 194, 239, 241, 251, 263–264, 330, 340, 345–346
Horn, Mike, 208, 210, 228, 232, 276, 291–293, 297, 328
  conquering or expedition of North Pole and Arctic Circle, 209, 219–227
  inducted as member of Laureus World Sports Academy in 2007, 209
  influence on Mark Boucher, 296
  received Laureus Alternative Sportsman of the Year award in 2001, 209
  sharing stories of preparation, 294
  training camp in Swiss Alps, 290, 294, 297
  into zone of death, 210–219
Howse, Jarrad, 344, 346–347
Hughes, Phil, 345
humility, 24, 31, 33, 35, 124, 126, 270, 277, 297, 352

Hussey, Mike, 26, 115, 251, 313, 335, 337–340, 343, 345–347
hyperventilating, 339

ICC Champions Trophy (2009), South Africa, 148–150
inclusion, 277
Indian Cricket Board (BCCI), 54, 139–140, 233
Indian cricket team, 17, 79–80, 82, 136, 211, 239, 251
Indian Premier League (IPL), 30, 72, 74, 106, 176, 178, 245, 249, 256–257, 260, 269, 317, 319, 332, 335, 353
individualism, 80
Indo-Pakistan war in 1971, 79
information and technology, 19
  first use of computers and video analysis in professional cricket, 38
Inglis, Greg, 346
Insight Timer app, 180
instinct, 149–150
instruction, 40–42
  -based coaching method, 28, 45, 173
intellectual excellence, 42
internal coaching focus, 42–48
international backpackers, 3
International Cricket Council (ICC), 55–56, 63, 77–78, 269
intrinsic motivation, 150
intuition (or gut-feelings), 149–150, 177, 179
intuitive leadership, 176–177
Irish Lions rugby team, 250
Iyer, Raghu, 256

Jadav, Umesh, 105
Jadeja, Ajay, 119
Jaques, Phil, 342
Jayawardene, D.P.M.D., 237
Jesus Christ, 22, 120
Jobs, Steve, 120
Johnson, Ben, 22, 112
Johnson, Mitchell, 84, 309

Jones, Bobby, 114
Jones, Marion, 22, 112
Jujimoto, Shun, 203

Kabbalah, 113
Kallis, Henry, 346
Kallis, Jacques, 1, 16, 19, 69, 156, 229, 242–243, 268, 281, 292–293, 297, 300, 307, 340, 343, 345–346
Kallis, Janine, 346
Kandalama Lake, 141
Kapugedera, C.K., 237
Karate Kid, 312
Karlovi, Ivo, 186
Katich, Simon, 309
Khan, Zaheer, 56, 89, 105, 233, 237
Khawaja, Usman, 309, 347
King, Greg, 99–100
King Jr., Martin Luther, 323–324
Kirsten, Gary, 1, 11, 16, 20, 28, 39, 49, 53, 93, 95, 136, 139–140, 142, 156–158, 160, 169, 177–178, 182, 188–189, 242, 285, 288–290, 292–294, 302–303, 305, 311, 313, 332–350
  actualisation included spiritual aspect, 16
  appointed as head coach of Indian national cricket team
    achievements, 24
    approach by Sunil Gavaskar in 2007, 53
    to chose your battles wisely, 83–84
    ego management among players, 127
    fitness coach/trainer, role as, 98–102
    India at War narrative, 78–80, 83–84, 234
    intuitive leadership, 176
    journey as head coach, 241–245
    lessons from Asia Cup loss in Karachi (2008), 191–197
    looking same things in different perspective, 104–106
    mental conditioning coach, 199
    optional practices sessions, 86–91
    preparation for Asia cup series (Sri Lanka) in 2010, 141–143
    relationship with Yuvraj Singh, 180–181
    reprimand for reprimanding, 129–132
    research and experience, 60
    resigned from South African cricket team head coach, 322
    Robin Singh as fielding coach, 78
    role as strategic leadership coach, 77
    sex dossier, 136–140
    starting strategy, 57
    storytelling problem and Gautam Gambhir, 91–97
    strategy to players, 56
    and success strategy, 111–117
    TEAM India strategy, 82–83
    Test series against South Africa in 2008, first assignment, 62
    World Cup preparations, methods to be adopted, 142–146
  Boxing Day Test, Durban, 15
  encourage players to make decisions themselves, 23
  and fear, 201–202, 205
  and god, 205–207
  feelings of surfer experience, 198
  golf putting stroke, 39
  as head coach of Rajasthan Royals, 106–108
  learn master the self, 17
  observation on professional sportsman, 20
  personal mastery of, 270–280
  Rahul Dravid request to join coach of Rajasthan Royals, 249–251
  scored 210 in Manchester, 15
  surpassed Hanif Mohammad score, 16
  and World Cup 2011
    beat Bangladesh, England,

Netherlands, West Indies, 228–230
and contribution of Yuvraj Singh in winning World Cup, 231–233
final against Sri Lanka at Wankhede stadium (Mumbai), 234–237
lost to South Africa, 229–230
morning after, 238–240
and role played by Mike Horn, 210–227, 235
semi-final against Pakistan, 233–234
Klusener, Lance, 1
knowing, 160–161
knowing in brain, 176
Kohli, Virat, 54, 103, 150, 173, 186, 203, 229, 235–237
Kolb, David, 44
Koran, 113
Kreese, John, 312
Krige, Corné, 344–345
Kulasekara, K.M.D.N., 237
Kumar, Bhuvneshwar, 259
Kumble, Anil, 54, 56, 61, 111
chief guest in Shakti Foundation's annual fundraiser programme in Chennai, 110
felicitation ceremonies in 2008, 109
test and ODI career of, 109
valued rest and private time, 119

Lahore Qalandars, 27, 319–320
Lancaster, Stuart, 332, 346
Laos, 3
Lara, Brian, 1
late developers, 67
Laureus World Sports Foundation, 8, 209
Lawrence, Johnny, 312
Laxman, V.V.S., 24, 56, 61, 79, 84, 96, 104, 113, 313
Leadbetter, David, 39
leadership, 60, 115–117, 132, 136, 167, 241–245, 250, 253, 303, 305, 308, 320–321, 337, 348, 351–352, 355
aim of, 285

approaches in business world, 17
changing landscape of, 27, 50, 241, 351
effectiveness, 285
methods to help others
abdicating, 29
advising or suggestion, 28
coaching, 29–31
instruction, 27–28
mentoring, 28–29
performance and personal focus approach of, 49
strategic coach, 53, 77
terrain, 102
transactional, 43
transformational, 43, 189
learned optimism, 172
learned skill, 64–65, 72
Lee, Brett, 28, 232
Lee, Bruce, 312
Lehman Brothers, 116
Levi, Richard, 72
loyalty, 118–119, 121, 269, 307, 309

Maguire, Madge, 346
Mahatma Gandhi, 22, 120, 323–324
Malinga, S. Lasith, 96, 155–156, 237
Mandela, Nelson (Madiba), 1, 22, 120, 323–325, 327, 353–355
Mandrax drug, 11
man-management, 49
Man's Search For Meaning (Viktor Frankl), 298
mantra, in sports and business, 175
Mantra Surf ashram, Mulki, 233
map of mental errors, 152–155
Maradona, Diego, 22, 116
match-fixing, 263
Materazzi, Marco, 313
Mathews, Mark, 337–338, 345, 347
McCay, Clint, 87
McDonald, Andrew, 338
McKechnie, Brian, 114
McMillan, Brian, 1
medical care, 19
meditation, 179

Melbourne Stars, 347
mental conditioning, 245
mental meltdown under pressure, forms of, 203
mental toughness, concept of, 165
    amongst elite athletes, 167
    definition of, 166–167
        as a failed concept, 169–174
Mental Toughness Q48 (MTQ48), 165–166
mental work, 244
mentoring, 28–29
Messi, Lionel, 54, 187
Middlesex University, 17, 37, 167
Mills, Kyle, 182–185, 188–190
mind
    distracted, 152–155
    focused, 151–152
Mishra, Amit, 105
modern-day knowledge-era coaching approach, 244–245
Mohali Test, 103–104
Mohammad, Hanif, 16
Morgan, Eoin, 340, 349
Morkel, Morné, 62, 156, 229, 300–301
Morris, Chris, 26
Moses, Edwin, 8
Mother Teresa, 22, 323–324
motivation, 32–33, 43, 68, 145–146, 150, 218, 243, 323–325, 327, 330, 340–341, 343
Mouse, Mickey, 129
MTN, 2
Mumbai Indians, 350
Mumbai terrorist attacks of 2008, 233
Muralitharan, M., 237
mystery of coaching, 35, 37

Nadal, Rafael, 187, 238
Nair, Arjun, 39
Nair, Karun, 258
name-droppers, 273
Nannes, Dirk, 282–283, 286
Narine, Sunil, 39, 267
National Alliance for Youth Sports, 348
natural distribution curve (or Bell curve), 150

need, 160–161
negative
    emotion, 131, 171, 326
    feedback, 132
Nehra, Ashish, 233
Netflix, 269
Newlands Cricket Ground, 354
New Zealand, 72, 114, 126, 160–161, 182, 184–185, 188, 191, 230
Nike, 2, 54, 58, 275
Noakes, Tim, 19, 38
Norgay, Tenzing, 343
Norrises, Chuck, 22
Now, Discover Your Strengths (Marcus Buckingham and Donald Clifton), 71, 73, 75
Ntini, Makhaya, 62
nutritional supplements, 19

Obama, Barack, 170
O'Brien, Bill, 283
occasional personality clashes, 2
Ojha, Pragjan, 84, 105
One Day International (ODI), 3, 25, 28, 56, 70, 82, 109, 125–128, 144, 146–147, 156, 186, 229–231, 233, 238, 268–269, 271, 285, 288
One Day side (Indian), beating New Zealand in home series in 2010, 182, 184
on-field mistake, 253–254
Oppo, 54
optimism, 170–171
optional training, 86–91, 123, 340
Originals (Adam Grant), 252
Otago, 267
Otten, Kai, 346
Ousland, Børge, 223
Outliers (Malcolm Gladwell), 66
over-stressed zone, 200

pain of losing, 317–320
Pakistan, 80, 115
    and India, World Cup 2011 semi-final between, 232–234
Pakistan Super League, 27, 245, 319–320, 332

panic, 203–204
Parsee Cyclists Sports Club, 260
Patel, Munaf M., 229, 233, 237
Pattakos, Alex, 328–329
Pattanaik, Devdutt, 78
Pattinson, James, 309
PCA stadium, Mohali, 83
Perera, N.L.T.C., 237
performance coaching focus, 48–50, 163–164
performance phase of team, 321
Performance Psychology Centre, at University of Michigan, 239
personal coaching focus, 48–50
personal mastery, 4, 20, 270–271
    and coaching, 276–279
    definition of, 22
        as journey, 279–280
        journey towards to live successfully as human being, 21
        to know and play to your strengths, 23
    leads through all of life, 24
    pursuing success, 23
    shift in/from
        attitude, 22
        expecting to be told, 23
        importance of looking good outwardly, 22
        thinking, 22
personal values, 21, 24, 113, 117, 120
Perth Scorchers, 281
pessimism scale, 170
Petersen, Alviro, 290
Philander, Vernon, 300
planning, 9, 38, 43–45, 56, 74, 88, 106, 130, 147, 177, 189, 193, 195, 197, 206, 238, 260, 339
player-centered coaching approach, 40–41, 244, 283
PlayStation, 269
Pollard, Kieron, 319
Ponting, Ricky, 83, 231–232, 302–303
Popper, Karl, 352
Porta, Hugo, 8
Port Douglas, 302

Port Elizabeth, 3, 15
positive interaction, 132
post-match, 315
    debriefs/meetings, 45, 82, 253, 342
    nightclub or pub brawl, 314
    reviews, 339
    routines, 254
Post-Olympic Depression Syndrome, 239
Powell, Neil, 277
power games, 2, 58
practice (optional), 86–91
Prasad, Venkatesh, 111
premeditation, 155
Presley, Elvis, 120
pressure, 159–160
Prince, Ashwell, 19
professional mastery, 21, 271
Prophet Muhammad, 22
psychopaths, 167–168
    out-and-out, 169

Raghuvir, Vasanth, 110
Rahane, Ajinkye, 258–259, 265–266
Raina, Suresh, 231–232, 237
Rajasthan Royals (RR), 74, 106, 244, 249–250, 253, 256, 262, 284, 310, 314–318, 321, 341, 350
Rambos, John, 21
Rana, Sameen, 27
Randiv, S., 237
Rayudu, Ambati, 318
Red Beard and Co., 281
Red Bull High Performance Centre, Los Angeles (LA), 333
Red Bull Stratos, 333
rehabilitation, 19
reverse-swing, 115
review after loss, 193–194
reviewing, 45, 47, 146, 197
Rhodes, Jonty, 1, 185
Richardson, Dave, 1
Richard the Lionheart, 312
Rio Olympic Games (2016), 239
Rivonia trial of 1964, 324
Robbins, Tom, 202

Rohr, Richard, 35
Ronaldo, Cristiano, 187
Roux, Adrian le, 99–100
Rowing Blazers (Jack Carlson), 85
Royal Challengers Bangalore (RCB), 258
Royal Marines, 283
rugby, 1, 3, 8, 18, 28, 38, 46, 67, 130, 152, 155, 160–161, 216, 250, 255, 277, 283–284, 300, 312–313, 332, 344, 346
Rugby World Cup
    1995, 161
    2003, 250, 283

Samaraweera, T.T., 237
Samson, Sanju, 256, 258–260
Samurai Warriors, 312
Sangakkara, K.C., 237
Saratoga, 37
Sawai Man Singh Stadium, Jaipur, 315
science, 43, 47, 334
    contribution to cricket, 19
    of coaching, 175
    of cricket, 42
    sport, 19, 351
Sehwag, Virender, 62–64, 72, 104, 156, 158, 228–229, 235–237
selection in cricket, 341
self-awareness, 283–287
self-doubt, 212
self-mastery, 278
Seligman, Martin, 71, 170, 172
Senge, Peter, 21
sentimental (or past-oriented people), 154
sentimental pessimists, 154
servant leadership, concept of, 60, 277
    definition of, 31
    Eastern Washington University (EWU) study of, 32–33
    features of, 31–34
service, 33, 277, 355
    humble, 31
sex dossier, 136–140
Shahzad, Ajmal, 229

Shakti Foundation, 110
Sharma, Ishant, 84, 100, 105, 118
Shastri, Lal Bahadur, 79
Shaw, George Bernard, 172–173
Shaw, Heath, 346
Shetty, Panish, 251
Shukla, Rahul, 267, 316
Silence of the Heart (David Frith), 274
Simons, Eric, 94–95, 142, 147, 230, 235, 353
Sinek, Simon, 326–327
Singh, Harbhajan, 56, 89, 101, 105, 112, 233, 237
Singh, Robin, 78
Singh, Yuvraj, 58, 82, 180–181, 222, 229, 231–233, 235–237
Skype, 349
Slater, Kelly, 150
Smith, Graeme, 84, 96, 203, 229, 242, 291–293, 297–298, 302–303, 305, 307–308, 311, 344–345
Smith, Jordy, 344–345
Smith, Steve, 84, 107, 115–117
social-conscience perspective, 138
solutions designing, positive experience of, 132
solutions-focused conversations, 132
South African cricket team (Proteas), 1, 3, 15–17, 19–20, 23, 26, 28, 39, 49, 63, 72, 85, 96, 98, 115, 131, 135, 204, 208, 210, 226, 229–230, 242, 244, 251, 258, 268–271, 274, 288, 290–291, 295–297, 299–302, 305, 308, 311, 319, 322–324, 327, 329–334, 336, 340, 344, 354
    beat India in World Cup in 2011, 229–230
    coaching methods employed by provincial and national coaches, 18
    psyche in ICC tournaments, 77–78
    ranked number one side in three formats in 2012 by beating England, 288–289
    re-entry into international sport, 18
    test series

    with Australia in 2012, 299–302
    with India, 85–86
    top level coaching, 18
spider cams, 258
spot-fixing scandal, in cricket matches, 119, 261, 272, 284, 316
Springbok (South African) rugby team, 18, 67, 155, 160
Sreesanth, S., 105, 119, 237, 261–263
Sri Lanka, 96, 101, 127–128, 141, 144, 147, 155, 233–235, 237, 285, 307
Stagg, Amos Alonzo, 278
Stamford Bridge (Chelsea Football Club), 332
Stealing Fire (Steven Kotler and Jamie Wheal), 330
Steinhoff, 116
Stellenbosch University Business School, 26
Steyn, Dale, 62, 97, 229, 256–260, 312, 344–345
Steyn, Rory, 354
stoke, 198
Stoll, Sharon, 277
storytelling problem, 91–97
Stransky, Joel, 160–161
Strauss, Andrew, 229
Street Universe, 6, 11
strengths, 23, 58, 62–63, 71–74, 81, 87, 146–147, 150, 189, 201, 203, 211, 213, 241, 263, 276, 317
    development into excellence, 68–70
    mental, 208
    of character, 22, 279
    playing to, 64–65, 157–159
    talent development into, 66–68
    ways to understand your, 75
Suarez, Luis, 187–188
subconscious mind, 204
subordinates, 39, 307
substance abuse, 274
success, 111–117
Sunrisers, 258–260, 264
supportiveness, 150
support staff, 39, 57, 85, 184, 230, 250, 291, 320
    functions of, 58

surfers, 198
Sutton, John, 346
Swann, Graeme, 229
Switzerland, 297–298
Sydney Olympic Park, 349
Sydney Sixers, 342
Sydney Thunder, 26–27, 39, 87, 158, 178, 251, 268–269, 281, 334–335, 337–339, 342, 344–345, 347, 349–350, 353

T20 cricketers, 31
T20 cricket league/tournaments, 72–73, 86, 106–107, 122
transform cricket into entertainment industry, 271–272
T20 World Cup
    2009, 90, 144
    2014, 331
Tahir, Imran, 296
Tait, Shaun, 263
talent, 2, 8, 17, 22, 31, 64–65, 67, 69, 71, 73, 75, 113, 124, 162, 172, 185, 206, 240, 249, 310, 330–331
    development into strength, 66–68
    natural, 63, 66, 68, 73
    special, 273, 276
    sporting, 345
Tambe, Pravin (PT), 74, 256, 260, 262, 264–267
Taylor, Bob, 114
team first attitude, 255
Team Hoyt, 186
TEAM India, 25, 55, 80, 82–83, 139, 143, 239–240, 343
team work, 150
Tendulkar, Sachin, 1, 21, 49, 56, 59, 69, 86, 94–95, 99, 101, 104, 113, 118, 124, 126–127, 140, 143, 208, 226, 229, 231, 235–237, 283
Thailand, 3
Tharanga, W.U., 237
The Antidote: Happiness for People Who Can't Stand Positive Thinking (Oliver Burkeman), 171
The Dominion Post, 188

The Inner Game of Tennis
  (Timothy Gallwey), 48
The Once and Future King (T.H. White),
  76
The Open Society and its Enemies
  (Karl Popper), 42
The Way of the Superior Man
  (David Deida), 200
The Winner Stands Alone
  (Paulo Coelho), 274
Thompson, Daley, 8
Titans, 267, 296
Tolle, Eckhart, 273
touchy-feely way of thinking, 176
Trevor, Chappell, 114
Trinidad and Tobago, 267
Troillet, Jean, 217
trust, 150, 157, 277
  importance in coaching, 30
Twitter, 263
Tyco, 116
Tyson, Mike, 22, 112, 312–313

Unadkat, Jaydev, 105
unintended consequences, of actions,
  286–287
United States Anti-Doping Agency
  (USADA), 168
Upton, Paddy, 61, 78, 133, 139, 170,
  226, 265, 287

value-creation exercises, 119
value(s)/value system, 20, 33–34, 43, 54,
  57, 77, 83, 91, 106, 111–113,
  117–120, 145, 159, 175, 179, 197,
  251–252, 257, 268, 271, 276–279,
  285, 310, 312, 329, 331, 337–342
  associated coaching, 32
  checklist, 121–122
  -creation exercises, 119
  of listening, 289
  personal, 21, 24, 113
  sportsmen differ in, 118
  team, 43, 57
van Zyl, Corrie, 295
Vas, Richie, 347

very short delivery, 106
video analysis programme, 16, 19,
  38–39
Vietnam, 3
Vince, James, 349–350
Viswanath, G.R., 114
Volatile, Uncertain, Complex,
  Ambiguous (VUCA) world, 130
vulnerability, 20, 72, 145, 201, 263,
  310, 340

Wallace, William, 312, 323–324
Walshe, Andy, 333
Wankhede Stadium, Mumbai, 54, 234,
  236, 261, 350
want, 160–161
Ward, Callan, 347
Warner, David, 115, 186, 336–337
Warne, Shane, 1
Watson, Jessica, 346
Watson, Shane, 83, 251, 257–258,
  263–269, 309–310, 315, 343, 345,
  353
Watson, Tom, 282
Waugh, Steve, 1
WBBL title, 347
weakness
  necessity to fix, 71–72
  problem with fixing, 70–71
Western Australia Cricket Association
  (WACA), 281, 302
Western Cape prison system, 5, 9, 11
West Indies, 78
What's important now (WIN), 155–156
Whiteman, Sam, 281–282
Whose Line Is It Anyway TV series, 334
Wilber, Ken, 42
Williams, Dale, 20
win-at-all-costs attitude, 348
Wisden Leading Cricketer, 63
wives and girlfriends (WAGS), 289
Woods, Tiger, 22, 188, 275
Woodward, Clive, 249–250, 283–284
Woolmer, Bob, 1–2, 19, 38
World Anti-Doping Association
  (WADA) study, 119

Worldcom, 116
World Cup (ICC Cricket), 55, 84, 142, 146, 148, 155, 157–159, 162, 180, 322
    1983, 54, 147
    1999, 226
    2007, 56, 144
    2011, 54, 77, 82, 101, 119, 124, 144, 149, 159, 171, 181, 196, 208–240, 305, 332
    2015, 54

yoga, 179
Young, Mike, 134
Younis, Waqar, 115
YouTube, 39, 186, 327

Zander, Benjamin, 189
Zidane, Zinedine, 116, 313
zone (or state of flow)
    definition, 149
    deliberately focused, 155
    distracted mind, 152–155
    focused mind, 151–152
    gateways to, 157
    mechanisms of, 150
    personalised pathway to, 161–162
    report, 149